W9-AVM-406

The Queen's Agent

The QUEEN'S AGENT

Sir Francis Walsingham
and the Rise of Espionage in Elizabethan England

JOHN COOPER

PEGASUS BOOKS
NEW YORK LONDON

The Queen's Agent

Pegasus Books LLC
80 Broad Street, 5th Floor
New York, NY 10004

First Pegasus Books cloth edition 2013

ISBN: 978-1-60598-410-0

10 9 8 7 8 6 5 4 3 2 1

Printed in the United States of America
Distributed by W. W. Norton & Company, Inc.

For my father

Contents

Illustrations

11. Drawings of the trial and execution of Mary Queen of Scots, Robert Beale? © The British Library Board.
12. Title-page of *General and Rare Memorials pertayning to the Perfect Arte of Navigation*, John Dee, 1577 © The British Library Board.
13. *Image of Ireland*, John Derricke, 1581 © Edinburgh University Library (De.3.76).
14. *Captain Christopher Carleill*, Robert Boissard after unknown artist, c.1593, line engraving © National Portrait Gallery, London.
15. *Indian Woman and Young Girl*, John White, 1585–6, watercolour © The Trustees of the British Museum.
16. *The Spanish Fleet off the Coast of Cornwall on 29 July 1588*, Augustine Ryther (engraver) after Robert Hood, 1590, engraving © National Maritime Museum, Greenwich, UK.

England and Ireland in the Sixteenth Century

Prologue

On the feast day of St Bartholomew 1572, a marked man picked his way through the streets of Paris towards the residence of the English ambassador. The Sieur de Briquemault had just seen his sons murdered in front of him, two victims among the thousands of Protestants who were being cut down by their Catholic neighbours. His own survival now depended on reaching Francis Walsingham without being recognised. The road to the suburb of Saint Marceau was well known to Briquemault, who had visited the English embassy several times since Walsingham's arrival in January 1571. But informants were on the lookout for Protestant Huguenots fleeing the mob justice which had taken hold of the city. Carrying a side of mutton on each shoulder, the aristocratic Briquemault tried to lose himself among the porters and carters who worked the medieval streets of Paris. When he stumbled and fell at the city gate, friendly hands helped him up and hoisted the meat onto his back. The French guards watching for any trouble outside the embassy had no interest in a delivery man, and Briquemault made it inside.

Walsingham could have refused to help the Sieur de Briquemault. As English subjects and Protestant heretics, the ambassador and his staff were already under threat from the Catholic crowd rampaging through the city. Briquemault had been close to the Huguenot leader Admiral Coligny, whose murder on the king's orders had unleashed the torrent of violence pouring through Paris and provincial France. Giving asylum to such a prominent fugitive could threaten the lives of others, English nationals and their Protestant allies, who had taken refuge in Walsingham's house. Then there was the safety of his own family to consider, his pregnant wife and his young daughter. The decision was one of the toughest which Walsingham would ever face: to trust in God's providence and give sanctuary to Briquemault, or to play the politician and turn him in. When the Frenchman refused the offer of money and horses and pleaded on his knees, Walsingham chose to follow his conscience. Briquemault was disguised as a groom and hidden in the embassy stables. His discovery after several days was blamed on one of his own servants, who was spotted in the city and made to reveal the whereabouts of his master. The king demanded that Briquemault be handed over, adding that he would force his way into the embassy if necessary. Even now Walsingham did not give up on his friend, accompanying him to court in a closed coach to petition for his life. It did no good: Briquemault was tried and executed on a charge of plotting with his fellow Huguenots to overthrow the Valois monarchy.[1]

The incident passes unnoticed in the traditional version of Walsingham's career, yet it says a lot about the courage of the man who served Queen Elizabeth as ambassador, principal secretary and chief of security. His efforts to save a fellow Protestant from being slaughtered were recorded by Walsingham's agent Tomasso Sassetti, in one of the comparatively few coherent accounts of the St Bartholomew's Day massacres. A reader of Machiavelli and a friend of the historian Lodovico Guicciardini, Captain Sassetti had volunteered for Elizabeth's army in Ireland before Walsingham recruited him for his embryonic secret service. He took his place in a network of news and intelligence which would ultimately stretch from Constantinople to the new-found lands of Canada and Virginia. Francis Walsingham is justly famous as a spymaster, a pioneer in cryptography and an expert in turning his enemies into double agents paid by the state. Catholic plots against Elizabeth were allowed to run just long enough to expose the full extent of their support. Less familiar is Walsingham's role in Elizabethan foreign policy, his long struggle with the issue of the queen's marriage and his promotion of English plantations in Ireland and America. His life in royal service saw him fighting other battles, against the canker of court faction as well as the illness which was gradually poisoning him. Where others would have crumpled under the burden of government, Walsingham stayed by Elizabeth's side until the twin threats of the Queen of Scots and the Spanish Armada had been neutralised.

Walsingham often wielded power over the lives of others. The destruction of Mary Stuart has been attributed to him by both critics and admirers, though Walsingham exonerated himself of any blame: she had conspired to destroy his mistress, and consequently she deserved to die. The execution of Catholic missionary priests is harder to justify. Walsingham was responsible for protecting the queen from assassination, and he saw it as his duty to use every weapon in his arsenal. Imprisonment, torture and a state-sponsored campaign of intimidation were all employed to drive Catholics into conformity with the established Church of England. Walsingham's agents infiltrated the English Catholic community at home and in exile, tempting the radicals in their midst to break cover by standing up for what they believed.

Modern lawyers would condemn this as entrapment, but again Walsingham's conscience was clear. Hidden treason would always reveal itself in the end, just as a witch could never fully conceal the pact which she had made with the devil. England was engaged in a war; literally so in the Netherlands and on the oceans from the mid-1580s, but also in spiritual combat against the forces of the Antichrist, whether in the form of the pope or the Guise family or Philip II of Spain. The need to convince

Elizabeth of this fact was Walsingham's most urgent priority during the two decades which he spent as her adviser and principal secretary. He presented himself to the world as the queen's agent, carrying out her policies and protecting her from harm. The full picture may surprise anyone who thinks that Tudor England was governed solely by personal monarchy. Walsingham was loyal and true to Elizabeth, devoted his life to her service; but he also cajoled her, clashed with her, and ultimately authorised the beheading of Mary Stuart without her knowledge. Queen Elizabeth I believed that she was in command of the ship of state, but Francis Walsingham was often at the tiller.

1 Exodus

In 1529 a London lawyer named William Walsingham used the proceeds of his thriving practice to buy the manor of Foot's Cray, a dozen miles out of town on the road to the Kentish coast. As he and many like him were discovering, it was a good time to be a barrister. The name of Walsingham was well known in London, and William was able to trade on his contacts in city government and the royal household. King Henry VIII chose him to report on the possessions of the disgraced minister Cardinal Wolsey, and he was elected to a prestigious readership at Gray's Inn. In 1532 he was appointed under-sheriff of London, the highest position which a city lawyer could hope to achieve. His wife Joyce had already given him daughters who could be married into prominent families; all that he now lacked was a son.

Regular registers of baptisms weren't introduced until the later 1530s, so the year of Francis Walsingham's birth is uncertain. But if we count back from his admission to King's College, Cambridge then it was probably 1531 or 1532, the twenty-second year of King Henry's reign. Nor is the place known for sure, although Foot's Cray seems more likely than the family's London home near Aldermanbury in Cripplegate ward; mothers of means usually chose to have their babies away from the filth and pestilence of the city. Francis would have been christened as soon as he could safely be carried to the parish church, in a rite that was rich in sacramental ceremony. The devil was exorcised with salt and holy oil before the baby was immersed in the font and wrapped in a chrisom cloth. Children who died before they could be cleansed of original sin were believed to go into limbo rather than heaven, hence the urgency of getting them to baptism.

Some pedigrees trace the ancestry of the family back to the village of Little Walsingham in Norfolk. It would be ironic if Francis Walsingham, who grew to loathe Catholicism, could be connected to one of the greatest sites of pilgrimage in medieval England. Henry VIII prayed at Walsingham in thanks for the birth of his short-lived son Henry in 1511, before the Reformation swept away its shrine to the Virgin Mary. But the link with Norfolk is probably apocryphal. The earliest reliable evidence dates from fifteenth-century London, where the Walsinghams emerged as property-owners and members of the prestigious Vintners' Company. In 1424 the merchant Thomas Walsingham bought a country manor at Scadbury near Chislehurst, so staking his claim to be a member of the gentry. It was a pattern that would define the English upper class for centuries to come: owning land was a social passport out of the world of commerce. Thomas's grandson James had a long career, serving Henry VII as sheriff of Kent in 1486–7 and travelling to France with Henry VIII in 1520. He witnessed the fantastical Field of Cloth of Gold as one of the king's honour guard. James Walsingham had two sons, Edmund – who inherited the estate at Scadbury – and William, who was Francis's father.

Edmund Walsingham scrambled a rung or so higher up the social hierarchy. He earned a knighthood fighting the Scots at Flodden, and accompanied his father to France in 1520. Two years later he attended King Henry during the visit of the emperor Charles V to England. The sword and helmet that once hung above his tomb are now preserved at the Royal Armouries Museum in Leeds. His wife Anne owned a jewel depicting Henry VIII within a golden heart, a visible statement of her family's standing at court. In 1521 Sir Edmund was appointed lieutenant of the Tower of London, giving him day-to-day responsibility for the prisoners held there. He found himself guarding both the Protestant translator John Frith, burned for heresy in 1533, and Frith's great enemy Thomas More, beheaded in 1535 for his refusal to accept Henry VIII's supremacy over the Church of England. John Fisher, Bishop of Rochester and another Catholic martyr, complained of harsh treatment at Walsingham's hands. The duties of lieutenant included supervising the torture of suspected traitors on the rack. Forty years hence, his nephew Francis would be authorising the same methods of interrogation.

William Walsingham had no prospects of a landed inheritance, so he turned to London and the law. Like Thomas More, he prospered on the legal business of the city. John Stow's *Survey of London* describes Aldermanbury as a street with many fair houses 'meet for merchants or men of worship', with a conduit of fresh water running down the middle. St Mary Aldermanbury had a churchyard and a cloister where the curious could see a shank bone reputedly belonging to a giant. William Walsingham asked to be buried in the church, and left its high altar a symbolic shilling in his will. Any monument to him would have been destroyed in the Great Fire of 1666, while the Wren church that replaced it was reduced to rubble during the Blitz and removed to Fulton, Missouri as a tribute to Winston Churchill. But a memorial to Sir Edmund survives in Chislehurst parish church next to a tablet to his grandson Thomas, who probably did some intelligence work for Sir Francis Walsingham and was a close friend of Christopher Marlowe.[1]

If William Walsingham enjoyed a degree of contact with the royal household, then his wife was even better connected. Joyce Walsingham was the younger sister of the Protestant courtier Sir Anthony Denny. As one of the principal gentlemen of Henry

VIII's privy chamber, Denny was the closest thing that the king had to a friend during the 1540s. His position as keeper of the privy purse made him responsible for Henry's huge personal expenditure on buildings, artwork and gambling. As groom of the stool, the gentleman in charge of the king's close-stool or portable toilet, Denny regulated access to the royal apartments during the last two years of Henry's reign. He also took charge of the dry stamp, a facsimile of the king's signature which empowered him to authorise documents as if they had been signed by Henry in person.

This was a remarkable concentration of power, based on closeness to the king rather than bureaucratic office. When the royal doctors decided that the time had come for Henry VIII to prepare for death in January 1547, it was Denny who had the unenviable task of telling the king. Denny kept his faith in reform even when Henry grew suspicious of Protestant radicalism, and he was among those who ensured that the young Edward VI was advised by councillors of the right religious persuasion. Protector Somerset appointed him as Edward's guardian during his own absences from London fighting the Scots, and he was still close to the throne when he died in 1549. One uncle entrusted with the Tower of London, another at the core of the king's court: these were powerful connections for a London lawyer's son. The tradition of royal service ran in Francis Walsingham's blood.

'Kent is the key of all England', wrote the traveller and antiquary John Leland in the 1530s. Henry VIII had spent much of his childhood at Eltham Palace, four miles from Foot's Cray. The Walsingham lands lay in a belt of arable farms and small estates that sent their wheat to the ever-expanding city of London. Livestock was raised on the salt marshes of the nearby Thames estuary. Timber and cloth travelled from the forests of the Weald, where an embryonic iron industry met the demand for cannon to arm Henry VIII's navy. To the east the road ran towards the River Medway at Rochester and onward to Canterbury, the ecclesiastical capital of England.

Kent was a landscape of ancient settlement, closely governed and prosperous. But its society was also experiencing some unsettling changes under the Tudors. Wealth was becoming concentrated in the hands of relatively few gentlemen and yeomen farmers, causing friction within a social order which was supposed to be fixed and harmonious. Population was rising fast, while people were increasingly on the move in search of work. As a justice of the peace for Kent and under-sheriff of London, Francis Walsingham's father was faced with the consequences of this demographic revolution in the form of growing problems of vagabondage and crime. At its most acute, economic discontent began to shade into politics. Kentish cloth-workers refused to pay a forced loan to fund the king's wars in France, following a tradition of resistance to unjust taxation which stretched back past Jack Cade's rebellion of 1450 to memories of Wat Tyler and the Peasants' Revolt.

The Church was traditionally a force for stability in turbulent times. Sermons and prayerbooks taught that people should submit to adversity and focus on the life of the world to come. But this bedrock was also shifting in response to events in Lutheran Germany, and its trade links with Europe meant that Kent was one of the first English counties to feel the tremors. In 1530 a joiner named Thomas Hitton was caught importing heretical books at Gravesend and burned at the stake on the orders of Bishop Fisher. Two priests and a carpenter who criticised devotional images and praised the works of Martin Luther were faced with a stark choice, to recant or to die for heresy. Kent had a history of religious radicalism to match its tradition of rebellion. The secretive community of the Lollards, who had been reading an English Bible and criticising the doctrine of purgatory for a hundred years, was strong in

Maidstone and the Weald. But figures like Hitton represented the advance guard of a new movement, inspired by Lutheran ideas about the priesthood of all believers and justification by faith; and unlike the Lollards, its converts were determined to evangelise.

Disturbed by the spread of heresy in their midst, Catholics received comfort from an unlikely source. Elizabeth Barton was working as a serving maid when her graphic visions of heaven and the deadly sins first brought her to the notice of the authorities. An investigation into the 'holy maid of Kent' pronounced her to be orthodox, and she subsequently took her vows as a Benedictine nun in Canterbury. But as the movement to break from Rome gathered pace, Barton's revelations acquired a sharply political edge. Having spoken in the pope's defence and called for the burning of Protestant books, she told the king that he would not survive a month on the throne if he divorced Katherine of Aragon. Henry was outraged, and put her under Sir Edmund Walsingham's guard in the Tower. She was hanged and beheaded for treason at Tyburn in 1534, alongside the Canterbury monks who had promoted her as a prophetess.[2]

Francis Walsingham was born during this watershed of the English Reformation. The king's personal dislike of Luther meant that it was not until the early 1530s that an official campaign got under way; and reform, when it came, was driven by Henry's need to settle the succession rather than any commitment to Protestant theology. In 1533 the Act of Appeals declared that 'this realm of England is an empire, and so hath been accepted in the world, governed by one supreme head and king'. A thousand-year allegiance to the papacy was not so much severed as declared to have been an illusion. The English Church was subject to kings rather than foreign potentates, just as it had been before the pope had usurped the rightful power of the crown. Printed for proclamation to the king's subjects, the Act unleashed a barrage of positive and negative propaganda. Henry VIII was hailed as the lion of Judah and Christ's lieutenant on earth, while the pope was vilified as the Antichrist. The royal supremacy over the Church was preached in every parish, taught in every school and catechism class. Heads of household had to swear an oath to uphold it.

Walsingham belonged to a generation of English men and women who had never known how to pray for the pope. Viewed from their perspective, the Reformation seemed like a rebellion of young people against their elders. Henry VIII's erratic relationship with religious reform left many causes for them to fight. Church services were still largely in Latin, incomprehensible to most of the people attending them. The king would not permit any dilution of the traditional teaching on the mass, a reworking of Christ's sacrifice in which bread and wine were miraculously transformed into body and blood. Chantry priests were still singing for the souls of the departed in purgatory. And yet the Bible was openly preached in English from 1539, while parish churches were being cleared of their images of the saints. Targets of the iconoclasm in Kent included the 'rood of grace' at Boxley Abbey, whose moving eyes and lips were exposed as a fraud in the market-place at Maidstone, and the sumptuous shrine of St Thomas Becket at Canterbury. Catholicism was becoming tainted with superstition and trickery. It was also increasingly derided as foreign, unpatriotic, 'Roman'. Protestant scholars such as John Leland and John Bale searched the historical record for proof of England's special place within Christendom. In Queen Elizabeth's reign this nascent sense of nationhood would peak in the belief that the English were an elect people, a new Israel en route for the promised land. It was a conviction which Walsingham would share.[3]

William Walsingham died in 1534, the year that saw Henry VIII proclaimed as supreme head of the Church of England and the holy maid of Kent carted to execution. Francis, his only son, was no more than three years old. William signed himself 'esquire' in his will, as did his own father James Walsingham. Sixteenth-century society divided itself up into ranks or orders marked out by forms of address, the order of precedence in church, even the cut and colour of their clothing. 'Esquire' places Francis Walsingham's father and grandfather among the lesser gentry. They owned land and displayed a coat of arms, became magistrates and sat on the commissions that monitored London's drinking water, but remained below the first tier of families which sent knights of the shire to Parliament and exchanged gifts with the king at new year. As for his soul, William committed it 'to Almighty God our blessed Lady Saint Mary and to all the holy company of heaven'. His work as under-sheriff would have required him to keep a watchful eye for heresy within his London jurisdiction. If he had any Lutheran leanings of his own, he kept them to himself.

Having provided for the marriage of his five daughters, William left the rest of his property to Joyce, 'my well-beloved wife', during his son's minority. Sixteenth-century legal documents are not known for their displays of emotion, so it seems that Francis's parents had developed a real affection for each other, perhaps had even married for love. Joyce was named as an executor, together with Sir Edmund Walsingham and one of William's fellow under-sheriffs. His death left Joyce a widow at twenty-seven, a property-owner with contacts at court and young enough to have more children. Within a couple of years she had married again. Her new husband was the courtier Sir John Carey, brother to the William Carey whose wife Mary Boleyn (the 'other' Boleyn girl) was Henry VIII's mistress for a time in the early 1520s. This proved to be another useful political connection. William and Mary's son Henry Carey, Lord Hunsdon, was Walsingham's near contemporary and a cousin (or, according to gossip, half-brother) to Queen Elizabeth.

Francis very probably went to live with his mother and stepfather at Hunsdon in Hertfordshire, a royal manor where Sir John was bailiff. Princesses Mary and Elizabeth and Prince Edward all spent time there in the 1530s and 40s, and Henry VIII is also known to have visited. In 1546 Edward had his portrait painted at Hunsdon, the gables and tall Tudor chimneys of the house visible through an open window behind the prince. Francis may also have spent time on Sir Anthony Denny's estates nearby, or with his grandfather at Scadbury. Frustratingly, nothing else is known about his childhood. Any private papers in the Walsingham archive were weeded out from the records of state after his death, taking much of his personal life with them. But assuming that Joyce Walsingham shared her brother Anthony's reformed religion, it is fair to speculate that she was the source of the Protestantism that defined Francis's world-view and career.[4]

The first formal record of Walsingham's education is his admission to King's College, Cambridge early in Edward VI's reign. The college accounts reveal that he was paying quarterly bills for food and lodging by June 1548. He matriculated as a member of the university in November and remained in residence for at least two years, leaving sometime in 1550–1. There is no evidence that he took a degree, although this was not unusual for someone of his rank: formal qualifications were mainly for those seeking a career in the Church. His background allowed Walsingham to claim the status of a fellow commoner, giving him social privileges over poorer scholars in chapel and hall. But conditions at King's would still have been spartan, closer to the life of a medieval monk than to the luxurious indolence enjoyed by later generations of gentleman students.

The college of Walsingham's day was cramped and cold, one small court huddled behind a fortified gatehouse. Land levelled a century earlier for a great complex of quadrangles remained empty and unbuilt on. The universities of Oxford and Cambridge still moved to the rhythms of the recently dissolved monasteries, private study and prayer interspersed with lectures in Latin and Greek. Student rooms were fireless, windows shuttered rather than glazed. Discipline at King's could be enforced by flogging and the stocks. But the college also provided security and fellowship, a combination of austerity and privilege in which a sense of communal identity could take deep root. Walsingham's time at Cambridge placed him among a body of five or six hundred men, many of whom would rise to become the governors, scholars and churchmen of Elizabeth's reign. It also put him at the fulcrum of England's spiritual renewal.

Cambridge students had been among the first to imbibe the new religious ideas coming in from the European continent. Opposite King's College lay the White Horse inn or 'little Germany', where Lutheran study groups had gathered in the 1520s. Officially the university took a strong stand against heresy. Under the chancellorship of John Fisher, graduates were required to repudiate the errors of Luther and John Wyclif and to affirm their belief in Catholic doctrine. But when Fisher was succeeded by Henry VIII's chief minister Thomas Cromwell, the orthodoxy changed dramatically. Royal injunctions abolished the teaching of canon law and revised the theology curriculum. The officers of the colleges and the university were ordered to surrender their 'papistical muniments' to the crown. King's advertised its loyalty by paying to have the injunctions painted on a board, while the whole university was required to attend mass in Great St Mary's to pray for King Henry VIII. There was to be no room for doubt about the new ordering of Church and state. The charter of Trinity College, drawn up a month before

Henry's death, specified the fight against the pope as part of its mission.[5]

Walsingham's arrival at King's in the spring of 1548 coincided with two major events in the life of the college. The first was the completion of the stunning sequence of stained glass that had been gradually installed in the chapel over the previous thirty years. The construction of King's Chapel had begun as a monument to Henry VI and the house of Lancaster, but its decoration was utterly Tudor. A pageant of royal iconography framed the lives of the Virgin and Christ that were celebrated in the glass: union roses, the royal arms, Prince Edward's fleur-de-lis, the badges of Anne Boleyn and Katherine Parr. The result rivalled the Henry VII Chapel at Westminster Abbey as a showcase of dynastic symbolism. One window dating from the 1520s pays homage to Henry VIII as Solomon receiving the tribute of the Queen of Sheba, a theme which was also taken up by the court painter Hans Holbein. With the break from Rome the image acquired a more specific resonance, the emperor who built a new temple in which his people could worship.[6]

The second event was the resignation of the provost of the college, George Day, and his replacement by John Cheke. They were similar men in some ways: Day a royal chaplain and frequently at court, Cheke a tutor to the royal children. Both were devotees of classical Greek, and indeed Cheke had been Day's pupil at St John's College. But the Renaissance humanism which they shared led them in different directions. Day supported the royal supremacy over the Church while remaining a conservative in terms of doctrine. Henry VIII approved of his loyalty and appointed him Bishop of Chichester. But when Henry was succeeded by Edward VI, the fellows of King's took advantage of the altered atmosphere to purge the Catholic practice of private masses from their college chapel. Day promptly resigned as provost. He was deprived of his bishopric three years later for refusing to replace altars with the wooden tables decreed by the new Protestant rite.

The new head of King's was a scholar rather than a clergyman. As a junior fellow at St John's, Cheke had attracted a circle of students devoted to the study of Greek. They set themselves apart by speaking the language in the style set out by the great humanist scholar Erasmus of Rotterdam. In the modern world, where knowledge of classical Greek has faded almost beyond recovery, it is difficult to comprehend why such a dry academic question should provoke the controversy that followed. Stephen Gardiner, who was appointed chancellor of Cambridge following Cromwell's execution in 1540, ordered harsh punishments for anyone using the Erasmian rather than the medieval pronunciation. Erasmus was no Protestant; but by opening up the question of biblical translation, his Greek New Testament made a breach in the old Church through which the floodwaters were cascading by the 1540s. Cheke backed down and was appointed tutor to Prince Edward in 1544, devising a curriculum based on languages, scripture and history. He continued in post after 1547, weaning the young king onto Cicero, rhetoric and finally Greek.

Cheke's duties kept him often at court, but his impact on Walsingham's Cambridge was profound. In 1549 he conducted a visitation of the university to test its compliance with Protestantism and refashion its teaching along humanist lines. He was appointed Lady Margaret professor of divinity the same year. His counterpart as regius professor was the eminent German theologian Martin Bucer, whose attempts to find consensus between the reformed churches of Europe may have moulded Walsingham's own belief in Protestant unity in face of a common Catholic enemy. Bucer lectured to large crowds on St Paul's letter to the Ephesians and contributed revisions to the Book of Common Prayer. When he died in 1551, his funeral procession ran to three thousand. Walsingham's tutor Thomas Gardiner wrote verses mourning his death. So complete was Bucer's identification with Protestantism that his bones were exhumed in Mary's reign and burned in a posthumous attempt to obliterate his heresy.

Walsingham drank deeply from this wellspring of reform. Cambridge refined the faith which his mother had taught him, while exposure to Bucer's teachings put him in touch with the European Reformation. An education in the classics induced another powerful impulse in Walsingham and his contemporaries, to enter the service of crown and state. Cheke's collaborator in Greek philology was Thomas Smith, professor of civil law, who was ambassador to France in the 1560s and worked alongside Walsingham as senior principal secretary between 1572 and his death in 1577. Cheke and Smith both taught Roger Ascham, who devised a programme of Christian and classical studies for Princess Elizabeth and was appointed her Latin secretary when she became queen. The most famous of Cheke's pupils was William Cecil, twelve years Walsingham's senior, who became an accomplished classicist and married Cheke's sister Mary. Cecil advanced to be the greatest statesman of his generation, lord treasurer and Baron of Burghley. For twenty years of Elizabeth's reign, the government of England would depend on the ability of Cecil and Walsingham to co-operate.[7]

The stained glass of King's College Chapel survived the iconoclasm of both the sixteenth and the seventeenth centuries and can still be seen more or less as Walsingham knew it, a final flourish of sacred Catholic art in England. Its depictions of the assumption and coronation of the Virgin Mary became controversial almost as soon as they were installed but were saved, ironically enough, by the Tudor royal imagery threaded through them. Beyond the sheltering walls of King's, Edward VI and his governors led the attack on the sin of idolatry. The compromise between tradition and reform which had held Church and state together during Henry VIII's last decade was swiftly abandoned by the council ruling in the young king's name. Churchwardens were ordered to deface or destroy all the devotional images that had survived the purges of the 1530s. Four thousand chantries and colleges singing masses for the dead were dissolved. Altars were removed and priests given permission to marry. The new English prayer book stipulated communion in both bread and wine and left out the symbolic elevation of the Host, provoking riots in several parts of the country and a full-scale rebellion in Cornwall and Devon. Further reforms in 1552 converted the Eucharist into an act of commemoration, and ended the practice of anointing the baptised and the dying. As the Protestant propagandist Richard Morison recalled during Mary's reign, 'The greater change was never wrought in so short space in any country since the world was'.

The king's own role in this is hard to quantify. There was no regency; Edward ruled. But he was also subject to the guidance of men like Walsingham's uncle Anthony Denny. What evidence there is suggests a boy who internalised everything that Cheke and his other tutors could teach him. When he was eleven, Edward collected scriptural passages on the subjects of idolatry and justification by faith and translated them into French as a gift for his uncle the Duke of Somerset. Another exercise was to compose a treatise on the papal supremacy. Deploying arguments for and against in typical humanist fashion, Edward came to the conclusion that the pope was a tyrant, 'the true son of the devil' and an Antichrist on earth. He also kept a notebook of the numerous sermons he heard at court. The contrast with his father, who had transacted royal business whilst listening to mass, must have been obvious.[8]

To Protestants who had suffered intimidation and occasionally active persecution during the closing conservative years of Henry VIII's reign, the liberation of the gospel under Edward was an act of divine providence. Here, at last, was a regime truly committed to reform. Preaching and print began to carry religious debate far beyond the clerical elite to which it had traditionally been confined. The gates of the kingdom of heaven, obscured for so long by ignorance and superstition, were being cleared of weeds and flung open. And yet there were many who struggled to make sense of the new teaching on salvation. A movement which identified itself as unshackling the word of God, giving it back to the poor and unlettered to whom it had been revealed in the time of Christ, also devalued the good works which had always been central to the spirituality of English men and women. Leading a good and charitable life was no longer enough; the Christian soldier must also have faith, defined not as broad belief but as a burning inner conviction, the faith of a convert on the model of St Paul. Only this could weigh against the intolerable burden of human sin on the day of judgement.

Nowhere did this evangelical energy pulse so strongly as in London, where Walsingham spent the final part of Edward's reign and possibly the first year or so of Mary's. He is last recorded in Cambridge in September 1550, although the relevant college accounts for the following year are missing, so he may have been in residence for a few months longer. He is remembered at King's in a portrait hanging in the hall, a version of the half-length attributed to the Dutch artist John de Critz in London's National Portrait Gallery. According to the Latin inscription which hung above his grave in St Paul's Cathedral, Walsingham completed his education with a pilgrimage to

Europe to study its languages and laws. He was certainly a gifted linguist, especially in French and Italian. It was probably the death of his stepfather Sir John Carey that recalled him to London. In 1552 he enrolled at Gray's Inn, where William Walsingham had been a reader and Cecil had also studied during the early 1540s. He may have been testing his vocation as a lawyer like his father, although this does not necessarily follow: having some learning in the law enabled a gentleman to defend his lands against the predatory litigation which increasingly occupied the Tudor courts. More than this, Gray's Inn offered Walsingham a billet close to Westminster and Whitehall, the hub around which king and court, the privy council and Parliament all revolved.

Walsingham was about twenty when he came to London. He found it in a ferment that was partly religious and partly social in character. Two years had passed since every altar in the capital had been ousted by a plain communion table. At St Paul's the iron grates of the choir had been bricked up to prevent traditionalists from engaging in any unauthorised veneration of the sacrament. Preachers denounced the rampant avarice of the ruling class along with the more conventional sins of the city, its want of charity and its addictions to gambling and prostitution. Ordinary people were experiencing sudden personal conversions. An apprentice allegedly turned away from his former riotous living when he heard the lectures at his local church. Other responses to change were more troubling to the authorities. Chroniclers recorded the stories of those who had seen strange omens, three suns in the sky or ghostly soldiers hanging in the air. The atmosphere was fevered, literally so when a mysterious sickness began to strike down both the rich and the poor. Courtiers who contracted the sweat were dancing at nine o'clock and dead by eleven, hence its given name, 'stop-gallant'. The price of bread rose to heights that had never before been seen, accelerated by bad harvests and the thousands pouring into London in search of work. With no modern economic theory to call on, the privy council blamed the crisis on the sloth of the mayor and aldermen. Preachers came to a different conclusion, detecting the punishing hand of God and calling on their congregations to repent.

Gray's Inn lay just outside the walls of the city of London in what John Stow called the 'suburbs' north of Holborn and Chancery Lane. The district was still almost rural, the houses and tenements of Gray's Inn Lane giving way to open fields. Walsingham learned to debate cases within the strict conventions of the common law, familiarising himself with the ossified Latin and Norman French in which writs were sued and judgements delivered. He would also have spent time observing the courts at work in the Palace of Westminster, which had been abandoned as a royal residence early in Henry VIII's reign. It must have seemed that he had entered a strangely medieval world. But life was not wholly limited to moots and learning by rote. The Inns of Court had a tradition of putting on Christmas plays satirising figures in authority (Cardinal Wolsey had been a target during Henry VIII's reign) and commenting on contemporary affairs.

Gray's Inn had a chapel of its own, where barristers and students gathered to mark the opening and closing of the formal legal terms. Its stained-glass window of St Thomas Becket had dutifully been removed on the orders of Henry VIII. But Walsingham would also have been aware of the radically Protestant 'Stranger Churches', the Dutch and French exiles who were offered the same emergency hospitality in London that Martin Bucer had found in Cambridge. The Strangers were given financial support by Edward VI's government, and the dissolved priory church of the Austin Friars in which to worship. Under their pastor John à Lasco, they created a miniature Zurich in England and prayed they would become a beacon of reform to their hosts. Walsingham's sympathies with the Stranger community are revealed in the contributions he made to its upkeep following the St Bartholomew's massacre of Protestants in Paris in 1572.[9]

Just when it seemed that English religion was being born again, calamity struck with a suddenness that left godly preachers reeling. In April 1552 King Edward contracted what he described in his diary as measles and smallpox. His health had apparently been robust until now, and he recovered to celebrate his fifteenth birthday in October. But the infection reactivated the tuberculosis which Edward must already have been carrying. His journal suddenly broke off in November 1552, implying that his condition had begun to deteriorate. By Christmas he was clearly ill, and by March 1553 the Venetian ambassador reckoned that he was dying. Edward knew it too, and began to draft a document known as the 'Devise' to alter the succession to the throne as ordained by Henry VIII.

The next few months witnessed some of the most extraordinary political manoeuvring of the entire Tudor era. Determined that the Reformation should continue after his death, Edward overturned his father's will and a 1544 Act of Parliament by asserting the claim to the throne of his Protestant Grey cousins. His two sisters were excluded from the succession: Mary on account of her Catholicism, Elizabeth for her illegitimacy – or, perhaps, the threat which her future marriage might pose to the cause of religious reform. His preferred solution was to name his cousin Frances Grey, Duchess of Suffolk, as 'governess' of the realm pending the birth of a Protestant male heir, either to Frances herself or to one of her three daughters. But as he grew weaker, Edward changed his mind in favour of advancing the eldest daughter, Jane, to the throne in her own right. He made the alterations to the 'Devise' in his own hand, one of his last acts as king.

Lady Jane Grey was Edward's exact contemporary, and a confirmed Protestant. John Foxe records the story that she scorned to curtsy to the consecrated Host when walking through Princess Mary's private chapel. In May 1553, just days before Edward decided that she would succeed him, Jane reluctantly married the son of his chief minister and de facto governor the Duke of Northumberland. The high politics of Edward's reign were often self-serving, but even by the standards of the time this was a naked attempt by Northumberland to play the kingmaker and splice his own family into the royal line. The king's own lawyers sensed treason, protesting that Edward was too young to make a will, but personal monarchy prevailed. Jane was proclaimed queen on 10 July 1553 to a muted and apprehensive London crowd. Nine days later the same crowds were ringing their bells and lighting bonfires for Mary's accession. Northumberland was executed but Jane Grey spared for the moment, both courses of action calculated to appeal to the people.

The surge of support which brought Mary to the throne is sometimes quoted as being the only successful Tudor rebellion; the irony being that it was pro- rather than anti-Tudor. Many of the families who rallied to her standard at Framlingham Castle in Suffolk in the summer of 1553 were stalwarts of the old faith. Mary had defied the heresies of her brother's reign, preserving the mass in her own household and flaunting her forbidden rosary beads when she rode through London in 1551. Images of the saints appeared in London windows following her accession, evidence that Catholics had been cowed but not converted by King Edward. But Mary enjoyed a broader base of support than this implies, at the start of her reign at least. The Protestant Earl of Sussex commanded her army of supporters in East Anglia. Sir Peter Carew, another committed reformer, saw to it that Mary rather than Jane was proclaimed in his native

Devon. Ordinary seamen of the royal navy forced their officers to declare for Queen Mary. To all of these, Henry VIII's chosen successor seemed preferable to a *coup d'état* engineered by the Duke of Northumberland.

Within a few months, however, the situation had changed dramatically. In the spring of 1554 Mary faced a Protestant rebellion of three thousand men, defectors from the London militia among them, which marched from Kent as far as the gates of the city before their leader Sir Thomas Wyatt surrendered to prevent unnecessary bloodshed. His force was barely a tenth the size of the Pilgrimage of Grace that had mustered against the religious reforms of Henry VIII, but Wyatt was an experienced military commander, and he came closer to deposing a ruling monarch than any other rebel leader during the Tudor age. Rumours of a revolt had forced Wyatt to act before he was fully ready. Given a few weeks longer to prepare, the uprising in Kent would have been one thrust of a co-ordinated national rebellion. The Duke of Suffolk had planned to raise Leicestershire, while Carew was deputed to secure the ports of the south-west so that supplies could be run in by the French navy. The revolt claimed to be a protest against Mary's marriage alliance with Philip of Spain, and this is probably what many of its foot soldiers believed. But its leaders were planning something closer to a revolution: the marriage of Princess Elizabeth to Edward Courtenay, Earl of Devon, and the proclamation of a Protestant monarchy. Elizabeth could well have been executed in the fallout, although in the event it was Jane Grey who suffered, beheaded in the courtyard of the Tower whilst reciting the fifty-first Psalm.

Where was Walsingham in all of this? If still at Gray's Inn, he would have watched the royal commander the Earl of Pembroke deploy his cavalry along Holborn; he would also have seen the queen's forces part to let Wyatt's men through, apparently with the aim of attacking the rebels in the rear, although they may have been waiting to see which side the city itself would take. But there is another possibility. Walsingham had recently reached the age of twenty-one stipulated in his father's will for coming into his inheritance. The manor of Foot's Cray was now his. The adjacent estate at Scadbury had passed from Sir Edmund Walsingham to his eldest son Thomas, Francis's first cousin. The Walsingham lands lay in a belt of parishes in north-western Kent that sent men to join Sir Thomas Wyatt's army. Wyatt himself was well known to the Kentish gentry, having served as MP for the county in 1547 and sheriff in 1550–1. Members of Walsingham's extended family were implicated in Wyatt's revolt, just as they had supported Jane Grey. Did he join them? If Walsingham did get himself involved in treason in 1553–4, his decision to flee Queen Mary's England may have been impelled by politics as much as faith.[10]

The failure of Wyatt's rebellion to depose Queen Mary faced Protestants with a bleak set of choices: to compromise, to resist, or to go into European exile. For the majority who could not afford to emigrate, the dilemma was starker still. The poor had to decide whether to return to the abomination of the mass or be forced beyond the walls of the Church. Excommunication carried with it the growing danger of imprisonment and a violent death. Paying lip-service to the Catholic religion while attempting to remain pure in heart was condemned by Protestant ministers as Nicodemism, named after the Pharisee who would worship Christ only under cover of darkness.

In London, the sheer size of the city and the complexity of its parish structure offered possibilities for Protestants to gather at its margins. Secret conventicles met in a cloth-workers' loft and a ship moored at Billingsgate, or took their Bible study groups out into the fields; a kind of internal exile. Their ways of coping were strikingly similar to the tactics that would be used by Catholics when they were driven underground by Walsingham and the forces of state surveillance during the 1570s and 80s. But this sort of zealotry was unusual, even in the capital. Looking back on Mary's reign, John Foxe numbered the Londoners who had held fast to the faith in the dozens rather than the hundreds. Some form of accommodation with the new environment was far more common, among the political elite as well as the broader population. A Parliament which had voted for evangelical reform in the 1530s proved surprisingly willing to repeal it again once the private ownership of ex-monastic land had been guaranteed. Provincial government continued to function effectively, implying that gentry with Protestant sympathies put their loyalty to the crown before the requirements of their religion. William Cecil had been knighted for his services to Edward VI's government, but still found himself able to stay in Mary's England and accept the mass back into his household chapel.[11]

Walsingham interpreted his scripture differently from Cecil. In autumn 1555, eighteen months after the failure of the Wyatt–Carew conspiracy and at a time of mounting persecution for Protestants, he arrived in the Swiss city of Basel accompanied by three of his Denny cousins. Henry, the eldest, was fifteen. He and his younger brother Anthony had previously matriculated at Pembroke College in Cambridge. They now registered at the university of Basel, together with Charles Denny and Walsingham himself. All four are described as *nobilis* in the university register, a mark of their superior social status. Walsingham very soon moved on to Padua in the Veneto region of Italy, leaving the Denny boys in the care of the English community, but he would return to Basel in 1556 and probably remained there for the rest of Mary's reign. Late in life he recalled his time among the 'true-hearted Swiss' with an ageing man's longing for the clarity of his youth.

Walsingham and his cousins joined a band of exiles about a thousand strong, sprawled across the Protestant towns of the Holy Roman Empire and the Swiss Confederation: Frankfurt and Strasbourg, Geneva and Zurich. Like Walsingham and the Dennys, most were wealthy or well connected. Gentry families and clergymen ejected from the universities mixed with merchants who acted as bankers to the English exodus. John Calvin had published the first edition of his *Institutes of the Christian Religion* in Basel, and the city was still known for its radicalism twenty years later. Its English congregation elected elders and conducted services according to the reformed Book of Common Prayer. From 1557 they gathered in a rented former convent, the Claraklosten, which combined a dormitory with a chapel: an ersatz Cambridge college in which Foxe could work on his *Acts and Monuments* or 'Book of Martyrs'. Three of Foxe's books would be dedicated to Walsingham, reflecting the affinity between the two men.

If Basel represented the Reformation to Walsingham, then Padua was an education in the Renaissance. In 1555–6 he was elected *consiliarius* or spokesman of the small English 'nation' of students at the city's law university. Governed by the republic of Venice, Padua lay outside the imperial sphere of influence which had come to dominate Italy. It was a favourite destination for English travellers. Recent alumni of its universities included the diplomat Richard Morison and the political theorist Thomas Starkey as well as the Catholic humanist and activist Reginald Pole, condemned as a traitor by Henry VIII and invited back to England by Mary to become her Cardinal Archbishop of Canterbury. Artists from across the Italian peninsula had studied in fifteenth-century Padua, and its churches and civic buildings were decorated with frescoes by Giotto and Mantegna. Its rich deposit of Catholic iconography makes Padua appear a curious place for Francis Walsingham to be, but in fact the city had a reputation as a refuge from the Inquisition. English *consiliarii* could avoid making any formal declaration of the Catholic faith, with the result that the intellectual traffic between England and Italy survived a Reformation which might otherwise have severed it.

This may not have been Walsingham's first visit to Padua. In 1554 a large number of English refugees of conscience had arrived in the city, including the three Denny brothers and Sir John Cheke, pardoned by Mary for supporting Jane Grey but shaken by his imprisonment in the Tower. It's a fair guess that Walsingham was among this group of émigrés. Both Sir Anthony Denny and his wife Joan were dead, making him the obvious choice to act as protector to their sons in exile. Cheke's presence in Padua reinforces the likelihood that Walsingham travelled from England to Italy in 1554 following the failure of Wyatt's rebellion. Cheke passed his time lecturing the English community on the *Orations* of the Greek statesman Demosthenes. His students included Thomas Wilson, a fellow of King's and a future privy councillor specialising in the interrogation of political prisoners, and maybe Walsingham too. Wilson would subsequently publish his own translation of the *Orations*, comparing the tyrant Philip of Macedon with Philip II of Spain. He and Walsingham would work in tandem as principal secretaries to Queen Elizabeth during the Anjou marriage negotiations in the late 1570s.

If this chronology is correct, we may imagine Walsingham following his former provost and other King's men to Padua in 1554, taking his Denny cousins with him, before escorting his young charges to Basel. He then spent a year in Padua before a final period in Basel, or other travels unknown. If the details are uncertain, the conclusion is clear: Francis Walsingham was moulded by the intellectual culture of Renaissance Italy as well as the theology of Reformation Germany.

At Gray's Inn Walsingham had learned about the law as a practical tool of justice and government, debated between barristers and determined by precedent. In Padua he studied civil or Roman law, and the manner of teaching was very different. Lectures focused on the *Corpus Iuris Civilis* of the emperor Justinian and other canonical texts, glossed by medieval commentators. English law was common law, so becoming a 'civilian' was of little practical use in the English courts. But civil law still made an impression on the theory and practice of Tudor government. Its pan-European status made it a good training for diplomats like Walsingham and Wilson. More subtly, it taught that statecraft itself was a virtuous pursuit. Thomas Starkey had seen the civil law as the ideal preparation for what he called the 'politic life', and its ideas fed into the royal supremacy that Henry VIII declared over the Church of England. It quickened the calling to serve which Walsingham had inherited from his family, although the republican context of his studies in Padua is also significant in light of his later thinking about the state. Principal Secretary Walsingham is too often presented in one dimension, a dour Puritan motivated solely by fear and hatred. The contrast with this image is illustrated by two small domestic details of Walsingham's time in Italy: he bought a quantity of wine and he invested in a clavichord, a keyboard instrument specially suited to composition.[12]

Walsingham recalled his education many years later in a letter to one of his nephews about to travel abroad. It would be hard to find a clearer manifesto of the value of ancient learning to the study of statecraft, a central tenet of the Renaissance mindset. Walsingham prescribed a daily routine of prayer, scripture and translation: specifically an epistle of Tully (Cicero) into French, and out of French into Latin. History came next. 'For that knowledge of histories is a very profitable study for the gentleman, read you the lives of Plutarch,' he wrote, 'also Titus Livius and all the Roman histories, as also all books of state both old and new'. The intention of all this reading was to 'mark how matters have passed in government in those days' in order 'to apply them to these our times and states'. He should also keep his eyes open, study foreign fortifications, and observe the men of state around princes, captured by Walsingham in an architectural metaphor as 'conduit pipes, though they themselves have no water'. In 1580 the soldier poet Philip Sidney penned a similar letter to his friend Edward Denny, another of Walsingham's cousins, recommending the same core ingredients – 'an hour to your Testament, and a piece of one to Tully's *Offices*' – but adding Machiavelli and Holinshed's *Chronicle* to the mix.[13]

By comparison with their countrymen scattered through Switzerland and Germany, the English émigrés in Venice and Padua were closely knit and politically active. Their individual biographies reveal a web of connections to the executed Duke of Northumberland and the Wyatt–Carew plotters. Several had estates in the west of England, where any Protestant liberating force was likely to land first. The grandest of the exiles was the Earl of Bedford, who had carried messages between Wyatt and Princess Elizabeth in 1554 and was now assembling a household of disenchanted Protestant aristocrats in Venice. The Cornishman Henry Killigrew had sailed to France to secure royal backing for Wyatt's rebellion; his manor house commanding Falmouth harbour might prove crucial to any future attempt to oust Queen Mary. John Ashley, whose wife Kat was Elizabeth's governess, was suspected of smuggling anti-Marian propaganda from Padua into England. The Venetian authorities encouraged any such political agitation against Mary and her husband Philip because it suited their anti-Spanish foreign policy.

In January 1556 Edward Courtenay, Earl of Devon, enrolled to study law at the university of Padua. Courtenay's father the Marquis of Exeter had been a first cousin to Henry VIII, a gentleman of the privy chamber and a personal friend of the king. But as Henry became increasingly paranoid in his later years, so Exeter's Yorkist lineage had come to tell against him. His execution on a fabricated charge of treason in 1538 left his son as one of very few remaining noblemen with royal blood in his veins. Thomas Wyatt had hoped for a marriage between Elizabeth and Edward Courtenay, a Protestant and English regime as opposed to a Catholic and largely Spanish one. Courtenay survived the furore by turning informer on his co-conspirators, yet he remained obsessed by his lineage and alive to any initiative that might make him a king consort. The Venetian ambassador in England encouraged Courtenay's pretensions to power in 1554, supplying Wyatt with artillery from a ship in the Thames. Now Venice itself became the focus of Protestant plotting. The adventurer Henry Dudley wanted to lead a French invasion of Devon and Cornwall, seizing Exeter as a bridgehead before marching on to London. Courtenay got as far as selling land to pay for men and supplies, but he died in suspicious circumstances in September 1556; murdered by poison, it has been suggested, on the orders of Philip of Spain. Francis Walsingham was the English *consiliarius* during Courtenay's time in Padua. He also seems to have been close to the Earl of Bedford, since he was elected to Parliament early in Elizabeth's reign to represent towns within Bedford's gift. Beyond these bare facts, his role can only be guessed at. But whether as observer or agent, Walsingham was apprenticed in Padua into a world of subversion and conspiracy.[14]

How much ought we to read into the fact that Walsingham chose exile during Mary's reign, while William Cecil made his peace with the new regime? Cecil's behaviour was not quite the dignified retreat that might be expected of a man who had been a royal secretary and privy councillor during the most radical phase of Edward VI's Reformation. He positioned himself for two possible futures, serving Queen Mary on two diplomatic missions but also acting as steward of Princess Elizabeth's lands. His new year's gift of gold to the queen in 1555 hints that he was open to a place in government, and he developed an unlikely friendship with Cardinal Pole, the spearhead of the Counter-Reformation in England. While Walsingham was sharing the Clarakloster with John Foxe, Cecil dined with Pole and gratefully accepted the stewardship of his manor of Wimbledon.

Cecil was a dozen years older than Walsingham, with a lot more to lose by going into exile. He was already an experienced administrator, with links to Elizabeth which could bear fruit if Philip and Mary failed to produce an heir. He was married, with a young family and a growing portfolio of property to defend. Walsingham's public life had barely begun; compared to Cecil, he had little to detain him in England. The different situations of the two men make their decisions easier to understand. But character must also have come into it. Walsingham wasn't forced into exile, unlike the married Protestant ministers or the London printers who lost their livelihoods under the new administration. He could have trodden the broad path of conformity and compromise, making the most of his father's reputation in the law and the city or cashing in his Cambridge connections to find a position in royal service. He could have copied his cousin Thomas Walsingham, who attended Cardinal Pole as he travelled through Kent on his triumphal return to England in November 1554. Instead he chose the narrow path, banishing himself in Basel among the theology students whose company he had shared at university. Cecil and Walsingham had many aspects of their outlook in common, but their experience of Mary's reign creates a sharp divide between them: one with a politician's pragmatism, the other unwilling to be a reed bending before the wind.[15]

In the spring of 1555, grim news began to reach the exiles about their co-religionists back home. The re-Catholicisation of England had begun positively enough, recovering and repairing devotional art, replacing altars and images, and celebrating mass with all the veneration that could be mustered. Money which might have restored the monasteries went instead to the universities and new seminaries to train up a better class of clergy. Dissidents were to be won over by education and preaching, and there was talk of a Catholic Bible in the English language. Many people must have welcomed the certainty of ceremony. With the return of the mass, however, came the means to police it. In December 1554 Parliament voted to resurrect the medieval heresy laws which Edward VI had repealed. Since church courts could not carry out a sentence of death, the condemned were handed back to the crown for execution, tainting the queen with the persecution which soon followed. The penalty for heresy was to be burned alive: a foretaste of the fires of hell but also a total destruction of the body, leaving nothing to answer Christ's call on the day of resurrection.

The incineration of heresy began with the Bible translator John Rogers at Smithfield in early February 1555. Executions in Gloucester and Suffolk soon signalled that Protestants in the provinces had as much to fear as those in the capital. Lichfield, Chester, Exeter and Guernsey would all witness public burnings over the next three and a half years. Two hundred and eighty-four people were executed in all, the last five of them at Canterbury only days before Mary's death. Another thirty died in prison of trauma or neglect.

The burnings swiftly accrued their own world of ritual. Protestants tried to die with fortitude, singing psalms and reassuring each other of the better world to come: they were convinced there was no purgatory to fear. The condemned kissed the stake or prostrated themselves in prayer before it, echoing the traditional Good Friday ceremony of creeping to the cross. Their supporters made flimsy white shrouds for them to wear, a reference to the army of martyrs in the Book of Revelation but also grimly practical: thick clothes prolonged the agony in the flames. The Kentish martyr Christopher Wade dipped himself in pitch and cried out to the crowd to beware the Whore of Babylon before he burned with his hands held to heaven. Watching him die was the nine-year-old Richard Fletcher, who would preach at the execution of Mary, Queen of Scots at Fotheringhay in 1587. While relic-hunters scrabbled in the ashes for fragments of burnt bone, the Church unloosed a fusillade of sermons and print. Miles Hogarde's *The Displaying of the Protestants* mocked the willingness of heretics to die in a 'fool's paradise'. Catholic spectators at Wade's execution pelted him with wooden faggots when he tried to shout down the chaplain preaching next to his pyre.

Accompanying the executions was an extraordinary campaign of surveillance and coercion. Eamon Duffy has drawn attention to the 'microscopic' scrutiny to which ordinary people were subjected during Mary's reign. Adoration of the body of Christ during mass was non-negotiable. Congregations were monitored for anyone looking away during the elevation of the Host or choosing to sit behind a pillar. A magistrate from Kent known as 'Justice Nine-Holes' bored through the restored wooden rood-loft so he could spy on the people of his parish. Weekly communion and Lenten confessions could not be evaded. Women who chose not to receive the sacrament before childbirth were reported as suspect. Men known to have good voices in

Edward VI's reign were forced to join the church choir. Anyone who refused the traditional rites of the Church on their deathbed was denied Christian burial. In Queen Mary's England, the beauty of holiness was restored by force.

The holocaust reached its height in London. Sixty-five people were burned in or close to the capital, and many more in the wider diocese of London. Eighteen men and women went to their deaths in just six weeks in the spring of 1556. One of them was blind, another disabled. At a mass burning at Stratford-le-Bow only the men were tied to stakes, leaving the women loose among the flames. The Bishop of London was Edmund Bonner, more a lawyer than a preacher and prone to outbursts of violent anger. Four years' imprisonment in the Marshalsea prison in Edward's reign had given him a searing sense of grievance, and he presided over the excommunication of heretics in his diocese with meticulous attention to detail. Enraged by the stoicism of a Protestant weaver from Shoreditch, Bonner seized his hand and held it over a candle until the flesh peeled. To Foxe he was Bloody Bonner, 'persecutor of the light and a child of darkness'.

Historians have tried to deal with these events by putting them in context. They point out that both Protestants and Catholics accepted that burning was a suitable death for a heretic. They note the relative insignificance of the English statistics on a European scale of persecution. But if the idea of burning for heresy was less shocking than we might think, the identity of the victims sent shudders of horror through a society which truly valued the ties of community and neighbourliness. Senior clergy like Bishop John Hooper and Archbishop Cranmer might have been regarded as legitimate targets, although even this cannot be assumed. The authorities were clearly nervous about public support for Hooper, and hooded him during his final journey from London to Gloucester. But high-profile heretics were followed to the stake by a procession of lesser martyrs: popular preachers, tanners and fullers too poor to escape into exile, the elderly, those too young to have experienced pre-Reformation Catholicism. Fifty-six of them were women. The campaign to eradicate false doctrine had strayed far beyond its initial mandate from Queen Mary to 'do justice to such as by learning would deceive the simple'.[16]

Spurred on by the news from England, a handful of the English émigrés began to question the doctrine that monarchs were the Lord's anointed. These radical thinkers were a minority voice even within the community of exiles, and they had little enough impact at the time. The *Shorte Treatise of Politike Power* by the former Bishop of Winchester John Ponet summoned an array of biblical and historical examples to argue that it was lawful to depose a tyrant, but its publication in 1556 came too late to influence the actions of Thomas Wyatt or Peter Carew. John Knox's *First Blast of the Trumpet against the Monstrous Regiment of Women* argued passionately that the idea of a woman ruling over a nation was 'repugnant to nature' and 'the subversion of good order'. But the book appeared in 1558, the year of Mary's death. The significance of these texts was only truly felt in Elizabeth's reign, when this subversive strand of English political thought was supplemented by the writings of Dutch and French Protestants; men close to Francis Walsingham. His exile in Basel and Padua provided Walsingham with more than a taste of the Reformation and Renaissance, more even than an apprenticeship in spycraft and conspiracy. It altered his perception of monarchy itself, and ensured that his relationship with Queen Elizabeth would never be as simple as that of mistress and servant.[17]

2 Massacre at Paris

On 6 November 1558 Queen Mary, childless and ravaged by fever, yielded to the inevitable and named Elizabeth as her successor. Her husband Philip of Spain had not been seen in England for more than a year. Hopes that the queen would give birth to a child had turned to ashes. Any chance of sustaining the Catholic faith to which Mary had devoted her life now depended on her half-sister, the offspring of Anne Boleyn and their father's break from Rome. By recognising Elizabeth as her heir, maybe Mary hoped to coax her into maintaining the rites and rituals which she had tenderly restored over the previous five years. If so, then she was deluding herself. Although Elizabeth had outwardly conformed to Catholicism during the reign of her sister, Protestants knew that she was a true reformer at heart. The deaths of Queen Mary and Cardinal Pole on the same day, 17 November, were taken as proof that the providential course of history had been restored. In later years Elizabeth's accession day would become an annual festival marked by bonfires and patriotic sermons.

The bells ringing across the nation to announce the peaceful transfer of power sounded a reveille to the English Protestant diaspora. Several hundred clergy, merchants and gentlemen were soon streaming home to pick up the threads of their lives. They might not have had a master plan for the future shape of the Church of England, but collectively the Marian exiles would make a deep impression on the age of Elizabeth. All but one of Queen Mary's bishops resigned in 1559, compelling Elizabeth to look to the émigrés to recruit the next generation of Church leaders. Fourteen of the twenty-five bishops who sat in the 1563 Convocation or synod had taken refuge in Germany and Switzerland. Protestantism in England had previously been moulded mainly by Luther and Bucer. Now it was infused with Calvinist ideas: the predestination of the elect to salvation and the structuring of the Church along presbyterian lines, with authority invested in congregations rather than bishops. This second wave of religious reform came with its own Geneva translation of the Bible, cheaper and easier to carry than the Great Bible of Henry VIII's reign.[1]

Political thought had also moved on during the time of exodus. Queen Mary and her ministers had regarded Protestantism as a disease which could be cut out of the body politic, driving John Knox and John Ponet to pioneer theories of resistance to royal power. Now that Elizabeth was on the throne, the threat that had sparked such radical thinking had faded. But the principle of absolute monarchy had been questioned, and the genie could not be put back in the bottle. It was no longer enough to preach the gospel of obedience: the crown would have to engage with those who saw the power of any earthly monarchy as limited by God. The sovereignty of a woman threw up even greater challenges. Mary's reign had been a time of persecution, popular rebellion and a disastrous foreign war; Elizabeth could hardly call upon her sister as a precedent.

Elizabeth's government was full of men who had tailored their religion to suit the fashion dictated by Queen Mary's regime. William Cecil had acted like an evangelical in King Edward's day, yet he allowed the Catholic mass back into his household and courted the friendship of Cardinal Pole. Robert Dudley jousted at Mary's court and fought in her army in France to atone for his family's role in the Jane Grey conspiracy. The Earl of Sussex defended London against Wyatt's rebels in 1554 and was appointed a gentleman of King Philip's privy chamber.

Sir Thomas Smith advised Mary on the economy and was paid a handsome royal pension. Sir Nicholas Bacon quietly carried on his work for the Court of Wards while his wife served as a gentlewoman of Queen Mary's privy chamber. None of this is to deny the Protestantism of Elizabeth's principal councillors, but it does mark Walsingham out among his peers: a man who could not be lured from his faith by the promise of patronage.

Walsingham was back in England by the spring of 1559, when he was elected to Parliament for the seat of Bossiney in Cornwall. A hamlet skirting the ruins of Tintagel Castle seems an unlikely start for one of the great political careers of the sixteenth century. Bossiney was condemned as a rotten borough by the Reform Act of 1832, and barely even registers on a modern map. Walsingham probably never saw the place, but he did understand its significance. As part of the estate of the duchy of Cornwall, Bossiney was effectively under the control of the crown. Elections were managed by the lord warden of the stannaries; in this case Francis Russell, Earl of Bedford and Walsingham's fellow exile in the Veneto. There was a natural affinity of faith between the two men. Bedford had studied with Heinrich Bullinger at Zurich and corresponded with Calvin following his return to England, using his position in the Lords to denounce the papacy as 'a sink of crime and a cess-pool of iniquity'.

Elizabeth's first parliament opened in January 1559 with a service at Westminster Abbey. Its dissolved Benedictine community had been re-founded by Mary, but the new queen had no time for monasteries. When Abbot Feckenham led his monks to meet Elizabeth at the abbey door, she objected to their processional candles: 'Away with these torches, for we see very well'. It was a signal that the devotional world of saints and altars, lights before images and the elevation of the consecrated Host, would soon be gone for good. After three months of debate, the constitution and liturgy of the Church were settled by statute. The Act of Supremacy restored the sovereignty of the crown which had been asserted in 1534, though with one important difference: Elizabeth was styled as 'supreme governor' rather than 'supreme head' of the Church of England. This was an astute piece of politics, the queen outmanoeuvring objectors on both sides of the religious divide. The mystical union between monarchy and priesthood asserted by her father and her brother did not easily translate into the rule of a woman. But the altered title also reflects the humility before God detectable in the prayers which Elizabeth composed throughout her life.

The second pillar of the Elizabethan Church was the Act of Uniformity. Services would be conducted according to the Book of Common Prayer; anyone absent without good cause would be fined a shilling a week. The liturgy was based on the more thoroughly Protestant prayer book of 1552, but again there was an attempt to soften the impact of change. Ministers were required to wear a surplice, not quite the sumptuous vestments of the Catholic past but still a visible mark of their ordained priesthood. The order for holy communion manoeuvred the conservative formula of the 1549 Prayer Book, 'The body of our Lord Jesus Christ, which was given for thee, preserve thy body and soul into everlasting life', into the more commemorative rite of 1552, 'Take and eat this in remembrance that Christ died for thee, and feed on him in thy heart by faith with thanksgiving'. By combining the two, it was hoped the Eucharist would revert to what it once had been, a celebration of communal peace in which all could take part.[2]

Walsingham was one of nineteen Marian exiles elected to Parliament in 1559. The Commons had swollen to a total of four hundred MPs by the beginning of Elizabeth's reign, and the queen would enfranchise another thirty-one boroughs of her own. Putting this in perspective, the House of Commons was two-thirds its modern size at a time when the total population of England and Wales was about one-twentieth of today's. Henry VIII and Cromwell had created a new role for Parliament, extending its jurisdiction over spiritual affairs and using it to justify the break from Rome. What Parliament had created only Parliament could modify, hence Elizabeth's use of Lords and Commons to revive the royal supremacy over the Church in 1559. Once this framework had been rebuilt, however, she wanted to see no more wrangling over religion. The ambiguities in Elizabeth's Church settlement may have offended the hotter Protestants on her council, but they also appealed to the conservative majority of her people. In her opinion, the question of religion was now a matter for the queen alone.

Elizabeth's interpretation of her royal prerogative provoked a series of skirmishes in the parliaments that followed, with controversy focusing on the Book of Common Prayer. William Strickland introduced a bill in 1571 aimed at Protestantising the Prayer Book, while Peter Turner tried to replace it with the Genevan order of service in 1584. If a Puritan ideology of opposition did exist in the Elizabethan House of Commons, as some historians have claimed, then there is no evidence that Walsingham shared it. His attitude to royal power was shaped by the writings of resistance theorists as well as his deep Protestant faith, but Parliament was not the place to pursue reform. Walsingham never made a major speech in the Commons, unlike his firebrand brother-in-law Peter Wentworth, who described Parliament without freedom of speech as 'a very school of flattery and dissimulation and so a fit place to serve the devil' – a challenge to the crown which carried him to the Tower. Walsingham's strategy was distinctly different. In 1578 he urged the English community of Merchant Adventurers in Antwerp not to abandon the Prayer Book for a more Protestant service:

> I would have all reformations done by public authority . . . If you knew with what difficulty we retain that we have, and that the seeking of more might hazard that which we already have, you would then deal warily in this time when policy carrieth more sway than zeal.[3]

Whatever his private doubts, he could appreciate the political value in having one form of public prayer.

In 1563 Walsingham was returned to the Commons for Lyme Regis, another borough under the Earl of Bedford's influence; he would subsequently sit as a knight of the shire for Surrey. Cecil took an interest in his election, noting in a memorandum 'Mr Walsingham to be of the House'. Sir Walter Mildmay, who had married Walsingham's elder sister Mary in 1546, may have played a role in bringing him to Cecil's notice. Mildmay was another Gray's Inn lawyer, an administrator rather than a politician who had worked with Cecil as a commissioner and councillor in Edward VI's reign. His presence on the privy council from 1566 adds Mildmay to the list of crown servants, courtiers and parliamentarians who were related to Walsingham. Peter Wentworth was married to Francis's sister Elizabeth. Another sister, Christiana, married firstly John Tamworth, keeper of the privy purse – a position once occupied by Sir Anthony Denny – and then William Dodington, an official in the royal mint. Katherine Astley, Queen Elizabeth's first chief gentlewoman of the privy chamber, was Denny's sister-in-law and thus related to Walsingham by marriage.

The closest of these family connections threading through government was also the longest-lived. Robert Beale was the senior clerk of the privy council, a Marian exile who had studied in Strasbourg and Zurich. He worked for Walsingham as a secretary during the Paris embassy of 1571–3, and later deputised for him as secretary of state during Walsingham's frequent absences from the council table. Friendship became kinship when Beale married Edith St Barbe, sister of Walsingham's second wife Ursula. Beale was a strong reformer, favouring the Protestant 1552 Prayer Book over the compromise settlement of 1559 and arguing that the power of bishops should be reduced. To Walsingham he was 'my brother Beale', a political ally and a friend.[4]

Apart from his election to Parliament, much of Walsingham's life during the 1560s is a frustrating blank. Robert Beale helps to explain why the documentary trail goes cold. A lengthy essay dating from 1592 describes the office of principal secretary which his brother-in-law had filled for so long. Aware of his own advancing years, Beale was worried about the continuity of government. He was particularly keen that paperwork should be maintained and passed on intact to the next generation of crown servants. In Henry VIII's reign there had been a chamber in the Palace of Westminster where the records of state were kept separate from the private papers of the principal secretary. But the practice had fallen into neglect, 'whereby no means are left to see what was done before or to give any light of service to young beginners'. The result was that, following Walsingham's death, 'all his papers and books both public and private were seized on and carried away'.

Beale's plea for a permanent archive is remarkable for its day. It would ultimately be answered by the creation of the Public Record Office in 1838, when piles of mouldering manuscripts were moved out of the Tower of London and Westminster Abbey into purpose-built accommodation in Chancery Lane. Victorian editors created order out of chaos, sifting out the principal records of government and sewing the individual manuscripts into volumes. Much of the Walsingham archive came to rest here, in the domestic and foreign series of the state papers. Other material descended to the British Museum, originally belonging to the records of state but extracted by antiquaries and collectors like Robert Harley, Earl of Oxford, whose portrait greets visitors to the manuscript reading room of the British Library at King's Cross.

Walsingham's public career can be reconstructed in forensic detail. But the letters and account books which might have recreated the texture of his domestic life – the hospitality and patronage which he dispensed, the furnishing of his houses, his private thoughts and devotions – are nearly all lost. Of no use to later secretaries, they were simply thrown away. If Walsingham had founded a political dynasty in the manner of William Cecil, his personal archive might have been preserved as Cecil's was at Hatfield House. As it is, only hints and fragments remain. We know that Walsingham enjoyed falconry because Sir John Forster, warden of the middle march with Scotland, presented him with a prized gyrfalcon. Other gifts included plants collected from the new worlds overseas which the English were beginning to explore. Walsingham noted that he went to see a garden while ambassador in Paris in 1571. His journal for 1583–4 couples the planting of elms and hawthorn in his own garden with urgent issues of state: the making of ciphers, the interrogation of Catholic priests and traitors, and the fortification of Dover harbour. Distinctions between public and private had little meaning for Walsingham. A garden was simultaneously a place of retreat and display, its triumph of order over nature a recognised metaphor of statecraft during the Renaissance. The portrait of Prince Edward at Hunsdon had made the same claim, the garden beyond the window symbolic of the royal estate which he would all too soon inherit.[5]

At least something of Walsingham's family life can be recovered. In 1560 his mother Joyce died and was buried beside her husband in the church of St Mary Aldermanbury. When Francis chose to marry two years later, it was within the same London merchant community that he looked for a bride. Anne

Carleill was recently widowed, a woman of means with a young son and an older daughter. Her late father, Sir George Barnes, was Lord Mayor of London in 1552–3 and had helped to put Lady Jane Grey on the throne. They had no children of their own, although Walsingham supported his stepson Christopher Carleill during a military career spent mainly in the Netherlands and Ireland. Anne's father and first husband were founder members of the Muscovy Company, incorporated in 1555 to spearhead England's trade into Russia, while her daughter Alice Carleill married the Baltic trader Christopher Hoddesdon; his reports kept Walsingham informed about shipping movements and dissident Catholics during the 1570s and early 1580s.

By marrying Anne Carleill, Walsingham strengthened his family ties with the city of London and gained admission to a circle of speculators in the new frontiers of English trade. In 1569 he became an 'assistant' or director of the Muscovy Company. For her part Anne acquired a guardian for her son during his minority, and the social cachet of a husband with connections to the royal court. Foot's Cray was sold, and the couple leased the manor of Parkbury in Hertfordshire. Walsingham had his first taste of crown service as a justice of the peace. But their marriage of mutual convenience was short-lived. Anne made her will, 'sick of body', in July 1564. Within four months she was dead, bequeathing Francis £100 and the custody of her son Christopher, with an earnest entreaty to see him 'virtuously brought up in learning and knowledge'. The contents of her wardrobe were distributed among Walsingham's sisters, suggesting the women had become friends: a damask gown with a kirtle of satin for Christiana, a pair of sables for Elizabeth, and a purse of purple silk and gold for Mary. Other bequests included a diamond, a 'book of gold' with a chain, and several sums to purchase remembrance rings – a Protestant alternative to the masses and obits of the past. A feather bed with bolster and blankets, its valance of needlework and curtains of sarsenet in red and green, offers a glimpse of the costly fittings at Parkbury.[6]

Walsingham did not mourn for long. In 1566 he married again, and this time it would last until his own death twenty-four years later. Ursula St Barbe was the daughter of a Somerset gentleman. Her first husband Sir Richard Worseley had been a landowner in the Isle of Wight, and Ursula brought the estates of Carisbrooke Priory and a house at Appuldurcombe as her dowry. Wight was burned by a French raiding party in 1545 and the Worseley house seems to have been fortified, since Ursula's two sons were killed there by an explosion of gunpowder soon after their mother's remarriage. A legal dispute over rights to the property grumbled on for several years. Walsingham's earliest surviving letter is a request to a friend for help in wooing Ursula 'from her resolution of sole life', and the couple continued to correspond when royal service kept them apart. Mary, the younger of their two daughters, died as a child in 1580. But Frances, named after her father, would wed two of the brightest-burning courtiers of the Elizabethan age: the poet Sir Philip Sidney, who died in 1586 fighting the Protestant cause in the Netherlands, and then the doomed royal favourite the Earl of Essex.

Ursula Walsingham's presence can best be detected in the ceremonial life of the court. She followed her husband to Paris when he was made ambassador, and was entertained by the French royal family in April 1571. As Francis rose in status, so Ursula took her part in the rituals of gift exchange which surrounded Queen Elizabeth. At new year 1579–80 she presented the queen with a pair of gloves set with gold buttons: an astute choice, since Elizabeth was known to be deeply proud of her hands. The following year she gave a jewel in the form of a scorpion, wrought in agate and gold with sparks of diamond and ruby. In 1581 Ursula took custody of a valuable diamond belonging to the Portuguese royal pretender Don Antonio, his pledge of support for a planned attack on Spanish colonies in the Caribbean. Walsingham described her in his will as 'my most well beloved wife', 'my most kind and loving wife'. She would outlive him by twelve years, her own will listing a resident minister among her numerous other servants. Two cooks were left an annuity of £3 each while a waiting-woman, Alice Poole, received a generous £50. Other bequests were made to the minister and the poor of the parish of Barnes, indicative of her godly faith. A portrait once thought to be Dame Ursula and datable to 1583, depicting a strong-featured woman in ruff and cap with a chain around her neck, has now been demoted to an 'unknown woman' by the National Portrait Gallery.[7]

Ursula's main occupation was running the household, initially at Parkbury and from 1579 at Barn Elms on the south bank of the Thames. Robert Beale's house was in Barnes, and Richmond Palace was close by. So was the company of the scholar and astrologer Dr John Dee, and his magnificent library, at Mortlake. From his stair down to the river Walsingham could be rowed with the ebbing tide to Westminster and onwards to Elizabeth's other great palace at Greenwich. The queen visited Barn Elms several times during the 1580s, the movement of the court marked by church bells ringing at Lambeth. She is also known to have stayed at another of Walsingham's houses, Odiham in Hampshire. In November 1578 Walsingham invited the Earls of Leicester and Warwick for 'a Friday night's drinking after the ancient and catholic order' at Odiham, a rare example of his sardonic sense of humour.

A survey taken in 1589 records sixty-eight horses stabled at Barn Elms, implying that this was the headquarters of Walsingham's formidable postal system. Little else is known about the house, which was demolished long ago. But there is a tantalising clue as to how it once looked. A three-quarter-length portrait traditionally thought to be of Francis Walsingham includes a fashionable gabled house set in a formal garden, visible through an open window and clearly the property of the sitter. The artist can only be guessed at, and in recent years the date has also been challenged. Roy Strong argues for the 1620s on the basis of the similarity of the architecture to the prodigy houses built by ambitious courtiers during the reign of James I. And yet the face is unnervingly similar to the authenticated portraits of Walsingham: the angular features and narrow nose, the dark hair beginning to recede, the same cut of moustache and beard. The ruff and embroidered doublet and cuffs are more elaborate than in other portraits, but the black garb clearly denotes a senior man of government rather than a country gentleman. The modest size of the property seems right for a principal secretary whose income was nothing like that of William Cecil, who was capable of building on the grandest scale at Theobalds and Burghley. Conyers Read evidently believed in the portrait, which forms the frontispiece to his 1925 three-volume biography of Walsingham.

If this is Francis Walsingham and his house on the Thames, then Barn Elms was modelled on strict Renaissance principles of order and symmetry. Dutch gables would still have been a novelty in Elizabeth's reign, but they had begun to appear on a number of other gentry houses. Walsingham was a strong supporter of the Dutch revolt against the Habsburgs, and it is conceivable that this is reflected in his choice of architectural style. The central tower suggests a banqueting house of the sort often found in Elizabethan mansions, a place for host and guests to withdraw to dessert. The garden is accessed by a grand doorway flanked by classical columns, a tunnelled arbour with domed pavilions giving way to flower beds and lines of fruit trees. Judging by the forty-odd books dedicated to Walsingham, his library at Barn Elms included works of philosophy, exploration and music as well as religion. John Cosyn's *Music of Six and Five Parts* was a collection of psalm settings 'for the private use and comfort of the godly'. But the mixed consort pieces 'Sir Francis Walsingham's good morrow' and 'The Lady Walsingham's conceits', presented by the gifted young lute-player Daniel Bacheler, brought a lighter tone to their life together.[8]

A gentleman with court connections and an education in the Renaissance, well-travelled, skilled in languages and the law: such was Francis Walsingham on the eve of his entry into state service. If he did assist Sir Nicholas Throckmorton during his embassies to Scotland in the later 1560s, as the *Oxford Dictionary of National Biography* tentatively suggests, then it went unrecorded. Walsingham at this point seems barely distinguishable from a host of other gentlemen in the Commons or on the magistrates' bench, engaging each other in litigation over land and dabbling in the commercial opportunities offered by the widening arc of English trade. In fact, he was more alert than he appeared. Walsingham's experience of exile had sharpened his senses, attuning him to the heartbeat of the global Protestant cause. When he accepted Secretary Cecil's request to do some undercover work for the crown, it was to meet a host of threats which would bring England to the brink of invasion and justify the execution of an anointed queen.

Mary Stuart had a surprisingly strong claim to the kingdom of England. Her father James V, whose death in 1542 catapulted Mary to the Scottish throne at only six days old, was the son of Henry VIII's older sister Margaret. This meant that both Elizabeth I and Mary, Queen of Scots were direct descendants of Henry VII, Elizabeth as his granddaughter and Mary his great-granddaughter. Mary's lineage made her an enticing prospect to the English. A determined effort was mounted in the 1540s to win her as a bride for Prince Edward, initially by diplomacy, and when that failed by the rougher wooing of an English invasion. But devastating defeats on the battlefield had the opposite effect from the one intended, driving the Scottish crown into a renewal of its alliance with England's oldest enemy. Mary was betrothed to the dauphin Francis and taken to France to be educated, crushing English hopes of creating a united kingdom on their own terms. They were married at Notre-Dame in 1558, Mary's uncle the Duke of Guise acting as master of ceremonies. Francis was proclaimed king the following year.

Under different circumstances Mary's descent from Henry Tudor would have amounted to little more than a diplomatic flourish, the English royal arms emblazoned provocatively on her plates and furniture during her eighteen-month reign as Queen of France. But when Mary returned to Scotland following Francis's premature death, several factors came into play which made her seem much less distant from the crown of England. The first of these was the absence of male children in the royal family tree. Henry VIII had tried to deny it, but the descendants of his sister Margaret Tudor were senior in line to those of his younger sister Mary as represented by Lady Jane Grey. Then there was the fallout from the break from Rome and the Reformation. Catholics could not accept the legitimacy of Henry's marriage to Anne Boleyn, nor of the child that had resulted from it. Bizarrely, opponents of Elizabeth's claim to the throne could cite the king himself in their support. Henry had annulled his union with Anne when presented with evidence of her adultery, making Elizabeth illegitimate by royal proclamation as well as the strictures of the Catholic Church. Parliament might retrospectively validate the Boleyn marriage, but sufficient doubt remained to be exploited by Catholic propaganda.[9]

The third factor was the arrival of the Queen of Scots on English soil. On 16 May 1568 Mary crossed the Solway Firth to Cumberland in a fishing boat. Her army had been routed at the battle of Langside, closing a seven-year chapter in which a Catholic and culturally French queen had attempted to govern Scotland in parallel with the same Lords of the Congregation who had overthrown the old Church in an English-sponsored Protestant revolution. The political credit which Mary accumulated during hundreds of miles of progresses around her kingdom was squandered firstly by her marriage to Lord Darnley, which made a bitter enemy of her half-brother the Earl of Moray, and then by her suspected complicity in Darnley's death by strangulation and explosion in February 1567. Mary could hardly be blamed for her subsequent abduction and probable rape by the Earl of Bothwell, but it was her own decision to marry Bothwell, the prime suspect in Darnley's murder, within three months of her late husband's body being found in the garden of the provost's lodging at Kirk o' Field. Threatened with execution by the Lords and slandered as a whore by the Edinburgh crowd, Mary was forced to abdicate in July in favour of her son James and a regency government led by Moray. That she then summoned the strength to escape from Lochleven Castle in an attempt to regain the throne illustrates Mary's astonishing reserves of self-belief, a resilience every bit as steely as that displayed by Mary Tudor when she faced down Wyatt's rebels, or Elizabeth when she scorned the Spanish Armada.

The Queen of Scots was not seeking permanent political asylum in England. What she needed was a resting-place to rally her forces, and she immediately called on her cousin Elizabeth for help. What she found was an endless house arrest and the barely-concealed hostility of the queen's chief ministers. Cecil did all he could to deaden Elizabeth's instinctive sympathy for Mary. A tribunal examining the 'casket letters', a cache of incriminating documents allegedly written by Mary to the Earl of Bothwell, was guided towards its verdict that she had ordered Darnley's murder. Walsingham's conclusion was even starker: the Queen of Scots was the agent of the devil. Isolated both from Scotland and the English royal court, powerless to protect James from the Calvinist republicanism being thrashed into him by his tutor George Buchanan, Mary was reduced to calling on France and Spain to agitate for her release. When petitioning failed, the only options were capitulation or conspiracy.[10]

On the morning of 19 August 1568, Walsingham went to see Cecil to discuss a matter that was too sensitive to commit to paper. Cecil had been receiving some alarming reports from the English ambassador in Paris, Sir Henry Norris, about the activities of the Guise family in support of their kinswoman Mary Stuart. It was believed at the French court that thousands of Englishmen were ready to rise in Mary's support. Writing partly in cipher, Norris recommended that Cecil should employ an Italian soldier named Captain Franchiotto to investigate. He had been working for the French for many years, but his Protestant faith had now convinced him to defect. Walsingham, who read Italian, became his handler. Franchiotto soon proved his worth, producing lists of suspected agents and warning the queen to beware of poison in her food or her bedding. In October Walsingham heard that twelve troopships were being prepared at Marseilles for an expedition against the north of England. Franchiotto was the veteran in this relationship, Walsingham a mere novice. He had a lot to learn. But he was also able to mobilise his own contacts among the London elite, instructing the lord mayor to provide him with weekly reports about the movement of strangers around the city.

In December Walsingham received information from Paris

that France and Spain were engaged in an operation in England 'for the alteration of religion and the advancement of the Queen of Scots to the crown'. Details were few, and he hesitated before troubling Cecil with such a vague report. But the 'malice of this present time' had convinced him; every scrap of intelligence had to be taken seriously. He concluded with statements which were already defining his outlook on the world: 'there is less danger in fearing too much than too little', and 'there is nothing more dangerous than security'. What Walsingham was warning against was a *false* sense of security, the complacent assumption that the queen's safety would be guaranteed by the love and loyalty of her people. It was an alert to the most powerful man in government that the danger of rebellion and assassination was real and urgent. Within months Elizabeth was facing a crisis of the sort which had most haunted her father, a Catholic rising in the northern reaches of the realm. Unlike the Pilgrimage of Grace, however, the rebellion of 1569 was prepared to call on foreign support to secure a Catholic succession.[11]

The heartland of the northern rising was in Yorkshire and Durham, the same counties which had risen against Henry VIII's Reformation. The protesters marched under the banner of the Five Wounds, symbolising the presence of Christ in their midst. Richard Norton, Sheriff of Yorkshire and a living link with the Pilgrimage of Grace, had worn the same badge of the Five Wounds more than forty years before. Foot soldiers, priests and horses were dressed in tabards painted with a red cross, the ancient symbol of the Crusades. A flag bearing the slogan 'God Speed the Plough' recalled earlier generations of rural revolt. Images of the saints and heraldic pennons added to the gorgeous array.

Mass was celebrated wherever the rebels went. At Kirkbymoorside in the North Riding, the plain communion table stipulated by the Prayer Book was symbolically cast aside. The women and young people of Sedgefield rebuilt their altar and holy-water stoup and warmed themselves round a bonfire of Protestant books. A mother from County Durham entrusted her baby to a midwife to be christened by a Catholic curate. The most spectacular offering of the mass was at Durham Cathedral, which had recently witnessed the burning of St Cuthbert's banner and now sought absolution in the name of the pope. By 18 November, when they paused at Boroughbridge on the great north road, the rebel force had swollen to six thousand. The majority were yeomen farmers rather than labourers, men of substance in their communities and the backbone of the militia. Their faith bound them together, and they mustered like an army.

The 1569 rising was led by two magnates whose families had ruled large swathes of the north for centuries, nominally for the crown but often on their own account. Charles Neville, Earl of Westmorland, was a cradle Catholic adrift in the restored Church of England. He was now in his mid-twenties, and gloomily aware that Neville influence was fading. Even so, he would probably have remained loyal to the crown had it not been for his wife Jane, a sister of the Duke of Norfolk. A plan had recently been hatched by Leicester and Throckmorton to marry Norfolk to Mary Stuart, who was in the process of divorcing the Earl of Bothwell. Privy councillors saw a chance for a peaceful union with Scotland if Elizabeth had no heir. To Mary it offered a dignified route out of captivity, and maybe a future role as queen mother. The problem was Elizabeth herself. Furious that the succession had been debated behind her back, she recalled Norfolk to court and flung him in the Tower. Fearing a similar fate, Westmorland raised his standard in a Catholic plot to capitalise on the Queen of Scots.

His brother in arms was Thomas Percy, Earl of Northumberland. Revolt in the name of religion ran in Northumberland's blood. His father Sir Thomas Percy had been executed following the Pilgrimage of Grace. Like Westmorland he had been forced to watch as royal appointees trespassed on his territory. In 1568 the crown awarded itself the profits from the copper mines on his estates, an affront which may have quickened his decision to be reconciled to the Catholic faith. When the two earls took their stand, they did so in the name of protecting Queen Elizabeth from the heretical advisers who surrounded her. Their proclamations called on the people to rise 'as your duty towards God doth bind you, and as you tender the common wealth of your country'. They said nothing about the Queen of Scots, but this was sheer calculation. Interrogated by Lord Hunsdon before his execution in York, Northumberland denied that they had intended to depose Elizabeth while freely admitting the importance of Mary:

> What was the intent and meaning of the rebellion? Ans., Our first object in assembling was the reformation of religion and preservation of the person of the Queen of Scots, as next heir, failing issue of her majesty, which causes I believed were greatly favoured by most of the noblemen of the realm.

The leaders of the rebellion concealed another element of their plan from their followers. Northumberland had made contact with Don Guerau de Spes, the new Spanish ambassador in London. De Spes was a religious militant, eager to snatch at any opportunity to reconvert the English to Catholicism. Westmorland would ultimately join the Spanish army in the Netherlands when the rebellion fell apart. Both of the earls hoped for military support from the 'Iron Duke' of Alva, the Governor of the Netherlands, hence their diversion to capture the port of Hartlepool where Spanish troops and supplies could be landed. Yet they boldly played on fears of invasion and the patriotic duty of English subjects: 'divers foreign powers do purpose shortly to invade these realms, which will be to our utter destruction, if we do not ourselves speedily forfend the same . . . if foreigners enter upon us we should all be made slaves and bondsmen to them.' This can only have been a deliberate smokescreen. The rank and file believed they were marching in a loyal Catholic crusade, while their leaders were deeply steeped in treason. Would the northern earls have been content with recognising Mary as Elizabeth's 'next heir' if their cavalry had succeeded in capturing her? The government recognised the danger and moved Mary from Staffordshire to Coventry, thereby depriving the revolt of its key objective. Threatened by a royal army and deserted by their captains, the rebels surrendered to the queen's mercy; hundreds would be hanged under martial law.[12]

Walsingham had been reluctant to ring the alarm bell too soon. He knew he lacked experience, hence the caveats in his letter to Cecil of December 1568. But his source in Paris was insistent: the monarchies of France and Spain were conspiring to undermine English security. As the northern rising and events in London soon proved, he had every reason to be concerned. Within days of Walsingham's warning, de Spes had called on the French ambassador in London with a bold proposal. The two powers should sink their differences and force Elizabeth to get rid of her chief minister. De Spes said he knew 'of no greater heretic in this world' than William Cecil. Even more remarkably, the queen should be told to return to the Catholic fold or face a total trade embargo. De Spes exceeded his brief, and soon found himself confined to quarters. But he had a collaborator, a man whose story would be told by English propagandists long after de Spes had been forgotten. His name was Roberto di Ridolfi, and his manoeuvring was so deft that we still cannot be sure whose side he was on.

To the London merchant community, Ridolfi was a respectable

Florentine banker and a financial agent for William Cecil. Unknown to the English, however, he was also a secret envoy of the pope. Since 1566 he had been handling the money sent by Pius V to fund political Catholicism in England. Ridolfi was the ideal choice for this kind of work. His profession as a merchant gave him freedom of movement around the courts of Renaissance Europe. Banking contacts in Florence enabled him to move money around by bills of exchange, avoiding the problem of transporting large quantities of coin. In September 1569 he used this method to transfer the best part of £3,000 from de Spes to the Bishop of Ross, Mary Stuart's representative in London. But a transaction on such a huge scale was hard to conceal. Suddenly nervous that Ridolfi might be more than he seemed, Cecil and Leicester ordered him taken to Walsingham's house for questioning.

In 1569 Walsingham's London home was the building known as the Papey in Aldgate ward, a converted medieval hospital for the relief of poor chantry priests. Here Ridolfi could be interrogated while his cover, which might prove useful to the English government, was preserved intact. Cecil and Leicester wrote to Walsingham as 'our very loving friend', illustrating how high he was rising in their confidence. Gradually Ridolfi began to talk to his captors. He knew about the conspiracy to marry Mary to the Duke of Norfolk. The money which he passed on to Norfolk's servants and the Bishop of Ross had originated with the pope. Elizabeth herself became involved in the investigation. Observing that some of Ridolfi's answers were 'far otherwise than the truth is', she offered to be lenient in exchange for a frank disclosure of his dealings with the Queen of Scots. Walsingham was authorised to search his house for evidence. Finally, a month after he had taken Ridolfi into custody, Walsingham was told to free him on bail with a lecture not to meddle any more in affairs of state.

Elizabeth claimed to be acting out of clemency, the love which she bore to Ridolfi's countrymen. Something about this does not ring true. Ridolfi was freed two days after peals of church bells in Yorkshire and Durham had raised the countryside in revolt – sheer folly, unless Cecil and Walsingham had some purpose in mind. Nothing is made explicit, but the shadow of a deal lurks behind Ridolfi's order of release: the promise of information in return for a suspended sentence, perhaps, or the prospect of advancing in royal service. If this did not persuade him, there was an unmistakable note of threat behind the queen's words. A harsher examination, she said, would reveal more than Ridolfi had so far volunteered. Walsingham was to impress on him just how fortunate he was.

Was Ridolfi turned during his weeks in Walsingham's house? There are two contrasting ways of reading the rest of his story. Before the northern rebellion ignited, Ridolfi had told the French ambassador that he held a commission from the pope to work with sympathetic English nobles, specifically the Duke of Norfolk, to restore Catholicism to England. On regaining his liberty, he apparently returned to the task he had been set. In March 1571 he made his way to Rome, where the pope endorsed his plan for another Catholic uprising, led by Norfolk and backed by Spanish troops, to put Mary on the English throne. But when the Bishop of Ross's courier Charles Bailly was arrested at Dover, the web of threads between Ridolfi and Mary Stuart's agents was severed. Norfolk was beheaded on Tower Hill in 1572. Mary survived for the time being, protected by the queen from a Parliament which was baying for her blood. Ridolfi slipped away to serve the Medici dukes in Florence, where he retired many years later as a senator.

Maybe Walsingham and Cecil made a catastrophic error of judgement in November 1569, leaving Ridolfi at liberty to plot against queen and state. Philip II was genuinely won over to an active policy against England. Had the Duke of Alva not been such a sceptic, it is possible that a Spanish armada could have been launched in the early 1570s rather than 1588. If Ridolfi was working as a double agent, then his cover was exceptionally deep, and his handlers were playing a dangerous game. And yet there are indications that this is just what he was doing. Ridolfi left England for Rome after a personal interview with the queen, who gave him a passport and two horses as her blessing. He was surprisingly lax about security, writing to Mary in plain text. Other letters were ciphered, but Elizabeth somehow got hold of a key. The Ridolfi plot precipitated Norfolk's downfall, which suited Cecil, and it might have done the same for the Queen of Scots.

There is another snippet of evidence that Walsingham persuaded his man to change sides. A year after the northern rebellion, Ridolfi and Walsingham were in conversation once again. The subject this time, so he reported to Cecil, was England's relationship with Flanders and France. Evidently he still thought of Ridolfi as an asset. The way Walsingham wrote about him suggests that the two men had discovered a rapport during their strange experience of sharing a house. They were direct contemporaries after all, both from merchant families, and they had Italy in common. Walsingham told Cecil that Ridolfi 'would deal both discreetly and uprightly, as one both wise and who standeth on terms of honesty and reputation'. Honesty and reputation seem like curious words to use of Roberto di Ridolfi. Either Walsingham had begun his career in royal service with an intelligence coup of major proportions, or he had been utterly and humiliatingly fooled. The queen, at least, seems to have believed his side of the story. By the time that he wrote this letter, Francis Walsingham had been named as the new English ambassador in France.[13]

†

English attitudes towards the French during the sixteenth century mingled fear with admiration. The 'auld alliance' between France and Scotland meant that English monarchs often faced a war on two fronts. Henry VIII revived the ancient claim that kings of England were rulers of France as well, but the footholds which he won in Normandy were fleeting. Boulogne was sold back by the government of Edward VI, while the garrison town of Calais was reconquered by the French in the dying days of Mary's reign. France was a great power, boasting a population six times that of England. Its taxation system could sustain lengthy campaigns overland and a modern naval base at Le Havre. Yet centuries of war had bred something else between the two nations, a shared belief in chivalry and a common language of power. King Charles IX was inducted into the Order of the Garter early in Elizabeth's reign, while the English were keen to copy the ceremonial of the French court. The religious gulf, too, was less than it might appear. The French Calvinist Church was one of the largest in Europe, with artisans and nobles proving the quickest to convert. The crown may have remained Catholic, but it was also resistant to any increase in the power of the pope. As a centralised monarchy ruling over a religiously plural people, France was more akin to England than either Spain or the Holy Roman Empire. It was also the most likely place for Queen Elizabeth to seek a husband.

English Protestants had particular reason to keep a close eye on France. By the early 1560s a million Huguenots, as French Calvinists were known, were engaged in bloody struggle for survival. The French wars of religion were played out against a dynastic backdrop uncannily similar to that of Tudor England. Like Henry VIII, King Henry II of France was succeeded by three of his children in turn following his death in a jousting accident in 1559. Francis II became king at fifteen but died in

December 1560, leaving Mary Stuart as a widow. His brother Charles inherited the throne aged just ten. The seizure of the regency by the queen mother, Catherine de' Medici, prompted a struggle for power which soon slid into civil war. Catholic churches were despoiled from Rouen to the Rhône. A vicious guerrilla campaign was fought in the Midi. As France tore apart along fault-lines of faith, communities fell into grisly crowd violence. Not content with violating devotional images and Protestant Bibles, people began to turn on their neighbours. Atrocity stories gained rapid currency, inflated by propaganda but based on murders and mutilations which were only too real. On progress through Maine in 1564, the king was told about a widowed Protestant noblewoman slaughtered in her own house alongside her children and chambermaids, their corpses left for pigs to feed on. Gangs of young Catholic men patrolled the towns of Provence, stoning Protestants to death and burning the bodies. Huguenots were dehumanised as vermin, a polluting stain which had to be washed out of French society.[14]

The French wars of religion were a mixed blessing to the English. A nation divided against itself was less capable of pursuing an aggressive foreign policy, and more likely to seek accommodation with its ancient enemy. But there was also the possibility that the uproar in France would foretell, or even spark, a similar conflagration in England. The fear that France represented an alternative destiny was fed by rumours of Catholic armies waiting to be mobilised in the north and west of England. It was also heightened by English memories of their own civil wars a century before. An obvious remedy was to ally with the Huguenots, and a deal was duly struck in 1562 with their leader the Prince of Condé. English troops would occupy Le Havre and Dieppe in exchange for the return of Calais when the Protestants won the war. But the towns proved difficult to hold, the Huguenots made peace with their Catholic countrymen, and the expedition collapsed amid a savage bout of plague. English honour had been hazarded and forfeited, while the queen's aversion to war had been vindicated. Persuading her to pursue a hawkish foreign policy would henceforth be more difficult than ever.

Francis Walsingham landed in France on New Year's Day 1571 and made his way to Paris for an audience with Charles IX and his mother. There were no permanent embassy buildings in this period; ambassadors had to make their own arrangements. It has always been assumed that Walsingham lived in the Faubourg Saint Germain, an expensive suburb colonised by nobles retreating from the bourgeois values of the city. In fact a document written by the soldier and agent Tomasso Sassetti reveals that Walsingham's house was in Saint Marceau. South of the city walls and on the left bank of the Seine, this was a very different place from the fashionable Saint Germain. Cloth-workers and tanners toiled in small workshops, where the smell of dyestuffs and animal hides hung heavy in the air. Its location and industrial character made Saint Marceau a natural centre of Protestant activism. Calvinists could worship openly in the building they called the Temple, while the English ambassador could entertain aristocrats and intellectuals like Hubert Languet and Petrus Ramus without arousing too much attention. Captains Sassetti and Franchiotto also visited the embassy, implying that Walsingham was already building up a network of operatives in Paris.[15]

Sixteenth-century ambassadors were more than civil servants. They represented the person of the prince as well as the state, and were treated with the courtesy which their dignity demanded. The French court was widely hailed as the most splendid in Europe, although Walsingham's letters home typically focused on policy more than pageantry. Describing a dinner put on to welcome him, he noted that 'we lacked no store of good meat';

pomp and ceremonial did not come easily to him. Sir Thomas Smith partook of French hospitality with much more relish when he joined the embassy a year later:

> Nine or ten cooks in my kitchen, butlers, victuallers, and officers of the king's house appointed to serve me. Of meat, wine, bread, candles, plate, and all such things as if I were a young prince, and all of the king's charges. Minstrels and music more than I would have and a controller of the king's house to see me served, from time to time attending on me as if I were a duke; two messes [meals] a day served with all delicacies.

The Spanish ambassador in Paris, admittedly not an unbiased witness, described Walsingham as blunt and uncourtly, a man who dressed entirely in black. Yet he was also a natural negotiator, and he soon managed to achieve a clear line of communication with Catherine de' Medici.[16]

Walsingham's predecessor Sir Henry Norris was eager to be relieved. His pro-Huguenot stance made him unpopular with the French royal family, while Elizabeth pestered him with unrealistic demands about the return of Calais. Norris had been made to attend the Catholic mass at court, his post tampered with and his servants arrested. Then there was the cost of maintaining a suitable household and horses, employing secretaries and couriers, paying informants and bribes. Elizabeth always had an eye to economy, and she expected her envoys to contribute to the costs of their embassy out of their own pockets. When Walsingham protested that he could not afford the posting to France, the queen replied by raising his daily allowance to £3 6s 8d: a little more than Norris had been paid, but still diplomacy at a discount. He was soon complaining that the expense was 'like to bring me to beggary'. In September 1571 he petitioned Cecil, now ennobled as Lord Burghley, for relief from 'the continual increase of charges that groweth on me far above her majesty's allowance'. The compensation lay in the close working relationship he developed with Burghley and Leicester, the contact with leading Huguenots, and the chance to promote the Protestant faith. Unlike his royal mistress, Walsingham defined the success of English foreign policy in terms of 'spiritual fruit' and the 'advancement of the gospel'. Four months into his embassy, he set out his political creed in letters to Leicester. 'Above all things,' he wrote in April 1571, 'I wish God's glory and next the queen's safety'.[17]

Walsingham had arrived in France during a lull in the wars of religion. The 1570 peace of Saint Germain gave four fortified towns into the hands of the Huguenots. Condé had been killed in battle, leaving Gaspard de Coligny, the Admiral of France, in command of Protestant forces. Coligny was pro-English and hoped for a marriage between Elizabeth and France, whether in the person of Charles IX's younger brother Henry, Duke of Anjou, or the Huguenot leader Henry of Navarre. He made a point of assuring Walsingham of his devotion to Elizabeth when he came to court in September 1571. Walsingham was encouraged. 'Generally all those of the religion,' he wrote to Burghley, 'who are the flower of France, do make like protestation, assuring her majesty that when occasion or trial shall be offered, she shall find them no less ready to serve her than if they were her own natural subjects'. But Walsingham knew the Huguenots were in a minority. Fiercely opposed to any such alliance were the ultra-Catholic Guise of Lorraine, temporarily out of favour but burning to regain their previous dominance of the court. Soldiers of the Duke of Guise had ignited the first civil war by massacring fifty unarmed Protestants in their makeshift church at Wassy. His brother the Cardinal of Lorraine had a powerful hold over the intensely pious Anjou, who grew pale from his perpetual fasts and vigils. Never far from the Cardinal's thoughts was his niece Mary, Queen of Scots. As the rightful ruler of

England and a potential bride for Anjou, Mary could seal the union of France and Britain under one Catholic crown.[18]

Elizabeth had briefed her new ambassador a few days before his departure. Walsingham must keep watch over 'all manner of their doings there, as well private as public, that may be prejudicial to us or our estate'. He was to support English merchants, and maintain the free flow of trade between England and France. A lengthy clause set out Elizabeth's attitude to the Huguenots, whose welfare was explicitly linked to the 'quietness of us and our realm'. Walsingham should impress on the French king how the peace of his own nation depended on observing the rights granted to the Protestants at Saint Germain. Elizabeth addressed Charles conventionally as 'our good brother', but she could not resist an arch comment on the wars of religion. Because of his treatment of his Huguenot subjects, Charles had 'seen and felt the continuance of the troubles of his realm'. A reference to the Queen of Scots and warships in Brittany explains the chill in Elizabeth's voice. Charles had recently threatened to send French troops into Scotland, where an English army was fighting to prevent Mary's faction from regaining control. With hindsight, this was the moment when Mary Stuart came closest to being freed from her imprisonment. Elizabeth actually considered it for a day or so, until the privy council gave its judgement: restoring the Queen of Scots could only undermine the crown of England.[19]

There was another matter, critical to both France and England even though it was unstated in Walsingham's formal instructions: the marriage of Queen Elizabeth and the Duke of Anjou. Perhaps the match never looked very likely. Elizabeth was thirty-seven, Anjou nineteen. Elizabeth was supreme governor of a church whose theology and bishops were clearly Protestant; Anjou had fought against the Huguenots, and regarded Elizabeth as a bastard and a heretic. Walsingham's description of

'Monsieur' Anjou was guardedly positive at best, 'his body of very good shape, his leg long and small but reasonably well proportioned', three fingers taller than Walsingham himself but his complexion and colour worryingly sallow. Walsingham said nothing about it, but Anjou's sexuality is also open to question. Following his accession as Henry III in 1574, critics remarked on his fondness for cross-dressing and earrings (in both ears), and his troop of male minions in long hair and bonnets.

And yet the marriage had its attractions to everyone except Anjou himself. Catherine de' Medici spotted a way to detach her son from the Guise. Charles resented his younger brother's popularity and wanted him out of France. England would gain a military ally against Spain. The queen herself gave it to be understood that she was determined to take a husband. Much has been made of Elizabeth's words to her first parliament in 1559: 'And in the end this shall be for me sufficient: that a marble stone shall declare that a queen, having reigned such a time, lived and died a virgin'. Less often quoted is an earlier part of the same speech: 'whomsoever my chance shall be to light upon, I trust he shall be . . . as careful for the preservation of the realm and you as myself'. Elizabeth modelled her monarchy on that of her father, and she knew it was her duty to settle the succession.[20]

Walsingham can hardly have relished the prospect of another foreign Catholic becoming King of England. The Earl of Leicester, a committed Protestant and a distant cousin of Ursula Walsingham, might have seemed a better candidate. But recent English history rang some warning bells. Edward IV's marriage to Elizabeth Woodville had been an accelerant in the Wars of the Roses, showing how destabilising a match between monarch and subject could be. Leicester's reputation had also been scarred by the rumour that he was involved in the death of his wife Amy Robsart. For Walsingham, a French match was a necessary concession within a much bigger strategic game. As ambassador in France he had a chance to build a defence alliance against the gathering forces of Spain. Extracting Anjou from the clutches of the Guise would strike a blow against the partisans of Mary Stuart. In the longer term, and God willing, there might be an heir. The birth of a child – better still, a male child – would calm the waters which had been rocking the ship of state since the 1540s. This is how Walsingham came to collaborate with Burghley to make a success of the Anjou match. As he explained to the French diplomat Paul de Foix, if he failed it would 'be for lack of judgement and experience, and not for lack of goodwill'.[21]

Discussions began in secret on 12 March 1571 in the garden of the new Tuileries Palace, where Catherine de' Medici met Elizabeth's personal envoy Lord Buckhurst. Twelve days later, Walsingham was instructed how to reply to the possibility of a proposal. Elizabeth explained how the 'solicitation of our loving subjects generally did induce us, for their sakes, to hearken to motions of marriage'. She dropped a hint that she might welcome an approach from Anjou. In everything that counted, however, the queen was uncompromising. Her starting point was that she would accept nothing less than Emperor Charles V had offered in 1554 when the marriage treaty was sealed between Mary and Philip of Spain. This was a fair demand in one sense: English honour would be compromised if Elizabeth was treated any less handsomely than her sister had been. A similar pre-nuptial agreement had been proposed to another of Elizabeth's suitors, the archduke Charles of Austria, in 1565. But the Spanish marriage had been a remarkably good deal for England. Philip was denied the dignity of a coronation, exercising sovereignty through the person of his wife. His Spanish retinue was debarred from holding English offices. It was an unacceptably emasculated kind of kingship, and Philip forswore the treaty before he signed it. Persuading Anjou to accept the role of royal consort on this model would require some hard bargaining.

At least Philip and Mary had shared a common Catholic vision. For a prince as pious as Anjou, the religious restrictions which Elizabeth laid down were every bit as objectionable as the limits on his political power.

> Monsieur shall not have authority to exercise the form of religion in England, that is prohibited by the laws of our realm . . . And as for his allowance of our religion, although we wish he might in conscience like it (and if he did understand the form thereof, truly we do not mistrust, but he would not mislike it) yet we shall only require his presence in our oratories and churches.[22]

The Anjou match allows us to glimpse the personal religion of a queen who famously didn't want to make windows into men's souls. Elizabeth is often portrayed as a *politique*, her Church settlement the genesis of a cosy Anglican compromise. Yet the prayers that she composed, and the music which she patronised in the Chapel Royal, reveal a queen whose faith was every bit as intense as that of her brother and sister. Her defence of sacred ritual was sometimes misinterpreted as Catholic in its sympathies, but to Elizabeth there was no contradiction between tradition and reform. The key, for her, was ordered worship. A queen who kept a crucifix in her private chapel could also deny her husband the Catholic sacrament of the altar.

Elizabeth's instructions placed Walsingham in a dilemma. He strongly approved of the hard line she was taking, and adopted a similar stance when French counter-proposals required the 'free exercise' of religion for Anjou and his servants. Allowing the mass in Anjou's household, he argued, would alienate the queen from her loyal subjects and encourage the spread of sedition. But Walsingham could also see that Elizabeth's stipulations, if presented in the manner that she proposed, would scotch a marriage which was the best hope of preserving the stability of the English commonwealth. That is why he decided that 'somewhat swerving from the precise course of her majesty's instructions' – in short, keeping quiet about religion when necessary – was the best course of action. Walsingham was robust with de Foix, pointing out that Anjou had flirted with Protestantism when younger, 'and therefore that if it please [Anjou] to water those seeds, he should be able easily to discern that the change of his religion should breed unto him no dishonour at all, it being no less fault to continue in error, than commendable to come from error to truth'. But his flexibility also reveals Walsingham's subtlety as a politician, working closely with Burghley to secure the alliance on which English security depended. If that meant moulding the words of the queen to fit the circumstances, so be it.[23]

Talks about talks dragged on through the spring and summer of 1571. Anjou wanted a coronation immediately after the wedding, a full role in government and a mint of money to run his household. The sum of £60,000 was suggested, equivalent to one-fifth of Elizabeth's annual income, which he expected to keep as a pension if she died childless. For her part, Elizabeth accepted that Anjou would not be forced to take communion as part of the wedding service. But she refused his request to practise his Catholicism 'in secret place and manner' on grounds that it would encourage others to flout the law. Nor would she allow him to be crowned. When Catherine complained to Walsingham about the harshness of English demands, Elizabeth offered to salve Anjou's conscience by sending him a copy of the Book of Common Prayer. This contained, she alleged, 'no part that hath not been, yea that is not at this day used in the Church of Rome'. If its English language was unpalatable, then Anjou was free to worship from the Latin translation of the Prayer

Book in use at Oxford and Cambridge Universities, or the French version prepared for the Channel Islands.[24]

This was disingenuous on Elizabeth's part. Whatever language it was in, holy communion according to the 1559 Prayer Book was very different from the Catholic mass. But nor was it intended to be a wrecking tactic. Elizabeth had a lot to gain by marrying, and she continued to signal her willingness to be courted. In conversation with Walsingham, Anjou was prepared to praise Elizabeth for her gifts of mind and body, 'the rarest creature that was in Europe these five hundred years'. Regarding freedom of religion, however, he was as immovable as the queen herself. He was also quoted as saying that marriage to a heretic was out of the question. Walsingham clutched at straws, hoping that the match could still be salvaged. Anjou's Catholicism derived from his mother's influence, he explained to Burghley on 21 June. De Foix had offered assurances that within a year Monsieur 'would be as forward to advance religion as any one within our realm'. Freed from the conventions of diplomatic language, Walsingham opened up with startling frankness in a private letter to the Earl of Leicester. The marriage was simply too important to let go:

> when I particularly consider her majesty's state, both at home and abroad, so far as my poor eye-sight can discern; and how she is beset by foreign peril, the execution whereof stayeth only upon the event of this match, I do not see how she can stand, if this matter break off.

In July the focus of attention shifted from France to Hampton Court. Anjou's captain of the guard, Grimonville de l'Archant, met the queen to discuss an embassy to conclude the marriage. Again, the religious obstacle proved insuperable. Burghley blamed de l'Archant, but in truth Elizabeth was just as inflexible. Aware that time was running out, Leicester and Burghley suggested that the issue simply be ignored in the marriage treaty.

But Elizabeth would have none of it: without 'plain dealing', she told Walsingham, there could only be more controversy. By September de Foix, who had replaced de l'Archant at the English court, was moving the deadlocked debate towards new ground. He called for the appointment of a special envoy from Elizabeth to Charles, or failing that, 'if the marriage shall not take place, to enter into the treaty of some straiter alliance or confederacy'. It was tacit recognition that the Anjou match was finished. In October the duke declared unequivocally that he would never marry Elizabeth. In spite of all his efforts, Walsingham had failed.[25]

The months of diplomacy and despatch-writing, the vexatious meetings with Anjou and his mother, all took their toll on Walsingham's health. In August 1571 Charles IX ordered foreign ambassadors south to the Loire, where he would be meeting the Protestant leader Admiral Coligny at Blois. Walsingham's departure was delayed 'by the necessity of taking physic', and he was soon petitioning Burghley to be allowed back to Paris: 'my disease groweth so dangerously upon me, as I must most humbly desire her majesty to take some speedy order for someone to supply my place. I hope my life shall stand her in more stead than my death.' Prompting this letter was a urinary infection which kept Walsingham bedridden between November 1571 and February 1572, and would continue to plague him for the rest of his life. His letter to Leicester also mentions his poor sight, a condition which was worsened by years of close document work by candlelight. In January 1588 he complained of a 'defluction' of fluid seeping from his eyes, explaining the marked deterioration in his handwriting as he grew older. Making a diagnosis at this distance is far from easy, but the combination of symptoms – the trouble with his eyes, an inability to pass water, the times when he felt close to death – makes it possible that Walsingham was suffering from diabetes. If this is right, then the quantities of sugar and saturated fat consumed by the typical Tudor gentleman must have cruelly aggravated his condition. Thomas Smith described the food at the French court as 'pheasants and partridges, red and white legged, and young peacocks and all other such fine meats, covered and seethened with lard'. Walsingham noted in his journal for November 1571 that his doctors had put him on a new diet. Several of his physicians would double as his couriers and agents during the 1580s.[26]

Walsingham continued to work in spite of his illness. Late in January 1572 he received some frightening news from Burghley in London. 'I perceive through God's good providence', he wrote in reply, 'your lordship hath escaped the danger of a most devilish Italian practice'. A pair of plotters had planned to shoot Burghley on his way back from court and rescue the Duke of Norfolk from the Tower using a rope bridge. The identity of one of the conspirators must have shaken Walsingham to the core. Edmund Mather had been secretary to Sir Henry Norris at the Paris embassy, the equivalent of Robert Beale to Walsingham himself. State secrets would have flowed across his desk every day. Mather confessed under interrogation to being a devotee of the Queen of Scots. Once Burghley was dead, Queen Elizabeth would have been his next target.

Mather had talked about his plans in Italian to a Welsh merchant and sometime pirate named William Herle. What Mather didn't know was that Herle was Burghley's agent, drawing out the plot to see who else would be implicated. It was a tactic which Walsingham would copy when he took charge of the queen's security in the later 1570s. Treason at home, his frustration at the Anjou match and his own gnawing illness came together in an outburst of loathing for the Queen of Scots. 'So long as that devilish woman liveth,' he exclaimed, 'neither her majesty must make account to continue her quiet possession of her crown, nor her faithful servants assure themselves of safety of their lives. God therefore open her majesty's eyes to see that which may be for her best suertie [protection]'. It was a *cri de cœur* which Burghley shared. Elizabeth reluctantly consented to Norfolk's execution under pressure from her privy council, but she blocked a bill in Parliament against the Queen of Scots. Burghley confided to Walsingham that he was 'overthrown in heart'. Fifteen years would elapse before they saw Mary finally brought to justice, giving others the opportunity to follow in the footsteps of the northern earls and Edmund Mather.[27]

The embassy was taken over by Thomas Smith and Henry Killigrew pending Walsingham's recovery. They found the king and his court at Amboise, dancing to mark the end of the twelve days of Christmas. A brief attempt was made to resurrect the Anjou marriage, Catherine restating her son's demand to attend mass in his own household. Smith's retort was bold: 'Why madame, then he may require also the four orders of friars, monks, canons, pilgrimages, pardons, oil and cream, relics and all such trumperies, which will seem so strange to our countrymen, that in no wise can be agreed.' Business then turned to the second part of Smith's commission, a defensive alliance between England and France. Walsingham rejoined the delegation in February, although Smith's voice continued to dominate their joint reports. Scotland was a potential stumbling-block. The king made a show of loyalty to the auld alliance and the Queen of Scots, 'my kinswoman, and my sister-in-law, and she was my sovereign'. At this point Killigrew stepped forward, and his reply was as frank as Smith's had been:

> Fire and water cannot be together, the one is contrary to the other. The league is made for a perpetual and strait amity betwixt you and the queen's majesty of England, and you would treat for the queen's most mortal and dangerous enemy. This cannot stand together, you must take her now for dead.[28]

On 17 April 1572 Smith was able to inform Burghley that 'at last Mr Walsingham and I have concluded the league'. Neither party would assist the enemies of the other, and the French agreed not to intervene in Scotland on Mary's behalf. True, the succession was no nearer to being resolved. But as the queen mother pointed out, there was always the Duke of Alençon, seventeen years old and sporting the beginnings of a beard. The task of formally ratifying the treaty of Blois fell to Edward Fiennes de Clinton, Earl of Lincoln and lord high admiral. Lincoln had fought with Henry VIII in Normandy, and supervised the English withdrawal from Boulogne in 1550. Simultaneous ceremonies were held on both sides of the Channel in June 1572, Smith's reports bringing out all the colour of the celebrations in Paris. Lincoln travelled to the Louvre in the king's coach, while Walsingham and Smith followed with the Duke of Anjou. The treaty was sworn on the high altar of the Church of Saint Germain, the English delegation sitting in a side chapel while vespers was sung (to 'very good musick', according to Smith). Supper was held in an open banqueting house in the garden of the Tuileries, where Walsingham and Smith were presented with gifts of gold and silver plate weighing 472 ounces. Days of dining, acrobatics and fireworks culminated in a massive bonfire, into which a bag of live cats was dropped from a crossbar for the benefit of the king, who particularly enjoyed entertainment of this sort.[29]

The treaty of Blois signalled a sea change in English foreign policy. It severed a relationship with Spain which had been sealed by Katherine of Aragon's marriage to Arthur Tudor more than seventy years before. The friendship with Burgundy, as the Spanish Netherlands were sometimes still known, stretched back even further. Renouncing alliances which had served England so well required a major shift in the psychology of government. Fortunately for us, Walsingham addressed this problem by putting down his thoughts on paper. The result, 'Whether it may stand with good policy for her majesty to join with Spain in the enterprise of Burgundy', is an awkward document in several ways. The title is confusing to a modern reader. 'Join with' means to join in battle with, to oppose. The manuscript exists in several copies of a lost original, its attribution dependent on the similarity of its language to Walsingham's official letters. This particular text, however, was never intended to be seen by the queen, which is precisely what makes it so valuable. Within an analysis of the pros and cons of war, Walsingham set out his thinking about being ruled by a woman.

Like Leicester and other hawks at the English court, Walsingham was eager to fund the Protestant revolt led by William of Orange and his brother Count Louis of Nassau against the Duke of Alva. 'If God had not raised up the Prince of Orange to have entertained Spain,' he wrote to Leicester in July 1572, 'a dangerous fire ere this time had been kindled in our own home'. Since conflict with Spain was bound to come, Elizabeth should seize the initiative by striking first. But persuading her would not be easy, 'for that her majesty being by sex fearful, cannot but be irresolute, irresolution being an ordinary companion to fear; a thing most dangerous in martial affairs, where opportunities offered are to be taken at the first rebound'.

The queen's counsellors were faced with a choice. If Elizabeth could be convinced that an expedition to the Netherlands would succeed, 'then fear giving place, reason shall have his full course to direct her majesty to be resolute'. (For Walsingham, reason was gendered male.) The alternative was to threaten her with the consequences of doing nothing, 'the ruin of her self and state'. This presentation of the queen as a factor to be coaxed and overcome is extraordinary. Her advisers clearly thought like this, may sometimes have talked to each other in these terms, but they rarely put such radical ideas in writing. The potential gains justified the means. Joining the enterprise would 'advance the cause of religion throughout all Christendom, an act worthy of a Christian prince'. An evil neighbour, and a tyrannical government in the Netherlands, would be overthrown. If Elizabeth refused to commit then Spain could only grow in strength, 'whose pride is such as he thinketh he may give law to all Christendom'. With the signing of the treaty of Blois and the possibility of English intervention in the Netherlands, Walsingham may have thought that the skies were brightening. In fact, the Protestant faith was about to be shaken by a thunderbolt.[30]

In January 1593 the company of actors known as Lord Strange's Men put on a new production by Christopher Marlowe at the Rose Theatre. *The Massacre at Paris* depicts a bloodbath of Protestants at the hands of the Guise family and the Duke of Anjou. Multiple murders are played out in full view of the audience. Admiral Coligny is brutally slain and strung up on stage. Huguenots kneeling at prayer are stabbed to death. The Old Queen of Navarre is poisoned by a pair of gloves. Catherine de' Medici presides over the play, directing the killing to maintain herself in power. But Marlowe lingers longest over Duke Henry of Guise, psychopathically Catholic and as ambitious as Doctor Faustus:

What glory is there in a common good
That hangs for every peasant to achieve?
That like I best that flies beyond my reach.
Set me to scale the high Pyramides
And thereon set the diadem of France;
I'll either rend it with my nails to naught,
Or mount the top with my aspiring wings,
Although my downfall be the deepest hell. (I, ii, 40–7)

As everyone in the theatre would have known, Marlowe based his play on real events that had taken place in France twenty years before. The St Bartholomew's massacres of August 1572 began with a royal wedding. On 18 August Margaret de Valois, the king's sister, married the Protestant Prince Henry of Navarre at Notre-Dame. The celebrations brought the Huguenot aristocracy en masse to Paris. Sectarian tension had been tinder-dry for months. Catholics were enraged when a memorial cross erected on the ruins of a Protestant house was removed on Coligny's orders. Forty Huguenots were killed when they mocked a procession of the consecrated wafer representing the body of Christ. It was rumoured that the king had sent troops to support Louis of Nassau's fight against the Spanish in the Netherlands. As Catholic preachers thundered against the pollution of a Protestant royal marriage, Coligny was shot and wounded on his way back from an audience with Charles IX. The bullet was fired from a house owned by a servant of the Guise. If Coligny had fled Paris at this point, the Huguenot leadership would have followed him. Instead, he accepted the king's offer of protection.

Sunday 24 August was St Bartholomew's Day, honouring the apostle of Christ who was flayed and beheaded for his faith. Early that morning, Coligny was murdered in his bed by a company of soldiers mustered by the Duke of Guise. Several dozen Huguenot noblemen suffered the same fate at the hands of the king's Swiss guards and the personal retinue of the Duke of Anjou. As news spread across the waking city, the festivities of a saint's day deteriorated with terrifying speed into a general assault on the Protestant population. The orgy of violence lasted for three days. Huguenots were cut down wherever they could be found, in their houses and in the street, some subjected to ritualised desecration and others run through on their doorsteps. It was an intimate killing. Catholics who had lived cheek by jowl with Protestants knew where to find their neighbours when they tried to hide. According to one narrative,

> the rascal multitude, encouraged by spoil and robbery, ran with their bloody swords raging throughout all the town. They spared not the aged, nor women, nor the very babes. In joy and triumph, they threw the slain bodies out at the windows, so as there was not in manner any one street or lane that seemed not strawed with murdered carcasses.

Two thousand Protestants died in Paris, and probably another three thousand in provincial France. The rioters struck at property as well as people, sacking six hundred houses in the capital. Prior to the French wars of religion, a 'massacre' had referred to a chopping-block used to carve up meat; now it took in the butchery of human beings.

Aside from its sheer numbers, the most difficult thing to grasp about the St Bartholomew massacre is the carnival atmosphere in which the slaughter was carried out. Victims were paraded as if they were caught up in a Mardi Gras game. Corpses were dismembered and dragged through the streets, body parts offered for sale in a grisly parody of the butcher's cart. The killers went about their work in good humour, laughing and joking, stopping off in taverns to drink and sing songs. It was the medieval theme of the *danse macabre* translated into flesh and blood. The perpetrators believed that they were in the right, doing no more than the king had told them. When a long-dead hawthorn tree in the cemetery of the Holy Innocents began to bloom, it was interpreted as a sign that they were carrying out the work of God.[31]

Huguenots both living and dead were dumped into the Seine in acts of ritual purification. More than a thousand bodies were washed up on the banks of the river over the next few days, a horrifying image which resurfaces in Marlowe's *The Massacre at Paris*. As Anjou stabs the Protestant scholar Petrus Ramus in his study, Guise and his brother Dumaine discuss the slaughter raging outside:

> GUISE. My Lord of Anjou, there are a hundred Protestants,
> Which we have chas'd into the river Seine,
> That swim about, and so preserve their lives.
> How may we do? I fear me they will live.
> DUMAINE. Go place some men upon the bridge,
> With bows and darts, to shoot at them they see,
> And sink them in the river as they swim. (I, vii, 57–63)

Maybe Marlowe talked to Walsingham about what he had witnessed in the summer of 1572. The idea is tempting, although the playwright also had ample printed evidence to work from: François Hotman's *De Furoribus Gallicis* was republished as *A True and Plaine Report of the Furious Outrages of Fraunce* a year after the massacres. Hotman's biography of Coligny was also translated for an English audience, as was a scabrous attack on the queen mother by Henri Estienne.[32]

Walsingham's family was with him in the English embassy. His daughter Frances was about five years old, and Ursula was pregnant with their second child. Robert Beale was there too, working as Walsingham's secretary. By chance the young poet Philip Sidney was also in Paris. St Bartholomew forged a close bond between Walsingham and Sidney, reflected in their political ideas and ultimately in Sidney's marriage to the sixteen-year-old Frances in 1583. The physician Timothy Bright, who witnessed the massacres as a student, described Walsingham's house as 'a very sanctuary' for Protestants who would otherwise have been slaughtered. Lord Wharton took refuge there when his tutor, an English clergyman, was cut down by the crowd. An Italian historian named Pietro Bizari, who seems to have been working as an intelligencer for Lord Burghley, attributed his own survival to Walsingham's protection. As we have seen, the Huguenot nobleman the Sieur de Briquemault was not so lucky. The Spanish ambassador in Paris, who decked out his servants in scarlet cloth in celebration of the massacre, claimed that Walsingham himself was lucky to escape with his life.[33]

No narrative of St Bartholomew survives among Walsingham's papers. Knowing that diplomatic despatches could be intercepted, he may have preferred to send a messenger who could recite his report from memory. But simple shock may also have come into it: relatively few witnesses of the massacre were ever able to write about what they had seen. One of the few who did was Robert Beale, who compiled a 'Discourse after the great murder in Paris & other places in France' which was probably intended for Lord Burghley's eyes. The preservation of the queen and English liberty was tied to the survival of Protestantism in Europe:

> I think it time and more than time for us to awake out of our dead sleep, and take heed lest like mischief as has already overwhelmed the brethren and neighbours in France and Flanders embrace us which be left in such sort as we shall not be able to escape.

If England continued to slumber then Anjou would be married to the Queen of Scots, 'which matter hath been long a brewing', and a French battle fleet would follow. Beale saw a direct parallel with the Norman invasion of 1066, when defeat had dissolved the laws and commonwealth of England. Anjou and Mary would be free to divide the land among their followers, just as William the Conqueror had done. England's defences were weak, her queen desperately vulnerable to poison or treason. The fall of the Huguenot stronghold at La Rochelle, or the defeat of William of Orange, would allow the forces of Catholicism to concentrate exclusively on England. 'But the chiefest mischief is to be found inwardly,' he went on, 'I mean the faction of the Queen of Scots and papists in this realm'.

English Catholics were only pretending to be loyal, and would desert at the first opportunity. Beale had a clear remedy to prescribe: nothing less than 'the death of that Jezebel', the Queen of Scots, could save England from civil war. Delay any longer, and 'our musters, our keeping of watch and ward, our ships will do us little good'. The urgency of Beale's argument, the repeated references to history and the fate of Christendom, all echo Walsingham's own rhetoric.[34]

For several days it was too dangerous for Walsingham to leave the embassy. When Ursula tried to make her escape, two of the ministers in her escort were recognised and beaten up by the guards at the city gate. Consequently it was Beale who went to court to hear the official explanation for an uprising which the queen mother nonchalantly described as 'the late accident'. What, he asked with icy courtesy, was he to tell his royal mistress? Walsingham got his answer at a royal audience on 1 September. The king had been protecting himself and his mother against a conspiracy planned by Coligny and his supporters; he desired nothing more than to preserve his friendship with his sister Elizabeth. Walsingham replied in kind. The alliance which his majesty had made with England was firmer than anything achieved by his predecessors, and should not be compromised by recent events. As a diplomat Walsingham was doing exactly what was required of him, protecting the treaty of Blois from those who would have preferred to go to war with England. As a Protestant, however, he was appalled by the turn of events in France. When Walsingham raised the issue of the three English victims of the riots, Charles promised to prosecute the offenders if they could be found. Walsingham's reply was acid: 'I showed his majesty it would be hard to produce them, the disorder being so general, the sword being committed to the common people'. This was a loaded reference. The sword in royal iconography represented the power to execute justice; it rightfully belonged to the king, not the crowd. It was as close to direct criticism as his position allowed.[35]

Burghley offered Walsingham some spiritual comfort, although his conclusions were hardly encouraging: 'I see the devil is suffered by the Almighty God, for our sins, to be strong in following the persecution of Christ's members.' The massacre was a call to repentance, a belief which Leicester expressed even more forcibly. God had visited his people with 'the scourge of correction', he told Walsingham, 'but our sins deserve this and more'. The only proper response was to hold fast in the faith and pray that God would let them live to see 'the fall of His and our enemies'. There was a solitary ray of hope: the queen had authorised her ambassador to announce his 'unwillingness to tarry' at the French court. Yet Charles IX proved resistant, threatening that Walsingham's recall would be taken as a breach in diplomatic relations. Sir Thomas Smith likened him to a pin stuck in a hole, needing another to get it out. Walsingham was hundreds of pounds in debt, forced to sell land and to borrow in anticipation of his salary. Pleas to increase his allowance went unanswered. It took until April 1573 for Valentine Dale to be despatched as Elizabeth's new envoy to France. 'I daresay you will wish him a speedy passage,' wrote Burghley with a wry smile.

A month after St Bartholomew's Day, Walsingham briefed the privy council on his analysis of Anglo-French affairs. The Huguenot community had been assaulted 'without pity and compassion, without regard had either of age or sex, without ordinary form of justice'. England was a valuable export market for the wines of Bordeaux, yet the French still looked on its people with loathing. Walsingham's life was threatened by 'the disquietness of this state'. All in all, it was a litany of failure:

Seeing now there is here neither regard had to either word, writing or edict; seeing the king persecuteth that religion with all extremity that her majesty professeth; seeing that they that now possess his ear are sworn enemies unto her majesty, and nourishers of the late amity are separated from him; I leave it to your honours now to judge, what account you may make of the amity with this crown. If I may without presumption or offence say my opinion, considering how things presently stand, I think less peril to live with them as enemies, than as friends.[36]

No marriage or resolution of the succession, a peace treaty that was rhetoric rather than substance, and the Catholic party triumphantly ascendant in France. Sailing home in the spring of 1573, Walsingham must have wondered whether the Lord had forsaken the English nation.

3 Armed with Innocence

The St Bartholomew massacre sent a shockwave through the Protestant community in England. Francis Walsingham had gone to Paris at a time of relative toleration for the Huguenots, but he departed from the front line of a confessional war. The carnage in France was a lurid stimulus to the imagination. A service was rapidly printed for use in parish churches, summoning the English to repent or face a similar punishment: 'The ungodly bend their bows, and make ready their arrows within the quiver: that they may shoot at those that call upon the name of the Lord'. Preachers called for public fasts in imitation of ancient Israel, but the book trade was hungry for atrocity stories. The survival of the reformed faith seemed to be at stake, not only in France but in the Netherlands, Scotland, even England itself. As Robert Beale put it, now was the time to awake out of sleep.[1]

It had all looked so different earlier that same summer. The signing of the treaty of Blois was commemorated in a group portrait of the English royal family now known as the Allegory of the Tudor Succession. According to its inscription, the painting was presented by Queen Elizabeth to Francis Walsingham as a 'mark of her people's and her own content'. The artist didn't sign his name but was probably Lucas de Heere, a Flemish Protestant who fled to England with his family in the 1560s. He later acted as an envoy between Walsingham and William of Orange. Like so many images of the time, the Allegory was intended to be decoded as well as admired. The setting is a throne room in one of the royal palaces. Henry VIII presides under the Tudor coat of arms, surrounded by his three children. Edward VI kneels beside his father, accepting the sword of justice, but it is Elizabeth who dominates the foreground of the painting. She is pictured entering the chamber hand in hand with Peace, a goddess with an olive branch. Weapons are trampled and burst into flames, while Plenty follows behind with her cornucopia. To the rear of the royal dais stand Queen Mary and Philip of Spain attended by Mars, god of war.[2]

The painting plays riddles with perspective and motion. Henry VIII sits squarely at the centre of the composition, but the angling of his body allows Queen Elizabeth to become the focal point. She accepts the viewer's gaze at first, then redirects it by pointing towards the figure of Peace. Elizabeth seems to be walking while her father, brother and sister are frozen in place. An accompanying verse describes the portrait as a 'show', and indeed a similar tableau was acted out during a torchlit pageant at Whitehall in June 1572, when Peace arrived in a chariot to seek the help of the queen. De Heere's method may have been sophisticated, but his meaning was plain enough. Edward and Elizabeth represent the legitimate, and Protestant, line of the royal succession. Where Mary's Spanish marriage had brought war and persecution, Elizabeth was allowing peace to return. Her diplomacy had won the objective which Henry VIII, with all his massive military spending, was never able to attain: an acknowledgement from the French crown that England was its equal.

The Allegory was a handsome gift. The queen rarely commissioned the portraits which created a cult of devotion around her, preferring to receive them in tribute from her courtiers. For Walsingham, however, its message must have been bittersweet. The language of friendship exchanged by the English and French legations at Blois had done nothing to protect Huguenots from the massacre at Paris. The figure of

Edward by his father's side was an uncomfortable reminder that the Tudor succession was still unresolved. The portrait spoke of peace at a time when England was heading for war: not a princely contest governed by the rules of chivalry, but a wholly new threat to the survival of true religion. Walsingham's eyes would inexorably have been drawn to the background of the canvas, where the forces of Catholicism rushed in through an open door.

For a brief while after returning from France, Walsingham was left alone with his family. The final fruitless months of the embassy left him with loans to restructure and debts to repay. His health had taken a hammering. The physical strain of following the French court had compounded the psychological scars left by St Bartholomew. He needed time to reflect and recuperate. The birth of their second daughter helped Francis and Ursula come to terms with the trauma of what they had witnessed in Paris. But the urgency of the times meant that he would not be allowed to rest for long. A new role was already being mapped out for him. Writing to Walsingham in January 1573, the Earl of Leicester had referred to 'the place all men would have you unto, even for her majesty's sake'. This could only mean one thing: a seat on the privy council as principal secretary to the queen.

On Monday 21 December 1573 Walsingham rode out from the city of London to Whitehall, the sprawling Henrician palace where the queen liked to keep Christmas. The terse note in his journal, 'I was sworn secretary', hardly captures the scale of the responsibility that he was taking on. From this day forward, Walsingham was wedded to the royal presence. As Sir Thomas Smith knew to his cost, Queen Elizabeth expected her secretaries to be constantly on call. Smith had cut his teeth as a secretary during the late 1540s, when the Duke of Somerset ruled in King Edward's name and the march of reform had seemed unstoppable. His 'Discourse of the Common Weal' had been a pioneering piece of economic analysis. But under Elizabeth, Smith was hobbled by having to obey every petty summons:

> what can I write when I can have nothing with daily attending, for the most part three or four times in the day. It makes me weary of my life . . . I can neither get the other letters signed nor the letters already signed sent away . . . I would some other man occupied my room who had more credit to get things resolved in time.

Although Smith remained the senior of the two secretaries until his retirement in 1576, it was Walsingham who increasingly took the initiative in managing the queen and council. Smith was in his sixties, tired by government and brought low by cancer of the throat. His youthful social conscience had been eclipsed by the more conventional concerns of the Tudor gentry, the building of a fine house and tomb to perpetuate his memory. In October 1573 his only son was killed on a colonising expedition to Ulster. Smith's religious commitment, never the dominant feature of his personality, was by now little more than lukewarm. He was not the man to press a Protestant agenda on the queen. Francis Walsingham, by contrast, fully intended to put his faith into action.[3]

The potential power of a principal secretary had been amply demonstrated in Henry VIII's reign. Thomas Cromwell used his access to the king to oversee a radical overhaul of Church and state during the 1530s, transforming the secretaryship into one of the great offices of state. Queen Elizabeth had no reverence for Cromwell: he had been instrumental in the death of her mother. But the trust she placed in William Cecil produced a rather similar kind of government. In fact Cecil exceeded even Cromwell in his remit as principal secretary, because a queen was believed to need instruction as well as advice. In 1572 Lord Burghley, as Cecil had now become, exchanged the burden of constant attendance on Elizabeth for a new role as lord treasurer. Walsingham inherited the tasks which had underwritten Cecil's power during the first dozen years of the reign: setting the agenda for the privy council, presenting crown policy in the Commons, and sifting the information which was presented to the queen.

The principal secretary's symbol of office was the signet, the most personal of the three royal seals which authenticated orders to officials and grants of crown patronage. The privy seal traditionally had its own keeper, while the great seal was held by the lord chancellor. But when Lord Howard of Effingham died in 1573, the post of lord privy seal was left unfilled. Walsingham was able to profit from the queen's economy. Custody of the privy seal had passed to him by the mid-1570s, tightening his grip over the writs and warrants generated by the crown. Burghley was still chief minister; no one could rival his personal relationship with Elizabeth. But Walsingham had become the kingpin of English government.[4]

As he recorded in his journal, Walsingham was soon in conference about the gathering political crisis in Ireland. Several days of shuttling between the queen, the privy council and Lord Burghley were concluded by Elizabeth's departure on 12 January for Hampton Court, with Walsingham in close pursuit. A principal secretary was never out of the saddle for long. In March the queen moved on to the palace at Greenwich where she and her father had both been born. This was the familiar rhythm of Elizabeth's court, and her council had learned to live with it. Much more disruptive were the queen's progresses around the south of England. Elizabeth spent the summer of 1574 making her way in slow stages to Bristol, where she was saluted by pageants and a fusillade of guns, and Walsingham was briefly reunited with his wife. A schoolboy dressed as Fame squeaked the city's speech of welcome:

No sooner was pronounced the name, but babes in streets gan leap;
The youth, the age, the rich, the poor, came running all on heap,
And, clapping hands, cried mainly out, 'O blessed be the hour,
Our queen is coming to the town, with princely train and power'.

The return journey was equally unhurried, taking in Sir John Thynne's building works at Longleat and the Earl of Pembroke's house at Wilton, then onward to Salisbury and the royal houses of Oatlands and Nonsuch. By the time that she returned to the centre of her realm, the queen and her government had been away for four months.

Elizabeth I did not travel light. Hundreds of baggage carts transported all the regalia of monarchy into the shires, from the queen's wardrobe to the accoutrements of the royal kitchens. Progresses connected the Tudor crown to the nobility and gentry who governed the shires. For Elizabeth they also addressed a more personal need, convincing her that she was loved by her people. In the country as at the royal court, magnificence was the handmaid of her rule. And yet Smith was exasperated by what he called 'this trotting about in progress', which made 'many things to be unprofited and longer deferred than is convenient'. Walsingham shared his irritation. 'Banqueting and pastime' took the queen out of the physical context of government, giving her the opportunity to dodge and delay. Elizabeth revelled in the confusion, altering itineraries on a whim and throwing months of planning into disarray. In privileging drama and display over administrative detail, she was her father's daughter.[5]

Where the queen led, her ministers and favourites had to follow. The privy council had long since outgrown its origins as the meeting of a king with his warrior aristocracy. In the words of its clerk Robert Beale, the Elizabethan council was responsible for despatching 'matters of estate either at home or abroad'. No

Act of Parliament declared that the queen had to heed her councillors' advice, but neither did anyone doubt their competence to act for the crown. The nobility had their place around the table more on merit than on rank. George Talbot, sixth Earl of Shrewsbury and the custodian of Mary, Queen of Scots, looked the most like a medieval regional magnate. The other earls on Elizabeth's council – Leicester, his brother Warwick, Sussex – owed their titles to the Tudors. They joined Burghley as lord treasurer, the two principal secretaries, and the chief officers of the queen's household. The full council numbered sixteen members in 1574, although some of these were backwoodsmen and attended mainly on ceremonial occasions. Urgent business was transacted by an inner circle formed around Burghley, Walsingham and Leicester.

When it wasn't trailing the queen on progress, the privy council often met in the Star Chamber in the old royal palace of Westminster. The room overlooked the Thames, its ceiling of azure blue emblazoned with stars of gold leaf. Tapestries of Tudor roses and the royal arms reminded councillors that they exercised the power of monarchy. Two or three times a week, more frequently as the reign drew on, the council came together to agree how the realm should be governed. Reports from ambassadors and bishops were received, debated and acted upon. The preparedness of coastal defences and the navy was constantly reviewed. Foreign trade and the conduct of English merchants overseas were monitored. Endless letters flowed in from the magistrates and town corporations who enforced crown policy in the provinces. With a change in props, a green cloth on the table instead of the usual red, the council was transformed into the court of Star Chamber with a special jurisdiction over riot. The separation of powers meant nothing in the sixteenth century.[6]

Tudor government can look like a Heath Robinson machine,

an intricate assembly which had no very obvious way of functioning. Yet the Elizabethan privy council managed to address an astonishing range of issues while keeping even the remote reaches of the kingdom under surveillance. On 31 May 1574, for instance, ten councillors gathered at Greenwich to face a typically eclectic agenda. Burghley, Smith and Walsingham sat alongside five peers of the realm, including Lincoln as lord admiral and Sussex as lord chamberlain of the royal household. The first item for discussion was the Inns of Court. Regulations were issued covering every aspect of their activities, from the conduct of moots to the attendance of students at divine prayer. The council then moved on to provincial business. Orders for military musters were sent to the sheriffs and justices of the coastal counties. A religious dissident named John Appleyard was consigned to the care of the Dean of Norwich. An arrest warrant was put out for an Italian goldsmith who had been counterfeiting coins in Scotland. Arbitration was offered in a long-running rent dispute in Dorchester. A docket was issued for the transportation of timber from the New Forest for the fortification of Guernsey. All this in just one meeting, on one relatively uneventful day. A principal secretary had to 'understand the state of the whole realm', from its geography and military resources to the hotspots of Catholic recusancy and the strength of the nobility.[7]

Beale's 'Treatise of the Office of a Councillor and Principal Secretary to Her Majesty' was one of two advice manuals written in 1592 by men who had served under Walsingham. The second, a 'Discourse Touching the Office of Principal Secretary of Estate', was the work of Walsingham's confidential secretary and agent Nicholas Faunt. The coincidence in date suggests that the secretaryship was being re-thought following Walsingham's death in 1590. Beale's treatise examined the relationship between secretary, queen and council while Faunt's focused on the staff in his household, but on two key matters they spoke with a single voice. The first was the remarkable range of business handled by the principal secretary, from foreign affairs to the maintenance of the common peace: 'staying the ill affected from evil courses, encouraging the well affected, making arbitraments and good agreements betwixt subjects', as Faunt put it. Burghley and Walsingham are sometimes cast in modern terms as prime minister and foreign secretary, but this distinction simply doesn't work. Walsingham's role as royal secretary, and his growing responsibility for the queen's safety, meant that he was deeply absorbed in domestic affairs.

The second point of agreement is more surprising. Both authors were openly critical of Walsingham's lax attitude towards security. 'Burthen not yourself with too many clerks or servants as Sir Francis Walsingham did', cautioned Beale. 'Let your secret services be known to a few', copying the good example of Lord Burghley. Faunt's critique of his former master was even sharper:

> by experience I can say that the multitude of servants in this kind is hurtful and of late years has bred much confusion with want of secrecy and despatch in that place. For if in a principal servant to the secretary, secrecy and faithfulness be chiefly required, what trust can there be reposed in many? And if many be employed in matters of secrecy, who shall think himself principal in trust?

Walsingham's modern reputation depends more than anything on his work as a spymaster, his ability to infiltrate and expose the Catholic plots which were attempting to dethrone Elizabeth. As we shall see, this image is based on a good deal of hard evidence. But in the judgement of his own staff, the men who acted on his orders and deputised for him when he was sick, Walsingham also made some serious mistakes. His operatives wrestled with each other for position, offering rival opinions and weakening his ability to react quickly and decisively. Far better, counselled Faunt, for a principal secretary to select one man to be 'his own pen, his mouth, his eye, his ear, and keeper of his most secret cabinet'.[8]

Queen Elizabeth was determined that the royal supremacy claimed by her father would not be eroded while she was on the throne. Policy flowed from the sovereign rather than her ministers, at least in theory. But Elizabethan England was far from being an absolute monarchy. All the queen's majesty and rhetoric, her delaying tactics and her tears, could not alter the fact that her dominions were ungovernable without the co-operation of the council. Elizabeth rarely attended meetings of the full council, preferring to summon her advisers one by one to avoid a united front. But the queen's absence also allowed an *esprit de corps* to grow among her councillors, which began the reign as a shared sense of frustration and ended it approaching a theory of mixed government. A council had ruled the realm once before, in Edward VI's reign. If Elizabeth would not or could not take the decisions necessary to ensure national security, then there were those in authority who judged it their duty to act without her.

Having tackled the technicalities of being principal secretary, Robert Beale turned to a far more sensitive question: how to manage the queen. His advice was startlingly frank. A great deal depended on her emotional state. If she was well disposed, a secretary had a good chance of getting her signature. If she was not – and Elizabeth was notorious for her explosive temper and bouts of depression – then government could simply grind to a halt. A wise man established her state of mind before seeking the royal presence. Hence the political significance of the privy chamber, the gentlewomen who acted as Elizabeth's companions and personal servants. 'Learn before your access her majesty's disposition', cautioned Beale, 'by some in the privy chamber with whom you must keep credit'. An entertaining anecdote while she signed any documents would make the process run more smoothly. Every chance should be taken to favour her family on the Boleyn side. When she was angry, the queen should not be approached 'unless extreme necessity urge it'.

Beale had another lesson to teach Walsingham's successor: court faction could leave a secretary vulnerable and exposed. 'When there shall be any unpleasant matter to be imparted to her majesty from the council,' he warned, 'let not the burden be laid on you alone, but let the rest join with you'. That way no one could subsequently say it was all the secretary's doing. Walsingham's correspondence with the people he trusted the most contains similar references to the queen, his letters to Henry Hastings, Earl of Huntingdon, being particularly revealing. Huntingdon governed huge swathes of England as president of the council of the north. He was also a convinced Protestant, using his influence to deploy evangelical clergy in strategic parishes and to organise preaching tours of the north. Huntingdon's interests were represented at court by his wife Katherine, whom Walsingham described as 'a most diligent solicitor' on his behalf. The northern counties were regarded by the government as a crucial buffer zone against potential attack from Scotland. The problem, as so often in Elizabeth's reign, was one of money: the queen was reluctant to fund a costly military establishment on a permanent footing. Walsingham's solution was to advise Huntingdon to send his requests for resources directly to the privy council, promising that when they were received 'I will devise some way that your lordship shall have entertainment without troubling of her majesty'.

Knowing full well what Elizabeth's reaction was likely to be, Walsingham was attempting to outflank her. Whereas Huntingdon took a generally positive view of the region under his command, Walsingham was more pessimistic. He doubted the loyalties of those who currently made a show of allegiance to the queen, predicting that many of them 'would be found very dangerous and doubtful in obedience' if a second northern rising began to muster. This was why he wanted 'her majesty still to doubt the worst, and the worst accordingly to be provided for'. Regulating the flow of information received by the queen placed real power in the principal secretary's hands. But Elizabeth was not so easily outmanoeuvred: despite Walsingham's best efforts, Lord Hunsdon was ordered to disband all but five hundred of the soldiers mustered in the north. 'By which account', wrote Walsingham bitterly, 'I see that Scotland is clean lost, and a great gate opened thereby for the loss of Ireland'. The council had faithfully discharged its duty to protect the kingdom from harm, 'but God hath thought good to dispose otherwise of things, in whose hands the hearts of all princes are'. There were times in Elizabeth's service when the only option left was to pray.[9]

Among all the offices of state, observed Nicholas Faunt in 1592, 'there is none of more necessary use, nor subject to more cumber and variableness, than is the office of principal secretary'. 'Cumber' has fallen out of modern English, but Faunt used it to mean the relentless pressure of government. Walsingham's day started when he was still in bed, making notes in a memoranda book on problems to be addressed, scoring out any which had been despatched and carrying over the many that had not. He would still be at work late at night, writing the reams of letters on which the authority of the Tudor crown depended. The only way to cope was to 'divide and measure the day' according to the urgency of business. Faunt's treatise paints a picture of Walsingham's servants clustering around him, ordering the bundles of papers on his table, fetching cipher alphabets to decode reports from agents abroad, and digesting the most valuable intelligence into ledgers to ensure that it wouldn't be lost.

It was a punishing routine, and Walsingham was soon paying a high price. In March 1574 he fell ill and had to withdraw from the court for several days. A more serious bout of sickness in December kept him away for nearly four months, although he continued to write letters from his bed. By September 1576, after two more summers on progress, Walsingham had almost reached the end of his endurance. He had only one request to bring before the queen, he told Burghley, namely 'to be quit of the place I serve in, which is subject unto so many thwarts and hard speeches'.

If Walsingham had acted on his threat he would be remembered in similar terms to Sir Thomas Smith, a modestly successful diplomat defeated by the sheer weight of Elizabethan government. The difference between the two men was that Walsingham could always find fortification in his faith. As he later wrote to the Earl of Huntingdon, 'a Christian man armed with innocence never taketh harm by the knowledge of suchlike thwarts, for that they minister rather cause of comfort than grief; when they be argument of God's love towards us, who doth correct those that he loveth'. Walsingham's drive to serve the state can be explained in different ways: his brooding fear of invasion, and the civil war which would follow it; his loyalty and patriotism; the desire for power and personal advancement, to which even he was not immune. But his obligation to queen and country was tightly bound with his duty to God. If the two ever came into conflict, Walsingham would unhesitatingly follow his conscience. The comparison may seem eccentric, but there are times when his priorities echo those of Henry VIII's secretary Thomas More, 'the king's good servant, but God's first'.[10]

For a ruler who cast herself in the image of her father, Elizabeth I was notably reluctant to go to war. The Tudor family portrait which she presented to Walsingham in 1572 praised her for banishing conflict from her kingdom, allowing peace and plenty to flourish. A seam of pacifism ran through the Christian humanism in which the young Elizabeth had been schooled, and it is possible that she had taken this to heart. Then again, her brother and sister had been educated in much the same way, and both of them pursued an aggressive foreign policy. Other explanations for Elizabeth's caution seem more likely. The consequences of earlier military campaigns were clear for all to see: the treasury emptied and the coinage debased, Calais lost and nothing gained in exchange. The Earl of Warwick's Newhaven expedition of 1562–3 ended in humiliating surrender at Dieppe and Le Havre. True, Queen Elizabeth's navy was comparatively strong. But she was shrewd enough to recognise that land armies ate resources on a scale which the crown could not sustain. There was another, more nakedly political, reason for keeping England out of the European theatre. Defending Le Havre had cost Elizabeth more than a year's regular income, forcing her to call on Parliament for a subsidy; remaining neutral might protect the royal prerogative from interference from the Commons.

Francis Walsingham did not see things Elizabeth's way. For him, national security and the survival of Protestant Christendom depended on a pre-emptive strike against Spain. With its small population and limited taxation base, England was in no position to launch an assault into Iberia; military ambition on that kind of scale had died with Henry VIII. But there was a battleground closer to home in which the English could land a blow against Spain and Catholicism. Since 1566 the Calvinist towns of the Low Countries had been gathering in revolt against the rule of Philip II and his regent in the Netherlands, his half-sister Margaret of Parma. Elizabeth's stance had so far been guardedly neutral. The prosperity of her crown and nation depended on trade, and English merchants were heavily committed in

Antwerp. Rebellion of any sort was anathema to the queen. On the other hand the emerging leader of the Protestant opposition, William of Orange-Nassau, was a prince in his own right. A sovereign ruler could hardly be a rebel. And if liberty and true religion were ground underfoot in the Low Countries, then England might be the next target of the Catholic league.

With its urban mercantile culture and intellectual traditions of humanism and anticlericalism, the Netherlands was natural terrain for Protestantism to take root. Printing presses had been disseminating radical ideas amongst Flemings and Walloons since the early 1520s. Forty years on, the persecution of the Huguenots was pushing French migrants over the border into Artois and Flanders. Protestants gathered in open-air rallies to sing psalms and hear the gospels read by 'hedge-preachers' recruited from the crowd rather than the clerical elite. Sympathetic Calvinist ministers travelled on mission from Geneva. An outbreak of iconoclasm blazed through Dutch towns and monasteries, fanned by sermons and an economic downturn which had left many without employment. It was against this backdrop that three hundred noblemen, dressed as beggars but armed with guns, served a petition on Margaret of Parma demanding toleration for non-Catholics. Children in Ghent staged a sympathetic protest of their own, challenging devotional images to say 'long live the beggars' before decapitating them in the streets. When William of Orange resigned from Margaret's council of state and fled to Germany, the various strands of the Dutch revolt had a leader around whom they could rally.

Ghent had been the birthplace of Charles V, Holy Roman Emperor and protector to the Catholic Church. Charles did everything he could to eradicate Protestantism from the Netherlands, but at least his regime had been recognisably Burgundian. His son Philip II was born in Valladolid, and never attempted to speak either Flemish or French. Philip's solution to the crisis was to garrison the Netherlands with Spanish troops. Their commander was Fernando Alvarez de Toledo, Duke of Alva, a career soldier who had previously fought the Ottomans in North Africa and the French in Italy. His arrival in the Low Countries in 1567 has aptly been called 'a turning-point in European history'. Alva's army, which regarded all the Netherlanders as 'Lutherans', was billeted on loyal and rebel towns alike. Amidst a thousand executions for heresy and the mass burning of Protestant books, William of Orange was condemned as a traitor.[11]

Given its centuries-old trade links with the Netherlands, England could hardly remain aloof from the Dutch revolt. The Orangist resistance was kept supplied by the 'Sea Beggars', a fleet of irregulars under the nominal command of William's brother Count Louis of Nassau. Some of these ships were paid for by Dutch refugee congregations under the protection of the English crown. By 1570 there were close on ten thousand exiles living in London and Norwich and Sandwich, enough to merit a separate province of the Dutch Reformed Church. When Alva overran the Protestant ports of the Dutch coast, Dover offered the Sea Beggars a safe harbour. As funds dried up and the Beggars turned to piracy to keep themselves afloat, the exile community ashore helped to sell the prizes which were being seized.[12]

Remembering his own time in exile, Francis Walsingham was a strong advocate for the Dutch Calvinists and their revolt. His first meeting with Louis of Nassau was in 1571, when the count was in France seeking support for his campaign against the Duke of Alva. To Walsingham he was the answer to a prayer, an agent sent by God to defeat the tyranny of Spain. The Habsburg dynasty, he explained in a letter to Leicester, 'is become the pope's champion, and professed enemy unto the gospel, and daily practiseth the rooting out of the same'. They should be thankful that God had given them the opportunity to advance His glory and to secure the queen's safety. It was time for England to commit to the war on false religion.

Walsingham was a hawk, but he was also a realist. Advising a prince to go to war was fraught with danger, because war was unpredictable. And yet sometimes not going to war was the more perilous course. It was characteristic of Walsingham that he thought this problem through on paper. An essay on what he called 'the enterprise of Burgundy' helped him marshal his thoughts before making a case to the privy council. 'As colours by their contraries are best discerned', he proposed, so 'the best and soundest resolutions are taken by comparing commodities with inconveniences'. Objections were first anticipated, then answered one by one as if in a court of law. Walsingham had no illusions about the resort to military action, 'wherefore the success is doubtful, the benefits that ensue thereof small or none, the harms most manifest'. By sea as well as land, England lacked the capability of Spain. The queen herself was 'irresolute', uneasy about backing the rebellion of the Netherlanders against their sovereign prince. War for 'ambition of ground' was unlawful. But defensive war was another category altogether.

Striking against Habsburg power in the Netherlands could be justified on grounds that Spain had already proved herself England's enemy. The northern rebellion had been kindled by the Spanish ambassador, and rebels against Elizabeth were still being fostered in Flanders. Philip of Spain was a protector to the Queen of Scots, 'her majesty's capital enemy', while Alva had been given 'the donation of England' by the pope. The soldier and privateer Thomas Stucley, a defector from Tudor service who dreamed of being created Duke of Ireland, had been warmly received at Philip's court. Queen Elizabeth was being openly derided on the streets of Spain. Intervention in the

Netherlands was not only legally defensible and strategically necessary; it was also the will of God. Supporting the Protestant uprising would 'advance the cause of religion throughout all Christendom, an act worthy of a Christian prince'. The King of Spain and the Guise between them aspired to rule the Christian world; only England stood in their way. Should all these reasons still not prove sufficient, Walsingham slyly played on the queen's vanity. The Netherlands enterprise could add 'increase of domination unto her crown' – as much to Elizabeth's honour as the loss of Calais had been a disgrace to her sister.[13]

For a while Elizabeth flirted with Walsingham's plan. In March 1571 she instructed him to find out, typical of her, 'what are the meanest sums of money to be demanded'. By the following month she had had second thoughts and abandoned the enterprise. She was simply not prepared to fund Count Louis on the scale which was required. The involvement of the Duke of Anjou, whom the Dutch rebels saw as a potential protector, was a major factor: there was no sense in spending English money to establish French supremacy in the Low Countries. Burghley also had a hand in the decision, arguing that English trade with the Dutch ports had to take priority. Walsingham was dismayed at the queen's attitude, but he cannot really have been surprised. Fifty thousand crowns spent now, he wrote gloomily to Burghley, might have saved three hundred thousand in the future. Spain had been provoked and would not forget the insult, 'as shall well appear when opportunity of revenge shall be offered'. When the Sea Beggars were evicted from Dover in March 1572 and captured the port of Brill, England lost the chance to shape the Dutch revolt in its own image.[14]

Walsingham had wanted intervention in the Netherlands as an act of state. The queen, and probably Burghley too, preferred that English engagement should be led by volunteers. Theirs was the subtler strategy, enabling Elizabeth to play up to

Protestant expectations while retaining a degree of deniability. In July 1572 the Devon gentleman Sir Humphrey Gilbert transported more than a thousand troops across the Channel to skirmish with the Spanish in Zealand. A graduate of the increasingly savage war in Ireland, Gilbert had forced any Gaelic Irishman hoping to parley to approach him along an avenue of severed heads. His troops in the Netherlands were under orders to maintain the fiction that 'they went without either licence or knowledge of her majesty, to do nothing but relieve the native people from their oppression'. In truth the privy council kept a close eye on Gilbert, directing him to secure Flushing and Sluys against the French as well as the Spanish. He was recalled to England in November, apparently in disgrace, although Walsingham would have need of him in the future.[15]

So long as he was an ambassador Walsingham enjoyed a certain freedom of movement, carrying out the queen's wishes but also formulating foreign policy on the ground. As principal secretary, however, he was one relatively junior voice on the privy council. Walsingham was forced to watch as Elizabeth and Burghley patched up the relationship with Spain. A trade embargo, imposed in 1569 after some diplomatic sabre-rattling over the detention of four Spanish bullion ships, was lifted in 1573. The queen was outraged when Orange impounded English merchantmen attempting to run his blockade on the River Scheldt. A new governor of the Netherlands, Don Luis de Requesens, exchanged envoys with Elizabeth's court. When she requested that English Catholic exiles be expelled from the Spanish Netherlands, Requesens agreed on condition that Elizabeth ejected the Dutch rebels from her own dominions.

Walsingham was deeply alarmed. Such a show of amity was 'but entertainment for a time', he told the diplomat Daniel Rogers, 'for Christ and Belial can hardly agree'. Belial, from a Hebrew word meaning wickedness or destruction, was a scriptural synonym for the Devil. Walsingham was quoting St Paul's exhortation to shun idolaters: 'what communion hath light with darkness? And what concord hath Christ with Belial?' The arrival in 1574 of a new envoy from Spain, Don Bernardino de Mendoza, prompted Walsingham to write to Burghley in protest. Mendoza came with honeyed words to 'lull us asleep for a time, until their secret practices be grown to their good and full ripeness'. He concluded with a prayer, 'God be merciful unto us'. The imagery of sleep recurs in a letter exhorting Burghley to return to court in January 1575. The queen urgently needed to look to her estate, Walsingham warned, not to 'slumber as she doth in a weak security'.[16]

The collapse of peace talks between Requesens and the Dutch rebels in summer 1575 signalled the end of a movement which had portrayed itself, however tenuously, as a loyal protest for religious toleration. William of Orange finally renounced the sovereignty of Philip II, and revolt turned into revolution. A delegation was soon in England to request aid for the independent States of the Netherlands. It was led by Philip Marnix, Baron de St Aldegonde and one of Orange's most trusted aides. Orange had described Walsingham to Daniel Rogers as 'the chiefest friend he had in England'. Now he told his agents to put themselves in Walsingham's hands. Their mission was simple: to offer Queen Elizabeth the overlordship of the Netherlands. If she refused, then the French crown would be next in line.

Walsingham knew what the royal reaction was likely to be. True to form, Elizabeth retreated into her privy chamber and slammed the door on the court, denying access to everyone until her gentlewomen threatened to break their way in. The council was left to come up with a response. Leicester, Bedford and Mildmay thought that England should openly support the rebels. Sir Nicholas Bacon agreed that assistance should be sent to Orange, but only in secret. Walsingham rehearsed the arguments which he had put before queen and council during his embassy in France. Wars in pursuit of dynastic ambition, to enlarge the dominions granted to a ruler by God, were unacceptable. But wars 'grounded on necessity, not for sovereignty but for safety, not to enlarge but to retain', were entirely just. Spanish councillors had denied the Dutch their legitimate request for 'freedom of conscience and the maintenance of their liberties'. Spain made no secret of its hostility to England, and a Netherlands under Spanish domination was a threat to national security. These were practical justifications, but Walsingham also made a compelling spiritual case. A Catholic league had been formed 'for the rooting out by violence of all such as profess the gospel'. What could be more proper than for a prince to fight for true religion?[17]

Walsingham's devotion to the Dutch cause provoked the queen into one of her periodic rages. According to the Baron de Champagney, who acted as an envoy between Requesens and the English court, Elizabeth gave Walsingham a public dressing-down for his interference and cuffed a lady-in-waiting in her fury. This wasn't out of character; Elizabeth hated being pressed to make decisions, especially in matters which she regarded as her personal prerogative. Her relationship with her principal secretary was often tense. In 1586 she threw a slipper in Walsingham's face when she discovered he had been playing down the threat of a Spanish invasion to prevent resources being diverted from Leicester's campaign in the Netherlands.

But Elizabeth also had a flair for the theatrical in politics. The rebuke to Walsingham may have been staged for the ambassador's benefit, and indeed Champagney came in for some histrionic treatment. One moment the queen was in full flow against Spanish tyranny: 'Your master's intention is to draw a girdle around my realm, thinking that he has only to do with a woman. My father would never have allowed you to go so far as you have done, and I, woman that I am, will know how to look to it'. Soon afterwards she was bidding him to pull up a chair, so the two could talk as friends. Champagney knew where he stood with Walsingham, 'not so much a Calvinist as a Puritan – or even worse'. But he departed England bewildered about Elizabeth's true intentions, like so many of her own servants. His one consolation was that St Aldegonde had fared no better. A mooted loan of £100,000 dissolved into thin air when the queen guillotined debate in the House of Commons, so that he too left with nothing.[18]

Starved of foreign capital and facing dwindling tax revenues from towns disrupted by the fighting, Orange was forced to detain the fleet of the English Merchant Adventurers at Flushing. Elizabeth came close to taking this as an act of war. Walsingham joined in the general condemnation, though he had reasons of his own for doing so. The actions of the rebels 'will marvellously exasperate her majesty against them', he wrote in anger to Beale, 'and draw her to make herself a party perforce against them'. His solution to the crisis took him far beyond the remit of a principal secretary to the queen. In a letter clearly intended for Orange, Walsingham explained what he needed to do 'for the satisfaction of her majesty'. Point by precise point, he set out the terms in which Orange should apologise to queen and council: how his overthrow by the Spanish would place England in peril, and how he might be forced to turn to the French if Elizabeth should abandon him. Orange took the advice, and a collision between Elizabeth and the States of the Netherlands was avoided. Walsingham knew the queen's habits better than anyone, and he had put his knowledge at the disposal of a foreign prince. There could be no clearer example of a foreign policy driven by faith.[19]

For a time it looked as if the Dutch revolt might end in a truce. In January 1577 the States-General, representing most of the Netherlands except Holland and Zealand, voted to accept Philip II's brother Don John of Austria as governor in return for the withdrawal of Spanish troops. More remarkably, the States also promised to maintain the Catholic faith. The southern Netherlands had been slower to convert to Calvinism than the merchant towns of the north, and the nobility was growing fearful of the gospel of liberation which the masses were finding in the Bible. Orange rejected the peace and petitioned Elizabeth to sign a treaty with the Protestant provinces, but she continued to deal with both sides. Walsingham was ill again, and could do little to help him. Fortunately for Orange, Don John's willingness to negotiate with rebels finally snapped. The citadel of Namur was seized as a base from which he could crush the States-General once and for all. A month later the South American treasure fleet arrived in Seville with two million ducats of bullion, allowing Philip II to raise loans to begin the reconquest of the Netherlands.[20]

The forces of Spain and the States met on 31 January 1578 at the abbey town of Gembloux. Spanish cavalry inflicted a crushing defeat on a larger rebel force, slaughtering several thousand and forcing the rest into headlong retreat. The rout had major consequences for the future geography of the Low Countries. Flanders and Hainaut now began to seek an alternative destiny as the 'obedient' provinces of the Spanish Netherlands, leaving the north to fight on alone. The turnaround left Elizabeth facing a dilemma of the kind which she hated so much: to commit English troops, with all the risks this might entail, or to do nothing, leaving the future of the Dutch revolt to be determined by the French. A loan to the German Calvinist leader John Casimir enabled him to march an army against Don John and bought Elizabeth some time, but it was far from being a long-term solution. Her two chief ministers offered conflicting opinions, indicative of their diverging attitudes to foreign affairs.

Walsingham urged the queen to intervene. Once properly fortified, the Dutch towns would be more than capable of resisting a Spanish reconquest. Burghley was sympathetic, but sceptical that the rebel States could survive a sustained assault. Mediation was the better course; and as so often, it was Burghley's advice that appealed. Turning down Leicester's request to lead the resulting peace mission to the Low Countries, Elizabeth opted instead for Lord Cobham and a reluctant Francis Walsingham.

There was no skimping on the scale of the 1578 embassy. Walsingham and Cobham were accompanied by more than sixty English gentlemen when they landed at Dunkirk on 21 June. Money and gifts were liberally cast about. Walsingham's expenses alone came to £1,300, sending him further into debt. The showiness was all part of the queen's strategy, a demonstration of English power to the States and Spanish alike. Cobham was the tenth baron of his line, with a career as a royal envoy stretching back to the reign of Edward VI. As lord warden of the Cinque Ports and constable of Dover, he knew a lot about fortifications. Elizabeth hoped to broker a peace in the Netherlands, but she also wanted an expert assessment of the strength of Orange's camp. Walsingham and Cobham despatched riders to reconnoitre the Dutch coast and hinterland and assess the attitude of the population to the rebel cause. Sir William Pelham and George Carew reported on Ghent, which they judged to be both well defended and spiritually sound. Sermons were being preached in former friary churches, and the citizens were eager for English support. Don John and the pope were derided as 'devils scattered upon the face of the earth', while Orange and Elizabeth were welcomed as the instruments of God.

Walsingham was awestruck when he was taken to see the States' army outside Antwerp, ten thousand foot soldiers and another eight of cavalry. 'If God, who is the disposer of victory, withdraw not courage from them', he enthused to Leicester, 'there is great hope of their good success'. Orange himself was 'the rarest man in Christendom'. It was clear to the ambassadors that the States would neither compromise on religion nor voluntarily yield any territory. Seeing little prospect of a settlement in the Netherlands and hearing rumours of Don John's support for the Queen of Scots, Walsingham and Cobham came to a firm conclusion: England must take the initiative before the French decided to do so.

They got their answer in a letter from the privy council. The queen was not inclined to lend any more money to the States. Worse, she was now making demands for the return of such loans as had already been advanced. Walsingham's friends at court alerted him that he was suspected of a lack of commitment to her chosen policy of peace. Burghley, who understood Elizabeth's changeability only too well, attempted to console him: 'however she misliketh matters at one time, yet at another time she will alter her sharpness, specially when she is persuaded that we all mean truly for her and her suerty'. Leicester was more angry, and less inclined to forgive. His hard words to the queen had had no effect, he told Walsingham in a letter written on the night of 20 July. 'Never stood this crown in like peril.' Since the entreaties of her counsellors had come to nothing, only God could now defend her.

Walsingham was shattered by the news. 'It is an intolerable grief to me,' he confided to Sir Christopher Hatton, 'to receive so hard measure at her majesty's hands'. The worst he could be accused of was having more regard to the queen's safety than to her treasure. The two ambassadors were reduced to raising £5,000 as a private loan to preserve any degree of credit with the States. But it wasn't enough to restore English honour, which was being held in contempt. Walsingham poured out his frustrations in a letter to Burghley. Those involved in such 'sour service' as they were needed to have patience, 'being almost ashamed to show our faces abroad'. The States had been entertained with the hope of royal favour, then abandoned when they stood in greatest need. John Casimir was rueing the day that he had ever left Germany. The queen's behaviour risked making her 'hateful to the world'. It had also deflected the Dutch into the arms of a new protector in the form of Francis Hercules, Duke of Alençon and brother of the King of France. And to the dismay of Elizabeth's Protestant councillors, a royal wedding was suddenly back on the cards.[21]

When a collection of documents illustrating Elizabeth's marriage negotiations was published under Dudley Digges's name in 1655, the compiler drew a contrast between the two French princes who had successively wooed the queen. The Anjou match of 1571–2 was little more than a ruse to draw the Huguenots into the net at Paris, 'I mean the barbarous and bloody massacre on St Bartholomew's eve'. But an alliance between Elizabeth and the Duke of Alençon had been 'really intended', by senior figures on the English privy council as well as by the French themselves. As to Elizabeth's own mind in the matter, 'a thing doubly inscrutable, both as she was a woman and a queen', he was forced to admit defeat.

Digges's evidence and related manuscripts in the National Archives and the British Library reveal that Elizabeth's own ministers were every bit as mystified about what she really wanted. 'I would to God', wrote Walsingham to Burghley in 1581 during another doomed mission to the French court, 'her highness would resolve one way or the other touching the matter of her marriage'. Walsingham entered the negotiating process more open to a French alliance than his Protestant ideology might imply. His visceral objection to a Catholic king-consort was offset by other priorities, to resolve the succession and to secure an ally against the menace of Spain. But the St Bartholomew's Day massacre left him haunted by another royal wedding between a Catholic and a Protestant, one which had ignited a pogrom against the Huguenots of Paris; 'of which most horrible spectacle I was an eye witness', as Walsingham recalled in the margin of a treatise setting out the pros and cons of the Alençon match. The longer the talking went on, moreover, the less chance that a prince would be born.[22]

The idea of Elizabeth marrying Alençon was first mooted in the spring of 1572, during the negotiation of the treaty of Blois. Following the Duke of Anjou's declaration that he could never marry a heretic, Catherine de' Medici had swiftly offered up his younger brother in his place. Alençon had just turned seventeen, while Elizabeth was thirty-eight. The gap between their ages really mattered to the queen, as the Duke of Montmorency discovered when he brought Alençon's proposal to England under cover of the celebrations for the new alliance. The French delegation had to work hard to convince Elizabeth of the benefits of the match. Marriage would make her throne more secure, as well as satisfying the desires of her subjects. Alençon's youth was actually an advantage for the queen, '*parcequ'elle estoit accoustumeé à commander seulle*'. Sir Thomas Smith sent extravagant encouragement from his own vantage-point in France. Alençon was as rich as Anjou while also being more moderate, more flexible and altogether 'the better fellow'. Admittedly, Anjou was taller and fairer. But Alençon was 'not so obstinate and froward, so papistical, and so foolish and resty like a mule as his brother is'. In short, he was ten thousand times superior to Anjou. Foreseeing Elizabeth's likely reaction, Smith urged Burghley to bring his own pressure to bear: 'My lord I pray you, move the queen's majesty to lose no time, and not to procrastinate as her highness is wont'.[23]

Walsingham was more reticent about singing Alençon's praises, not least because of the young duke's appearance. A bout of smallpox had left him disfigured, and he also suffered from an irregularity of the spine. Elizabeth later devised a pet name for him, 'Frog', perhaps a reference to his bandy legs; it predates English jokes about frogs and the French by two centuries. The queen was already sensitive to the lewd gossip which marriage to a much younger man could bring. Alençon's pockmarked face and lack of height made matters worse, potentially compromising the royal magnificence which Elizabeth held so dear.

The 'delicacy of her majesty's eye' was not the only just impediment. Walsingham repeatedly complained about English courtiers who spoke against the marriage simply to keep themselves in royal favour, 'having neither regard unto her majesty nor to the preservation of our country from ruin'. Elizabeth was, in Walsingham's famous phrase, 'the best marriage in her parish', while Alençon was the best suitor to have wooed her. But the 'necessary remedy' prescribed by Parliament was being thwarted by the corruption of court politics, bringing him to despair of the queen's safety.

Walsingham laid out the advantages of the Alençon match in a letter to Lord Burghley. If his looks could be discounted, the duke had many of the qualities to be desired in a husband for the queen. There were also grounds for hope regarding his religion. Walsingham reckoned that Alençon could be guided to conformity with the Church of England once detached from the influence of his family. Sir Thomas Smith agreed. Now that Anjou had become a partisan of the ultra-Catholics, Alençon's household was a 'refuge and succour' for Huguenots seeking royal service. From an English perspective, his degree of distance from the French throne actually made him a more attractive prospect than his brother. If Queen Elizabeth's husband inherited the kingdom of France, then England might be reduced to a satellite state. Beyond such high political concerns was the expectation, shared by Elizabeth's male counsellors, that marriage (and, by implication, sex) could only improve the queen's indifferent health. Childbirth was good for women because, in Smith's memorable phrase, it 'doth clear their bodies, amend their colour, prolong their youth'. The pains which afflicted Elizabeth in her cheek and face were attributed by Burghley to her spinsterhood.[24]

Alençon's proposal demanded a response from the queen. On 23 July 1572 she wrote to Walsingham from her summer progress to tell him that she could not agree to the marriage, citing the 'absurdity' which the world might see in her choice of partner. The gap in their ages was simply too great. The queen had also received a fuller description of the scars on the duke's face, about which Walsingham himself had remained tactfully quiet. Four days later came another letter to Walsingham, which Elizabeth claimed was consistent with her first answer but actually modified it in one very significant detail. Because she valued the French alliance so highly, she was willing for Alençon to 'come hither in person' to present his suit. Only then would she finally make up her mind. Recognising that France would lose face should the duke be rejected on grounds of his appearance, Elizabeth suggested that the visit could be secret and private, 'without any outward pomp or show'.

If Alençon had been bluffing when he offered to meet the queen, then Elizabeth had called it. Why these two contradictory letters, sent in such close succession? Walsingham was instructed to present them both at the French court, where they caused a good deal of confusion. Perhaps this was the point: if Elizabeth had no intention of taking a husband, then there was at least a clear diplomatic advantage in keeping negotiations going as long as possible. Shifting her stance might also help to quieten the clamour in the council chamber and Parliament for her to marry. Or maybe the two letters represent what Susan Doran has called the queen's 'perplexity', the sheer difficulty of making up her mind on an issue in which domestic and foreign policies were so densely intertwined. This would fit with what we know about Elizabeth's character, her shunning of decisions on many of the great questions of state.[25]

There is an alternative explanation, unmistakably hinted at in Walsingham's instructions. The queen was willing to consider marrying Alençon, but only if the French could offer something extra in return. Elizabeth was fully aware that the duke's youthfulness was a weak excuse for breaking off the marriage talks. The French delegation could reasonably argue that if this was such a sticking-point, she should have been plain from the start. Artfully anticipating this objection in her 23 July letter to Walsingham, Elizabeth explained that she had been waiting to see if 'any such further matter might be offered with this match, as might counterpoise in the judgement of the world, the inconvenience of the difference of the age'.

All parties knew what this meant: the return of Calais to the English crown. This isolated remnant of Henry V's empire in France had been taken by the French only months before Elizabeth acceded to the throne, and she felt the loss as painfully as her half-sister Mary had done. In practical terms, the capture of Calais was not of much significance. English merchants had little difficulty in porting their operations elsewhere, and men of government probably welcomed the saving to a hard-pressed exchequer. The French were understandably affronted at the idea that Elizabeth should be compensated for deigning to marry Alençon. Her ministers could see what the queen could not, that there was little strategic value in one vulnerable garrison town in northern France. But Calais was symbolic of English sovereignty, and Elizabeth felt compelled to recover it. She clung to the belief that diplomacy could win back what her sister had lost through war – the same message that was encoded in Lucas de Heere's Allegory of the Tudor Succession.[26]

On 21 August 1572 Catherine de' Medici wrote to her ambassador in England proposing that Elizabeth and her son meet on a ship in the Channel between their two realms. The following day, the French Protestant leader Admiral Coligny was shot in Paris. Unlike his brother Anjou, the Duke of Alençon was not personally implicated in the massacres which followed, but he did take part in the siege of the Huguenot citadel at La Rochelle. Persuading the English public to accept a French king-consort would be far more difficult in the aftermath of St Bartholomew, even assuming that a political consensus had pointed in this direction. An exchange of envoys in 1573 kept the marriage theoretically in play, but each side remained courteously deaf to the arguments of the other.

At Easter 1574, while Charles IX lay dying, Alençon was confined to the fortress chateau of Vincennes outside Paris. He was suspected of plotting against his brother Anjou in collaboration with Henry of Navarre, the Protestant and Bourbon claimant to the throne. It must have seemed to Walsingham that the events of August 1572 were repeating themselves. Thomas Leighton was hurriedly sent as a special envoy to the Valois court, and Walsingham re-engaged his former agents in France in order to make contact with Alençon. The ciphered report which he received from Leighton was far from reassuring. Alençon reckoned that he would soon be in the Bastille, and was appealing to England for help. Burghley responded by sending money to bribe his guards, but without success. Elizabeth also attempted to intervene, offering to receive the Duke of Alençon at court, but the invitation was turned down by his mother. Meanwhile the Count of Montgommćry, the Protestant captain who had fled to England in 1559 after accidentally killing Henry II in a jousting accident, launched an assault into Normandy from his base in Jersey. The Anglo-French entente which had been hammered out at Blois was fast becoming a distant memory. The English diplomat Lord North was treated to the sight of Catherine de' Medici publicly mocking two dwarfs dressed up as Queen Elizabeth.[27]

As France slid back into its wars of religion, Walsingham put the case for military action to the queen. John Casimir's Protestant army in Germany was in desperate need of funds. The royal navy was ready for action and could be used to harry French commerce. The urgency of the cause called for plain speaking. 'For the love of God, madam,' he wrote in January 1575, 'let not the cure of your diseased state hang any longer in deliberation. Diseased states are no more cured by consultation, when nothing resolved on is put in execution, than unsound and diseased bodies by only conference with physicians, without receiving the remedies by them prescribed.'

Elizabeth responded by offering Casimir's father Frederick III a loan of 150,000 silver thalers, but only on condition that Calais be returned to her. When the money was actually sent, it had mysteriously shrunk to 50,000 thalers or £15,000 – too little, Frederick protested, to be of any real use. In September Alençon took matters into his own hands, breaking out of Vincennes and declaring himself protector of the commonwealth. From now on, the duke was an independent agent in French politics. Elizabeth was furious when the Huguenots subscribed to Alençon's 'Peace of Monsieur' the following year, but her unreliability as a patron had left them little alternative.[28]

A great deal had changed by the time that the uprising in the Low Countries put the Alençon match back on the agenda in 1578. The admission of the former Duke of Anjou, now Henry

III, that he would not be having children had nudged his younger brother Alençon a step closer to the French throne. Alençon had soiled his reputation in the interim by commanding an army against his Huguenot allies, but now he spied an advantage in leading the Dutch revolt against Spain. The Calvinist States of the Netherlands had been abandoned by Elizabeth and were threatened with potential annihilation; they had nowhere else to turn. As the Earl of Sussex bleakly put it to Walsingham in August 1578, 'the case will be hard both with the queen and with England if either the French possess or the Spanish tyrannise in the Low Countries'. The plotlines of the Dutch revolt and the Duke of Alençon, until now largely separate from each other, had become intertwined. Facing a shift in the European balance of power but unwilling to go to war, Elizabeth attempted to cash in her principal asset while it still had some value.[29]

When a marriage alliance had first been proposed during Francis Walsingham's embassy to Paris, the privy council and Parliament were broadly in favour while the queen repeatedly expressed her opposition. Once the Alençon negotiations resumed, however, it soon became clear that the tables had turned. Elizabeth let it be known that she wanted to be wooed. When Alençon's personal envoy Jean de Simier arrived in January 1579 bearing gifts of jewels, he was swept into a bizarre world of courtly love by proxy. Elizabeth dallied with him at masques and jousts, hosted intimate interviews and pressed him with love-tokens for his master. He became her 'Ape', apparently a pun on the Latin version of his name, although something else may have been implied: monkeys symbolised sensual pleasure in Renaissance art.

Elizabeth's advisers watched her display of coquetry with disbelief and growing alarm. Sir Walter Mildmay was openly opposed to the match, addressing a personal appeal to his fellow councillors: which of them would want to see his own daughter married to a papist? Burghley's opinion is more difficult to read. Memoranda in his hand which apparently promote the match can also be read within the rhetorical conventions of the time, as identifying a case in order to counter it. When he did offer his verdict on the marriage, initially to Elizabeth and then to the rest of the council, it was to speak against it. Only Sussex welcomed the marriage, citing the assurances of Alençon's entourage that he was content to become Elizabeth's 'servant and defender', and arguing that this was the best way to deflect the duke from his ambitions in the Netherlands.[30]

Walsingham's attitude to Alençon had cooled since the duke's escape from house arrest at Vincennes. When Elizabeth demanded that her councillors put their individual assessments of the marriage down on paper, Walsingham replied with a treatise on 'the diseased state of the realm, and how the same may in some kind be cured'. This picked up the imagery of sickness and medicine which he used to harangue the queen for her failure to commit to the Protestant cause in Europe. As a diagnosis of the threats to her regime at home and abroad, it made for grim reading. Her subjects were unnerved by the queen's unwillingness either to marry or to name a successor. There was no religious unity in the realm. Popular devotion was diverting towards the Queen of Scots 'in respect of religion and the expectation she hath of this crown'. The rulers of France and Spain were both enemies to Elizabeth, and might act against her when their internal troubles had calmed. Then there was King James of Scotland, soon perhaps to make a foreign marriage alliance of his own, which would leave England encircled by hostile states.

Having reviewed the state of national security, Walsingham turned specifically to the Alençon match. There was the personal impact on the queen to consider. Elizabeth would be in physical decline while the duke was still in his prime; a common cause of unhappiness in marriage, as Walsingham pointed out. Given the queen's unwillingness to take a husband, any pressure to do so might hasten her death. This objection was less plausible in 1579, when Elizabeth was doing as much of the running as her suitor, but another was sharply relevant: 'the danger that women of her majesty's years are most commonly subject unto by bearing of children'. Elizabeth was in her forty-sixth year, improbably old by Tudor standards to be delivering her first child. For Walsingham and her other Protestant councillors, the chance to settle the succession had offset their opposition to a Catholic consort. Now the birth of an heir had to be weighed against the risk that Elizabeth would die in the attempt, leaving England's future to be determined by a French duke and a Scottish queen. Far from healing the lesions in the body politic, the marriage could easily 'breed some broil in England'.

Walsingham's greatest fear was the 'diversity in religion' which would follow in Alençon's wake. For him this was the crux of the issue, 'a matter principally to be weighed by Christian counsellors in giving advice to a Christian prince'. The prosperity of a kingdom depended wholly on the goodness of God. The people must place their trust in providence, not be 'carried away by human policy'. History had proved that mighty potentates were bridled when they defied the will of God. Walsingham's thoughts returned again to the massacre at Paris: 'And what success is to be looked for of those marriages that are not made *a domino*, grounded upon human policy, let the dolorous success of the King of Navarre's marriage teach us.' Faith alone, 'soundly without wavering', was sufficient to secure God's protection – a message stretching from the sixteenth-century reformers back to St Augustine and the epistles of St Paul.[31]

These were the terms in which Walsingham preached to the queen and council. The blots and scribblings out, the arguments carried into the margins and the frenetic handwriting, bespeak the speed and passion with which he wrote. Walsingham's treatise matched the mood of many other Protestants in court and country. A Lenten sermon in the presence of the queen called the martyrs of Bloody Mary's reign to mind. The government banned the exposition of any scriptural texts which could be construed as relevant to the match, but popular culture proved less easy to censor. A recycled ballad about the marriage began to do the rounds, a skit on the queen's pet name for Alençon. It was still in circulation centuries later as a children's song:

A frog he would a-wooing go. Heigh-ho, says Rowley!
A frog he would a-wooing go,
whether his mother would let him or no,
With a roly-poly, gammon and spinach.

In July a bullet came close to the barge in which Elizabeth and Simier were being rowed. The queen chose to see it as an accident rather than a failed assassination, and pardoned the terrified waterman who had fired it. Even so, it was thought prudent to tighten the gun laws within the precincts of the court.

The arrival of Alençon in person in August 1579 sparked a fresh outburst of anti-French feeling. As the duke disappeared for a fortnight into the queen's privy chamber, pamphlets and sermons combined in a collective howl of patriotic protest. An anonymous poem was nailed to the door of the Lord Mayor of London, proclaiming allegiance to Elizabeth so long as she defied the 'foreign yoke' and openly threatening the duke:

Therefore, good Francis, rule at home, resist not our desire;
For here is nothing else for thee, but only sword and fire.[32]

One of the boldest critics was a London lawyer and Protestant polemicist named John Stubbs. His *Discoverie of a Gaping Gulf whereinto England is Like to be Swallowed* was a scorching indictment of the Alençon match, 'the straightest line that can be drawn from Rome to the utter ruin of our church'. Marriage to a Catholic was a sin which would bring down the wrath of God, and draw queen and country into captivity under the French. The duke himself came in for a thunderous attack. Alençon was a serpent come 'to seduce our Eve, that she and we may lose this English paradise'. Since Elizabeth was being led 'blindfold as a poor lamb to the slaughter', it was the responsibility of others to wake her from her bewitchment. Stubbs concluded by calling on the English people to heed his warning: first the nobility and privy council, as 'tutors to the common weal'; then bishops and royal courtiers, who might have some influence with the queen; and finally the common folk, though their role was restricted to praying that this plague be lifted from 'Christian Israel'.

Elizabeth knew how to parry Protestant agitation in church and Parliament. But Stubbs went further than her sternest critic in the Commons would have dared. He had pinpointed a moment of political crisis, and his solution seemed dangerously close to republicanism. Worse, his opinions had been broadcast to the shires in a thousand printed copies. When she first heard about Stubbs's *Gaping Gulf*, the queen wanted him dead. Although she was persuaded to settle for a lesser charge than treason, the punishment meted out was horribly symbolic: Stubbs's writing hand was chopped off in three blows, watched by an ominously silent Westminster crowd. The victim managed the obligatory 'God save the queen' before he blacked out, but his scaffold speech had pointedly referred to the lack of mercy shown to him. It did the government no favours that Stubbs was prosecuted under a revived Marian statute devised to silence Protestant writing and preaching.[33]

It was whispered around the court that Walsingham had something to do with the *Gaping Gulf*. Stubbs alleged under interrogation that a privy councillor had prior knowledge of the pamphlet and did nothing to halt its publication. Walsingham has speculatively been identified as this unnamed patron, although it could just as well have been Leicester or Hatton or Mildmay. He may well have had some sympathy for Stubbs, but he would not have welcomed every aspect of his argument. Walsingham's obsessive care for the queen's safety made him cautious about Puritan petitioning in the Commons and beyond, and the portrait of Elizabeth as a lovelorn maiden leading her nation towards ruin was not one which he would have wanted hawked around in public. John Stubbs was enough of a lawyer and politician to have come up with his arguments for himself.[34]

There is no doubting Walsingham's closeness to a more eminent commentator on the Alençon match. Philip Sidney's 'Letter to Queen Elizabeth touching her marriage to Monsieur' was probably written in the weeks before Stubbs produced his *Gaping Gulf*. Sidney had watched the St Bartholomew's massacres from the uncertain safety of Walsingham's house in Saint Marceau, and the two men had become friends. By the time he was appointed royal cup-bearer in 1575, Sidney had soaked up much of what the literary and artistic Renaissance had to offer. In Paris, he met the Huguenot political thinker Philippe Duplessis-Mornay; in Venice he was painted by Veronese. At the English court, by contrast, his career signally failed to launch. For the son of a viceroy of Ireland, this lack of employment was achingly frustrating. Poetry became both a personal release and a means to influence the Elizabethan regime. This was the context in which *Arcadia* was begun; to entertain his sister, claimed Sidney, though it sought to do a good deal more than that. Before the allegory of *Arcadia*, however, came a more direct attempt to dissuade Elizabeth from marrying Alençon.

Sidney's travels had schooled him in the gallantry required of a Renaissance courtier, and he knew how to craft an appeal to

Elizabeth. His words came from 'the deep wellspring of loyal affection', and they were addressed to an absolute princess. His supplication was intended solely for the 'merciful eyes' of the queen. Sidney spoke rhetorically; the 'Letter to Queen Elizabeth' circulated in manuscript, as he intended that it should. But there was a world of difference between Sidney's mannered prose and the public marketing of Stubbs's *Gaping Gulf*. The 'Letter' called on age-old metaphors of the state: as a ship sailing through calm waters, or as a healthy human body. Alençon threatened this equilibrium because of his religion. According to Sidney, the Catholic faction in England was looking for a figurehead. No monarch had ever been held in higher esteem than Elizabeth, but the history of Tudor rebellions offered sobering lessons in how the people's allegiance could be squandered. Sidney's oratory was polished, but his assessment of the situation was no less damning than that offered by his uncle the Earl of Leicester: 'there can almost happen no worldly thing of more evident danger to your State Royal'.[35]

For five solid days in October 1579, the privy council met at Greenwich to find a way around the impasse. Burghley repeatedly spoke in favour of the marriage; whether out of altered conviction, or a sense of duty to the queen herself, is unknowable. Walsingham did not attend the debates, and indeed removed himself from court for the following three months. The gossip at Paris was that Elizabeth had dismissed him as a 'protector of heretics'. The queen was certainly angry with him, although his chronic medical condition seems to have flared up at the same time, so perhaps this was more than a tactical withdrawal. At any rate, Walsingham wasn't there to witness Elizabeth's tears of rage at the majority council decision against the marriage. When she rejected their advice and ordered a group of loyal advisers to draw up a treaty which Simier could carry back to France, her principal secretary was not included.

Elizabeth condemned her councillors as so many sieves, their courage draining away when forced to face their sovereign. Perhaps this was no more than coincidence, but the year of Alençon's visit also saw the first in a series of portraits of Elizabeth carrying a sieve in the style of the Vestal Virgin Tuccia: so chaste, the legend had it, that she could carry a sieve of water from the Tiber to her temple without a drop leaking away. One was commissioned by Sir Christopher Wray, the judge who had passed sentence on John Stubbs; another by Sir Christopher Hatton. A cameo brooch with the same sieve motif was presumably made to be worn by a supporter of the campaign against the marriage. During her final years, Elizabeth embraced the identity of the Virgin Queen as a way of sustaining her hold on power. But in the context of the Alençon match, an icon of maidenhood functioned as exhortation as much as praise. The queen regularly made use of art to communicate with her political nation; the sieve portraits prove that the traffic was two-way.[36]

The privy council was the monarchy's voice in Parliament. Without its wholehearted support, the queen had little hope of persuading a truculently Protestant House of Commons to accept a Catholic as their co-ruler. The bishops in the Lords, many of whom had chosen exile in Queen Mary's reign, were also likely to offer spirited resistance. The recent incursion of missionary priests onto English soil was another factor, stoking anti-Catholic feeling in both Parliament and the pulpit. By the time that Walsingham returned to court, the marriage of Elizabeth and Alençon had been provisionally agreed on paper. But the treaty was a phantom; a clause allowing the duke the free exercise of his religion in private effectively guaranteed that it could never be ratified. Nor is there reason to suppose that Elizabeth had wavered in her own convictions since she denied the mass to the Duke of Anjou.

The parody of love-making dragged on for another eighteen months. In the spring of 1581 Elizabeth welcomed a huge French delegation to the English court to settle the marriage once and for all. Statesmen and the officers of Alençon's household were presented with all the pageantry of the cult of Elizabeth at its zenith. A fantasy wedding ceremony was drawn up by the French, to be concelebrated by Catholic and Protestant bishops in a temporary theatre planned for Westminster. In a remarkably insensitive twist, the wedding service would be modelled on the one worked out for Margaret de Valois and Henry of Navarre.

The English commissioners, Walsingham included, solemnly agreed to all these demands. But a 'triumph' staged at Whitehall for the benefit of the visiting ambassadors told a different story. Surveyor of the queen's works Thomas Grave spent weeks constructing a banqueting house at one end of Henry VIII's tiltyard, assisted by a small army of artists and craftsmen. The result recalled the prefabricated palaces built by Henry VIII and Francis I at the Field of Cloth of Gold. Its canvas ceiling was painted with clouds and sunbeams, while oranges and pomegranates seemed to grow from the walls. The chronicler Raphael Holinshed counted 292 panes of glass in its windows. Elizabeth's presence transformed the structure into a Castle of Perfect Beauty, where tiers of spectators watched a mock battle unfold over the course of two days. Four knights and their retainers set scaling ladders against the fortress before bombarding it with poetry and roses. But the Children of Desire were forced to withdraw, defeated by the Virtue which would not allow them entry. The castle which they had assaulted belonged to 'the eye of the whole world'. For Philip Sidney, who took the role of one of the knights caparisoned in blue and gilt armour, the allegory must have been especially satisfying.

The French delegation sailed home soon afterwards, carrying

a treaty that was signed but impotent. When Walsingham followed them to France a month later, it was to angle for an alliance detached from the marriage. Elizabeth sent him with a kind of blessing: 'as she doth know her Moor cannot change his colour, no more shall it be found that she shall alter her old wont, which is always to hold both ears and eyes open for her good servants'. Walsingham had been readmitted to royal favour with a nickname, perhaps a pun on his habitually black clothes. It was an honour reserved for those closest to the queen.[37]

4 The English Mission

On 30 November 1577 a Cornish town paused from the hurly-burly of market day to watch the death of a traitor. Public executions were a familiar enough sight to the sheep-farmers and hawkers who clustered around the gibbet in Launceston. Felons were regularly hanged in the precincts of the derelict Norman castle. But the condemned man was not a murderer, nor had he levied war against the crown. Cuthbert Mayne was a Catholic priest, one of the first Englishmen to be ordained at a seminary at Douai in the Netherlands. He took a long time to die. The noose was severed while Mayne was still breathing, and he dashed out an eye as he fell against the scaffold. The hangman then set about him with a knife, ripping out his heart at last to offer to the crowd. His corpse was quartered and displayed across Cornwall and his native Devon. It was a calculatedly brutal warning to any local families tempted to shelter missionary Catholic clergy.

Walsingham's career so far had focused mainly on international affairs, the question of the queen's marriage and the threat to the Protestant faith in the Netherlands. The discovery of Cuthbert Mayne opened his eyes to the danger of the enemy within. Mayne had been captured at Golden Manor near Truro, home to the gentleman courtier Francis Tregian. The raid on Tregian's house was led by Sir Richard Grenville, Sheriff of Cornwall and a former captain in Queen Elizabeth's army in Ireland. Grenville had returned from Munster convinced that Catholicism had to be rooted out of English society. He thought like a soldier, and it was in the same terms that he regarded

Cuthbert Mayne. The priest's true allegiance was betrayed by the Agnus Dei which he wore around his neck, a wax disc depicting Christ as the Lamb of God which had been blessed by the pope. A search of Mayne's chamber turned up 'divers other relics used in popery', 'pernicious trumperies' contrary to the laws of England.

Mayne was placed in chains following his arrest and questioned in Launceston jail. Reflecting his higher status, Tregian was imprisoned in the Marshalsea in London before being summoned before Walsingham and the privy council. Mayne's final interrogation was recorded by a clerk and survives among the state papers in the National Archives. His neat, sloping signature affirms it to be a fair transcript of his replies. Mayne explained that he had arrived in England two years before, his true mission unsuspected by the government agents who were keeping watch on the ports. He was eager to return to his native West Country, and enlisted the help of the Catholic underground in London to secure him a stewardship in Tregian's household. His cover left Mayne free to roam his protector's scattered estates, celebrating mass and offering absolution to the Cornish people.[1]

Had he been a relic of the medieval world, carrying on his ministry as if the Reformation had never happened, Walsingham might have been less concerned. Catholic clergy ordained in Henry VIII's or Mary's reigns were a temporary problem, whittled away by the passage of time. But Mayne fell into a much more dangerous category, the fresh convert to Catholicism. Educated at Oxford University in the early 1560s, he served the established Church as a chaplain at St John's College before his escape to the seminary at Douai in 1573. Mayne had willingly traded a promising career in the Church of England for the hunted existence of a Catholic missionary priest. He had renounced his loyalty to the queen as supreme governor of the

Church. Walsingham knew that there were more young men like him, training in the Low Countries or already at large in England.

Mayne's position on the Church of England was uncompromising. No true Catholic should attend his parish church, while taking communion under the new Elizabethan rite was out of the question. This was the language of the continental Counter-Reformation, agreed in Italy in 1564 at a meeting of the Council of Trent. Still more alarming, Mayne hinted at a political dimension to the English Catholic mission. If a foreign prince invaded a realm to restore it to the pope (the Cornish clerk wrote 'Bishop of Rome'), then Catholics were bound to assist 'to the uttermost of their powers'. Mayne spoke in the abstract, but the implications of his words were chilling. Cornwall and Devon were the front line of defence against any French or Spanish naval armada, sent on a crusade to reclaim England for the Holy See. Mayne had found shelter with Sir John Arundell of Lanherne, a kinsman of Francis Tregian and virtually a magnate in the West Country. A generation earlier, in Edward VI's reign, an Arundell had led a huge rebellion in Cornwall and Devon against the Protestant Reformation. It was a disturbing reminder of Catholic strength in England's exposed western peninsula, nearly twenty years since Queen Elizabeth's accession.[2]

Cuthbert Mayne was the protomartyr of the English Catholic mission: the first of two hundred priests and laypeople to die for their faith prior to the accession of King James in 1603. When England was threatened with foreign invasion in Henry VIII's and Edward VI's reigns, the crown was able to respond by investing in coastal forts and gun foundries and the royal dockyards. In the 1570s, all of a sudden, the danger seemed to come from within. The coming of the English mission led Walsingham into a bleak landscape of plots and snares, informers and renegade priests, ciphers and torture. Intelligence-gathering and surveillance had traditionally focused on foreign courts; now the national gaze was turning in on itself.

The influx of priests in Cuthbert Mayne's image brought a harsh new clarity to English politics. Compromise was denounced and loyalties defined ever more rigidly on both sides of the religious divide. Facing the oblivion of their faith, some Catholics began to contemplate the sort of active resistance to which radical Protestants had been driven in Queen Mary's reign. As Francis Walsingham exposed successive conspiracies during the 1580s, Protestant prayers and sermons celebrated the last battle against the Antichrist of Rome. Simply to be a Catholic was to renounce the natural duty of a subject to his sovereign.

The story which is about to unfold, pitting Walsingham and his agents against those who sought to overthrow the Elizabethan regime, is deeply contested. The myth that Catholicism is somehow alien to Englishness has had a long and corrosive effect on the national memory of the British Isles. Focusing on Francis Walsingham inevitably carries the risk of seeing the past through the eyes of the victors. Since Victorian times, Catholic apologists have been fighting back to create their own Elizabethan historical tradition. The restoration of the Catholic hierarchy in 1850 created an urgent need to develop a respectable identity for the English Catholic community. A new history emerged to rival that of the Protestant establishment: a tale of Catholic heroes and martyrs, recalling the persecution of the earliest Christians under the Roman Empire. Research on the reign of Elizabeth was commissioned by the Vatican. In 1886 many of the clergy executed during the English Reformation were beatified, in company with some of the layfolk who succoured them. The campaign has continued into modern times. Several sixteenth-century martyrs were canonised as saints in 1970, including Cuthbert Mayne. Walsingham has no public memorial, whereas Mayne has given his name to a church and several schools. He is remembered on a pilgrimage at Launceston every 30 November.[3]

Its actors may be long dead, but the drama of the English Catholic mission remains relevant in a way that few events of the sixteenth century could claim to be. Opinions still polarise along confessional lines. The priests and Jesuits who challenged the Church of England are variously cast as traitors or martyrs. Walsingham appears both as the saviour of Queen Elizabeth and the agent of a tyrannical Tudor state. The reality of politics, however, is rarely this simple. Allegiance might be concealed, loyalties could shift, true conversion was always a possibility. We cannot assume that everyone caught up in the English mission acted out of high principles: intensity of faith, or certainty of political ideology. As we shall see, several of the spies – and some of the clergy – entered this hall of mirrors for their own gain, or the sheer thrill of playing a double game.

Our own verdict on Walsingham, his effectiveness as a statesman and his political morality, depends on one question above all others. Did English Catholics conspire to undermine the Elizabethan regime and kill the queen? Walsingham claimed to have thwarted numerous attempts on Elizabeth's life. The most famous of these were led by venerable gentry families, Throckmortons and Babingtons, who dreamed of freeing the Queen of Scots from her English imprisonment. Had Walsingham been less alert, had his security services been less able or attuned, then England might have slumped into the same wars of religion which were crippling France. His critics protest that Elizabeth's Catholic subjects were loyal to her person, even if not to her religion. The pope may have plotted to destroy her, but the seminary priests of Douai and Rheims were on a spiritual mission; other interpretations reek of Protestant propaganda. The most striking allegation against Walsingham, from the pen of a modern Jesuit, is that he fabricated the Babington plot in a Machiavellian scheme to obliterate Catholicism from the map of England.[4]

The massacre at Paris had been a moment of revelation for Walsingham. As in other Protestants of his generation, it annealed a world-view forged in the fires of Mary's reign. By the later 1570s, however, the fight for true religion was leaching from Europe into England itself. The Catholic mission from Douai and Rheims propelled Walsingham into an unfamiliar role, from ambassador and administrator to statesman and spymaster. Searching for a metaphor to capture Walsingham's achievement, the seventeenth-century biographer Sir Robert Naunton described him as the 'engine' of the Elizabethan state. 'Engine' meant two things to Naunton's audience: a machine used in warfare, and an instrument of torture.[5]

The radicalisation of English Catholicism gave Walsingham the chance to rise in power and status. Birth mattered as much as education and ability in the Elizabethan firmament, and Walsingham was a commoner surrounded by peers. He lived at the heart of the Elizabethan regime, but was hardly a courtier in the sense that contemporaries understood the word. Walsingham wore black in a court obsessed by beauty, and had little time for the gaudy magnificence of monarchy. His plangent Puritanism aggravated the queen. But she knew that he was loyal, and she continued to trust his judgement. The death of Sir Thomas Smith in August 1577 left Walsingham as her senior principal secretary, a promotion which he celebrated with a day's hunting.

In December he was knighted, allowing him to deal with the county gentry on an equal footing. The following year he was appointed chancellor of the Garter, England's noblest order of chivalry now recast in a Protestant format by Edward VI.[6]

In Elizabethan English, 'secretary' still meant 'keeper of secrets'. Walsingham's principal secretaryship brought a special responsibility for the queen's safety. In principle the government had collective responsibility for the Catholic question, but Walsingham's fellow councillors soon began to defer to him. Within days of Cuthbert Mayne's arrest, the Bishop of London was complaining that 'the papists marvellously increase both in numbers and in obstinate withdrawing of themselves, from the church and service of God'. Catholics were turning into recusants, refusing to have anything to do with their parish church – precisely what Mayne had been teaching his Cornish flock.[7]

What the Bishop of London had detected was a quiet revolution in the culture of Catholic England. The state church re-established by the 1559 Parliament was solidly reformed in character. The liturgy was translated from Latin into English, as it had been during Edward VI's reign. Mass became communion, and doctrine began to shadow the language of Calvinism. The clergy had to swear to their belief in predestination – that God had chosen those who will be saved 'before the foundations of the world were laid'. But the Elizabethan religious settlement left many feeling bewildered and deprived, especially in the remoter parts of the kingdom. Anyone over fifty would have remembered the rich devotional world of damask vestments and processional banners which had existed before Henry VIII's break from Rome. A younger generation had seen the fabric of Catholicism restored by Queen Mary, when empty niches were refilled with images and the great festivals of Corpus

Christi and Rogationtide were revived. Even relics had re-emerged. Looking back on his childhood in Queen Mary's reign, the Catholic author Nicholas Roscarrock could remember seeing the casket of St Piran paraded through the Cornish countryside.[8]

Traditionalists regretted the vigorous stripping of the altars which was carried out in Elizabeth's name after 1559, yet the great majority were able to compromise with the regime during its early years. Parish records and bishops' visitations prove that medieval or Marian church fabric often escaped the initial assault of the Elizabethan iconoclasts. Surviving altars and holy-water stoups provided a link with the liturgical past. Numerous churches retained the rood screens which divided the priest's domain of the chancel from the laity in the nave, while some had held onto their carved images of Christ and the saints. Clergy with distinctly un-Protestant opinions were able to weather the Elizabethan Church settlement. Until a new ministry could be trained in the universities, the Church of England had to rely on priests ordained before the Reformation or in Mary's reign. The vicar of Morebath, a sheep-farming community on Dartmoor, came to the village in 1520 when Henry VIII was still a devout Catholic. He was there fifty years later, still brewing beer to sell in aid of church funds.[9]

Another explanation for Catholic conformism can be found in the English parish. The celebration of holy communion reinforced the ties of community; a service according to the Book of Common Prayer was better than none at all. Recusancy risked excommunication, and this was a dreadful sanction in a society that feared isolation from church and neighbours. The excommunicated were barred from the essential rites of passage provided by the Church: marriage, baptism, even burial on consecrated ground. In December 1584 the family of a Leeds Catholic named Richard Lumbye attempted to bury him in the churchyard, only to be halted at the lychgate by the curate and churchwardens. Because Lumbye had chosen to withdraw from his neighbours in life, he had no right to lie with them in death. Time, and parish fellowship, were powerful allies of the Church of England.[10]

A third factor was the queen herself. Elizabeth's own faith was a curious hybrid, combining Lutheran ideas with a respect for traditional structure and liturgical dignity. Her unwillingness to concede Alençon the freedom of Catholic worship contrasted with the crucifix and candles which she stubbornly kept on the altar of the Chapel Royal. Her bedside cabinet contained a book of Latin prayers which Elizabeth had copied out as a gift to her father, and her patronage of William Byrd ensured the survival of English sacred music. Pope Pius IV offered to confirm her settlement of religion if she would only recognise his jurisdiction in England. The first generation of Catholic intellectuals who took refuge in Louvain in the 1560s did not find it difficult to reconcile their theological stance with a continuing sense of loyalty to the queen. Thomas Dorman affirmed that Elizabeth was 'the image of God in earth in all civil and politic government', while Thomas Stapleton protested that Catholics were her 'most loyal and obedient subjects' except in matters of conscience. Until the early 1580s, Catholic political thought was dominated by the doctrine of non-resistance.[11]

If the tide of government policy had turned against the Catholics, then the ebb-and-flow history of the earlier Reformation suggested that all was not lost. Time, and God's providence, might revive their fortunes. So they generally came to church, listened to the English collects and psalms, and prayed for the safety of the queen. A new term of art entered the English language: the 'Church papist', who took part in the rites of the established Church in spite of his or her traditional faith. The bravest of the Church papists advertised their contempt for

Protestant services by reading devotional works of their own, or muffling their ears during offensive sermons. Women, who were less likely to be literate, could pray their outlawed rosary beads. Most Catholics, however, were content not to draw attention to themselves. The requirement to take communion two or three times a year could be dodged by claiming to be out of charity with a neighbour. At home, a quiet regime of fasting according to the old Catholic cycle – on Fridays, Ember days, during Lent – perpetuated the memory of the pre-Reformation calendar.[12]

What disturbed this equilibrium, forcing Walsingham and the powers of the Elizabethan state to redefine English Catholics as traitors, and hound their priests as outlaws? A decade after Elizabeth's accession, a biting anxiety began to afflict the Catholic community. Unless it took more positive action, it might soon cease to be. Parishes which had initially hung onto their costly Catholic fabric were now disposing of their obsolete chalices and vestments. The failed uprising of the Catholic northern earls in 1569 convinced the churchwardens of Morebath that their silken tunicle, worn by a sub-deacon during the old Latin liturgy, had become a liability. With an eye for economy, they recycled it into a covering for the wooden communion table that had replaced the ancient altar. Like a myriad similar decisions by wardens in other parishes, it was tacit recognition that the Catholic mass would never be sung again.[13]

Numerous secret Catholic congregations survived the early years of Elizabeth's reign, served by priests who resigned their posts in protest at the 1559 settlement of religion. By the mid-1570s, however, the supply of breakaway clergy was dwindling as death claimed the pre-Reformation generation. Deprived of their Latin primers and annual saints' plays, the English people were beginning to forget their Catholic devotions and old processional routes. Meanwhile, parish life was becoming attuned to the reformed rhythms of the Church of England. The turning of the seasons was measured by the collects of the Book of Common Prayer rather than by saints' days and sacred drama. From the later 1560s, bell-ringing and bonfires for the queen's accession day offered a replacement for the medieval holidays of Candlemas and Corpus Christi. The privy council was sufficiently confident to release prominent Catholic prisoners from the Marshalsea in 1574, including John Feckenham, the last abbot of Westminster Abbey. There was a new spirit of English patriotism in the air. 'Our England', exclaimed Bishop Horne of Winchester, 'is sailing with full sails and a prosperous breeze'.[14]

Within and beyond the walls of the established Church, Catholic culture was in danger of bleeding away. The tourniquet was supplied by an exiled Lancashire gentleman and Oxford academic, William Allen. Walsingham and Allen were direct contemporaries: their characters were both formed by the political and religious upheavals of the mid-sixteenth century. But their response could hardly be more different, since Allen was destined to become a cardinal and the spiritual leader of the English Catholic community. In 1568 Allen set up a college in Douai in the Netherlands to educate Catholic émigrés from the English universities. At first he was content to play a waiting game. When God chose to strike down the heretical regime of Queen Elizabeth, Allen would be waiting to deploy a new church leadership in England. But when the rising of the northern earls and the 1571 Ridolfi plot both failed to restore a Catholic government to England, Allen began to see a different meaning in contemporary events. God must have another purpose for the English students who were by now flocking to Douai. Looking back to the persecution of the early Church, 'the old example of the Apostles in their days', Allen found the model of the missionary priest: a preacher in private houses rather than a parish church, free to move between congregations.

Allen's missionary priests absorbed the intensive piety of the Counter-Reformation. Personal discipline was paramount, so they followed the spiritual exercises pioneered by the Society of Jesus. When they studied scripture, it was in a new English translation rather than the Latin Vulgate. In this sense, they had learned lessons from their Protestant enemies. In 1574, six years after Allen founded his seminary, its first three clergy sailed for the English mission. In 1576 sixteen priests were despatched, and the college at Douai had 236 students. Many of them were fresh out of Oxford and Cambridge, eager graduates whom the Church of England could ill afford to lose.

The evisceration of Cuthbert Mayne in 1577 did nothing to staunch the flow of Catholic ordinands. When the English college was expelled from Douai the following year, it moved to Rheims and continued to flourish. In 1579 the English hospice in Rome was converted into a second seminary, and colleges in Spain would follow. By 1580, the year in which the English Jesuits Edmund Campion and Robert Persons joined the mission, Allen had sent a hundred Catholic priests into England. The total rose to 471 by the end of Elizabeth's reign; small beer compared to the astonishing fifty thousand priests in England before the Reformation, but a serious challenge to the monopoly of faith demanded by the Elizabethan Church establishment.[15]

The young Francis Walsingham had chosen exile in Basel and Padua rather than compromise with the Catholic regime of Queen Mary. His character was moulded by his studies at Cambridge, and the evangelical energy that pulsed through the colleges during Edward VI's reign. So too with the students and tutors who left for Douai a generation later. When Elizabeth inherited the throne, there was still a spiritual excitement about the quadrangles and common rooms of the English universities, but this time it was on the Catholic side. Two Oxford colleges, Trinity and St John's, had been founded under Queen Mary, and Caius was re-founded at Cambridge. Under the guidance of Cardinal Pole, the universities had become the forcing-houses of Catholic renewal. Pole's tenure was short, but his achievement is attested by the Oxford men who toiled to disrupt the Elizabethan Church. Marian Oxford educated nearly thirty of the seminary priests ordained after 1559, plus at least seven Jesuits. Catholic influence continued strong in Elizabethan Oxford. Cuthbert Mayne, Edmund Campion and Gregory Martin (who translated the New Testament studied by the Douai ordinands) all spent time at St John's early in Elizabeth's reign. Reputed for its Catholic humanism, New College haemorrhaged scholars in the 1560s. Thirty-eight fellows were deprived by Elizabeth, or chose to flee Oxford. They found sanctuary in the Netherlands, firstly at the University of Louvain and later at Douai.[16]

To Walsingham, their theology was repugnant and their politics subversive. Yet the principal secretary and the seminary priest had more in common than either would have admitted. Both were formed by the common life of university and exile; both perceived past and current events through the lens of religious ideology. To that extent, they inhabited the same mental world.

If English Catholicism had been looking frail by the early 1570s, the mission from Douai gave it a shot in the arm. Its clergy travelled in disguise, changing their names, clothes and horses to throw spies off the scent. As they dispersed throughout the kingdom, preaching and administering the sacraments, Catholic recusancy began to gain ground. The seminary priests who came to England were not missionaries in the stamp of the Jesuits who travelled to seventeenth-century Japan, or the Baptists who brought the Bible to Victorian Africa. England was not virgin terrain; it had known, and rejected, the true apostolic faith. William Allen distinguished between the 'Catholics' who could be brought back within the fold, and the 'heretics' who were beyond redemption. The Jesuits who came to England from 1580 had similar instructions. Shunning the company of Protestants, they were to preach to the converted and discourage any waverers from attending their parish church. Above all, they were to concentrate their efforts on the gentry.

Jesuitical distinctions between Catholics and heretics meant little to the Elizabethan regime, which saw the invasion from Douai as a general assault on the establishment of Church and state. As the mission began to stabilise and reinvigorate the English Catholic community, it brought a more intense surveillance and persecution in its wake. Walsingham responded rapidly when reports of Cuthbert Mayne's capture and the growth of recusancy reached the privy council in June 1577. A conference of councillors and bishops was summoned to consider how those who were 'backwards' and 'corrupt' in their religion could be brought within the fold of the Church of England. Up-to-date intelligence was a priority. Bishops were ordered to make a survey of those refusing to attend their parish church – and, ominously, the value of their lands and goods. Abbot John Feckenham and other Catholic figureheads were re-arrested. Education of the young was identified as a paramount concern. Schools were to be purged of suspect masters: men like Nicholas Garlick in Derbyshire, who shipped three of his boys to the seminary at Douai before entering the priesthood himself.[17]

The census of recusant England began in October 1577. Lists of people who refused to attend church were hastily compiled for each diocese: a total of 1,562 names. Within an English population of perhaps three and a half million in the 1570s, this figure looks tiny. Modern evangelical churches regularly poll a congregation of this size every Sunday. Within the statistics, however, was a deeply worrying trend: fully a third of the recusants identified in 1577 were gentlemen. The decline of the feudal magnates under Henry VII, and the dissolution of the monasteries under Henry VIII, had left the gentry manor house as the dominant institution of the English countryside. A gentleman did not exist in isolation: he was lord of his own household, governing the behaviour of his clients and tenants. As Cuthbert Mayne's case had demonstrated, a Catholic squire could do a lot to ensure that the old religion survived in his 'country'. The authorities also feared the social disruption implicit in recusancy. A gentleman ought to be seen in his parish church, a visible symbol of hierarchy and good order. By staying away, he neglected his duty to the Tudor commonwealth. Recusancy, in short, was an encouragement to sedition.[18]

The July 1577 conference mapped out a strategy to bring Catholics back into conformity with the Church of England. They were initially to be encouraged to rejoin the fellowship of their parish church. If negotiation failed, then an ascending scale of action was proposed: fines, an oath of allegiance, and ultimately imprisonment. Since there were many more Catholics than prison places to hold them, Walsingham and Burghley toyed with the idea of using castles to segregate 'the better sort of recusants'. Deprive Catholic areas of the natural leaders of society, and the faith of the 'baser sort' would wither. But the plan could not be implemented, not least because the crown entirely depended on the gentry for effective local government. The punishment of crime, ensuring that the poor had access to cheap bread, the maintenance of coastal gun batteries: all would suffer if the Catholic gentry were stripped out of provincial life.

Given the hierarchical nature of Tudor society, it is hardly surprising that the missionaries from Douai also focused on what they called the 'better sort' of men. William Allen had a vision of his clergy as latter-day Apostles, carrying the gospel from house to house; in practice this meant seeking shelter under the roofs of the aristocracy. A grand Catholic household, with its routines of confession and mass, allowed the seminarians to sustain the spiritual life that had formed them at Oxford and Douai. Where prominent local families had already fallen into heresy, they shook the dust from their feet and moved on. When Protestant heresy crumbled in England, it was vital that Catholics should be ready to answer the call as magistrates, lords lieutenant and members of Parliament. In any case, and as Allen observed, many of the English missionaries were high-born. Their education, their manners, even the language that they spoke, made it easier for them to move among the gentry without detection.

Country-house Catholicism focused disproportionately on the south of England. Walsingham ordered the ports of Dover and Rye to be watched for seminary priests, but the descriptions issued to the local authorities were often vague and inaccurate. A high proportion of missionaries who slipped through the net chose to become chaplains to the gentry of the southern counties. In 1580, six years into the English mission, half of its forces were mustered in London, the Thames Valley and Essex. Docking at Dover that same year, the Jesuit Robert Persons was shocked to find no priests serving in Wales or the far north of England. These were communities with residual Catholic sympathies, where vigorous preaching and evangelisation might have made a difference. Persons exaggerated to make a point, or perhaps he didn't have the full picture; an agent informed

Walsingham in 1585 that priests were making use of boats sailing from France to Newcastle to collect coal. But in all too many locations, the seed planted by the secret Catholic congregations of the 1560s was becoming choked with thorns.[19]

The nature of the mission made a permanent impression on the English social landscape. For the next three centuries, Catholic England would remain aristocratic and inward-looking, sustaining itself in country houses rather than parish churches. Radical change only came with Victoria's reign and the mass immigration of the Irish working class. Yet the Catholicism that Evelyn Waugh mourned and celebrated in his novels was still that of the recusant gentleman. On converting to Roman Catholicism, Waugh chose to write a biography of the Elizabethan Jesuit Edmund Campion as his work of piety. In *Officers and Gentlemen* the elderly and gentle Mr Crouchback, called up to teach in a wartime school, could reliably be distracted into lengthy reminiscences about the penal times under the Tudors, when the Blessed Gervase Crouchback was martyred for the Catholic faith.

How did Catholics experience their religion in Walsingham's England? While the Church settlement was still becoming established, traditionalists had been able to dress up the new religion in the clothes of the old. But the sinews of the Tudor state were strong, the pressure of crown and bishops inexorable. One by one the altars were broken up, the devotional images profaned and holy wells filled with rubbish. In 1567 the Reformation caught up with Aysgarth, a village in Wensleydale which offered a home to the rood screen from Jervaulx Abbey following the dissolution of the monasteries. Parishioners who had hidden their 'idols' and 'old papistical books' were forced to burn them and stand barefoot in white sheets in a public shaming ritual.[20]

Deprived of its traditional places, the practice of Catholicism was forced beyond consecrated ground. Missionary priests celebrated mass in safe-houses, barns and farmyards. In the West Country, sheets were spread on hedgerows at crossroads to indicate when and where to congregate. Country houses of this period often had their own chapels attached, but government surveillance made them too visible for Catholics to use. Attics and upper chambers were more secluded. To an older generation who remembered the sumptuous ritual of the past, the recusant liturgy must have seemed a pale imitation. Vestments and sacred vessels were rudimentary by comparison with the silk chasubles and silver-gilt chalices of Henry VIII's reign. Sacred music, such a striking feature of the pre-Reformation English Church, was limited to what the congregation could sing for themselves. In the 1590s William Byrd composed mass settings in three, four and five parts to meet their needs. His patrons, the Pastons of Norfolk, felt secure enough to sing in open procession around their gardens, though few other families could be so bold. But Catholics took heart from the history of the early Church, when Christians had gathered in private houses to worship.[21]

The English mission was a grim war of attrition. Of the three hundred-odd seminary priests who had come to England by 1586, thirty-three had been executed, fifty were in prison and another sixty had been arrested or banished. This was an unsustainable wastage rate. Travel without obvious cause was inherently suspect in Tudor England, and communities kept a close watch for vagrants and gypsies. Catholic priests needed a good disguise and a strong alibi to avoid arrest by village constables and magistrates. A chaplaincy offered an alternative, but Catholic households were themselves increasingly liable to being raided by the authorities. Walsingham's pursuivants or 'priest-hunters' could search properties for hours or even days, ransacking possessions and intimidating servants, women and children to reveal any hidden secrets.

Catholic houses began to acquire secret hiding-places where a missionary could shelter with his chalices and vestments in the event of a raid. The first priest-hole that we know about was built in York in 1574, the year that the English Catholic mission began. Early examples were often crude. Sheriffs soon learned to search the dead space in eaves and attics, or below garderobes and latrines, to flush priests out of hiding. They brought measuring-rods to discover cavities behind walls and fireplaces. The ringing of a bell could reveal a hollow echo.

By the later 1580s hides were becoming far more sophisticated thanks to Nicholas Owen, a carpenter from Oxford known to his friends as 'Little John'. Two of his brothers were ordained as Catholic priests, while a third was apprenticed to the university printer and later set up a secret press in London's Clink prison. Nicholas had a craftsman's ability to visualise his art in three dimensions. Recruited by the superior of the Jesuit mission Henry Garnet, he became a master of architectural concealment. Owen understood perspective: he could visualise the ways in which a search party would scan the lines of a building. Choosing places where gables and towers met and making use of changes of level, he was able to construct priest-holes that were virtually invisible from the outside. In the words of the Jesuit John Gerard, he designed hiding-places 'in all shires and in the chiefest Catholic houses of England'. Some allowed their inhabitant to be fed via a trapdoor, or a hollow quill through which broth could be dripped. An example of Owen's craftsmanship survives at Oxburgh Hall in Norfolk, accessed via a pivoting floorboard and complete with a feeding-trap. In 1606 Owen himself survived a four-day search in a hide at Hindlip in Worcestershire before being starved out. Ten further 'secret corners and conveyances' were found in the same house. As Gerard pointed out, Owen could have done more to undermine the Catholic cause than anyone else in England, but he died under torture in the Tower without revealing anything. He was canonised as a martyr in 1970.[22]

Many Catholics, however, had little or no chance of attending mass. The concentration of priests in southern England left much of the realm bereft of spiritual comfort. Nor can we assume that the Catholicism of the great house was always welcoming to the countryside that surrounded it. The risk of betrayal meant that the sacraments were often restricted to the immediate household. Where formal provision was sporadic or non-existent, Catholicism retreated to the hearthside: the reading of devotional manuals in a family setting, or prayers recited over a baby's cradle. When the Elizabethan injunctions banned the hallowing of wax tapers for the feast of Candlemas, Catholics in north Wales transferred the ceremony into their own homes and placed candles in their windows each 2 February. Women were particularly active in sustaining this Catholicism of the hearth. The state was often satisfied if a husband attended the parish church, leaving wives to tend the embers of the old faith within their own domestic domain.[23]

Church papism, country-house Catholicism, a religion of women and the hearth: three ways of experiencing traditional religion in Walsingham's England, and each of them personal and secretive. In the prisons and on the gallows, however, Catholicism found a more public stage. Well over half the missionary priests who came to England in Elizabeth's reign spent a period behind bars before being deported or executed. Life for Catholic clergy in an Elizabethan prison could follow a bizarre sequence of brutality and relative freedom of movement. Physical and psychological torture was commonplace, and plague and jail-fever were a constant terror.

Yet for those with money or connections, visits from the outside were easy to arrange. Servants and sympathisers were allowed in and out, and supervision was so lax that the Catholic mass became a common feature of Elizabethan prisons. A report on London's Newgate in 1583 informed Walsingham that the mass was being openly celebrated in the common jail, and privately in the prison-keeper's house. Three years later, one of his agents found two priests in Newgate attended by several Catholic gentlewomen: 'Sir, if you mean to stop the stream, choke the spring: for believe me, the prisons of England are very nurseries of papists'. John Gerard's autobiography describes how Catholic priests in the Marshalsea were able to smuggle in books and liturgical equipment. One search by the prison authorities yielded a cartful of Catholic paraphernalia. Subsequently imprisoned in the Clink on London's Bankside, Gerard found himself able to carry out 'all the tasks of a Jesuit priest' thanks to fellow Catholic prisoners who fabricated him a key for his door. The situation was no better in the provinces. Thomas Bell, a daring seminary priest who later made a spectacular conversion to become a Protestant polemicist, broke into York Castle in 1582 and sang high mass complete with a sub-deacon and music. In October 1586 Sir John Horsey and George Trenchard complained to Walsingham about the dismal state of security in Dorchester jail. The result of having a prison system run for profit by 'persons of no credit' was that 'all justice is subverted, and papists live at ease, and have their conventicles in despite of us, do what we can'.[24]

Incarceration was not the end of the line for a Catholic priest: paradoxically, it offered real opportunities to evangelise. Confessions were heard, the sacrament of the altar distributed, even marriages solemnised without fear of discovery or the incrimination of a host family. Missionary work could be undertaken among the felons imprisoned in close proximity with the clergy, often with startling success. The possibilities for priestly ministry, and the affirmation of Catholic identity offered by imprisonment, help to explain why so few priests sought to escape. A handful of clerics actually sought a martyr's death and glorified in their capture, although this was viewed with disapproval in Douai and Rome. More commonly, the room for manoeuvre enjoyed by imprisoned Catholic priests made life on the outside seem less spiritually fruitful. Just as the English mission was modelled on the journeys of the Apostles, so jailed priests could find solace in the scriptural imprisonments of St Peter, St Paul and John the Baptist.

Openly proclaimed in the prisons, the English Catholic mission found its apotheosis on the gallows. By 1592 ninety-six Catholic priests and thirty-six laypeople had been executed in full view of the Elizabethan crowd. Many of these died at Tyburn, near London's Marble Arch, where they are now venerated as martyrs by a house of Benedictine nuns. Others suffered a provincial death, such as the fourteen priests who were moved away from London to be executed in the Armada year of 1588. Two years earlier Margaret Clitherow, a butcher's wife who ran a safe-house for fugitive priests in the Shambles in York, had been pressed to death on a toll-bridge over the Ouse river for refusing to testify. The site was marked with a commemorative plaque in 2008.

Public executions in this period usually had a carnival atmosphere, especially if a celebrity criminal was dying. But the reactions of the crowds witnessing the death of priests were complex, even in Protestant London. Executions were imagined in the language of the playhouses that had sprung up on the south bank. The participants in this grisly theatre – audience, executioner, the victims themselves – had roles that were scripted by contemporary expectations. The authorities wanted punishments to be exemplary, offering visible proof that Catholicism and treason were two sides of the same coin. Priests denied this equation by praying for the queen, and strove to live up to a burgeoning Catholic martyrology by dying in a state of spiritual calm. Mindful of Christ's actions on the cross, they offered absolution to the criminals who were executed alongside them.

The quest for a good death could create scenes every bit as macabre as those played on the Elizabethan stage. When Ralph Sherwin was hanged, drawn and quartered at Tyburn in December 1581 he prayed for the queen before kissing the hands of his executioner, still dripping with the blood of Edmund Campion. John Nelson managed to pray for Elizabeth during his own dismemberment. The crowd were impressed by equipoise of this sort, as the watching authorities noted with alarm. Walsingham himself was dubious about a policy of execution, not out of sympathy (he was content with a handful of deaths 'for example's sake') but because he recognised the raw political truth that persecution creates martyrs. As he wrote in 1586, the 'constancy or rather obstinacy' of executed priests and Jesuits 'moveth men to compassion and draweth some to affect their religion, upon conceit that such an extraordinary contempt of death cannot but proceed from above'. Such stoicism on the scaffold made people wonder if God wasn't on the Catholic side after all.

For some Catholic priests, the mission continued even after their deaths. Bodies which had been butchered by the state could be recovered, either for burial or for relics. So it was that Cuthbert Mayne's skull, removed by the Arundells from a pike at Wadebridge in Cornwall, eventually found its way to the convent that now inhabits their ancient family house at Lanherne. A year after the priest Robert Sutton was executed at Stafford, local Catholics were able to remove an arm from the corpse to venerate as a relic. The forefinger and thumb which pronounced the blessing when celebrating mass had not corrupted, thus proving Sutton's sanctity. Crowds fought to dip their handkerchiefs in the blood of despatched priests, just as they had done with the Protestant rebel Thomas Wyatt when he was hanged for treason against Queen Mary. They would do the same at Charles I's execution in 1649.[25]

The arguments witnessed on the Elizabethan scaffold – the authorities claiming that they executed Catholics on grounds of treason, the victims retorting that they suffered only for their religion – were also played out in a vigorous propaganda war. In 1583 Lord Burghley published a tract defending the policy of the Elizabethan regime towards the Catholic problem. *The Execution of Justice in England* was urgent and direct. Queen Elizabeth did not make searches into the consciences of those who differed from the Church of England in their religion. But since the pope was attempting 'to deprive her majesty of her kingdoms, to withdraw from her the obedience of her subjects, to procure rebellions in her realms', it was only reasonable to invoke the treason laws to head off the threat. Burghley seized on the cloak-and-dagger tactics of the missionary priests, their disguises and false names, as proof that they were 'secret espials and explorers in the realm for the pope', intent on fanning the 'flames of rebellion' in England.[26]

The *Execution of Justice* was translated into French, Dutch and Latin to maximise its propaganda value on the continent. It was known to William Allen in Douai, who soon replied to Burghley's 'libel' with a book of his own. *A True, Sincere and Modest Defence of English Catholics* flatly denied that Allen's seminary priests were tainted with treason. English Catholics were being persecuted 'for mere matter of religion', under statutes that had been devised specifically for this purpose. The *Defence* demolished

Cecil's argument that the Elizabethan state was simply enforcing ancient treason laws, pointing out that Cuthbert Mayne was martyred under new legislation for owning an Agnus Dei made of wax. But Allen, too, was selective in his presentation of the facts. If he schooled his priests to preach the Catholic gospel and face martyrdom with spiritual joy, Allen himself had only one end in mind: the renaissance of the English Catholic Church on the model of Queen Mary's reign. This was hardly possible without Elizabeth's deposition. Much of Allen's career was spent in lobbying the papacy, the King of France and above all Philip II of Spain to provide the military resources for a full-scale invasion of England. The bishopric of Durham awaited him if any of these schemes had proved successful.[27]

Historians tend to be shy of moralising about the past. The rightness of competing routes to salvation is best debated by the theologian and the philosopher. But if we are to make any sense of the English mission, it demands something more than a simple recitation of statutes and statistics. There are two compelling reasons for coming to a judgement about the actions of Francis Walsingham and his agents, Cardinal Allen and his priests. The first is that hundreds of Elizabethans died during this conflict, in prison or in prolonged torment on the scaffold. Many more lost their property, positions and status. The second lies in the way that these events have been interpreted. Stories and myths were born in these years, both Protestant and Catholic, that went on to make a deep impression on British culture. Identities and prejudices have been formed by the memory of the English mission; it is up to us to determine whether they have any foundation.

The keystone of Burghley's argument in the *Execution of Justice* was the papal bull issued against Queen Elizabeth by Pius V in April 1570. Citing her 'impieties and crimes multiplied one upon another', *Regnans in Excelsis* not only absolved English subjects of their allegiance to Elizabeth, but ordered them to disobey her laws on pain of excommunication. This seemed plain enough: no true Catholic could accept Elizabeth as queen. Parliament responded the following year, declaring it high treason to possess the papal bull or to call Elizabeth a heretic. But the impact of *Regnans* is questionable, not least because it was never generally broadcast in England. Most English Catholics never saw a copy, although one was successfully nailed to the Bishop of London's palace by John Felton, who was promptly executed for treason. The great majority of Catholic subjects would have been deeply uneasy about its splenetic attack on 'the pretended queen of England and the servant of crime'. Far from advancing the English mission, *Regnans* became a hindrance to the missionary priests who hoped to reconcile patriotic Catholics.[28]

The life of Sir John Arundell, the Cornish gentleman who protected Cuthbert Mayne, reminds us that English Catholic identity was more flexible, and more compromised, than the propaganda of the time would have us believe. The Arundells had served the Tudors as soldiers and sheriffs for three generations, and Sir John was no exception. He was knighted and appointed justice of the peace by Elizabeth, and surveyed Cornwall's coastal defences for the crown in 1574. Yet he consistently refused to subscribe to the royal supremacy over the Church, and he supported the seminary priest John Cornelius as well as Cuthbert Mayne. Following Mayne's execution, Arundell spent much of the rest of his life imprisoned or under house arrest. Fines for refusing to attend church, raised from a shilling per offence to £20 a month by the 1581 Parliament, meant that estates had to be mortgaged and sold. Under this punishing regime, what had been one of the greatest families of western England began to fade away. Why then did Sir John, to the end of his life, pledge allegiance to his sovereign over the pope in Rome?[29]

The truth is that the majority of English Catholics were keen to carve out a distinct identity for themselves, combining loyalty to the old faith and fealty to their queen. Had there been no mission from Douai and Rheims, official attitudes towards Catholicism in England would not have hardened in the way that they did. But the arrival of hundreds of seminary priests, undeterred by banishment, imprisonment and execution, was seen as undermining the stability of the state. In Burghley's words, Catholic priests had been trained up as 'seedmen in their tillage of sedition', sent to England to uphold the pope's 'anti-Christian and treasonous warrant' of deposition. Burghley was a skilled propagandist, yet the fears expressed in the *Execution of Justice* – that England faced 'imminent danger of horrible uproars' and a 'bloody destruction of great multitudes of Christians' – were real enough. With wars of religion raging across the Channel, as Walsingham had seen for himself, the breakdown of order in England seemed all too possible.[30]

There was another threat to the equilibrium of the many Catholics balanced between Church and state, and again it came from their own countrymen in exile. By the early 1580s, Paris had become a refuge for hundreds of English laypeople, mainly drawn from the gentry, who refused to compromise with the Elizabethan Church settlement. Paris was one of the great centres of the European book trade, and its English exiles actively collaborated with local printers to mobilise opposition to the Elizabethan regime. In 1583 Walsingham received a series of disturbing reports of events in the French capital. In July he heard from the outgoing ambassador in Paris, Sir Henry Cobham, that printing-houses in the city were supplying the market for illicit Catholic devotional material in England. In November the new ambassador, Sir Edward Stafford, sent word that obscene pictures of Elizabeth hitching up her skirts for the Duke of Alençon had been posted in the streets of Paris, with

English exile collusion strongly suspected. Meanwhile the English polemicist Richard Verstegan had produced a French-language broadsheet of engravings depicting the torments of Catholics in England. Such brazen propaganda had disturbing implications for royal authority in France as well as England, and Stafford successfully lobbied for his arrest. Four years later, however, Verstegan's polemic took physical form when a tableau of the tortures endured by the English Catholic martyrs was set up in the churchyard of Saint-Séverin, where it pulled in large crowds and sparked off a riot. Mary, Queen of Scots, recently brought to execution by Walsingham, was included in the display.[31]

It was in this context that Walsingham and Burghley tightened the screws of state. English exile propaganda was encouraging Catholics at home into a self-imposed apartheid from their Protestant neighbours, following St Paul's admonition to the Corinthians to shun the company of 'unbelievers'. Although most Catholic writers combined recusancy with political non-resistance during the first half of Elizabeth's reign, more radical voices could also be heard. Nicholas Sander's *De Visibili Monarchia*, published in 1571, reprinted the papal bull *Regnans in Excelsis* and justified deposing Queen Elizabeth as a heretic. To Sander, the rising of the northern earls in 1569 had been a miracle; those who were executed in its wake, martyrs for the faith. His explanation of the uprising – that it failed only because English Catholics were not yet aware that Elizabeth had been deposed – was taken by Walsingham and Burghley as clear evidence of the treachery inherent in Catholicism. Sander spent years petitioning Philip II and the papacy to fund the overthrow of the Elizabethan regime, writing to Cardinal Allen that 'the state of Christendom dependeth upon the stout assailing of England'. He died in Ireland in 1581, still campaigning against the 'she-tyrant'.[32]

In the early 1570s, Sander's politics were on the extreme. Ten years later, a radicalisation had set in among the English Catholic exiles. By upholding the pope's power to depose Queen Elizabeth, William Allen's *Defence* represented a turning-point in Catholic political thought. This ratcheting-up of the rhetoric was a response to the growing persecution in England, but it also demonstrates the power of ideologies to cross national boundaries. Faced with a Protestant heir to the throne since the death of the Duke of Alençon, French Catholics were developing a theory of legitimate resistance to the higher powers. Their deliberations struck a chord with the English exiles. Crucially, ideas similar to those of Sander and Allen crop up in the interrogations of the seminary priests sent to England. Cuthbert Mayne had stated that Catholics should be ready to rise in rebellion against the state if the pope sanctioned it. The Lancashire priest James Bell concurred, telling the judge at his trial that he would support the pope against the queen in the event of a foreign invasion to restore Catholicism. He also requested that his lips and fingers be cut off to punish him for his earlier adherence to the Church of England.[33]

The life of one man, Nicholas Roscarrock, can be taken to illustrate the personal impact of this complex fusion of faith and politics. We first met Roscarrock as a boy, watching the relics of St Piran in procession in his native Cornwall. In the early 1570s he spent some time at the Inner Temple, collecting medieval manuscripts and making friends with the historians William Camden and Richard Carew. Both Carew and Camden were Protestants, but this was no obstacle to their intellectual kinship with the Catholic Roscarrock. By the later 1570s, however, Roscarrock's identity and behaviour were becoming defined by his faith. Refusing to attend his parish church, he was indicted as a recusant at Launceston assizes and his lands were assessed for fines.

Persecution had the effect of radicalising Nicholas Roscarrock's religion. By 1580 he had joined an association of Catholic gentlemen in London, bound by an oath to support the priests of the English mission. Then he went on pilgrimage to Douai and Rome. Such activity brought him to the notice of Francis Walsingham, who ordered two agents to 'discover' him. Roscarrock was hosting a sermon by the missionary priest Ralph Sherwin when his house was raided. The two men were taken first to the Marshalsea, then the Tower. Accused of being a 'dangerous papist' and a 'practiser with foreign states', Roscarrock was forced to listen to Sherwin being racked before he too was tortured for information.

Sherwin was executed in 1581. His death was commemorated in a sequence of frescoes in the English College in Rome which depicted Edmund Campion and other recent martyrs alongside St Alban and St Thomas Becket, setting the priests of the English mission within a continuum stretching back to the earliest days of the Catholic church in Britain. Nicholas Roscarrock lived, but languished in prison for more than five years. The friendship he struck up with Lord William Howard in the Tower is commemorated in the 'Langdale rosary', now preserved in the Victoria and Albert Museum. Roscarrock subsequently found a degree of healing in the biographical register of British and Irish saints which he compiled in the 1610s and 20s.[34]

In the early years of Elizabeth's reign, a sort of doublethink prevailed among English Catholics. Obedience to the monarchy was justified, no matter what *Regnans in Excelsis* may have said, so long as spiritual allegiance was owed to Rome. By the early 1580s, this dualism was becoming increasingly difficult to sustain as both the English crown and the Roman Church demanded a monopoly over personal loyalty. Later Elizabethan Catholics were caught in a vice formed by their faith on one side and their nationality on the other. Most laypeople struggled with this twin identity until the end of the reign, attending mass when they could and quietly ignoring the shrill propaganda that was assailing them from the continent. Some, like Nicholas Roscarrock, went further by sheltering priests or suffering imprisonment and torture for their faith. And a handful crossed the line into open treason.

5 Security Services

There is something indistinct about Francis Throckmorton, the young Catholic gentleman executed in 1584 for plotting to put Mary, Queen of Scots on the English throne. There are no independent witnesses to his character; few clues to his motives for rejecting the quiet loyalism of the Catholic mainstream. Throckmorton's story has to be reconstructed from the records of his trial and the official propaganda campaign that followed it. We strain to hear his own voice above the babble. Historians write about the 'Throckmorton plot', and yet Francis himself had only a supporting role: the real directors of the drama were off-stage, in Paris and Madrid.

Throckmorton was an unlikely revolutionary. His forebears had clambered into royal service by cultivating the law and hunting out good marriages, not unlike Walsingham's own family. His father John rose to be vice-president of the council governing the Welsh marches, earning him a knighthood from Queen Elizabeth in 1565. Sir John must have conformed to the established Church to have held such a sensitive position, but he showed his true colours when he schooled his sons Francis, Thomas and George as Catholics. Francis Throckmorton's faith led him to Salisbury Court, the London house of the French ambassador Michel de Castelnau, where he dined and dreamed and went to mass. By Christmas 1581 Throckmorton had been recruited by an embassy official, Claude de Courcelles, to handle the secret correspondence between Mary Stuart and her English supporters. He was also spotted in the company of Don Bernardino de Mendoza, the ultra-Catholic ambassador of the King of Spain.

Salisbury Court was convenient for the River Thames, and Mary's letters were probably smuggled from Throckmorton's house at Paul's Wharf by boat. Under cover of the French diplomatic bag, the Queen of Scots could finally reach her supporters in Paris. In May 1582 her envoy James Beaton, Archbishop of Glasgow, met the Duke of Guise and the Scottish Jesuit William Crichton to discuss reclaiming Britain for Catholicism by force. Robert Persons, who had joined Edmund Campion on the first Jesuit mission to England, took responsibility for winning over Philip II of Spain. The plan was initially to send an army to Scotland, capitalising on the friendship between King James and his French-born cousin the Earl of Lennox, but the capture of the fifteen-year-old king in the August 1582 raid of Ruthven left Scottish government in the hands of the Protestant lords. When Cardinal Allen gained a seat at the table in June 1583, the target of the invasion shifted to England. Charles Paget, a leading figure among the Paris exiles and a member of Guise's household, was despatched to London to negotiate with Mendoza and reconnoitre the south coast.

The story is taken up in a propaganda pamphlet published shortly after Throckmorton's execution. *A Discoverie of the Treasons Practised by Francis Throckmorton* was written by someone close to Walsingham, possibly the diplomat Thomas Wilkes, to create the official record of the plot. When royal officials broke into Paul's Wharf early in November 1583, they surprised Throckmorton in the act of writing a letter to the Queen of Scots. A search produced further incriminating papers copied out in his own hand: a list of safe harbours 'for landing of foreign forces', with the names of Catholic aristocrats who could be relied on to support an invasion. Pedigrees detailing Mary's claim to the English crown left no doubt about his guilt. Taken to the Tower and 'somewhat pinched' on the rack, Throckmorton yielded further details of the conspiracy. An uprising of the

English Catholic nobility was to coincide with a naval assault led personally by the Duke of Guise and bankrolled by Philip II. Walsingham had feared a Catholic enterprise for years, but the Throckmorton plot was on a scale grander than even he had predicted.[1]

Contemporaries were mystified by Francis Throckmorton's descent into treason. The *Discoverie of Treasons* drew attention to his 'pleasant humour' in the company of friends, and the antiquary William Camden presented him as 'a gentleman well educated and of good wit'. How had this wealthy and popular young man become radicalised? His studies at Hart Hall in Oxford and the Inner Temple in London placed Throckmorton in the company of other idealistic young Catholics. By the later 1570s his family was dabbling in recusancy, attending the household masses celebrated by a missionary priest. But the turning-point seems to have been a meeting with the English exile and veteran plotter Sir Francis Englefield in the Low Countries, where Throckmorton was drawn into discussions about 'altering of the state of the realm'. He returned to England speaking a much more heated political language. When his father was ejected from the chief justiceship of Chester shortly afterwards, ostensibly for corruption but probably on religious grounds, Francis added family honour to his litany of grievances against the establishment.

Royal propaganda slotted the events of 1583–4 into a pattern of Catholic plots against crown and state. The *Discoverie of Treasons* contrasted Throckmorton's 'pretention' that he aimed at freedom of conscience for English Catholics with his 'intention' to depose Queen Elizabeth. It lingered over his confessions and retractions, defending the fairness of the trial and justifying torture as a necessary weapon against terror. Translations into Latin and Dutch targeted European support for any future uprising, while a printed ballad sang the same story to the English public. The queen was compared to the three children of Israel who refused to bow down before idols, miraculously preserved from harm in Nebuchadnezzar's fiery furnace. Throckmorton was pictured breaking down at his betrayal of the Queen of Scots, 'who was the dearest thing to me in the world . . . sith I have failed of my faith towards her, I care not if I were hanged'.[2]

Uncovering the Throckmorton plot was a coup for the government, apparent proof of the deadly efficiency of Francis Walsingham's network of agents and informers. According to the *Discoverie of Treasons*, 'secret intelligence' that Throckmorton had been acting as Mary's courier was not initially acted upon 'to the end there might some proof more apparent be had to charge him therewith'. Thanks to the detective work of John Bossy, we now know who supplied this information. Throckmorton was tracked from within the French embassy by Laurent Feron, a London-born clerk who kept Walsingham supplied with the contents of Ambassador Castelnau's diplomatic bag. The operation was concluded with an extraordinary Watergate-style raid on the French ambassador's files, in which Feron passed months of incriminating correspondence on to Walsingham's agent Walter Williams, risking 'not just dishonour but death' by doing so.

Secret services like to propagate myths about their own competence. Fear is a powerful deterrent, often outweighing any objective danger of being detected. In fact Walsingham had tried without success to infiltrate the household of the French ambassador until a priest living there, writing under the alias Henri Fagot, offered to recruit Castelnau's secretary on his behalf. This tremendous piece of luck allowed Walsingham to monitor the ciphered traffic between Mary, Castelnau and King Henry III of France. The principal danger, or so Walsingham had thought, was a pro-Catholic invasion from Scotland. When

Francis Throckmorton came into view, more or less by chance, Walsingham realised that his information was out of date. The real threat in 1583 was an army landing on the coasts of Sussex and Cumbria, paid by Spain and led by the Guise.[3]

To judge by the weight of the archival record, Francis Walsingham's main influence was as a diplomat and foreign secretary. The Elizabethan state papers depict him as the broker of England's foreign policy, struggling to reconcile his own Protestant internationalism with the isolationism of his sovereign. Archives, however, are selective in what they tell us. They can refract, as well as reflect a life. When those who had known him came to write about Walsingham after his death, they recalled a spymaster as well as a civil servant.

William Camden was the first historian to assess the character and achievements of Francis Walsingham. His *Annals* or 'History of Elizabeth' was printed in Latin between 1615 and 1625, the period of James I's 'personal rule'. The political context was gloomy. James's autocratic language had soured the relationship between crown and political nation, and the late Queen Elizabeth's reputation was enjoying a nostalgic revival. Walsingham had hounded James's mother Mary to her execution, and Camden had to tread carefully. In praising Walsingham as a Protestant, 'a most sharp maintainer of the purer religion', he was on safe enough ground. But Camden also remembered 'a most subtil searcher of hidden secrets', a clear reference to Walsingham's role in defeating the Catholic conspiracies which had promoted the cause of the Queen of Scots.

In 1634 Sir Robert Naunton included a portrait of Walsingham in *Fragmenta Regalia*, his celebration of the personalities of the Elizabethan court. Naunton was disgruntled at losing his position as secretary of state, and like Camden he contrasted his own times with the golden age of Elizabeth. He described Walsingham as a faithful servant of the queen, watchful over her safety and possessed of 'curiosities and secret ways of intelligence above the rest'. Naunton is a useful witness. He had met Walsingham in 1589 and knew what it was like to work undercover, having served the Earl of Essex in the 1590s as an 'intelligencer'. The word was freshly coined, a linguistic response to the new world order of plots and counter-espionage. Walsingham's success as a spymaster remained relevant to a generation which had witnessed the Gunpowder Plot of 1605. Protestants like Camden and Naunton saw Guy Fawkes as the latest in a line of Catholic conspirators stretching back into Elizabeth's reign. Their failure, time and again, was proof of divine providence: the English monarchy was under the special protection of God.[4]

Walsingham's career as a spymaster was no less topical when scholarly interest revived in the late nineteenth century. Writing in the original *Dictionary of National Biography*, its editor Sidney Lee credited Walsingham with developing a secret service capable of thwarting the 'furtive designs' of England's enemies. Biographers have a habit of seeing their own times reflected in their subject. Lee's essay was published in 1899, a time of growing apprehension about German agents and covert naval expansion. Erskine Childers caught the mood in his thriller *The Riddle of the Sands*, which fantasised about an invasion of England from the Frisian Islands. The Secret Service Bureau was established in 1909, soon to be restructured as MI5 and MI6. With the coming of the Second World War, the American scholar and businessman Conyers Read was able to put his vast research on Walsingham to practical effect. An Anglophile and an opponent of Nazism, Read combined his study of Elizabethan statecraft with employment on the British Empire desk of the Office of Strategic Services, precursor to the CIA.[5]

Scholars of Sidney Lee's era were happy to search Tudor England for the origins of the modern state: the rule of law, government by council and the germ of parliamentary democracy. Modern historians tend to be more sceptical. Strictly speaking, Francis Walsingham was not the founding father of MI5 and 6. The Elizabethan secret service was less a formal structure than a web of relationships. Walsingham turned his household into a seat of government, just as Henry VIII's chief minister Thomas Cromwell had done before him. His agents were his own servants and clients, operating as individuals rather than as cogs in a departmental machine. The gathering of intelligence was lubricated by patronage and profit. Yet it is this absence of bureaucracy which makes Walsingham's achievement so remarkable. Success or failure depended on his ability to keep alert, to spot the connections in the avalanche of information and to keep his people loyal. Camden says that 'he knew excellently well how to win men's minds unto him, and to apply them to his own uses'. One word recurs in his depiction of Walsingham: 'subtiltie' – the quality of the serpent that tempted Eve in the Elizabethan translation of the Bible.[6]

The twin threat of invasion from overseas and a Catholic fifth column at home shocked the Elizabethan state into a new scale of surveillance. Its effectiveness depended on the willingness of ordinary people to collaborate. English society had always watched itself closely for signs of difference or deviance, although in the ordinary run of things this came down to respectability more than politics. Scolding women were dunked in the village pond in a wooden see-saw known as a cucking-stool, and adulterers saw themselves paraded in effigy. But when the 'great matter' of Henry VIII's marriage morphed into a Protestant Reformation, the state came to take a far closer interest in the behaviour and beliefs of ordinary people. Parliament broadened the definition of treason to include crimes of thought and word as well as deed. Conversations in private chambers and arguments in taverns became politicised and were duly reported to Cromwell. Compulsory oaths of allegiance bound every subject to their sovereign.

The parallels between the 1530s and the 1580s are telling. Cromwell and Walsingham occupied the same office, principal secretary to the monarch. Both were responsible for policing a reformation among a population that was occasionally welcoming, often uneasy and sometimes actively hostile. The nature of Cromwell's secret service offers a point of comparison with Walsingham's fifty years on. Like Walsingham, Cromwell was credited at the beginning of the twentieth century with creating a 'system of espionage' and spinning a fine web of agents and spies. In fact, information flooded in through the normal channels of communication between the crown and the shires. Some of Cromwell's correspondents hoped for advancement: a lucrative parcel of monastic land, or marriage to a wealthy ward of the king. Others informed on their neighbours out of evangelical commitment, or in revenge against a rival. The majority simply saw it as their duty. In Henry VIII's reign as in Elizabeth's, the state encouraged this belief with a vigorous propaganda campaign to foster allegiance to the Protestant nation.[7]

In 1571 Parliament passed an updated version of the legislation introduced by Cromwell to protect the royal dignity from slander. Anyone who denied Queen Elizabeth's right to the throne, or called her a heretic or a tyrant, would be prosecuted as a traitor. An accompanying statute forbade Agnus Dei tokens of the sort worn by Cuthbert Mayne. A decade later, the perceived Catholic threat had increased still further. In January 1581 Sir Walter Mildmay, chancellor of the exchequer and Walsingham's brother-in-law, stood up in the Commons to deliver a lengthy broadside against the mustering forces of the English Catholic mission. Jesuits, 'a rabble of vagrant friars', were creeping into the houses of the gentry 'not only to corrupt the realm by false doctrine, but also, under that pretence, to stir sedition'. Mercy towards the papists had done England no good, he said. The time had come 'for us to look more narrowly and straitly to them'.[8]

As members of the privy council, Walsingham and Mildmay shared responsibility for piloting legislation through Parliament. The aggressive Protestant rhetoric of the 1581 session translated into a new statute 'to retain the queen's majesty's subjects in their due obedience'. This preserved the distinction between the spiritual and the political qualities of the English mission which was so crucial to government propagandists. Any priest who celebrated mass faced a year in jail and a fine of two hundred marks. If the fine could not be paid, the priest would stay in prison. His congregation was liable to a year's imprisonment and fines of one hundred marks. Far more crushing penalties were promised for those who actively campaigned for Catholicism. Anyone who sought to withdraw the queen's subjects 'from their natural obedience to her majesty', or to lure them 'for that intent' away from the Church of England, was declared a traitor. The formula 'for that intent' emphasised the official argument that Catholicism was treated as treason only if it became compromised with politics. In practice, it proved easy enough to construe Catholic priests as traitors by the nature of their calling. The same 1581 statute raised the financial penalty for refusing to attend the parish church to £20 a month.[9]

The Jesuit mission provoked a degree of loathing out of all proportion to the dozen or so priests and lay brothers operating in England. Unlike the religious orders of the past, the Society of Jesus exempted its members from wearing a habit and allowed them to conceal their identity. John Gerard dressed as a gentleman, and taught himself falconry and hunting to have a topic of conversation to match his character. Edmund Campion landed at Dover in June 1580 in the more humble disguise of a travelling jewel salesman from Dublin. He was arrested but then released, even though the government had circulated a description and woodcut portraits of Campion and his fellow Jesuit Robert Persons. Still more worrying was the internationalism of the Jesuit order. Active in Ireland and Scotland as well as England and with a single chain of command to the father general in Rome, the Society of Jesus had the ability to launch a co-ordinated assault on the reformed faith throughout the British Isles.[10]

Jesuits also made skilful use of the printed word. A keen advocate of Queen Elizabeth's deposition, Robert Persons set up the secret Greenstreet House Press on the outskirts of London soon after his arrival in England. When Walsingham began to close in, it was dismantled and moved to Stonor Park near Henley. Books printed before the press was seized in August 1581 included Campion's *Decem Rationes*, an academic attack on the intellectual emptiness of Protestantism. A young seminary priest in Oxford named William Hartley managed to smuggle copies into St Mary's Church, to the horror of the university proctors. Propaganda victories like these prompted Parliament to insert the last piece in the jigsaw of anti-Catholic legislation. In 1585 Jesuits and seminary priests were given a suitably biblical forty days to submit to the queen or flee the realm, on pain of high treason.[11]

The modern British security services occupy architecturally distinctive office space at Thames House and the 'Ziggurat' on Vauxhall Bridge, the subject of a million tourist photographs from the tripping boats on the river. The buildings proclaim the status of the agencies within them, intentionally drawing public attention to their existence. There was nothing so centralised, or so bureaucratic, about the Tudor state. If the Elizabethan security services had a headquarters then it was at Walsingham's own house in Seething Lane, lying in Tower Ward within the walls of the ancient city of London.

The 'fair and large' building noted by the Tudor topographer John Stow has long gone. A Victorian office block now occupies the site, its name – Walsingham House – and a portrait discreetly etched in glass above the entrance the only clues to what once stood here. But an inventory or 'table book' offers a window into Walsingham's study at Seething Lane in about the year 1588. The visitor was confronted with a slew of paper on every aspect of Elizabethan government, from copies of treaties and correspondence with ambassadors to descriptions of the queen's houses and the Order of the Garter. Plans for provisioning the navy and mustering the army competed for space with reports about the war against piracy. Bundles of manuscripts were sorted into a series of chests. The 'box of navy, havens, & sea causes' included descriptions of the fortification of Dover harbour and 'the discovery of unknown countries' by Sir Humphrey Gilbert and Martin Frobisher. A 'box of religion & matters ecclesiastical' contained lists of Catholic recusants and papers relating to the reformation in Wales. Chillingly, there was also a 'box of examinations' of papists and priests. Other furniture included a black desk and the 'secret cabinet' in which Walsingham's will was found after his death. A 'book of the maps of England' probably contained the county surveys by Christopher Saxton which were also prized by Lord Burghley.

The surveyor Arthur Gregorye supplied Walsingham with plans of Dover and the English plantations in Ireland.[12]

Along with his papers and his books, Walsingham assembled a household of godly administrators at Seething Lane. This cadre of men was doubly bound together by its Protestant devotion and its service of the state. Laurence Tomson, who acted as Walsingham's secretary for fifteen years, found time to translate the Genevan version of the New Testament into English (which he dedicated to Walsingham) as well as an edition of Calvin's sermons. Nicholas Faunt, another strongly committed Protestant, was an active intelligencer as well as a secretary to Walsingham, carrying despatches to English agents abroad and sending reports of his own. Robert Beale was also closely connected with Seething Lane, deputising as principal secretary when Walsingham was absent or sick. Their shared memory of St Bartholomew was a powerful bond between these men at the heart of Elizabethan government.

Conyers Read described Walsingham's household as 'a perfect hot-bed of Puritanism'. One man, however, stands out from the rest. Walter Williams was another veteran of the French embassy of 1571–3 who subsequently proved his worth delivering letters between England and the continent. By 1582 he was being redeployed in a surveillance operation at home. At the time of the Ridolfi plot, William Cecil had been able to gather valuable information from Catholic prisoners in the Marshalsea via his agent William Herle, imprisoned on a charge of piracy but actually working for the crown as an agent provocateur. A series of 'secret advertisements' between August and December 1582 reveals Williams operating in the same role, as an undercover agent eavesdropping on Catholics detained in Rye. His letters to Walsingham describe him sleeping on the floor 'among thieves and rovers', trying to persuade his cell-mate to talk. On this occasion, the haul was disappointing. Williams could find no evidence of a conspiracy against the queen beyond some vague talk about Scotland. A letter intercepted by Walsingham implies that the anonymous 'papist' had seen through his fellow prisoner, perhaps alerted by his request for a list 'of all the rebels beyond the seas, and where their abode is'. On 15 December Williams asked to be released, at which point Walsingham put him in charge of his headquarters at Seething Lane. By August 1583 he was acting as Walsingham's contact with Laurent Feron, the mole inside the French embassy. Conveniently, Feron's house in Mincing Lane was only two streets away.[13]

The challenge facing Walsingham and his secretariat was the sheer wealth of information pouring into his office. It is the perennial problem of those engaged in espionage – how to sift the useful intelligence from the international chatter of news and rumour, propaganda and gossip. Simply reading and archiving the reports filed by diplomats, agents and chancers of all sorts must have been a formidable task for a small team. How much more difficult to make sense of it; to extract the viable conspiracies out of the many that would never get beyond the dreams of a maverick Jesuit, or the posturing of an isolated exile.

There were times when the work seemed overwhelming. His correspondence shows Walsingham to have been haunted by the sickness and decay of the edifice that he sought to shore up. When sixteenth-century people thought about the state, they frequently likened it to the human body. In a letter of March 1575, Walsingham called on medical imagery to describe his relationship with Queen Elizabeth. He had recently discovered that Mary Stuart was in secret communication with the outside world with the aid of a London stationer. To Walsingham, this was a prime chance to be rid of the Scottish 'bosom serpent' once and for all. Yet Elizabeth stalled the investigation and forgave Lord Henry Howard, who was clearly implicated. 'Surely my lord', Walsingham wrote to Leicester in disgust, 'her majesty's strange dealings in this case will discourage all honest ministers that are careful for her safety to deal in the discovery of the sores of this diseased state, seeing her majesty bent rather to cover than to cure them'. The morbid language recurred throughout his life. Notes which Walsingham made on 'the decay and falling away in religion' in December 1586 pinpointed seminary priests and Jesuits as 'the poison of this estate'.

His choice of metaphor was poignant. Walsingham's own body was being progressively poisoned by a urinary infection that could incapacitate him for weeks, sometimes months on end. Physical torment could be reconciled with a godly life: Calvinists expected to suffer. But what of the spiritual doubts that may have lurked in his mind? Catastrophes on the scale of William of Orange's assassination in 1584 implied that God had tested the cause of the reformed Church and found it wanting. When Walsingham broke the news of the Throckmorton plot, it was devoured by Protestants of all classes as proof that England was, after all, a nation of the elect.[14]

The flow of intelligence into Seething Lane came from many different directions. The regular diplomatic channels of the Elizabethan state are sometimes forgotten in the rush to recreate Francis Walsingham as a spymaster. Like the foreign ambassadors resident at her own court, the queen's envoys to her brother princes were instructed to keep alert for information that might prove of political or military advantage. The recall of her representative in Spain in 1568 left only two permanent embassies, in Edinburgh and Paris, supplemented by temporary missions as necessary. Balancing the budget had always been a strain for the Tudors, and royal finances were seriously overstretched by Walsingham's day. Maintaining a magnificent presence in a foreign territory could be ruinously expensive. Small as it was, however, the diplomatic corps had a role to play in maintaining the security of the Elizabethan regime, and nowhere more so than in Paris.

For upper-class Catholics unwilling to compromise, Paris was proving to be an attractive place to sit out the reign of Elizabeth. About four hundred English expatriates were living in the city during the 1580s, many of them with families and servants in attendance. Paris offered safety from arrest and an intensely Catholic piety. For a few, it also provided the space to imagine the deposition of the heretical queen who ruled in their native land. Their presence forced Walsingham time and again to focus his attention on France. As Ambassador Sir Henry Cobham reported in 1582, it was depressingly easy for the émigrés to remain in communication with their kin in England. The continuing convulsions of the French wars of religion may have kept alive the prospect of a Protestant monarchy in that country, but they also spawned the threat of a Catholic invasion of England via the Channel ports. Aristocratic exiles like Charles Paget stood ready to assist.

In truth, King Henry III was not obviously keen to fund the English Catholics within his dominions. But they were sometimes observed parading at the royal court, as Sir Edward Stafford informed Walsingham at Christmas 1583. Furthermore, the French king's caution left the initiative in the hands of the fanatically Catholic Duke of Guise. In 1572 Guise had participated in the murder of Admiral Coligny, sparking an orgy of violence against the Huguenots. By the early 1580s he was courting funding for his Catholic League from the equally hawkish Philip II of Spain. As the Throckmorton plot chillingly demonstrated, Guise was eager to take the fight to England even if Henry III was not.[15]

Paris wasn't the only exile centre in France. Writing in 1585, an informer named Thomas Becknor warned Walsingham about the growing number of English exiles in Rouen. An Act of Parliament had theoretically cut off the revenues of those who travelled abroad without the permission of the crown, but local merchants were providing them with a rudimentary banking system in much the same way that Protestant exiles had been sustained during Mary's reign. Charles Paget was using a Rouen trader named Barthelemy Martin to deliver money which had been exchanged, for an appropriate fee, with another merchant in London. Catholic exiles were thus finding a way to draw on the rents from their estates, to the frustration of the Elizabethan government.[16]

The limitations of the traditional diplomatic channels were becoming increasingly evident. Language could significantly hinder the gathering of intelligence. Walsingham was unusual for his fluency in French and Italian, although he struggled with Spanish. Ambassadors who lacked his skills had to work through translators, greatly reducing their opportunity to detect sensitive information. Another problem was the elaborate ceremonial of the Renaissance court, which enveloped foreign envoys and kept them distant from the theatres of politics. Queen Elizabeth herself was a particularly skilled player of this game. Hunting trips and progresses into the shires could be used to dodge ambassadors who were seeking an audience with her. Itineraries were not advertised, and in any case Elizabeth altered them at will, leaving foreign delegations lost in the English countryside.[17]

The patronage system that regulated the Elizabethan regime could also hamper its response to threats from abroad. Walsingham regarded the business of diplomacy as his own domain and expected ambassadors to report directly to him, but he never quite achieved the monopoly he desired. One man in particular stood up to him, spurning his friendship and deliberately channelling despatches to Lord Burghley as an alternative patron. Sir Edward Stafford held the crucial embassy to Paris from 1583 until after Walsingham's death. Once installed as ambassador, Stafford became increasingly maverick in his behaviour. He pointedly bypassed Walsingham when reporting from Paris, and trespassed on his operations among the English exiles in the city. He openly proclaimed his support for Mary Stuart as Queen Elizabeth's heir. Incredibly, from 1587 he was also in the pay of the Spanish government as a spy.

The relationship between Stafford and Walsingham had begun well enough. Stafford's mother was mistress of the robes to Queen Elizabeth. He followed a conventional gentleman's route from Cambridge to the Commons and a minor office at court as a gentleman pensioner. In the 1570s he was active in French affairs as a courier and made a friend of the Duke of Alençon, hosting him at his own house in 1579. But when a posting to Paris seemed in the offing, Stafford scorned his previous co-operation with Walsingham and hitched his colours to Burghley's mast. The resulting feud between ambassador and principal secretary was partly personal, but no doubt also ideological, since Stafford did not share Walsingham's visceral support for the French Huguenots. Walsingham retaliated by directing his searchers to open Stafford's letters as they arrived at Rye. When Stafford protested, Walsingham replied that he would do well to put future letters 'in a packet directed to me' to prevent it happening again. Meanwhile the impetuous ambassador was building up heavy gambling debts in Paris. It was perhaps to pay these that he accepted, first an advance of six thousand crowns from the Duke of Guise for sharing the contents of his diplomatic bag, and then a further two thousand crowns from Don Bernardino de Mendoza, by now the Spanish envoy to France. The bearer of this second sum was Charles Arundel, the English Catholic exile and conspirator.

The jury is still out on the exact nature of Stafford's treason.

An agent returning from Paris to England in spring 1586 brought news of the cash-for-secrets deal with Guise and Arundel. And yet Walsingham did not strike, in part because Stafford remained in Burghley's confidence, but also perhaps to avoid blowing the cover of his informer. A more intriguing possibility is that Walsingham had decided to use Stafford to feed false or baffling information to his Spanish handlers. By 1587, when Stafford was recruited by Mendoza, a sea war between England and Spain was looming and naval intelligence was at a premium for both nations. In April of that year Stafford forwarded Mendoza news, recently received from Walsingham, that the queen was delaying sending out Francis Drake's fleet to harass Spanish shipping. This was the opposite of the truth: Drake had already sailed on his famous expedition to 'singe the King of Spain's beard' at Cadiz.

When he realised that Drake had put to sea, Stafford sent an urgent warning to Cadiz which arrived only a day after the town had been burned. Clearly he had other sources besides Walsingham. One of these was his brother-in-law Lord Howard of Effingham, the Lord Admiral of England, who inadvertently provided statistics on the firepower of the English fleet. Walsingham may have been playing Sir Edward Stafford, but he could not control him. Stafford's despatches to his Spanish paymasters undoubtedly compromised England's defence against naval attack. He was never called to account for his actions, and was honourably buried at St Margaret's, Westminster in 1605.[18]

Stafford's tenure of the Paris embassy for most of the 1580s challenged Francis Walsingham's position at the focal point of Elizabethan diplomacy. Sir Henry Cobham had been provided with a secretary by Walsingham himself, one Francis Needham, enabling him to monitor the ambassador's correspondence. Stafford's appointment changed all this, diverting the flow of information from Paris. As the customary sources of foreign intelligence dried up, so Walsingham was driven towards a new type of statecraft. The security of the Elizabethan regime increasingly came to depend upon a network of agents and informers, paid by Walsingham and reporting directly to him rather than to the queen.[19]

In 1592 Robert Beale recalled the 'foreign espials and intelligences' maintained by Walsingham during the last ten years of his life. The principal secretary ran his network using his own resources as well as an allowance from the crown. A list of 'sundry foreign places from whence Mr Secretary Walsingham was wont to receive his advertisements' spanned France, the Low Countries and Germany to Spain, Italy and the Ottoman Empire: a total of forty-six locations, from Constantinople to Algiers. Much of this was simply news, equivalent to the foreign affairs pages of a modern daily paper. The work of this sort of 'espial' would nowadays be the domain of the journalist. But among these thousands of despatches were some that were very valuable indeed. They enabled Walsingham to tail exiles in Madrid and Paris, to overhear conversations at the English colleges in Rheims and Rome, and to piece together the jigsaws of conspiracy against the crown.[20]

Elizabethan England may have lacked a large diplomatic establishment, but its power as a nation of traders was increasingly impressive. Francis Walsingham was able to make his own use of the merchants and factors of the great commercial companies, men who had legitimate reason to travel and linger abroad. Christopher Hoddesdon is a good example. Following several successful years trading in Muscovy and the Baltic, Hoddesdon rose to be master of the Company of Merchant Adventurers in Hamburg and a financial agent of Elizabeth I. He sent a steady stream of letters to both Walsingham and Burghley, full of the breaking news of Europe: royal marriages in the Holy Roman Empire, a Turkish siege in Hungary, exchange rates and shipping movements. Within this onslaught of information was more specific intelligence. In February 1578 Hoddesdon forwarded a report from his own agent in Rome describing Captain Thomas Stucley's attempt to launch an invasion of Ireland from Civitavecchia, an armada of one leaky vessel with four cannon and a mutinous crew. It helped that there was a family connection between Walsingham and his informant. Hoddesdon was married to Walsingham's step-daughter Alice, and he committed his son to Walsingham's care 'if God take me away before I return'. They may have shared an interest in falconry, since Hoddesdon sent him a goshawk. He continued filing reports from Emden and Antwerp in the early 1580s.[21]

Walsingham was a powerful patron for a man like Hoddesdon, whose wealth and status depended on the free flow of trade. As so often in early modern Europe, the quality of the gifts exchanged indicates the value of the relationship. In 1584 Walsingham received a unique and costly present from Constantinople, a leather carpet in the style of the inner apartments or seraglio of the sultan's palace at Topkapi. Its sender was William Harborne, a London merchant who had been resident in the Ottoman capital since 1578. The English were a welcome supplier of munitions to the Turkish war against Persia, and Harborne was able to negotiate a charter of privileges for English merchants from Sultan Murad III. Queen Elizabeth rarely missed an opportunity for economy, and in 1582 she appointed Harborne her 'orator and agent' on the expense account of the newly founded Turkey Company.

Walsingham, too, spied an advantage. Alliance with an Islamic empire that was perceived as the scourge of Christian Europe may seem a strange objective for a Puritan principal secretary, but the Ottomans were a great power in the Mediterranean sea.

If they could be induced to make war on Spain, Philip II would be forced to deploy ships which could otherwise be used against England. In 1585 Walsingham wrote to Harborne in cipher, 'your assured loving friend', instructing him to explain to the vizier how the rise of Spain was threatening the dignity of the sultan. The remedy that Walsingham prescribed was a military strike, either on Spain itself from the coast of Ottoman-controlled Africa, or an assault of naval galleys on Habsburg territories in Italy. Harborne dutifully spent the next three years petitioning the sultan to commit some portion of his forces against Spain, although it turned out that he was too committed to the conflict in Persia to open up another front against Catholic Christendom. In 1588 Harborne exchanged Constantinople for Norfolk, where he wrote an account of his Turkish experiences which was printed in Richard Hakluyt's *Principal Navigations of the English Nation*. Appropriately, the book was dedicated to Walsingham.[22]

Ambassadors and semi-official envoys like William Harborne inhabited a courtly world, defined – at least on the surface – by codes of chivalry and amity, and displayed in exaggerated etiquette. The queen's image abroad was one aspect of her government that Elizabeth treated with deadly gravity, since it was by her own reputation that the strength of her regime was assessed. England was underpopulated and militarily under-resourced by continental standards, and this made it all the more vital that the queen should visibly appear to emanate power and dignity. Where diplomacy shaded into espionage, it could not be allowed to compromise the public face of the English monarchy. This set a limit to the intelligence operations of the official channels of state.

Look underneath that patina of royal magnificence, however, and there was another layer to the Elizabethan security services: the semi-professional intelligencers who existed to collect, decrypt and interpret information regarding the enemies of the established regime. One of the remarkable features of Walsingham's secret service was its social inclusiveness, from young members of the gentry down to the jailbirds and petty criminals of the Elizabethan underworld. It is tempting to draw a comparison with modern agencies like Bletchley Park in the early 1940s, a melting-pot of grammar-school boys, dons and debutantes. At a time when even modes of dress were prescribed by Parliament according to hierarchy, Walsingham was willing to recruit talent wherever it lay.

At the social summit of the Elizabethan secret service lay men who were educated at university or the Inns of Court, fluent in classical languages and English common law. Robert Beale was one of these. Another, almost certainly, was the poet Christopher Marlowe. Speculation about his work for Walsingham in the mid-1580s adds just the required dash of spice to Marlowe's biography, which is otherwise scant in crucial details. It seems to provide a context for the subversiveness of such plays as *Dr Faustus* and *Edward II*. It might also explain his sordid death with a knife in the eye at a Deptford rooming-house. Marlowe's outrageous atheism, and his uncertain but passionate sexuality, contrast dramatically with the steely Puritanism of Walsingham's other administrators and agents in the field.

Unfortunately, this portrait of Marlowe rests on evidence that is both limited and tainted: an absence from his Cambridge college in the mid-1580s, and a slew of slanders after his death. Rumour clung to Marlowe in his own lifetime, courted by the poet himself, and his myth has only grown in the telling. But one place-name recurs in the sources, implying that Marlowe was somehow involved there: the French city of Rheims, home to

Cardinal Allen's college for missionary priests and the target of a sustained operation by Francis Walsingham.

We know that Marlowe's time as a spy was brief: a few months while reading for his MA at Corpus Christi in 1584–5, and a reprise in the Dutch port of Flushing in 1592. According to the ledgers of the college buttery (from *bouteillerie*, where the bottles are kept, hence an account of food and drink consumed) he disappeared from Corpus for the duration of Michaelmas term 1584. He was absent again between April and June 1585, and was noticeably more lavish in his spending on his return. Then silence until June 1587, when the privy council directed the University of Cambridge to award him his MA. It also wanted the rumour suppressed that Marlowe was intending to defect to Rheims. These unusual orders were justified on grounds that Marlowe had been employed 'in matters touching the benefit of his country'.

Who was Marlowe working for? Although he reported to Lord Burghley on occasion, there is circumstantial evidence that Francis Walsingham was his principal paymaster. Marlowe's life as a playwright was entwined with that of Thomas Walsingham, a young second cousin of Sir Francis who fashioned himself as a literary patron while couriering government letters between England and Paris in the early 1580s. If Thomas recruited Marlowe, then he may also have been his handler at Seething Lane. When the authorities came to arrest Marlowe in May 1593, they looked for him at Thomas Walsingham's manor of Scadbury in Kent. Within the month, Thomas was one of the mourners at Marlowe's funeral. The 1598 edition of Marlowe's *Hero and Leander* was dedicated to Thomas Walsingham by its editor. As for the nature of his secret service, Marlowe would have been too easily recognised to be a plausible plant in Cardinal Allen's seminary. Then again, he hardly needed to leave England to serve the state: he was already in a position to trail Cambridge men who were contemplating the road to Rheims.[23]

The two sides of Kit Marlowe, atheist and spy, come together in his relationship with Richard Baines, another Cambridge MA with a connection to Rheims. Baines was already working for Walsingham when he was ordained a Catholic priest there in 1581. He was a valuable mole within the seminary until he was identified as an *explorator*, a 'lurking spy' in William Allen's Latin. Marlowe knew Baines as a man whose career was virtually finished, scarred by the torture he had endured in the town jail in Rheims following his discovery. Walsingham's intelligencers varied in their response to the close quarters in which they were required to work. In some, it fostered an *esprit de corps* founded on patriotism or faith. Others found it stifling. Baines detested Marlowe, and made a record of his provocative conversation. His account of Marlowe's atheistical table-talk, his 'scorn of God's word', created an atmosphere around the poet that prompted others to think they could profit from his murder.[24]

Investing in Marlowe may have paid Walsingham a dividend of a different kind. A London playhouse was one of very few venues where politics could be publicly discussed, and consequently the crown took an interest in what was put on. For Walsingham Marlowe may have represented a man on the inside, a literary equivalent of Richard Baines in the seminary at Rheims. A parallel strategy was to offer protection to the actors themselves. In 1583 Walsingham instructed Master of the Revels Edmund Tilney to form the company of Queen's Men. Whatever his motives, Walsingham's patronage of plays and players forces us to refine the received image of a relentlessly dour Puritan.

Dogged by rumours of homosexuality and crypto-Catholicism, Marlowe lay at one end of the spectrum of agents employed by Walsingham. At the other was Maliverny Catlyn, who wrote

Aldermanbury, City of London. Walsingham's parents William and Joyce were both buried in the church of St Mary Aldermanbury.

Edward VI in front of Hunsdon in Hertfordshire (c.1546), the royal manor where Walsingham's step-father Sir John Carey was bailiff.

The south porch of King's College chapel, Cambridge University (c.1800). Walsingham's studies at King's profoundly influenced his future outlook and career.

Portrait traditionally thought to be of Dame Ursula (d.1602), Walsingham's second wife. Ursula witnessed the St Bartholomew's massacre alongside her husband.

Provisionally identified as Barn Elms, the house on the Thames where the Walsinghams received the Queen on progress.

Map of sixteenth-century Paris. The Huguenot district of Saint Marceau, where Walsingham lived during his time as ambassador, appears at the top.

Allegory of the Tudor Succession, attrib. Lucas de Heere, 1572, presented to Walsingham by Queen Elizabeth to mark the signing of the treaty of Blois.

Elizabeth I: Sieve Portrait, Quentin Metsys the younger, 1583. The globe behind the Queen alludes to England's aspiring empire at sea.

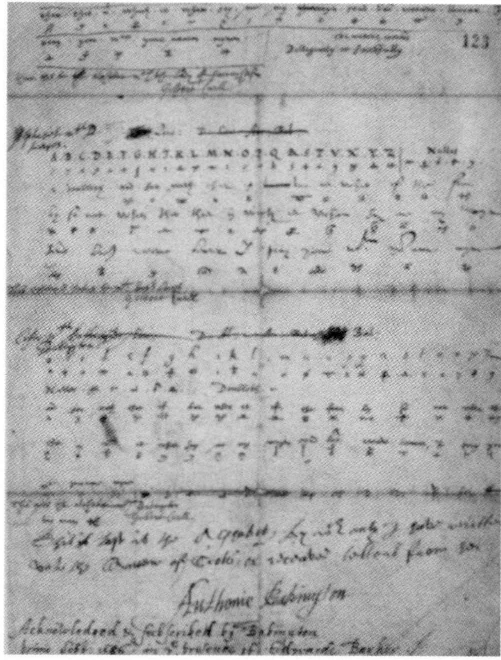

123

Anthonie Babington

Relic of the skull of St Cuthbert Mayne, the first priest of the English Catholic mission to be executed for his faith.

Cipher alphabet with which Anthony Babington communicated with the Queen of Scots.

Drawing of the execution of Mary Queen of Scots at Fotheringhay, 8 February 1587.

Title-page of *General and Rare Memorials pertayning to the Perfect Arte of Navigation*, John Dee, 1577. Elizabeth I sails the ship of state towards the new world.

Image of Ireland, John Derricke, 1581. 'An armed company of the kerne attack and burn a farmhouse'.

Captain Christopher Carleill by Robert Boissard (engraver) after unknown artist, c.1593. Lacking a son of his own, Walsingham remained close to his step-son from his first marriage.

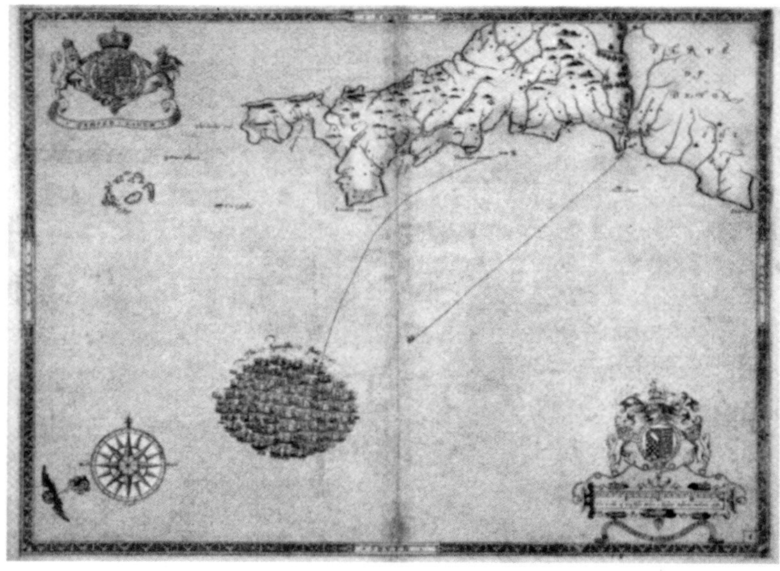

Indian Woman and Young Girl, John White, 1585–6. The girl holds an Elizabethan doll traded with the English.

The Spanish Fleet off the Coast of Cornwall on 29 July 1588, 1590. Lord Henry Seymour credited Walsingham with fighting Spain 'more with your pen than many have in our English navy'.

from Rouen in April 1586 promising 'such service as might witness my duty to religion, her majesty's person, and my country's preservation'. By his own account, Catlyn had served as a soldier in the Low Countries before successfully penetrating the English Catholic exile community in France. He revealed the true tone of his faith in a sermonic address to Walsingham on what he called 'the daily abuse of stage plays': 'such an offence to the godly,' wrote Catlyn, 'and so great a hindrance to the gospel, as the papists do exceedingly rejoice at the blemish thereof'. While two hundred proud players paraded in silks, five hundred people starved on the streets of London. Every theatre, declared Catlyn, should pay a weekly pension to the poor.

Notwithstanding his contempt for the Elizabethan stage, Catlyn must have been a convincing actor. Walsingham embedded him as a prison spy in Portsmouth and then the Marshalsea, where he was assured by one of the prisoners that a Franco-imperial invasion and a popular Catholic uprising would free them before the harvest was in. Catlyn forwarded the news to Walsingham 'with all speed, with all expedition'. As Walter Williams had found before him, the life of a stool-pigeon was never easy. Catlyn struggled to get hold of paper and ink and to allay the suspicions of his jailer, 'who in truth useth me like a prisoner committed for high treason, so that I was forced to charge him in her majesty's name to deliver this to your honour'. When Walsingham had discovered all he could, Catlyn was transferred to survey the strength of Catholicism in the north.

His diatribe against stage plays implies that religious zeal motivated Catlyn to volunteer for Walsingham's secret service. He identified the English nation with God's people in the Old Testament, numbering himself among the elect: 'the Lord of Hosts will surely forsake to dwell amongst the tents of Israel if the sins of the people do still provoke him'. Elsewhere, however, we find Catlyn attempting to serve both God and Mammon. His letter from Rouen called Walsingham's attention to 'my poor living, the defect whereof drives me sometimes to a non-plus; for being the youngest son of a younger brother, my position was only seven feet of inheritance, which has constrained me to seek my living *hic et ubique* [here and everywhere]'. A few months later he wrote again asking for money, or else 'I and mine are like to keep the coldest Christmastide that hitherto we ever tasted'. Walsingham sent him £5, hardly generous if Catlyn's household aspired to any sort of gentility.[25]

This seems to have been how Elizabethan spies were rewarded, ad hoc and for operations carried out. Again, it looks so different from the established security agencies of the modern state. But Walsingham's system had the advantage of keeping his operatives hungry to serve, and personally loyal to him. It also acted as a check on costs, a vital consideration given the queen's notorious reluctance to part with money. The financing of the Elizabethan security services is difficult to trace in the archives. Funds were authorised by warrants issued under the privy seal rather than voted by Parliament or paid through the formal crown machinery of exchequer and treasury. This made things easier for Walsingham, who had physical custody of the privy seal by the mid-1570s, but also problematic for the investigating historian, since a fire in 1619 consumed many of the privy seal warrants. The records which do survive, augmented by a list of payments 'for secret service' compiled by signet clerk Thomas Lake (nicknamed 'Swiftsure' for his efficient despatch of business), reveal an annual grant to Walsingham of £750 in 1582. This rose to about £2,000 in the mid-1580s and dropped to some £1,200 when the crisis of the Spanish Armada had passed. Ordinary crown revenue was about £300,000 per annum, implying that Elizabeth's security services accounted for two-thirds of one per cent of her government's spending. But this would be misleading, for two reasons. Intelligencers were often rewarded not in cash but in kind, for instance with the stewardship of a profitable royal estate. Secondly, Walsingham's substantial debts at his death suggest that he had been paying his agents out of his own resources when state subventions did not suffice.[26]

Walsingham's willingness to buy information greatly increased the reach of his secret service, but it also created unease among his peers. In Robert Beale's words, 'with money he corrupted priests, Jesuits and traitors to bewray the practices against this realm'. Beale was his colleague and brother-in-law, a fellow pilgrim in the journey towards the Protestant promised land. His advice to a future principal secretary included a warning not to copy Walsingham too closely: 'seeing how much his liberality was misliked, I do not think that you can follow the like example'. William Camden also hinted that Walsingham had crossed the line into entrapment: 'the Papists accused him as a cunning workman in complotting his businesses, and alluring men into dangers'. Camden's tone is defensive, but his epitaph and Beale's treatise provide some evidence from the Protestant side that Walsingham put his Protestant conviction before his respect for the law; just as Catholics have always claimed.[27]

Whatever its ethics, Walsingham's strategy of suborning the enemies of the English state to his own service produced some spectacular results. Through bribery, threats and a handful of genuine conversions to the Protestant cause, Walsingham was able to infiltrate English Catholicism at home and abroad. Defectors came from among both the laity and the clergy. In 1581 a wealthy Suffolk gentleman named George Gilbert, who had converted to Catholicism while touring the continent two years before, went into exile in Rheims and Rome. Travelling with him was his servant Thomas Rogers, who more often appears in the state papers under his alias of Nicholas Berden. For whatever reason, Berden had chosen to lead a double life. In 1583 he reported to Walsingham from Rome 'concerning the proceedings there touching the Queen of Scotland'. Somebody came to suspect Berden and he was imprisoned for a while, but was permitted to return to England on his release.

Berden's value to Walsingham lay in his credibility within Catholic circles, which evidently survived the Roman episode. By the spring of 1585 he was filing despatches every few days: dining with a Catholic priest here, talking to Cardinal Allen's agent there. It was a rich harvest of intelligence from deep within the Catholic underground. Berden reported on the safe-houses and prisons of London; on the priests and books stowed away on French coasters bound for Newcastle, where the queen's officer 'is a papist in heart'; on the networks that supported seminary priests and Jesuits in England. Walsingham learned that William Allen supplied his priests with £6 or £7 in money 'and a new suit of apparel to wear' when they embarked on their mission. In the summer Berden was moved to France, where he successfully re-established himself among the exile community and provided Walsingham with a valuable alternative to the Paris embassy compromised by Sir Edward Stafford.

Soon after he started working for Walsingham, Berden set down his motives for betraying the Catholic culture that had nurtured him. He wrote with a swagger which is rare in the archives of espionage, and it is worth letting him speak in his own words.

> When so ever any occasion shall be offered wherein I may adventure some rare and desperate exploit such as may be for the honour of my country and my own credit, you shall always find me most resolute and ready to perform the same . . . This only I crave, that though I profess myself a spy (which is a profession odious though necessary) that I prosecute the same not for gain, but for the safety of my native country.

Reading this letter in context, it almost rings true. The Elizabethan age praised those willing to face peril in the pursuit of fame. Berden's work was undoubtedly dangerous, and by Protestant standards counted as heroic. His political vocabulary is a plausible reaction to the nationalistic rhetoric that had become deeply rooted in English culture by the 1580s.

Almost rings true – but not quite; because Berden, like Maliverny Catlyn, also worked for money. Within Catholic circles, he cloaked his treachery by posing as someone who could influence Walsingham to be lenient through his own contacts at court – so long as the price was right. In accepting the bribes of Catholic gentlemen, he enriched himself while rising ever higher in their estimation. Berden literally held the power of life and death in his hands, annotating Walsingham's lists of captured priests as to who should be banished, who imprisoned and who hanged. He contrived to be convincing to all sides. His last letter to his master, written in April 1588 when his cover had finally been blown in Paris, thanked Walsingham for securing him the contract to supply poultry to the royal kitchens. He has no entry in the *Oxford Dictionary of National Biography*, but he surely deserves one.[28]

Perhaps it is not so surprising that the crucible of Tudor religion and politics distilled men like Nicholas Berden, who defended his own bloody advancement with the language of glory and patriotism. What remains astonishing is Walsingham's ability to recruit double agents from within the very brotherhood of Catholic priests that he was hunting down. The most notorious of these turncoats was Gilbert Gifford, who would play a central role in the Babington plot. Gifford was an unquiet soul, the son of a Staffordshire recusant and barely seventeen when he entered Allen's college at Douai in 1577. Having apparently challenged another student to a duel, he left for the English College at Rome but was soon expelled from there too. In 1583 Allen took Gifford back and he was finally ordained deacon. He then journeyed to Paris to meet the two leading figures of the expatriate Catholic resistance, Thomas Morgan and Charles Paget. Morgan wanted to open a channel of communication to Mary, Queen of Scots, who was at that point under house arrest at Chartley in Gifford's home county. But Gifford was too visible, too quick to temper, to make an effective courier. When he crossed the Channel to Rye in December 1585 he was swiftly arrested and brought to Walsingham to be interrogated.

Was Gifford already working for the English security services when he was picked up at Rye? One Jesuit writer alleges that Walsingham had turned him two years earlier, although Gifford's most recent biographer hedges his bets. If the accusation against him is just, then his dealings with Morgan and Paget in Paris look like a prime example of what Camden called Walsingham's 'complotting': a Machiavellian manoeuvre to tempt the English exiles into treason. From here it is an easy step to a conspiracy led by Walsingham and Burghley against the life of Mary Stuart. Certainly Gifford became a crucial link in the chain that led to Mary's traitorous last correspondence with Anthony Babington. A triumphant Walsingham granted him a pension of £100, an enormous sum in comparison to his payments to other agents. Gifford's behaviour, always difficult to interpret, then became very odd indeed. Rather than living out a comfortable life in England, he opted to return to Paris. Somehow he was ordained priest in March 1587, barely a month after Mary's death, and he spoke of travelling back to Rome. The depth of his vocation may be doubted, since he was arrested in a Paris bordello and died in the Archbishop's prison. Sir Edward Stafford condemned him as 'the most notable double treble villain that ever lived, for he hath played upon all the hands in the world'.[29]

Other Catholic priests were turned, or perhaps converted. An exile since childhood, Anthony Tyrell was ordained at the English College in Rome and sent into England in 1581. His work as a missionary was interleaved with political agitation, in Rheims with William Allen, in Paris with Charles Paget, and in Rome with both the pope and the father general of the Jesuits, or so he claimed. But when he was finally arrested in England in 1586, Tyrell was prepared to offer up a hoard of information on the whereabouts and contacts of his fellow priests. He was spirited into London's Clink prison to see what he could find out from the Catholics detained there. Tyrell was encouraged to hear confession and say mass before reporting on what he had learned. When he had exhausted his usefulness to the government, including preaching a Protestant sermon at Paul's Cross, he was re-employed as a Church of England clergyman on the Essex marshes. Trips to a London brothel, however, meant a further spell in prison. He ended his life in Naples, apparently a Catholic once again.[30]

It is difficult to know what to make of chameleons like Gifford and Tyrell. Marlowe's nemesis Richard Baines was a fraud from the start, seeking ordination as a priest only to infiltrate the seminary at Rheims. Tyrell and Gifford occupy a separate category, defying historians who want to divide Elizabethan Catholicism into neat groups of believers and apostates. The full picture is more complex, but also more psychologically plausible: hidden allegiances, partial conversions, and overlapping loyalties to Church and state. The febrile Anthony Tyrell, who changed religion six times within twenty years, was tormented by the fear that he had been possessed by devils during an exorcism. Gilbert Gifford's return to the Catholic Church following his destruction of the Queen of Scots is every bit as extraordinary. However they were turned, these double agents enabled Walsingham to create a perpetual anxiety within the English Catholic community. Congregations sheltering in barns and attics had good reason to fear discovery at the hands of an investigating magistrate or a royal pursuivant on the prowl. But betrayal might also come from a Judas within; and against this sort of threat, a watcher from a high window was no defence.

Studying the security services built up by Francis Walsingham allows us to piece together competing narratives of the Elizabethan state. One tells the story of a legitimate Tudor queen, served by able ministers and loved by her people, who was faced with assassination by Catholic zealots and the invasion of her kingdom by the great powers of Europe. To defeat this threat, Walsingham devised a secret service which worked, in the words of Sidney Lee, 'with a Machiavellian precision at home and abroad'. Espionage might be a murky business, but Walsingham managed to preserve his own integrity as well as the state which he served: 'in no instance is there conclusive proof that he strained law or justice against those whom his agents brought under his observation'. For Lee's generation, Walsingham seemed to embody values of loyalty, patriotism and fair play; a characterisation endorsed in its essentials by Conyers Read, whose account was based on years of painstaking research in the archives.

The Walsingham of the original *Dictionary of National Biography* has a doppelgänger, discovered by the Victorian Catholic priests who constructed an alternative narrative of the English Reformation. For them the Virgin Queen was a bastard and a heretic, and Mary Stuart the rightful successor to a kingdom which still yearned to be Catholic. Walsingham's web of informers and turncoats features large in this story too, but as the enforcement agency of a state power intent on utterly extinguishing the flame of English Catholicism. More recently, the Jesuit historian Francis Edwards has presented the Throckmorton plot as an attempt 'to bracket militants and pacifists and destroy them all' – in other words, to use one foolhardy dreamer to condemn the entire Catholic community. Throckmorton himself was a victim rather than a perpetrator, shy of committing treason but tortured on Walsingham's orders into 'false and feigned' confessions. For reasons which will be obvious, this is the image of Francis Walsingham which has appealed to modern film-makers.[31]

On balance, the Throckmorton plot represents an impressive victory for Walsingham's intelligence service courtesy of Laurent Feron, the embassy clerk who offered his services as a mole. It had been a close-run thing in November 1583. The Duke of Guise had successfully persuaded Philip II to fund an invasion of Cumbria and Sussex, where Throckmorton was to join him. Forces had already started to muster in Normandy. If we accept that Elizabeth was the rightful ruler of England, then we could justifiably cast Walsingham as a hero. A credible threat to overthrow the state had been averted, and Mary Stuart's supporters had been thrown into confusion. Deep down, however, Walsingham knew that the execution of one religious radical would not prevent others from stepping forward to take his place. Plotters against Elizabeth need be lucky only once; Walsingham had to be lucky every time.

6 Bonds and Ciphers

Early one morning in October 1583, a lone gunman set out from Warwickshire on a mission to kill the queen. For a man intent on assassination, John Somerville cut a conspicuous figure. He was obviously well born, yet he travelled without any servants to attend him. Then there was the heavy pistol slung at his side, a curious choice of weapon for a gentleman. Anyone meeting him along the way would have been struck by the ferment in his head. Stopped at an inn for the night, Somerville scattered feverish threats to shoot the queen and 'see her head set on a pole, for that she was a serpent and a viper'. His imprisonment in the Tower was swiftly followed by the arrest of his wife, sister and household.

Somerville was questioned on a charge of high treason. Secretary to the council Thomas Wilkes reported to Walsingham on 7 November that 'nothing could be learned except from the confessions' of Somerville and his family, a phrase that implies the threat of torture. English law had traditionally shunned torture, but the rulebook had been rewritten as society had fissured in the wake of the Reformation. Investigating reports in 1575 that Mary, Queen of Scots had been getting messages to the outside world, Walsingham admitted to Burghley that 'without torture I know we shall not prevail'. Queen Elizabeth remained squeamish about it, but the use of torture to extort information had become increasingly common. When the Jesuit William Holt was arrested at Leith in 1583 on suspicion (correctly, as it turned out) of gathering a Catholic alliance to make a holy war on England, Walsingham urged the English envoy in Scotland that he 'should be put to the boots and forced by torture to deliver what he knoweth': in other words, his feet would be crushed until he confessed or fainted. Within days of Somerville's ordeal in the Tower, Walsingham would be writing to Wilkes to authorise the racking of Francis Throckmorton.

Somerville's interrogators hoped that his detention could be used to force other traitors to break cover. Who were his accomplices, they demanded? Who had sown sedition in his mind? What was his connection to Hugh Hall, a Catholic priest who lived at the house of his father-in-law Edward Arden, disguised as a gardener? Given the oppressive political atmosphere, Somerville's conviction was never in much doubt. He was found guilty by a commission of oyer and terminer, a fast-track legal process which avoided the need for a conventional trial. He was dead within two hours of being moved from the Tower to Newgate prison to await the queen's mercy: strangled, it was explained, by his own hand. Arden suffered a traitor's execution at Smithfield the following day. Their severed heads were spiked on London Bridge.

To the historian with hindsight, John Somerville resembles a gnat biting an elephant. He was already under surveillance as a Catholic and known sympathiser with the Queen of Scots. Propagandists on both sides of the religious divide, Lord Burghley and Cardinal Allen, agreed that Somerville was 'furious' or mentally ill. His attempt at regicide was on a wholly different scale from Francis Throckmorton's, with its menacing coalition of Spanish money, French troops and English fifth-columnists.

And yet there were aspects of the 'Somerville plot' which explain why the crown, sensitive to the charge of tyranny, still chose to show him no quarter. The portrait that we can paint of John Somerville is a familiar one. He was young and privileged, due to inherit estates scattered across three counties on his twenty-fourth birthday. He entered Hart Hall, Oxford in 1576; Francis Throckmorton departed the same hall in the same year. Somerville's marriage to Margaret, the daughter of Edward Arden, consolidated the landholdings of their two Catholic families in Warwickshire and Worcestershire. Arden was a respected figure in his community, serving as Sheriff of Warwickshire in 1575. He was a distant cousin of Shakespeare's mother Mary Arden. More to the point – and this may have given Walsingham pause for thought – Edward Arden had married a daughter of Sir Robert Throckmorton.

It may be no more than coincidence that the Somervilles, Ardens and Throckmortons all had estates in Warwickshire and Worcestershire; that Margaret Somerville's mother was a Throckmorton; that John Somerville made his suicidal bid at the very moment that Walsingham was closing in on the Throckmorton plot. Perhaps Somerville and Francis Throckmorton did not cross paths at Hart Hall. But at a frenetic time at Seething Lane, when every day seemed to be turning up new conspiracies and connections, Walsingham and his aides could not afford to take chances. The state papers reveal that the Throckmorton and Somerville plots cohabited on Walsingham's desk. On 5 November the privy council pored over the interrogations of Somerville's family and household, and sent out its commission for his trial; Walsingham ordered the arrest of Throckmorton at Paul's Wharf the same evening. In Walsingham's 'ledger book' or diary, his notes on the Somervilles and Ardens are followed by the memo 'to appoint a new examination of Throckmorton': new, because the queen had now agreed to the use of the rack.[1]

Somerville made a less convincing martyr for the Catholic cause than did Francis Throckmorton, and he was much more quickly forgotten. Even by the standards of Tudor jails, his sudden death was suspicious. A report on Catholic activity dating from February 1584 refers to Somerville as having been hanged in prison 'to avoid a greater evil'. William Camden, whose *Annals* have Somerville 'breathing nothing but blood against the Protestants' and brandishing a sword, had heard some gossip that linked his strangling to the Earl of Leicester. Edward Arden had always made a virtue of his independence from Leicester, refusing to sell him property and dropping hints about his chequered marital history. By the early 1580s it was widely rumoured in Catholic circles that Leicester had murdered his wife Amy Robsart in order to get closer to the queen, concealing the crime as a fatal fall on the stairs. Arden's card was already marked; and when Somerville made his frantic gesture against the Elizabethan regime, both were left naked to their enemies.[2]

Having disposed of the Throckmorton and Somerville plots, Walsingham set about capitalising on them to promote a sense of national unity. The life and death of Francis Throckmorton was taken up by government propaganda and broadcast to the kingdom as a lesson in loyalty. The Renaissance mind searched for patterns in history which could cast light on contemporary events. The litany of conspirators who had failed to harm the queen – Ridolfi, Throckmorton, Somerville – endorsed the official rhetoric that Elizabeth and her loyal subjects were the chosen of God. As new traitors arose and were cut down by divine justice, so their names were absorbed by the books of prayers that carried the cult of Elizabeth into the shires: William Parry, the impenetrable MP who was hanged in 1585 for plotting the queen's murder; Anthony Babington in 1586; and Edward Squire, executed in 1598, a royal stable-hand who allegedly devised a potion to poison the queen's saddle. As late as the 1680s, Henry Foulis's *History of Romish Treasons and Usurpations* was preaching the same stories to a fresh generation of English Protestants.[3]

The plots against Elizabeth prompted another initiative to hold her people in obedience, far more audacious in scale and scope. In October 1584 the privy council bound the kingdom of England together in an association to protect the queen's life. News from the Netherlands was closely monitored by English Protestants, and it had been taking an ugly turn. In July 1584 William of Orange was murdered by a Catholic zealot, the victim of a political culture which increasingly regarded the assassination of rulers as a legitimate tactic. With Orange out of the way, Philip II's military commander the Duke of Parma lost little time in conquering Ghent and Flanders. The cause of true religion seemed to be faltering. What was needed was a new national covenant, to remind her people of the blessings of Queen Elizabeth's rule – and the painful fate of opposing her.

The result was the 'instrument of an association for the preservation of the queen's majesty's royal person', drawn up by Walsingham and Burghley and referred to as the bond of association. It required all subjects 'to the uttermost of their power, at all times, to withstand, pursue and suppress all manner of persons that shall by any means intend and attempt any thing dangerous or hurtful to the honours, estates or person of their sovereign'. Withstand, pursue, suppress: one of those Tudor trinities intended to sear themselves into the memory, as when congregations were instructed to 'read, mark and inwardly digest' the lessons of holy scripture. Those with long memories thought back to 1534, when Henry VIII's subjects had pledged themselves to the king as supreme head of the English Church. The Elizabethan oath imposed sacred duties, publicly sworn on a copy of the gospels: constant vigilance, being prepared to inform on others without regard to friendship or community, and a personal commitment to take up arms to defend the sovereign.

The bond of 1584 was a master-stroke of propaganda. The

majority of English men and women, especially those beyond the circuit of the royal summer progresses, can have had only the dimmest notion of the monarch as flesh and blood. Contact with their queen was limited to a scuffed image on a coin, or the engraving of Elizabeth on the title-page of a Bible. The bond aimed to span this gulf between ruler and ruled, fostering a cult of allegiance to the regime and demanding 'uttermost revenge' on anyone who threatened it. The bond is a fascinating counterpoint to the artistic magnificence of the royal court, where portraits and poetry emphasised the queen's godlike omniscience rather than her human frailty. It was signed in an atmosphere of solemn theatre. In Wigan the backdrop was a church, and volunteers came forward in order of social precedence, hatless and on their knees as if they were taking holy communion. Although the bond was aimed initially at the gentry, thousands of citizens also queued to add their names. In Yorkshire the Earl of Huntingdon collected enough signatures to 'fill a good big trunk'. Those who couldn't sign were allowed to make their mark: illiteracy was no bar to loyalty.

The spontaneity, however, was not quite what it seemed. Walsingham oversaw the operation as it spread out through the English shires, and he knew the bond had more value if it appeared to be a voluntary act of national fealty. In a letter drafted by Burghley, probably for circulation among the lords lieutenant who were the queen's principal representatives in the counties, Walsingham inserted some instructions of his own. 'Your lordship shall not need to take knowledge that you received the copy from me, but rather from some other friend in these parts', he wrote. It was important that the bond was seen to stem from 'the particular care of her well-affected subjects'. It was a sophisticated response to the climacteric of 1584, and it reveals just how skilled Burghley and Walsingham had become in the art of manipulating public opinion. At a spiritual level the bond represented the covenant between Christ and the reformed Church on earth, central to Calvinist theology. For its two drafters, it had the grimmer attraction of fixing its sights on the Queen of Scots. Mary met politics with politics, signing the bond in order to prove that she plotted no secret treasons against the English crown. It suited the persona that she created for herself, loyal to Elizabeth in spite of her wrongful imprisonment. For Walsingham, however, this was a document beyond price: a pledge of allegiance in Mary's own hand which could be quoted against her if she ever broke her oath. He kept it close, waiting and watching.[4]

In 1585 the bond was endorsed by an Act of Parliament 'for the surety of the queen's most royal person'. This sweeping new law justified itself in terms of the 'sundry wicked plots of late devised and laid, as well in foreign parts beyond the seas as also within this realm'. It made a blanket grant to the queen's subjects of the right to pursue to the death anyone engaged in an act of invasion or rebellion against her. In effect it legalised a type of vigilante justice that would have been inconceivable before the early 1580s. Addressing the parliament that passed the Act, Queen Elizabeth took comfort in this expression of her nation's devotion: 'No prince herein, I confess, can be surer tied or faster bound with links of your goodwills'.

The rhetoric of protecting the queen's person concealed some even more radical thinking. Who would govern if Elizabeth met a violent death? Parliament came close to authorising an interim executive formed of the privy council, selected peers and the legal officers of the crown, and recognising its own power to choose a successor. This was not an attempt at a Glorious Revolution a century early – the transfer of sovereignty would only have been temporary – but it still went further than anything that Parliament had attempted to do before. In imagining an emergency republic, Walsingham recalled the classical history he had learned in Cambridge and Padua, while Burghley looked to the more recent experience of Edward VI's reign. Both were familiar with the medieval doctrine of the 'king's two bodies' recently restated by the law reporter Edmund Plowden. His *Reports* of 1571 contrasted the body politic, 'consisting of policy and government, and constituted for the direction of the people, and the management of the public weal', with the body natural, the flesh-and-blood body of the prince that would wither and die like any mortal's. The theory had been developed to explain the royal succession, but it could also have been used to justify the exercise of the crown's authority in the absence of a king. In the event, Elizabeth detected a threat to her prerogative and would not waver from the principle of hereditary monarchy, a personal victory which kept her counsellors guessing until the very moment of her death.[5]

As the waters of the 1584–5 parliamentary session boiled around him, so William Parry, spy and MP for Queenborough in Kent, was forced up for air. Parry's biography is bewildering even by the standards of the shape-changers and quislings who populated the Elizabethan secret service. He began life among the large group of Welsh gentry whose landed income was barely sufficient to maintain their social status. Mounting debts, a commuted death sentence for burglary, and rumours that he was abusing the daughter of the wealthy London widow whom he had married, propelled him to Paris in hope of government service. He was received into the Roman Catholic Church and sank himself into the exile community in France, where he took a doctorate of law and debated the theology of tyrannicide with the Jesuit William Crichton. He was back in England by the summer of 1584, and somehow got himself returned to the House of Commons in November. Within the month he was apologising on his knees for denouncing legislation against seminary priests and Jesuits as full of 'blood, danger, terror, despair'. In February 1585 Parry was accused of discussing Elizabeth's assassination by an accomplice named Edmund Neville, and was tried for treason in Westminster Hall. He confessed, then recanted on grounds that he had been threatened with torture.

Parry posed as a government agent, working to 'prevent and discover all Roman and Spanish practices against our state'. At this distance we simply cannot tell where his true identity lay, whether an agent provocateur in the English seminary in Rheims, or a Catholic traitor engaged in a breathtaking double bluff. Perhaps he no longer knew himself; the multiple personalities that he assumed may have left his loyalties irredeemably confused and compromised. His contemporaries were equally uncertain, although Robert Persons concluded that Parry did plot with his friends to kill the queen. Raphael Holinshed has Walsingham pressing Parry to reveal anything which he might have said, even with the intention of trapping his Catholic targets, which could have brought him under suspicion of treason. Parry seems to have expected a royal pardon. But the advice he scribbled to Elizabeth in his last days in the Tower to 'cherish' the Queen of Scots as her 'undoubted heir in succession' was a bad miscalculation, and shows how out of touch with reality he was.

Like Francis Throckmorton, Parry died a traitor's death. The British Library contains a hand-written 'Report of Parry's Execution', dramatising his dying speech and loading it with advice for his fellow Catholics:

> I am not come hither to preach nor to make you any oration, I am come hither to die. And here I protest unto you all, I am clean of that I am condemned to die for: I did never intend to lay violent hands on her most sacred majesty: whom I beseech God long to preserve from all her enemies, and here I will take it on my death and seal it with my blood.

And you that be of my profession in religion, beware that you never offer to lay violent hands upon her, she is God's anointed: and before I die receive this comfort at my hands.

Those who watched Parry on the scaffold saw him taken down alive and heard him groan as his bowels were cut out. The 'Parry plot' ensured that the Act for the surety of the queen's person passed into law without further objection: a biting irony – or, perhaps, the government's intention all along.[6]

'The cipher I had from Thomas Morgan in France.' Thus Francis Throckmorton described to his interrogators how he had been communicating with Mary Stuart and her English supporters in Paris. William Parry had also consorted with Morgan during his time in France. According to Holinshed's *Chronicles*, Parry confessed to having bragged to Morgan of his resolve to do the Catholic Church some great service, even to kill the greatest subject in England. Morgan's reply was blunt: why not the queen herself? We have glimpsed Morgan before, trailed by rival Walsingham and Stafford surveillance operations in Paris, and we shall soon meet him again as a cog in Anthony Babington's treason of 1586. Morgan it was who recruited the Douai student and double agent Gilbert Gifford to be a courier for the Queen of Scots. Remarkably, he played his part in the Babington plot from within the walls of the Bastille, where he had been shut up at Queen Elizabeth's request following the Parry plot. In France as in England, a prison could be an effective headquarters for an aspiring revolutionary.

Thomas Morgan was the *éminence grise* of the expatriate Catholic resistance during the 1580s. Like Parry he was a Welshman from a minor gentry family, and was forced by dwindling finances to shift for himself. Early in Elizabeth's reign he worked as a scrivener or clerk for William Alley, Bishop of Exeter, and then as secretary to Archbishop Young of York. These were odd connections for a man who later claimed to be born of Catholic parents, since both Alley and Young were paragons of the Protestant establishment. Stranger still, Thomas Morgan's life was the reverse of that of his own brother Rowland, who began his career as a Catholic seminary priest and ended up in the Church of England. For Thomas, the moment of epiphany was his meeting with the Queen of Scots when he joined the Earl of Shrewsbury's household in 1568. His favours to Mary – tip-offs when her rooms were to be searched, help in hiding suspect papers – were sensed by the government at the time of the Ridolfi plot, and Morgan spent much of 1572 in the Tower. On his release, bail set at £10,000 could not prevent him from returning to the Scottish queen's service. In 1575 Morgan was named in connection with Henry Cockyn, a London stationer and bookseller who had been using his shop as a post office for Mary's letters, and Walsingham ordered his arrest once again. But this time he was more agile, and slipped away to Paris. In 1581 Mary began paying him a pension and found him a place in the household of Archbishop Beaton, her ambassador in France.[7]

Beaton put Thomas Morgan to work as a cipher clerk. Queen Mary used her Paris embassy to petition sympathetic powers abroad, and the bulk of this correspondence flowed through Morgan's hands. Given the precariousness of Mary's position in English custody, security of communication was paramount. Letters carried obvious risks. Couriers could be arrested and pressed in the Tower to reveal what they knew. Royal searchers at the south-coast ports knew where to look for papers concealed in imported bales of cloth, or bottles of wine, or the bindings of books. Once intercepted and digested, incriminating documents were often released to their intended destination to encourage plotters to betray themselves. Walsingham's servants included the forger Arthur Gregorye, who could restore the wax seals on letters 'that no man could judge they had been opened'.

Expecting to be searched, agents developed methods of concealing the secrets that they carried. In a treatise dating from the mid-sixteenth-century, the scientist and occultist Giovanni Battista della Porta of Naples explained how a solution of an ounce of alum and a pint of vinegar could be used to write a message on the inside of an egg, invisible until the shell was broken. Alum was a familiar compound to the cloth trade as a mordant or dye-fixer, and quantities were imported to feed the English wool industry. It was available to the imprisoned Queen of Scots, who excitably forwarded a recipe for invisible ink to the French ambassador in London: 'the paper must be dipped in a basin of water, and then held to the fire; the secret writing then appears white, and may easily be read until the paper dries'. We know this because the mole in Castelnau's household passed Mary's letter on to Walsingham, where it remains in his archive. In February 1586 Arthur Gregorye reported to Walsingham 'from my poor house, half blind' on his own investigations into the chemistry of secret writing. Alum, he explained, could indeed be 'discovered' by fire and water, but best of all with coal dust. At the foot of his letter, Gregorye gave his master an exercise to do. 'If your honour rub this powder within the black line,' he wrote, 'the letters will appear white'. Walsingham did as he was bid: four lines of Latin appear palely through a smudge of soot, no longer legible even under ultraviolet light.[8]

Other agents experimented with crushed onions, or citric acid. Walter Williams reported from Rye prison in 1582 on 'the plan of the traitors for conveying intelligence by secret writing with orange juice'. When nothing else was available, they used their own urine. Meanwhile Walsingham's constant battle against ill-health meant the hiring of physicians and druggists, and these could have briefed him on the chemistry of secret writing. One likely candidate is Roderigo Lopez, son of a Portuguese *marrano* or forcibly Christianised Jew, who treated Walsingham's kidney stones in Paris in 1571 and went on to become physician to the queen. Lopez milked his cousins within the *marrano* merchant community for news that he could pass on to Walsingham, although he also gained a reputation as a poisoner. Another source of advice may have been the alchemist John Dee, whom Walsingham called 'my very loving friend' on the basis of their discussions about the Gregorian calendar and the exploration of a north-west passage to China.[9]

The standard formulae for invisible ink were widely known, and offered limited defence against discovery. Secret writing was far more effective if encrypted by code or cipher. Italy led the field, attributable to the precocious diplomacy of its jostling city-states. The Venetian republic had three cipher secretaries in the 1540s, with an office located in the doge's palace and a school to develop their skills. The pope appointed a cipher secretary from 1555, and the duchies of Florence and Milan employed cryptographers of their own. Francis Walsingham's activities in Padua in the 1550s are thinly documented, but his Italian exile could well have offered training in espionage as well as the civil law. Meanwhile Philip of Spain, who married Mary Tudor in 1554, may have introduced sophisticated Spanish ciphers into England. In general, however, the English seem to have lagged behind Italy, France and the Habsburg states in their development of encrypted communication until Walsingham spotted its potential.[10]

Innovation was forced by the arrival of the English Catholic mission in the mid-1570s. If priests and conspirators against the Elizabethan state were communicating by cipher, then those ciphers would have to be broken. Sometimes the Protestant powers of Europe shared intelligence among themselves. In summer 1577 the Prince of Orange informed the English diplomat Daniel Rogers about the plans of Don John of Austria to land a Spanish army in England under cover of taking refuge from a storm. The information had been captured by a Huguenot general and deciphered by Orange's adviser the Baron de St Aldegonde. Rogers forwarded the news to Walsingham, who had co-operated closely with St Aldegonde during the latter's embassy to England in 1576. In March 1578 Walsingham turned to St Aldegonde once again to decode a letter from the Portuguese ambassador. It was revealed to be a lengthy, and all too plausible, complaint that Queen Elizabeth was avoiding an audience by feigning illness. Relying on sympathetic foreign statesmen was not a long-term solution, however, and so Walsingham cast around for an English talent whom he could nurture. He found him in Thomas Phelippes.[11]

We can build up a fuller biography of Phelippes than some of Walsingham's operatives, partly because his higher social rank has left more traces in the records. The son of a London cloth merchant, Phelippes may have studied at Trinity College, Cambridge in the early 1570s while maintaining his father's financial interest in the customs house. He inherited a property in Leadenhall Street and owned others in Chiswick, Holborn and beyond. Phelippes was urban well-to-do rather than landed gentry. The royal court was a natural place for him to seek employment. In class terms he was closer to Christopher Marlowe than to Walsingham's field agents like the ex-soldier Maliverny Catlyn or the gentleman's servant Nicholas Berden. A Thomas Phillips was nominated as burgess for Hastings in the 1584 and 1586 sessions of Parliament, and this may well be the decipherer. Unusually we have contemporary accounts of Phelippes's temperament (Elizabethans would have said 'humour') and appearance. The first, from his father, comments on his 'staid and secret nature'. The second comes from Mary, Queen of Scots, who met Phelippes when he came to stay at Chartley and tried to bribe him. She describes his slight build, his blond hair and beard, his shortsightedness and the smallpox marks that ravaged his face. Perhaps to compensate for his looks, he had taught himself to be a skilled mimic.

Phelippes had a gift for languages, ancient and modern. As with the crossword-solvers of 1940s Bletchley Park, this quickness with words must have been the foundation for his skills in cryptography. In June 1578 Principal Secretary Thomas Wilson wrote to Walsingham enclosing a ciphered letter with the advice that if St Aldegonde could not crack it, he should forward it 'to your servant young Philips, who is with our ambassador at Paris'. The ambassador was Sir Amyas Paulet, whose Puritan outlook and profound suspicion of the Queen of Scots matched Walsingham's own. When Paulet was recalled from the Paris embassy in 1579, Phelippes stayed on with his successor Sir Henry Cobham. In July 1582 he wrote to Walsingham from the university town of Bourges in central France, where he was toiling over an encrypted letter that was something to do with the Jesuits, 'against whose practices the Lord defend us'. The cipher was causing him a lot of trouble: 'these imperfect lines have been worn out of the hard rock. I have had to do, as you know, with many ciphers, but I never lit upon any wherewith I was more cumbered, nor wherein the observations which I serve myself of in these occasions did more fail me.' Phelippes admitted he was proceeding by guesswork, and could only recommend that Walsingham force the messenger to 'tell more plainly what is meant'.[12]

In explaining why he found this commission so challenging, Phelippes provides a clue to his method of working. The Jesuit letter was written in Latin. Of itself this was no obstacle, since Phelippes could read and write Latin fluently. The problem, for him, lay in the original rather than the ciphered version. Whoever wrote the document had a shaky grasp of Latin, and had made so many mistakes that Phelippes was thrown off the scent. Or perhaps the author was more subtle, deliberately misspelling words in order to frustrate an enemy intercepting his letter; this was a common tactic.

What were the 'observations' which normally served Phelippes so well? The answer qualifies him as perhaps the first English cryptanalyst, as distinct from cryptographer: someone with both the mathematical ability and the linguistic dexterity to apply frequency analysis to the decrypting of texts. The technique of counting the occurrence of individual letters or symbols in order to crack a cipher was known to the Arab-speaking world in the tenth century, but it took another five hundred years to percolate into Europe. By the time that Phelippes was working for Walsingham and Thomas Morgan for the Queen of Scots, cryptanalysis was becoming a science of its own, informed by parallel developments in algebra and linguistics. The makers of ciphers learned to change them regularly – Morgan is credited with forty separate alphabets for the Queen of Scots – while old ciphers were archived, and could be sent for if necessary.[13]

Phelippes shared his fascination with the shape of language with another graduate of Trinity College, Cambridge, the physician Timothy Bright. Walsingham had sheltered Bright and other Protestants in the Paris embassy during the carnage of St Bartholomew in 1572, and Bright dedicated his abridged edition of Foxe's *Acts and Monuments* to him. In 1585 a letter from Walsingham helped Bright secure a lucrative post at St Bartholomew's Hospital in London, which gave him the security to pursue his research into alphabets and cryptograms. While neglecting his patients, Bright devised an ingenious system of shorthand writing based on a system of eighteen symbols with a series of hooks, loops and lines to vary their meaning, and a list of over five hundred 'charactericall' words to be memorised. In 1587 he translated sections of *De Furtivis Literarum Notis*, a study of cryptography by Giovanni Battista della Porta, on instructions from Walsingham's assistant secretary of state William Davison. Bright may have served Walsingham as a personal physician, as the Portuguese Jewish intelligencer Roderigo Lopez had done.[14]

At its edges, the study of secret writing shaded into the mystical. Della Porta found his researches being scrutinised by the Inquisition. Some seventy years earlier, the Benedictine abbot Johannes Trithemius had apparently set out a system for communicating across great distances by means of spirit helpers. His *Polygraphia*, published posthumously in 1518, dealt straightforwardly with the subject of cryptology. His earlier *Steganographia*, by contrast, was hotly pursued by philosophers and occultists because it was said to have been delivered by a spirit in a dream. Trithemius had known the original Dr Faustus, and wrote treatises on alchemy and witchcraft. When he tracked down a manuscript of *Steganographia* in Antwerp, John Dee spent a purseful of money and a frenzied ten days in a lodging house transcribing endless tables and bewildering lists of names. For Dee, secret writing meant the realm of angels and demons. His 'skryer' or spirit medium Edward Kelley duly provided him with a fragment of a language taught by God to Adam. What no one realised until Trithemius's code was finally cracked in the 1990s is that the mysterious incantations taught in *Steganographia* are in fact codes and pangrams: wordplay rather than magic.[15]

The final downfall of the Queen of Scots is a tale that turns on the interception and interpretation of encrypted documents. The cipher alphabet which Mary used to correspond with her devotee Anthony Babington looks convincing enough at first sight: a curious assortment of twenty-three symbols, some like Greek letters or Arabic numbers, others reminiscent of musical notation. A further thirty-five stood for prepositions and other frequently used words: letter and bearer, send and receive, majesty, pray. Four 'nulls' or blanks signifying nothing, and another character that cued the reader to double the letter that followed it, made frequency analysis more problematic: the equivalent of an extra rotor on the Enigma machine. Technically this was a nomenclator, a hybrid of a cipher and a code. Who devised it? Not Morgan, presumably, since Mary had been unable to write to him for months. Perhaps one of her secretaries; or it could have been the queen herself. Mary was known to delight in emblems, working subversive iconography into the embroidery that filled the long hours of her inactivity.

As it turned out, Phelippes's ingenuity would barely be tested. Presented with the opportunity of smuggling letters out from house arrest, Mary took the obvious precaution of changing her ciphers, sending an alphabet to the new French ambassador Châteauneuf and her other correspondents. But what seemed like wisdom was in fact a gift to her enemies. Mary's route to her supporters had been provided by Walsingham and Phelippes, who now held the key to her deepest secrets.[16]

When Mary and her attendants had been moved to Chartley in Staffordshire on Christmas Eve 1585, it appeared that her fortunes were improving. Mary herself had requested the move from nearby Tutbury, where she had spent several hateful months under the piercing gaze of her new guardian Sir Amyas Paulet. Tutbury Castle was damp and neglected, its poky rooms empty of furniture and its latrines overwhelmed by the scale of Mary's household. Chartley was a timbered manor house in the grounds of an abandoned castle, surrounded by a broad moat. Perhaps it was this apparent slackening in the bonds of her confinement that encouraged Mary to believe that she could commune with her supporters without being detected. That, or the gnawing fear that her captivity could soon kill her. Either way, she was grievously deceived.[17]

Since her flight to England in May 1568 Mary Stuart had existed in a sort of limbo, in some ways accorded the courtesies of a foreign monarch and in others treated with cold contempt. For fifteen years she journeyed between the country houses of her keeper the Earl of Shrewsbury, trailing a retinue second only to the royal household. Her life was a parody of the royal progresses enjoyed by her cousin Elizabeth. The nearest that she came to normality was at Buxton spa, where Shrewsbury built her a secluded lodge so that she could take the waters, a kindness which provoked caustic comments from his wife Bess of Hardwick that he and Mary were having an affair. When the Earl was recalled to the privy council in London during the nightmare year of 1584, the venerable Sir Ralph Sadler briefly took his place. As Henry VIII's envoy to Scotland, Sadler had balanced the infant Mary on his knee; now he took her hawking by the river at Tutbury. It was this leniency that saw him swiftly replaced by Sir Amyas Paulet.[18]

Paulet was an unflinching jailer. A career administrator who served as Elizabeth's governor in Jersey before his stint at the Paris embassy, he had no patience for Mary's pretensions to royal dignity. Paulet's outlook on politics and religion can be read in his choice of a French Calvinist, Jean Hotman, as tutor to his sons. Hotman's father François was a prominent Huguenot legal theorist, one of a group of academics and lawyers whose theories of resistance to absolute monarchy earned them the description of 'monarchomachs' or king-killers. Like Walsingham, Paulet combined his Calvinism with an understanding of royal power as limited and conditional, although he was also utterly loyal to Elizabeth.

It is difficult to imagine a less sympathetic guardian of the

Queen of Scots. Mary received visitors under a cloth of estate, the sumptuous textile canopy that transformed her chair into a throne and her room into a royal presence chamber; Paulet tore it down. Mary had her own staff to cook her meals and change her linen; Paulet quarantined them and forced them to strip when entering or leaving the house. In September 1585 he informed Mary on Walsingham's orders that her letters could no longer be forwarded via the diplomatic bag of the French embassy, severing her contact with her devotees in Paris and beyond. Four months of this treatment left Mary defeated and brutalised. So when a young Catholic cleric named Gilbert Gifford materialised to tell her he could spirit letters out of Chartley concealed in barrels of beer, Mary swelled with excitement: at last she could regain some control over her life.

It is not difficult to see why Gifford appeared a plausible courier to the Queen of Scots. He had an impeccable Catholic pedigree: a Staffordshire recusant whose family were suffering for their faith, an exile who had studied both in Rheims and in Rome. His boyish looks made it less likely that his real identity would be suspected. Thomas Morgan assured Mary of his good character. When he travelled from Paris to England in December 1585, maybe Gifford really did intend to serve Mary rather than to betray her. On the other hand, we know that Walsingham had been secretly negotiating with his fellow exile and kinsman Dr William Gifford, whose longing to return to England Walsingham was able to play on. When he landed at Rye Gilbert was immediately escorted to Walsingham, implying that his arrival was expected and his arrest staged. If he wasn't already working for the English government, it proved an easy task to turn him. Gifford's letter of commendation from Morgan offered Walsingham the means not simply to monitor Mary's correspondence, but to ensnare the queen herself. What followed was the greatest triumph of Walsingham's career: Mary was caught in the act of rebelling against the Queen of England whom she had so recently sworn to protect from harm.[19]

Mary knew full well that, even when she had been allowed to write and receive letters via the French embassy in London, they had been read by Paulet and Walsingham. The trick was to convince her that some new way had been found to reach the outside world. Her hunger for news was an Achilles heel which Walsingham could exploit. Mary hoped that messages could be hidden in the boxes of shoes and silks that she was still allowed to order, but this proved impractical because everything was minutely examined before being allowed to reach her. The plan that Gifford put to her on 16 January 1586 was both more daring and more simple, taking advantage of a humdrum domestic routine. All great Tudor households consumed large quantities of beer, lighter than its modern equivalent and preferable to drinking unclean water. Chartley carted kegs of beer from nearby Burton rather than brewing its own, and therein lay their chance. Letters in and out could be concealed in a watertight container, slender enough to fit through the bung-hole of the beer barrel, to be passed on by the Burton brewer whose loyalty Gifford had bought. It seemed ingenious, a classic example of hiding a secret in plain view. In reality it was a sting devised by Walsingham and Gifford in collaboration with Thomas Phelippes, who spent the new year of 1586 at Chartley setting up the operation in company with his old master Paulet.[20]

Mary seized her chance. Gifford's arrest had given him the credibility in Catholic circles that he needed to play his part, and she entrusted him with an initial batch of letters to Morgan, Archbishop Beaton and the Duke of Guise. Châteauneuf in return handed Gifford all the mail for Mary that had been backing up at the French embassy since the Throckmorton plot: twenty-one packets of it, which Gifford promptly passed to Phelippes for deciphering before another carrier took it up to

Chartley. Elaborate safeguards prevented this unnamed agent and the Burton brewer from discovering that they were both in government service.

As messages passed and repassed over several months, apparently proving the security of the beer-barrel system, Mary became more candid about her feelings towards the usurper Queen of England. In May 1586 Walsingham discovered that she was deeply embroiled in treason. Her Paris agent Charles Paget had heard from a missionary priest named John Ballard that the time of reconquest was nigh. English Catholics were ready to rise, while Elizabeth's armies were tied up in the Low Countries. Mary strongly endorsed the idea of invasion, hoping to recruit her son James for the cause. She was also in communication with Mendoza, the former Spanish envoy to England who was now ambassador in Paris.

Before Anthony Babington even stepped onto the stage, Walsingham had enough evidence of her plotting to condemn the Queen of Scots. Why did he delay? Not out of any reluctance to strike; removing this 'bosom serpent' from Elizabeth's breast had been his objective since his earliest days in crown service. But Walsingham could see that Ballard was full of bluster, and that his story didn't quite add up. Invasion would come, Walsingham knew that, but he had also heard from his agents in Spain that Philip II wasn't ready to commit his formidable navy against England. In the meantime, listening in to the conversations of the Queen of Scots might bring other traitors to light.

Enter Anthony Babington. The plot that bears his name was the greatest challenge to Elizabeth's rule since the rising of the northern earls, although Babington was not the most radical of the conspirators and was reluctant to assume their leadership. Like the Throckmorton plot it threatened to unite foreign military support with an uprising of English Catholics. Its security was compromised from the start, and more than one of the plotters had connections with Francis Walsingham. It is fair to question how close they came to replacing Elizabeth and her ministers with a Catholic regime under Mary Stuart. That said, there can be no doubt about the importance of the Babington plot. It led directly to the execution of the Queen of Scots, a savage end to the dream that she might one day accede to a united British kingdom. By associating Catholicism with treason, the plot also accelerated the fusion between English national identity and the Protestant faith: a lasting legacy of the age of Elizabeth.

Anthony Babington was not quite twenty-five when he was executed for conspiring against queen and country. His family of Derbyshire gentry had clung onto their Catholicism ever since the days of his great-grandfather Thomas, Lord Darcy, beheaded by Henry VIII for supporting the Pilgrimage of Grace. Babington was well educated, had literary leanings, was highly regarded by his friends – qualities which remind us of Francis Throckmorton. Camden describes him as 'rich, pleasant witted, and learned above his age'. But he was also 'addicted' to the Roman religion, a phrase which already carried the sense of enslavement to a drug. His role in the plot that took his name can be reconstructed from a full series of confessions that he made shortly after his arrest in August 1586. In his later interrogations he was clearly responding to questions put to him, but his first and fullest explanation was volunteered to Sir Christopher Hatton and Lord Burghley at Hatton's London house. Babington seems keen to tell his story in his own words, ruefully at times, but without the fawning appeals for mercy that characterise the outpourings of other traitors against the Tudors.[21]

He began with his 1580 visit to Paris, where Morgan and Beaton recruited him for the Queen of Scots's service. If

Babington already knew Mary from his earlier service as a page in Shrewsbury's household, he made no mention of it. When he returned to London a year or so later, Castelnau's secretary persuaded him to use his contacts to send packets of letters to Mary, 'affirming the service to be very meritorious, full of honour and profit'. It was dangerous work, and Babington was troubled by doubts about what he was doing. He resolved to return to France or Italy and contemplated entering a monastery, but couldn't get a passport to travel. At this point, in about May 1586, the renegade Catholic priest John Ballard made contact with him, telling a tale similar to the one he had peddled to Charles Paget. The pope, the Kings of France and Spain, and the Dukes of Guise and Parma were all preparing for war against English apostasy. Passive support from English Catholics was not enough, said Ballard, since foreign troops 'would enter by right of conquest'. No one would be spared unless they had explicitly declared their support for the invasion. Babington was sceptical, and said so. Little could be done 'so long as her majesty doth live, the state being so well settled'. Ballard replied that this wasn't an obstacle; he had already found a way to deal with Elizabeth.[22]

In the summer of 1585, the English exile John Savage swore a sacred oath to assassinate Elizabeth. Savage had initially found his vocation as a soldier in Parma's army, but then took up residence in the English college in Rheims, where Gilbert Gifford witnessed his oath and Dr William Gifford suggested how it might be fulfilled. Savage could lurk in the gallery of the queen's chapel and stab her. Or he could shoot her in the royal gardens, or run her through when she took the air with the gentlewomen of her privy chamber. Savage duly returned to London, at which point Ballard became the link-man between his plot and Anthony Babington's. Tyrannicide was at the core of the Babington conspiracy from the start.[23]

Horrified and fascinated by the scale of the mission entrusted to him, Babington turned to his friends. The poet Chidiock Tichborne had been with Babington in France and was questioned for bringing 'popish relics' back with him. Thomas Salesbury was even younger than Babington, a gentleman's son from Denbighshire whose Catholic piety had intensified during his studies at Trinity College in Oxford. The state papers describe him as Babington's 'bedfellow', implying shared lodgings rather than anything more intimate. As Babington later explained to his interrogators, 'we seemed to stand in a dilemma': a stark choice between death at the hands of Protestant magistrates, and the invasion and sacking of England by foreigners.

Other young Catholics began to adhere to them as they talked, enticed by the prospect of power or martyrdom and linked to each other by minor court office. Charles Tilney was a gentleman pensioner to the queen, cousin to Master of the Revels Edmund Tilney who regulated the London playhouses. He was a recent convert to Catholicism, John Ballard acting as his confessor. Edward Abington was the son of Elizabeth's under-treasurer, Edward Jones the son of her master of the wardrobe. Jones was recruited by Salesbury, who believed he was of the same bloodline as Henry Tudor; the two of them were deputed to spark an uprising in Wales. Robert Barnewell, described by one of Walsingham's men as tall and pockmarked with a flaxen beard, had attended court in the service of the Irish peer the Earl of Kildare, and knew that the queen was sometimes lightly guarded. His presence added a further British dimension to the Babington plot. Henry Donne was a Londoner, a clerk in one of the revenue offices of the crown and probably a relative of the poet John Donne. The list builds up to fourteen names from various points of the compass: Southampton and Suffolk, Worcestershire and Derbyshire, Wales and the Irish Pale. As if aware of their place in history, they took time to have their portraits painted. Camden claims the canvases were secretly shown to the queen so that she could recognise the plotters if they came to court.[24]

The gravity of what they were attempting weighed heavily on the conspirators. They had to be sure that God would not condemn them for the death of an anointed sovereign. Babington's confession lets us hear them conferring urgently among themselves. Edward Abington would have preferred to kidnap the queen, take her to a safe place and surround her with Catholic councillors. Babington was wracked with doubts of his own, fearing that the realm would be brought into 'misery and wretched estate' and fought over by rival claimants: perhaps a reference to the Wars of the Roses, a time of strife which still haunted the Elizabethan mind. Again he felt the call of the cloister, a yearning to leave 'the practice of all matters of estate'. But always there was the figure of John Ballard, spreading news of the coming invasion, suggesting ways that English naval guns could be sabotaged, and above all hastening Babington into action.

Ballard seems to have been a genuine radical, willing to use any sort of violence to force a Catholic restoration. There is little evidence that he was playing a double game. As Walsingham would point out at Mary's trial, if Ballard had been working for him then why did he not reveal the secret and save his life? The same cannot be said for Robert Poley, 'sweet Robin' to Anthony Babington. The conspirators believed Poley to be a Catholic agent within Walsingham's household. He lived up to expectations by suggesting that Leicester and Burghley and Walsingham could be neutralised 'by poison or violence'. Even as he said so, however, he was working for Walsingham. Using Poley as an intermediary, Babington requested an interview with Walsingham at his country house at Barn Elms in early July 1586. What passed between the two men, plotter and spymaster, quarry and hunter? Babington later confessed to 'having made proffer of service in general terms' in return for licence to travel abroad. Suspecting that he was under surveillance, perhaps he was gambling on turning queen's evidence. Walsingham gave him a courteous reception, but no passport. Babington was far too valuable a property to be allowed to slip away; not because his band of poets, priests and dreamers had any real chance of killing the Queen of England, but because he was corresponding with the Queen of Scots.[25]

As we have seen, the lives of Mary and Babington first intersected in the early 1580s, when Babington forwarded some letters for her. They were reconnected now by Thomas Morgan, who counselled Mary in April 1586 to send a note to Babington declaring the faith that she still placed in him. Crucially, Walsingham did not initially pass on this letter to Mary once it had been deciphered. He only released it when he heard news from Poley in June about Babington's deliberations with Salesbury, Tichborne and Barnewell regarding the lawfulness of tyrannicide. When she received Morgan's message, Mary did as she was bid. She wrote to Babington as his 'assured good friend', exhorting him to locate packets of mail that had been unable to reach her. Paulet passed her letter to Walsingham, who made sure that it reached its destination. For months Babington had been frozen between obedience and revolt, 'indifferent betwixt the two states, and not very sincere unto either', as he put it in his confession. Now, flattered by Mary and urged on by Poley and Ballard, he made his choice and sealed the fates of all who were caught up in the conspiracy.[26]

Babington's ciphered reply to Mary was carried to Chartley by Thomas Phelippes himself. It was a bold pledge of fealty to a queen 'unto whom only I owe all fidelity and obedience'. Elizabeth is unnamed, reduced simply to 'the usurping Competitor'. In lofty language that suggested he was already thinking of himself as a royal councillor, Babington outlined an aggressive plan of campaign. An invasion from Catholic Europe would be assisted by loyal lieutenants appointed in Wales, the West Country and the north. Six noble gentlemen would see to 'the dispatch of the usurper', while Mary's rescue would be undertaken by Babington himself. The religious context is explicit throughout. Elizabeth's excommunication by the pope was also a deposition, freeing Catholic subjects of their allegiance to her. Babington hailed Mary as a sacred ruler miraculously preserved by God, 'the last hope ever to recover the faith of our forefathers, and to redeem our selves from the servitude and bondage which heresy hath imposed upon us with the loss of thousands of souls'. She had only to say the word, and her supporters would swear on the sacrament to risk their lives.[27]

For nine days, Mary considered her response. Few documents of this period have been so intently examined as the reply that she finally sent to Babington on 17 July. Eighteen years under house arrest, and the bitter disappointments of the 1569 uprising and the Throckmorton plot, had left their mark on the Queen of Scots. Although desperate to believe in Babington, she needed to be certain he could make good his claims. How many soldiers and horses could he muster, and what quantities of munitions and armour? Which ports were most suitable for a foreign landing? She pressed Babington with plans for her own liberation, favouring a midnight raid on Chartley to set its stables and barns ablaze, or using overturned carts to barricade the gatehouse while she was carried away on horseback. She urged him to organise a Catholic uprising in Ireland as a diversion, and a parallel action in Scotland to put her son James in her hands. As for Elizabeth, the 'queen that now is', there was no explicit endorsement of regicide; Mary referred simply to the 'time to set the six gentlemen to work'. But what she had written was already enough to condemn her under the 1585 Act for the surety of the queen's person. Phelippes knew it, and drew a gallows on the decrypt that he sent to Walsingham.

Babington was instructed to burn Mary's letter after reading, although he memorised its contents and provided his interrogators with a clear summary. The letter was dictated in French, Mary's first language, to her secretary Claude Nau before being translated into Scots English by his colleague Gilbert Curll; the absence of a manuscript in her own hand would weaken the government's case against her. When the empty barrel was opened and Phelippes got hold of the letter, he used his copy of Mary's cipher to add a postscript requesting Babington to name the six gentlemen who would be dealing with Elizabeth. This was a gamble on Phelippes's part: it might have yielded unknown traitors close to the court, but could equally have blown the whole operation. As events would unfold, Babington would not have the chance to reply.[28]

Although it left the details of Elizabeth's killing to others, Mary's letter clearly gave her blessing to the Babington plot. Babington himself had been coldly specific about what he termed 'that tragical execution', and Mary made no denials. Instead she responded to his rhetoric in kind, identifying her own cause with that of the true religion. Mary echoed Babington's note of urgency that persecution was sapping the life of English Catholics, who would soon 'become altogether unable for ever to arise again and to receive any aid at all'. It was now or never. The letter was delivered to Babington in London by 'a homely serving man in a blue coat', in reality a servant of Thomas Phelippes. With more time, Babington might have taken Mary's advice to recruit a Catholic nobleman as a figurehead (she named the Earls of Arundel and Northumberland as possibles) and the haul of traitors would have been even greater. But Walsingham's decision to arrest Ballard at Poley's lodging house on 4 August sent the plotters into a spasm of activity.

At last Babington took charge. Meeting Savage in Poley's garden, Babington urged him to carry out his oath while he rallied their friends. Killing the queen was their 'last and only refuge'. When Savage protested that he would never get near the court dressed as he was, Babington gave him money and a ring from his finger to buy what he needed. And yet even when he seemed to be drenched in treason, Babington was trying to strike a bargain with Walsingham. On 31 July he had sent word to Walsingham via Poley that he could reveal the details of a conspiracy against the state. When Poley was arrested with Ballard, presumably to preserve his cover, Babington went to a tavern in the company of another of Walsingham's agents named Scudamore. Why was he not already galloping towards Chartley, mobilising the fifth column about which he had boasted to the Queen of Scots? According to his confession, Babington aimed 'to obtain liberty for Ballard under pretence of better service': in other words to play on his relationship with Walsingham for long enough to enable the conspirators either to escape, or to activate their plans for invasion.

Camden explains how drama quickly collapsed into farce. During dinner, Scudamore received a message from the royal court. Suspecting that this was the warrant for his arrest, Babington offered to pay the bill at the bar and then fled, leaving his cloak and sword behind him. He hid out in St John's Wood, cutting his hair and soiling his fair complexion with green walnut shells. But it was not easy for a young Elizabethan gentleman to evade a manhunt on this scale, to merge into the society of the apprentices and groundlings that he previously had despised. After ten days on the run, sleeping in barns and dressed as a farm labourer, he was captured in Harrow. The city of London lit bonfires and rang its church bells as Babington and his fellows were paraded through the streets.[29]

Following a month of interrogations, fourteen plotters were

tried over three days of hearings at Westminster. Savage attempted to plead guilty to conspiracy and stirring up sedition while denying that he had assented to the murder of the queen, but the crown would not allow it. He agreed that he had confessed without fear of torture. Babington made a strong impression on the judges, tracing his pathway to treason 'with a mild countenance, a sober gesture, and a wonderful good grace'. He blamed Ballard for convincing him that the queen was excommunicate, and that it was therefore lawful to murder her. The most interesting exchanges came on the final day, when Edward Abington's plea of not guilty meant that a jury was summoned to hear him mount a vigorous defence. Abington called for writing materials so that he could record the allegations against him, but was denied. He cited the Elizabethan statute which demanded the evidence of two witnesses in treason cases, but was told he was indicted under the law of Edward III. A vehement protest, 'before heaven and earth, as I am a true Christian', that he did not know that Babington intended him to be one of the six gentlemen tasked with murdering the queen was countered with the evidence of a Holborn armourer that Abington was preparing armour for himself and others. The jury had little difficulty in finding him guilty.[30]

Justice followed swiftly. On 20 September seven of the convicted conspirators were taken to a gibbet newly constructed in St Giles Fields, the parish where their plots had been laid. Ballard, the only priest among them, was the first to die. Having been stripped of his clothes, he read from a borrowed copy of the meditations of St Augustine before climbing the ladder to the scaffold. An observer recorded his exchanges with the sheriff and Protestant minister who harangued him during these final minutes. Ballard was urged to confess his treason and pray for forgiveness. 'You would have killed the queen's majesty,' shouted the sheriff to a roar from the crowd, 'you would have sacked

London, and overthrown the state'. When Ballard replied that he trusted to be with the angels within half an hour, the gallows chaplain gleefully pointed out that he clearly didn't believe in purgatory: 'take heed of falling out of the world with a wrong faith, for then you go to the condemned angels'. Ballard ended the disputation by reciting the Lord's prayer and creed in their Latin versions, symbolic of the old faith. The eyewitness confirms that he was cut down alive before being castrated, disembowelled and cut into quarters. His head was put on a stake, the people crying out 'God save the queen'.

Six more men died on this first day. Tichborne, the poet who helped to decipher Mary's letters and fantasised about assassinating the lords of the council in the Star Chamber of Westminster Palace, confessed his guilt and blamed Babington for involving him in the plot. His oratory won the sympathy of the crowd, but it made no difference to his fate. Abington, who had proposed to capture Queen Elizabeth and compel her 'to grant toleration in religion', spat threats that a bloody reckoning was coming to England. Babington, who in happier times might have become a monk, went to his death crying out '*Parce mihi domine Jesus*', 'Spare me Lord Jesus', words adapted from the Book of Job for the medieval mass for the dead. Such an orgy of executions would have left the scene littered with heads and body parts, the hangman and his scaffold awash with blood. Aware that a measure of mercy was welcomed by the crowd, the queen and council directed that the second day's conspirators should hang until they were dead, and only then be cut to pieces. Londoners could soon buy a souvenir verse pamphlet addressed to the dead conspirators:

> Now mayest thou see what fruitless gain, from Antichrist doth spring
> And how to shamefull wretched end, the pope his people bring.

The Babington plot would provide fodder for balladeers and almanac-writers for a generation to come.[31]

It might seem as if Francis Walsingham held all the strings of the Babington plot. Partisan histories have sometimes claimed as much. But this would overstate the degree of his control over people and events. John Ballard did more than anyone to convert latent discontent into violent action, and he had been thinking about regicide since his 1584 pilgrimage to Rome to petition the pope to bless the enterprise. John Savage, the ex-soldier who haunted the English Catholic seminary at Rheims, took his assassin's oath of his own volition. Gilbert Gifford was an unpredictable agent of the crown. Given the task of tracking down Ballard, he chose to slip out of England in disguise a few days before Babington was taken. Walsingham received the news of Gifford's escape with alarm. Although he wrote a letter of apology from Paris, Gifford may have had a shadow of sympathy for the plot against Elizabeth. Certainly he was trading on his own account.

As for the forged postscript, apologists for the Queen of Scots have taken it as proof that the rest of Mary's 17 July letter, even the whole conspiracy, was the fabrication of Walsingham and Phelippes. Following his arrest, Mary's secretary Claude Nau wrote to Elizabeth to deny that his mistress had practised against her life. But he subsequently reaffirmed his initial testimony, that Mary's letter to Babington was genuine. His reward was to be allowed out of confinement to walk in Walsingham's garden. Burghley wrote on Nau's letter that it contained 'things of no importance', and since he and Walsingham effectively controlled Elizabeth's correspondence between them, there is a real chance that the queen never saw it.[32]

Was Mary Stuart betrayed by her own people, as well as ensnared by her enemies? Thomas Morgan has appeared in this narrative as a client of the Queen of Scots, a veteran of the

Throckmorton and Parry plots who was shut up in the Bastille but still true to the woman he had fallen for when she first fled to England. So many trails lead back to him: the cipher secretary who devised secret alphabets for Mary, the gentleman exile who recruited Babington as a courier in Paris, the author of the letter that persuaded Mary to believe in Gilbert Gifford. Morgan had counselled Mary 'to write three or four lines of your own hand' expressing her confidence in Anthony Babington. He knew Babington to be passionate but uncertain, susceptible to flattery: a personal letter had the best chance of persuading him to commit. Then again, to encourage Mary to provide an autograph record of her dealings with Babington, in plain text rather than cipher, was curious advice from the man entrusted with the security of her correspondence. When he travelled to Flanders following his release from the Bastille, Morgan was accused of spying for England and spent a further two years in prison. A rumour did the rounds that he had been seen in conversation with Walsingham's agents in Paris.

Maybe Morgan was loyal to the Catholic cause as he interpreted it. It is possible that he was hunting after some political advantage in the conflicts that were afflicting relations between Welsh and English exiles, seculars and Jesuits. His trust in Gilbert Gifford could perhaps be excused by his prison isolation. One piece of evidence, however, looks more damning. Morgan knew Thomas Phelippes; they had been close friends, or so claimed Gifford, who had himself lodged with Phelippes. Their association presumably dated back to the time when Phelippes was working for Ambassadors Paulet and Cobham in Paris. Phelippes could mimic Morgan 'to the life'; may even have been the source of his knowledge of ciphers. This does not necessarily make Morgan a traitor to the Queen of Scots. Gifford is a tainted witness, his true allegiance – if the concept is even appropriate in such a conflicted world – impossible to determine. But the connection between Morgan and Phelippes shows just how far Walsingham and his agents had penetrated the community of English Catholics in exile.[33]

Questioning Morgan's motives, exposing the treachery of Gilbert Gifford and the radical politics of Ballard and Savage, should not obscure the fact that Mary had also brought ruin upon herself. Elizabeth tried in vain to minimise references to her cousin during the trial of the 1586 conspirators. The prosecution named the Queen of Scots as having 'willingly allowed of these treasons', and charged her with writing letters to Babington that 'did animate, comfort and provoke' him to take action. Mary kept up a pretence of innocence, casting herself as Elizabeth's 'good sister and friend' when summoned to Fotheringhay Castle in Northamptonshire to testify before a royal commission. But she also based her defence on the principle that no monarch could be put on trial: 'I am an absolute prince, and not within the compass of your laws . . . for that I am equal to any prince of Europe'. Six of the forty-odd commissioners seem to have agreed, since they failed to attend the hearing on 14 and 15 October. Lord Burghley, who presided for the crown in the absence of a judge, told her differently: treason had to be answered, whatever the claims of sovereignty and privilege.[34]

The papers of Robert Beale contain a pair of ink-and-pencil drawings of Mary's two final appearances on the public stage, her trial in the great hall at Fotheringhay and her execution in the same chamber four months later. Each drawing has a key identifying the principal players. Burghley had planned the layout of the room with precise attention to detail. Elizabeth's presence was represented by an empty throne under a cloth of estate. Burghley sat close by, facing Mary and surrounded by the peers who lined two sides of the hall. Lawyers in caps and mortar-boards made notes at a central table which had been covered with a cloth. As a commoner, Walsingham sat on a bench that made up the fourth side of the square, facing Elizabeth's throne and accompanied by Paulet, Sir Walter Mildmay and Sir Christopher Hatton. The local gentry crowded at the back.

Walsingham watched in silence as Mary denied any knowledge of Anthony Babington or John Ballard. 'I am clear from all crime against the queen,' she recited. 'I have excited no man against her, and I am not to be charged but by mine own word or writing, which cannot be produced against me.' She called for trial before a free and full Parliament, and made artful legal objections to the procedure of the commission. What precedent could they cite for trying a monarch as a subject? Informed that her own secretaries had spoken against her, she retorted that this was the threat of the rack.

Mary knew that she was guilty. But the crown was also on uncertain ground, and not simply because the most thorough searches of her apartments at Chartley had found nothing incriminating in her own hand. Some of the commissioners were uneasy at placing so much emphasis on the testimony of Curll and Nau. Babington's confession presented another problem. It had to be cited with care, lest its reference to Phelippes's postscript taint the government's case with forgery. Mary had instructed Babington to burn the manuscript of her 17 July letter, so the paper being brandished by Burghley as evidence of her deceit must be a copy. And so it was: Burghley had acquired a facsimile of Mary's original letter, re-enciphered by Thomas Phelippes, to substitute for the original that Babington had destroyed. Denied legal representation and hemmed in on all sides, Mary realised that the evidence which the crown was placing before the commissioners was not what it appeared to be. But she could hardly play on this without admitting she had lied about knowing Babington.[35]

So Mary threw down a fresh challenge to her accusers.

Turning her gaze from Burghley to Walsingham at the other end of the hall, Mary spoke to the man whom she now knew had entrapped her. Counterfeiting ciphers was an easy matter, she said. Could Walsingham claim to be an honest man in his dealings with her? The principal secretary rose to his feet and stepped forward to the lawyers' table so that his words could be heard. 'Madam,' he said, using the coldly respectful form of address that Burghley had also adopted,

> I call God to record that as a private person I have done nothing unbeseeming an honest man; nor as I bear the place of a public person, have I done any thing unworthy of my place. I confess, that being very careful for the safety of the queen and realm, I have curiously searched out the practices against the same. If Ballard had offered me his help I should not have refused it; yea, I would have recompensed the pains he had taken. If I have practised any thing with him, why did he not utter it to save his life?

There is something cinematic about this scene, the first and last in which these greatest of enemies inhabited the same space. The encounter had wrung from Walsingham a recitation of his political creed, poised but also candid. Recent biographers of Burghley and Mary have called his words 'fabulously elusive', an answer worthy of Machiavelli. Is this the best reading? 'Curious' in Elizabethan times meant attentive, while 'practice' equates to deception or conspiracy. Walsingham justified his actions on grounds of state security. But he also felt himself vindicated in the sight of God. Machiavelli, the Florentine politician whose name was already a byword for chicanery by Walsingham's day, had a very different philosophy. He based his analysis of human history on a classical concept, *fortuna*, rather than the divine providence in which Walsingham so clearly believed. Walsingham's attitude is revealed even more clearly in the letter that he wrote to Leicester the following day: 'I see this wicked creature ordained of God to punish us for our sins and unthankfulness'. Walsingham saw Mary Stuart as a scourge, just as the Protestants of Mary Tudor's reign had interpreted their exodus as part of God's deeper plan for repentance and reformation. His service to God, as much as his allegiance to Elizabeth, demanded the death of the Queen of Scots.[36]

The obstacle was Elizabeth herself. As Walsingham explained to Leicester, a 'secret countermand' from the queen had interrupted the commissioners before they could come to judgement. Her strategy of delays was all too familiar. Elizabeth's objections to the trial had already sparked an exasperated outburst from Walsingham to Burghley: 'I would to God her majesty would be content to refer these things to them that can best judge of them as other princes do'. Now everything rested on whether she would sign a death warrant.

The intelligence operation against Mary had been Walsingham's alone. It is doubtful whether Burghley even knew about the trap before it sprang, although he subsequently took charge of the interrogations and the trial. But the two ministers had to work closely to persuade the queen to accept the consequences of the Babington plot. On 25 October the commissioners reassembled in the Star Chamber at Westminster. This was the same room where the lords of the council would have been gunned down if Chidiock Tichborne's plan had come to pass. Now they finally condemned Mary to death. A joint committee of both houses of Parliament, whipped by Burghley in the Lords and Hatton in the Commons, argued for a speedy execution. But Elizabeth havered, directing them towards 'some better remedy, whereby both the Queen of Scots' life might be spared, and her own security provided for'. Sentence was proclaimed in London 'in the most solemn manner that could be devised', to the sound of trumpets and in the presence of the mayor and aldermen in gowns of scarlet and chains of gold. Elizabeth responded by receiving embassies from France and Scotland to plead for Mary's life.[37]

Ill and exhausted, Walsingham retreated from the court to his house at Barn Elms. The signet and great seal, tools and symbols of his power, were left in the custody of the new junior secretary, William Davison. Walsingham's spirit had been sapped by news of the death of his son-in-law Philip Sidney in the Netherlands in October. His passing left Walsingham honouring £6,000 of Sidney family debts, and yet his request to the queen for assistance was rebuffed. As a spymaster this was the summit of his career, but it had brought him no material benefit and had actually distanced him from the queen's favour. Walsingham slid into weeks of sickness that were part physical and part psychological, a 'dangerous disease' brought on by what he called 'the grief of my mind'. Echoing Elizabeth's own metaphor of monarchy as theatre, he observed to Burghley that the happiest men in government were 'rather lookers-on than actors'. But life in the country offered little comfort. Walsingham could not rid himself of the dread that his mistress was in greater danger than ever.

His fears for the future are detailed in a document that Walsingham wrote before leaving London, a lengthy memorandum on the 'dangerous alteration likely to ensue both in England and Scotland' if Mary's execution should be delayed any longer. Her survival would increase both the numbers of English Catholics and their resolve to rebel: 'her friends will rather attempt some desperate remedy than to suffer her to perish without attempting anything'. Scotland presented the awful possibility that the impressionable James VI might be persuaded to renounce his Protestantism and strike against England, to liberate his mother and to pursue his own title to the English throne. As so often with Walsingham, the pan-British dimension of his thinking is striking.[38]

Elizabeth finally decided to sign Mary's death warrant on

1 February 1587, more than three months since the commissioners had come to a verdict. Recalling for a moment her father's cruel sense of humour, she quipped that the news would be a cordial to restore her principal secretary to health. Walsingham was back in London but still too weak to attend court. William Davison had to take responsibility for the warrant, and suffer the consequences of the queen's fury when she discovered that it had been despatched without her express permission. What merit Elizabeth saw in further delay it is difficult to say; perhaps she simply changed her mind. But the councillors of the monarchical republic had been one step ahead of her. For a few extraordinary days Burghley, Walsingham, Davison and Hatton effectively seized the initiative in government. Burghley quietly secured the support of the rest of the council, guarding the warrant and preparing for the mass detention of Catholic recusants. Beale was woken in the night and ordered to report to Seething Lane, where Walsingham told him that he would be carrying the fatal document to Fotheringhay. Walsingham also took charge of the executioner, who travelled in the clothes of a serving man with his axe in a trunk.

Elizabeth's reluctance to agree to Mary's execution is the stuff of legend. Towers of interpretation have been built upon it. For some it exposes the crippling indecisiveness of the queen. Others identify her behaviour as deliberate, consistent with her strategy of keeping her male ministers on the back foot, expressive of the kinship that one female ruler felt for another. To allow that the law had the power to discipline an anointed sovereign was a radical reversal in the theory of monarchy, and Elizabeth was justly nervous about where it might lead.

But Walsingham's correspondence reveals a darker facet of the queen's character, the politician who spotted the advantage of a quiet backstairs killing over a public execution. On 1 February, the same day that she sent Mary's death warrant to be sealed, Elizabeth directed her two principal secretaries to write to Sir Amyas Paulet expressing her disappointment that no one had acted under the bond of association to rid her of the Queen of Scots. In open court Elizabeth would weep for Mary, mourning the death of a sister monarch, but the raw truth was that she tried to arrange for her murder. Paulet was horrified and refused to make 'so foul a shipwreck of my conscience', although self-preservation must have also played its part: few would have been willing to leave themselves so politically exposed. He was saved by the arrival of Beale bearing the warrant, unknown to Elizabeth. The irony was that Walsingham, who had done so much behind the scenes to advance Mary Stuart towards her death, should guarantee her the relative dignity of a public execution.[39]

Mary was beheaded in the great hall at Fotheringhay on 8 February 1587. The second of the pair of drawings in Beale's papers traces the sequence of events. Mary appears three times: entering the chamber dressed as if for a festival, in gown and trailing linen veil and carrying a rosary; on a dais in the centre of the room, her missal and crucifix set down on a table and a man in breeches awkwardly holding her top dress; and kneeling at last for the half-naked axeman. Like all the great officers of state, Walsingham stayed away. The execution was left to the Sheriff of Northamptonshire and the Earls of Shrewsbury and Kent. A small crowd looks on from behind a line of soldiers armed with halberds. The Dean of Peterborough is speaking, although in reality Mary rejected the sermon that he had prepared and knelt with her servants to recite the Latin office of the Blessed Virgin Mary. A fire burns in the grate, where a man with a sword rests on one leg. It is a familiar image, but an upsetting one – its violence implied, about to happen: an axe poised, cartoon faces watching and talking, a few looking the other way as if distracted or bored with what they were seeing.

There is no triumphant depiction of Mary lying dead, but it captures the pose of the onlookers with a chilling intimacy.[40]

Francis Walsingham had coaxed the brags and dreams of a group of friends into a plot against the Protestant state. He offered Mary Stuart an apparently secure route to those who wanted to see her on the English throne, and calibrated the moment that her letter to Anthony Babington would have the greatest impact. The ethics of the episode are hard to judge. Walsingham had tempted Mary into an act of rebellion, but in truth she had already shown herself willing to depose her cousin Elizabeth. The criminal justice system of today would attempt to balance the degree of entrapment against the scale of the offence that it revealed. The shape of the Babington plot owed a lot to Walsingham and his agents, but its origins lay in the exile communities in Paris and Rheims. Mary can hardly be blamed for desiring her own freedom: she had come to England seeking sanctuary and had found an endless imprisonment. But Elizabeth could never have recognised Mary as her heir, for fear of sparking a Protestant revolution of the sort that had deposed Mary from the throne of Scotland. The result was that Mary Stuart signed the bond of association with one hand, and gave her benediction to a company of assassins with the other.

Babington's letter to Mary described the impending execution of Elizabeth as a tragedy, and it was in similar terms that the conspirators' own downfall was perceived. Sir Christopher Hatton made a memorable interjection during the arraignment of the principal plotters: 'O Ballard, Ballard, what has thou done? A sort of brave youths otherwise endued with good gifts, by thy inducement hast thou brought to their utter destruction and confusion'. Contemporary accounts of the Babington plot take on the tone of an Elizabethan morality play, a tale of talent tragically brought low by pride. The prosecution took care to remind the trial how Ballard was dressed when he came on his mission to England, not in the humble clothes of a man of God but the gorgeous apparel of a gentleman soldier: 'a grey cloak laid on with gold lace, in velvet hose, a cut satin doublet, a fair hat of the newest fashion, the band being set with silver buttons; a man and a boy after him, and his name Captain Fortescue'. Hatton ended by denouncing Ballard and other such Catholic priests who preyed on young Englishmen of 'high hearts and ambitious minds', carrying them 'headlong to all wickedness'.[41]

It served the interests of the crown to sensationalise stories of treason and plot. And yet the perpetrators seem to have shared the sense of theatre. Chidiock Tichborne delivered a remarkable oration about his friendship with Babington before he was given over to the executioners. 'Of whom went report in the Strand, Fleet-street, and elsewhere about London, but of Babington and Tichborne? Thus we lived, and wanted nothing we could wish for: and God knows, what less in my head than matters of State?' Tichborne framed his address as a warning to other young gentlemen, asking forgiveness of the queen and for some provision for his wife, sisters and servants. But his final prayer was for himself, 'that he hoped steadfastly, now at this last hour, his faith would not fail'. By acting out a role, he and his companions steeled themselves for the torment to come. Tichborne also sought solace in poetry, penning a wrenching elegy in his last days in the Tower:

I sought my death and found it in my womb,
I looked for life and saw it was a shade;
I trod the earth and knew it was my tomb,
And now I die, and now I was but made.
My glass is full, and now my glass is run,
And now I live, and now my life is done.[42]

Anthony Babington died for his vision of an English nation that was still viscerally Catholic. The north he assumed would rally to his cause, because Catholicism was still the religion of the common people, but also to revenge the harm that the region had suffered in the wake of the 1569 rebellion. Wales he judged to have the same complexion, and the West Country might also be sympathetic. Working inwards from 'the very extremities of the kingdom', supported by foreign troops and placing Catholic magistrates to govern the counties that he had already taken, Babington reckoned to squeeze the south parts of the realm into submission.

In much of this he was plainly deluded. The majority of Elizabethan Catholics wanted nothing more than to be recognised as loyal to the queen. Babington's plan for invasion was not welcomed by Abington, who told him 'I had rather be drawn to Tyburn by the heels for my religion than to have it reformed by strangers'. The papacy was less concerned for the plight of England than Babington believed it to be. As for the extremities of the kingdom, Walsingham had received assurances from the Earl of Huntingdon, president of the council of the north, that 'in no part of England is Queen Elizabeth more reverenced than she is here'. Two of Babington's predictions, however, were more alarming to his interrogators. The first was that the English people, labouring under a weight of unjust rents and taxes and the enclosure of the commons, would one day be ready to cut the throats of their landlords. The second was that, although his own conspiracy had failed, it would be followed by others; and next time, the plotters would know how to keep their secrets.[43]

7 Western Planting

In 1577 the scholar and astrologer Dr John Dee published a book announcing that it was time for the British to take command of the oceans. *General and Rare Memorials pertayning to the Perfect Arte of Navigation* was dedicated to Sir Christopher Hatton, a fast-rising royal favourite who enjoyed privileged access to the queen as vice-chamberlain of her household. Dee described the *Memorials* as a 'plat': literally a design for a building, but by implication also a plan of action, to construct or to reform. In this instance, it was the architecture of empire which the author had in mind.

Dee's argument was superficially simple. Piracy was a growing problem around the British Isles, shrinking the profits of trade and sullying the dignity of the crown. Foreign fishermen had taken to poaching in English waters. His solution was for the queen to create a 'petty navy royal', a fleet of eighty frigates built on sleeker lines than the heavy warships anchored at Portsmouth and Deptford. Elizabeth's little navy would be capable of outrunning the pirates, allowing merchants to ply their trade without fear. Securing the food supply would reduce the danger of any 'homish disorder' and make for a quieter commonwealth. The queen's enemies would be discouraged from invasion, while her subjects would be schooled in the art of navigation: the mathematics of sightings and soundings, how the tides ebbed and flowed.

Dee was troubled about national security, but he also had a more ambitious agenda to press upon the queen. The *Memorials* advertised a companion volume to follow it, which promised to set out the 'entitling of Queen Elizabeth to very large foreign dominions' on the grounds they had once belonged to her ancestor King Arthur. Books of navigational tables would supply the necessary proof, building up into a series under the collective title of *The Brytish Monarchy*. For Elizabeth to restore the ancient British empire was not simply expedient in Dee's eyes; it was her sacred duty. Once the overseas territories rightfully belonging to the monarchy had been 'recovered and used', many secret and wonderful things would be revealed by the power of God.

The *Memorials* was a carefully targeted piece of propaganda. A hundred copies at most were printed, implying that the argument was aimed at the courtly elite rather than the wider reading public. An elaborate title-page reinforced the case which Dee was making. Classical and Christian emblems are jumbled together in an allegorical landscape. An outsize Queen Elizabeth steers the ship of state towards the coast, watched over by St Michael and the Hebrew Tetragrammaton standing for the power of God in Protestant iconography. The rudder is emblazoned with the royal arms, which appear again with Tudor roses at the top of the page. The chi-rho (**XP**) monogram of Christ tops both the masts, while three councillors – Hatton, Walsingham and Burghley perhaps – stand on deck. A border in Greek sums up the image as a 'hieroglyph of Britain'.

Having crafted a deliberately complex image, Dee offered some guidance on how to interpret it. The woman kneeling on the shore represented *Respublica Brytanica*, 'earnestly soliciting the most excellent Royal Majesty, of our ELIZABETH, sitting at the helm of this Imperial Monarchy'. The Latin *respublica* meant different things during the Renaissance, but given the praise which Dee lavished on the majesty of monarchy an appropriate translation would be 'state' rather than 'republic'. The ship in the estuary flies an English ensign and is guarding against the marauding vessels to the left, one of the duties which

Dee expected of his petty navy royal. The walled town bottom right also has a homely look to it, with its churches and pitched roofs and defensive bastions. Perhaps this is meant to be England, basking in the protection of God and the queen.

But this isn't the only possible reading. Like her cousin the Queen of Scots, Elizabeth was fascinated by emblems and symbols. Dee knew that she would look for hidden meanings to decode. Perched above the city on a hill is the goddess of opportunity, holding a laurel wreath in the direction of the queen. Dee completed the *Memorials* in the summer of 1576, coinciding with the return of the privateer Martin Frobisher from his first voyage to Canada to locate the fabled north-west passage to China. Frobisher hadn't discovered what he set out to find, but he did manage to reconnoitre a previously unknown shore, and he had the evidence in the form of an Inuit man captured complete with his kayak off Baffin Island. The rumour soon spread that Frobisher had also stumbled across something far more lucrative, a lump of blackish ore which bore clear traces of gold. Both souvenirs caused a sensation in London. In this context, Dee's emblems of fertility and plenty – the two gentlemen exchanging a bag full of money, the forests, the ear of corn – allude to an altogether grander project than the construction of a new national coastguard. His vision of Elizabeth as the pilot of a ship, with the figure of Europa swimming beside her on a bull, was an invitation to the old world to capitalise on the new.[1]

Dee was not alone in presenting imperial images to the queen. When Elizabeth revived her love interest in the Duke of Alençon, court painters used their art to steer her away from a French alliance. George Gower's 'sieve' portrait of 1579* features a terrestrial globe behind Elizabeth's right shoulder, clearly

* See p. 123.

intended to chime with the classical symbol of chastity in her left hand. Another version was painted in about 1583 by Quentin Metsys the younger. Gower left his globe as a blank space, but Metsys mapped his out in detail: the British Isles glowing in the sun, with open seas to westward and ships under full canvas. Beyond Metsys's globe is the figure of Christopher Hatton, full of swagger in his role as captain of the queen's ceremonial guard. Unlike everyone else in the painting, Hatton looks the viewer boldly in the eye. John Dee's diary records a meeting with Hatton on 1 December 1577, when the vice-chamberlain received his knighthood from the queen. Francis Walsingham was knighted during the same ceremony.[2]

The sieve portraits and Dee's *Memorials* combined a hymn to the Virgin Queen with an appeal to found a new England overseas. Walsingham became a fulcrum for the various adventurers and ideologues who were competing to get noticed at court. Years before he entered the service of Cecil and Elizabeth, he and his family had been involved in promoting English trade and influence beyond the boundaries of Europe. Walsingham's earliest known connection as a private investor was with the Muscovy Company, which his first wife's father had helped to establish in Queen Mary's reign. Russian furs and the products of the White Sea whaling trade were exchanged for English wool and cloth. As principal secretary he was paid partly in licences to export the unfinished cloth which foreign merchants valued so highly. He also took a keen interest in the opportunities opening up to the east. The Ottoman Empire based at Constantinople was denounced by preachers as the scourge of Christian civilisation, but it was also the greatest enemy of Spain in the Mediterranean. Walsingham supported the efforts of the Levant Company to court the sultan's favour on political as well as economic grounds.[3]

Elizabethan traders pushing eastwards found that other

nations – Venetians, French and Portuguese – had got there long before them. In the new world to the west, the situation was very different. The American mainland north of Florida had scarcely been touched by European settlement. As Elizabeth's secretary and one of her closest advisers, Walsingham was ideally placed to coax the queen towards a policy of westward exploration and colonisation. John Dee, who coined the term 'British Empire', and Richard Hakluyt, the Church of England clergyman whose writings did so much to launch it, both wanted him for a patron. And as Hakluyt pointed out, England's ambitions in America were bound up with another one of Walsingham's responsibilities, the pursuit of a stable administration in Ireland. Trade between Ireland and the new-found lands could only have an improving effect on the unruly Irish people.

Walsingham was instrumental in translating the crown's policy of plantation from the provinces of Ulster and Munster to the land which the English called Virginia in honour of their queen. He was personally involved through his cousin Edward Denny, who was a soldier and then a planter in Ireland, as well as his stepson Christopher Carleill, who commanded the English garrisons at Coleraine and Carrickfergus and harried the Spanish West Indies in the company of Francis Drake. There were many more ties between Elizabethan Ireland and the Americas. When Hakluyt and other observers wrote about 'reducing' Ireland and America to a state of civilised government, they used the verb in its Latinate sense of *reducere*, to lead back or restore rather than destroy by conquest. But as the English diaspora became progressively bloody, the word gathered a bleaker set of connotations: 'to reduce' became to lay waste and to plant society afresh.[4]

When Thomas Lake drew up a catalogue of the state papers in Walsingham's possession in 1588, the index to the Irish material alone ran to twenty manuscript pages. Instructions sent to the Lord Presidents of Munster and Connaught fought for space with treatises on taxation and the founding of a university in Dublin. A 'box of Ireland' in Walsingham's study at Seething Lane contained 'a bundle of plots and devices for the reformation of Ireland' and papers relating to the first Earl of Essex's plantation schemes in Ulster. A note in a different hand refers to the lending of a book of plots and discourses to Sir Robert Cecil in 1596, revealing that the Walsingham archive continued to inform the government of Ireland years after his death. When King James I was shown the 'infinity of books and packets' in the State Paper Office in 1619, he drily remarked that 'we had more ado with Ireland than with all the world beside'.[5]

The order which Lake brought to Walsingham's papers was disrupted long ago. But at least one of the Irish documents which he describes can still be traced. The manuscript that Lake calls 'Mr Edmund Tremaines discourse of Ireland' survives in the Huntington Library on the outskirts of Los Angeles, part of the Ellesmere collection of English government papers acquired by the railroad magnate and philanthropist Henry E. Huntington. Edmund Tremayne went to Ireland in the late 1560s as secretary to Lord Deputy Sir Henry Sidney, before returning home to the clerkship of the English privy council. His 'Discourse' addressed a critical dilemma for Elizabeth's advisers: whether she should be counselled 'to govern Ireland after the Irish manner as it hath been accustomed, or to reduce it as near as maybe to the English government'. Tremayne completed his report in December 1573, apparently at the request of Sir Walter Mildmay. This was the same month that Walsingham was sworn principal secretary. The 'Discourse' was almost certainly among the documents being debated during six days of meetings on the Irish question in early January 1574, giving Walsingham his first taste of what it meant to govern on behalf of the queen.

For Tremayne, the rule exercised by a typical Gaelic Irish lord was nothing short of tyranny:

> he useth the inferior people at his will and pleasure. He eateth and spendeth upon them with man, horse and dog. He useth man, wife and children according to his own list, without any means to be withstanded or gainsaid. Not only as an absolute king, but as a tyrant or a lord over bondmen.

The Irish tradition of brehon law (from the Gaelic *breitheamh*, a hereditary judge) seemed to allow a lord to pardon or to punish as he saw fit. Disputes were settled by acts of vengeance instead of the queen's justice. The situation was little better in the nominally English areas of Ireland. Nobles claiming to be of 'the English race' still behaved as absolute rulers of their own countries, maintained in power by gangs of idle soldiers. Tremayne was swift to point out the implications for royal authority. Not only the revenues owed to the crown, but the very hearts of the people – 'which should be in deed the very fortress of a prince' – were being forfeit. In short, 'the Irish rule is such a government as the mightiest do what they list against the inferiors'.

By referring to bondmen and bands of armed retainers, Tremayne was deliberately evoking the world of medieval lawlessness and violence which the Tudors prided themselves on having banished from England. He aimed his appeal at councillors, Walsingham and Mildmay, whose duty was to persuade the queen 'to reduce that realm to a better government'. Religious and legal reforms were urgently required. But even Tremayne had to admit that these would not be enough; the body of Ireland was too diseased. Only a third kind of medicine – her majesty's army – could render the other two effective.[6]

How had Ireland come to be in this state? The history of England's attempts to rule, to settle and to understand its western neighbour was already very old when Elizabeth came to the throne. Anglo-Norman adventurers, the so-called Old English, had colonised large parts of the east and south in the twelfth and thirteenth centuries, with much smaller coastal enclaves established in Galway and Ulster. By 1300 something like two-thirds of Ireland was under the nominal control of the English crown. But the Black Death of 1348–9 cut a swathe through the market towns built by the incomers, and plague was followed by political fragmentation in England. By the time that Henry VIII assumed his new title of King of Ireland in 1541, the 'Englishry' had shrunk to less than half the island. Even here, the Old English had adopted a hybrid identity, passing estates to their eldest sons on the model of the English peerage, but offering hospitality to Gaelic poets and judging their tenants' grievances according to brehon law. New English commentators like Edmund Tremayne criticised their Irish dress and their horses without saddles, and mocked their Chaucerian patterns of speech. Gaelic culture seemed everywhere to be encroaching. Villages in productive farmland had been abandoned by farmers of English blood. Fields which historically had been ploughed for arable lay desolate. A landscape which had once been recognisable was reverting to Irish forest and scrub, a metaphor of cultural degeneracy.

Reformers in Dublin and Westminster hoped that raising Ireland from a lordship to the status of a kingdom would turn the Gaelic tide. Tremayne described Elizabeth as 'the natural liege sovereign' of both Ireland and England, and argued for their equal treatment – so long as Ireland conformed to English standards of civility. The instructions which Walsingham sent in the queen's name to her administrators and clergy referred to 'our realms of England and Ireland', as if parity existed between them. Ireland had a parallel jurisdiction of Parliament and privy council, lord chancellor and a reformed state Church. Efforts were made to refashion the native nobility on an English model. Successive lord deputies from the 1540s onwards persuaded leading Gaelic families to surrender their lands to the crown in order to have them re-granted as English-style peerages, with access to the royal court and a seat in the Irish House of Lords. Deals were sealed with the spoils of dissolved monasteries.[7]

For a few years, it seemed that this might be the answer. In June 1576 Francis Agarde, an English soldier and official who had based himself in Ireland since Edward VI's reign, wrote to Walsingham setting out his hopes for the future. The O'Donnells and O'Kellys had agreed to pay sterling rents into the Irish exchequer and to become loyal liegemen of the queen. Other Gaelic lords might soon follow their lead. In all his years of service, 'the likelihood of obedience (amongst the very Irish I mean) hath not been more'. Agarde was New rather than Old English, but his argument was not so different from the petitions sent to Westminster by earlier generations of would-be reformers. If the crown would only commit more resources to Ireland – Agarde's own plea was for the appointment of 'upright ministers' to bring proper English justice to the planted provinces – then peace was within its grasp. But surrender and re-grant had a fatal flaw. Gaelic society could not permanently be restructured on a feudal footing for the simple reason that land, in Irish law, belonged to the sept or clan and not the lord. The differences between English and Irish definitions of landownership would be spectacularly laid bare in 1595 when Hugh O'Neill, up till then a powerful ally of the crown in Ulster, cast off his title of Earl of Tyrone and was hailed as the O'Neill at the stone chair of Tullaghoge.

Agarde's optimism couldn't hide the truth of a deepening political and sectarian crisis in Ireland. Another of Walsingham's correspondents, William Gerard, hoped that his long experience of bringing common-law justice to the Welsh marches would transfer to his new posting as Lord Chancellor of Ireland in 1576. But he was dismayed to find that the Irish courts of King's Bench and Common Pleas were mere 'shows and shadows' of their English equivalents. When Gerard tried to hold the assizes at Trim in County Meath, he was faced with a courthouse resembling 'an English pinfold for cattle' and officers of the crown dressed worse than the peasantry back home. The town of Trim lay well within the ditch and stockade of the Pale; the country beyond it was even more unfathomable. Francis Agarde referred to the Gaelic territories as 'those foreign parts'. Agriculture in Gaelic Ireland was based on cattle rather than crops, a dramatic contrast with the ordered ploughlands of lowland England. The custom of transhumance, the people following their animals to their summer upland pastures, meant that settlements appeared temporary and insubstantial to English eyes. Dwellings were built of mud, turf and timber rather than stone. The native Irish came to be seen as slothful and shiftless, uninterested in cultivating the land which they occupied. English writers were fascinated by the Irish diet, its butter mixed with cow's blood and offal cooked on open fires.[8]

The belief that the Irish were under-using their land became an excuse for annexation. In a book of verse illustrated by detailed engravings, John Derricke contrasted the 'royal soil and fertile Irish ground' with the wildness of the 'woodkerne' or peasant soldiers who inhabited it. His 1581 *Image of Ireland* painted Gaelic culture as lost in rebellion, its natives drunk on whiskey and inflamed by the preaching of Catholic friars and bardic poets. Lodowick Bryskett, a clerk of the Irish privy council who sent Walsingham a series of reports in the early 1580s, was moved by what he called 'the universal disposition of this people to disobedience' to come to a damning conclusion about Ireland:

> the state whereof me thinketh I may well compare unto an old clock or garment often times mended and patched up, wherein now so great a rend or gash being made by violence, there is now no remedy but to make a new; for to piece the old again will be but labour lost.[9]

The attempt to govern, to reform and finally to conquer Ireland in Elizabeth's name generated a huge volume of paper. Walsingham and Burghley largely shared the work, either of them taking the lead according to circumstance. Burghley's position as lord treasurer meant he had more patronage to offer, and his personal relationship with Elizabeth was unrivalled. But Walsingham's control of royal correspondence could give him the edge. His chief clients in Ireland – the soldier turned administrator Sir Nicholas Malby, vice-treasurer Sir Henry Wallop, Sir Edward Waterhouse – bombarded him with reports and advice and requests for money. Maps of Ireland and its English plantations covered his desk and the walls of his study at Seething Lane. If the Elizabethan regime ultimately succeeded in extending its control over the whole of Ireland, then Walsingham could be credited with making progress where generations of English officials had foundered. But if Ireland had been pacified only through indiscriminate bloodshed, if victory came at the cost of ethnic and religious divisions which were more entrenched than ever, then Walsingham must also take his burden of the blame.

For a queen obsessed with her own sovereignty, the stunted royal establishment in Ireland was an acute embarrassment. Elizabeth was conflicted in her attitude towards her second kingdom. Sometimes she chose to protect the interests of her Irish subjects, instructing the Earl of Essex to ensure that local people bordering his Ulster plantation were 'well used'. But other voices were also competing for her attention. Her captains in the field clamoured for the all-out war which would make a reality of her rule, and win them estates and glory in the process. Knowing how the queen mourned the failure of her sister Mary to defend English ground in France, royal commanders skilfully exploited her fear that Ireland too might be lost. Lord Deputy Sidney explicitly compared the situation in Ireland to that of Calais. In 1579 the incoming Lord Justice of Ireland, Sir William Pelham, warned Walsingham that 'her majesty may say she *had* a country' unless a remedy could be swiftly applied.[10]

His mandate to protect the queen's safety required Walsingham to take a close interest in Ireland, where the survival of Catholicism was creating a tempting bridgehead for England's enemies. The Reformation failed to make much impression on Gaelic culture, largely because of its hostility towards preaching in the Irish language. Tudor Wales acquired a Prayer Book and Bible of its own, whereas Irish was widely shunned as a 'contaminant' of English civility. Even more alarmingly, the Old English began to reject Protestantism in their droves mid-way through Elizabeth's reign. Gentry families withdrew their sons from Oxford and Cambridge and offered them up to continental seminaries, just as their Catholic counterparts in England were doing. In 1576 the President of Munster informed Walsingham about the merchants' sons from Waterford who were slipping away to Louvain to be ordained as missionaries. Catholic recusancy was a minority faith in England, the danger which it posed generally more apparent than real. But in Ireland it threatened to drive a wedge between the crown and the governing elite.[11]

Walsingham's fear that a Catholic league was mustering took shape in Thomas Stucley, the English-born adventurer who spent the early 1570s shuttling between Madrid and Rome and Paris to recruit support for an invasion of Ireland. Stucley's biography reads like a work of fiction: a professional soldier who fought for France and Savoy as well as England; a part-time privateer who considered joining the French colony in Florida, but ended up in Ulster on an official mission to persuade the warlord Shane O'Neill to come to terms. Stucley tried to settle as a loyal subject in Ireland, but Elizabeth was understandably suspicious of his erratic loyalties and his foul language. In 1568 he was accused of saying that he 'set not a fart' for the queen or her office. His land claims were passed over in favour of his cousin and rival Sir Peter Carew, prompting an increasingly bitter feud between them. Stucley nurtured a growing grievance against the royal court, its 'pen and ink-horn' men like Cecil and its gadfly queen given to 'frisking and dancing'.

Honour and revenge propelled Stucley into open defiance of the sovereign whose patronage he had once craved. From 1570 he based himself in Spain, where Philip II gave him a pension and honoured him as Duke of Ireland. He soon repaid his master, captaining three galleys against the Turks at the victorious battle of Lepanto. But Philip had many other priorities besides Ireland. Stucley had to wait until 1578, more than thirty frustrating years since his career had begun in Henry VIII's service, before he could sail from Civitavecchia in an eight-hundred-ton warship with a force of Catholic exiles, a handful of made-up titles and a blessing from the pope.

Walsingham had heard from his merchant contacts that Stucley was coming. A warning was sent to Lord Deputy Sidney, and the authorities in Bristol were put on their guard. A proclamation to the Irish nobility was rejected in case it implied that Stucley posed a real threat to 'a prince of her majesty's power, armed with the goodwill of her subjects'. As chance would have it, his flame was snuffed out a long way from the coasts of Munster. Putting in for supplies at Lisbon, Stucley was recruited by the devoutly Catholic King Sebastian of Portugal to join an expedition against the pro-Ottoman regime of the Sultan of Morocco. Sebastian bought his loyalty by promising to send a fleet against Ireland once the Moors had been defeated.

Both men were killed in the ensuing rout of the Christians at Ksar el Kebir, Stucley losing his legs to a Portuguese cannon.

With one leaking ship and a few hundred raggle-taggle followers, Stucley can hardly have hoped to take on Elizabeth's army in Ireland. But his story was interwoven with that of a far more dangerous opponent of the crown. James fitz Maurice Fitzgerald, a cousin of the Earl of Desmond, was another rebel adrift in Paris and Rome looking to liberate Ireland from the English. Unlike Stucley, however, he was Irish-born and a cradle Catholic. Fitz Maurice had led an uprising in Munster in 1569, restoring the mass in the towns which he captured and demanding that Protestants be expelled. His revolt gave voice to an ideology of Irish resistance. English rule in Ireland, he argued, depended on a gift made by the pope to King Henry II. That grant of power had been annulled by Henry VIII's break from Rome, leaving Ireland free to seek a new ruler. The surrender of his allies had driven fitz Maurice into exile, but he continued to hawk his own brand of revolution around the Catholic courts of Europe. In July 1579 he came ashore at Smerwick on Ireland's south-western tip, leading a company including survivors from Stucley's escapade and the English Catholic resistance theorist Nicholas Sander. Fitz Maurice was killed a month later in a fight over some stolen horses, but Desmond took his place at the head of an uprising which Sander hoped to coax into a revolt of all Ireland. The royal official Nicholas Walshe explained the scale of the threat to Walsingham:

> and now that [Desmond] is got in arms . . . he doth not behave himself as other rebels are wont to do, which (however ill soever they intend) do still pray for the prince, but in skirmishing do cry, *papaboe*, as who should say God send the pope strength and victory.[12]

The Desmond rebellions brought the politics of the Counter-Reformation to England's own back door. Armed skirmishes and cattle raids were endemic to Irish culture, but the scale of the violence showed how traditional Gaelic warfare was changing in response to the threat from the English. Fitz Maurice and Sir Edmund Butler timed their attack on Enniscorthy in County Wexford to coincide with the summer fair, when the resident population was swollen by visiting farmers and traders. The menfolk were cut down in the streets while their wives and daughters were raped. Bodies were dumped in the river before the town was razed. The port of Youghal suffered a similar fate during the second phase of the Desmond rebellions, as Walsingham learned in a letter from Sir Henry Wallop. The Earl of Desmond had signalled his revolt by ritually defacing the royal arms in the town's courthouse. Now Youghal's defensive walls were demolished, its stores of corn looted and its buildings set ablaze. Only two stone houses survived. It was as if all traces of an alien culture were being erased from the landscape.[13]

When they sank to such brutality, the rebels were repaying atrocities meted out by successive royal armies since the 1540s. Prisoners taken by the English were regularly killed in cold blood, rather than ransomed according to Irish custom. In September 1580 there was a second landing at Smerwick harbour, a force of Spanish and Italian soldiers sent by the pope to shore up the Desmond rebellion. Their commander probably expected treatment according to the usual rules of war when they surrendered a few weeks later to a much larger English army under Lord Deputy Grey de Wilton. Richard Bingham, a naval captain who had fought with the Spanish against the French in Queen Mary's day, described to Walsingham what happened next. Lord Grey ordered the colonel and captains to 'deliver up their ensigns with order and ceremony', which they did without protest. But once the English soldiers had occupied the fort, they 'fell to revelling and spoiling and withal to killing, in which they never ceased while there lived one'.

Bingham estimated that between four and five hundred captives were slain, though Grey put it at nearer six hundred. The Catholic priests who had travelled with the expedition were hanged, together with any women and children unlucky enough to be found in the fort. All this took place after a white flag had been raised. Walsingham's cousin Edward Denny commanded a company at Smerwick, and a young Walter Raleigh was among the officers directing the killing. The poet Edmund Spenser, then serving as Lord Grey's secretary, was probably another witness. The phrase 'Grey's faith' entered the Irish language as an act of treacherous dishonesty.[14]

The appointment of Grey de Wilton signalled a hardening of the English government's attitude towards Ireland. Sir Henry Sidney had been a different brand of lord deputy, as much a courtier as a soldier. One of his initiatives had been to turn 'the old ruinous castle of Dublin' into a fitting headquarters for royal government, with better accommodation for the law-courts and a chamber in which the Irish privy council could meet. A narrative defence of his policies in Ireland, presented to Walsingham following his final recall, suggests that Sidney judged the people of Ireland by their actions rather than their ethnicity.

Lord Grey, by contrast, was a man of violence through and through. Before coming to Ireland, Grey had settled a dispute with a neighbour over the right to hunt deer by ambushing him with a cudgel in Fleet Street. Where Sidney showed some kindness to the future Jesuit Edmund Campion, Grey triumphed in the slaughter at Smerwick as a victory over false religion. The grovelling Spanish and Italian commanders were forced to listen to Grey's tirade against the pope, 'a detestable shaveling, the right Antichrist & general ambitious tyrant over all right principalities'. A letter of explanation which Grey sent to the queen rhapsodised over the Protestant confession of faith made by John Cheke, the only English officer to die in the engagement. But his account of the massacre itself betrayed no such fine feelings. Grey's sole regret was that useful munitions and food had been spoiled in the process, 'which in that fury could not be helped'. He confidently placed events at Smerwick within the compass of divine providence: 'so hath it pleased the Lord of Hosts to deliver your enemies into [your] highness's hands'. Grey's report to the queen was soon repackaged as a popular pamphlet hailing England's God-given victory 'against the foreign bands of our Roman enemies'.[15]

Seven thousand Irishmen may have died as a result of the Desmond rebellions, in battle with English and loyalist forces or by execution under martial law. The earl was slain in November 1583, by a rival Irish sept rather than an English bullet. His brother Sir John of Desmond was already dead, his head sent to Dublin as a gift to Lord Grey. The war in Munster brought a demographic catastrophe in its wake. Faced with an opponent fighting a guerrilla campaign from mountains and forests, English commanders took inspiration from their Roman military manuals and set about laying waste to the countryside. In October 1579 Sir Nicholas Malby informed Walsingham that he had torched the town of Askeaton and destroyed the crop in the surrounding fields. A year later Richard Bingham was reporting on reprisals against the people of County Kerry for their failure to maintain the English garrison at Tralee. Sir George Bourchier had been empowered 'to burn their corn, and spoil their harvest, to kill, and drive their cattle' to deny these resources to Desmond. In a macabre parallel to the killing of prisoners, thousands of head of cattle were slaughtered and left to rot.

The consequences for a society which depended on milk, meat and hides were calamitous. In February 1582 Justice John Meade wrote to Walsingham describing the hunger and sickness which the people of Munster were being forced to endure, 'and every plague so extreme that it is sufficient to destroy a whole realm'. Stocks of oats and barley were soon consumed, leaving nothing for animal feed or next year's planting. The Earl of Ormond informed Burghley in September 1583 that the harvest hadn't been gathered in Munster that year. Ireland was no stranger to hunger, but starvation and land-flight on this scale hadn't been witnessed since the fourteenth century. Spenser recalled in his 1596 *View of the Present State of Ireland* that the common people had resembled 'anatomies of death', forced to graze the ground in imitation of the beasts which they had lost. A modern estimate places the death toll at more than forty-eight thousand, close to a third of the pre-famine population of the province. The truly horrifying thing about Meade's report to Walsingham is his conviction that the Irish deserved their punishment, 'which is justly lighted upon this nation for their long continuance in offending and transgressing of God's laws and commandments, and now their unnatural rebellion against their liege sovereign lady the queen's majesty'. Meade found some comfort in the spectacle of Sir John of Desmond's headless body hanging in chains from a tower in the city of Cork, upside down 'like a tumbler or juggler' and visible from a mile away, to the terror of the rebels.[16]

Meade was a zealot, but his judgement that the Irish were rebellious by their very nature was shared by many other Englishmen. Much of this came down to their religion. The revolt of the Kildares against Henry VIII had cemented the connection between persistence in the Catholic faith and resistance to the rule of the English. The Desmond rebellions, the activities of Thomas Stucley and the presence of Nicholas Sander amongst fitz Maurice's supporters at Smerwick could all be taken as evidence that allegiance to the pope was incompatible with loyalty to the queen. The same equation between

Catholicism and treason which sent missionary priests to the scaffold in England could in Ireland be applied to an entire society. Some English observers went further, wondering whether the Irish could be considered Christian at all. Sir Henry Sidney doubted that children in Ireland were baptised, 'for neither find I place where it should be done, nor any person able to instruct them in the rules of a Christian'. The 'beastliness' of the Irish for Edmund Tremayne went deeper than their Catholicism, which at least contained the spark of true religion: 'they will swear, and forswear, murder, rob, ravish, burn and spoil, marry and unmarry at their pleasures with pluralities of wives without any grudge of conscience', sufficient to shock any Christian heart. All these aspects of English belief – that Gaelic lordship was oppressive and tyrannical, that fertile soil was literally going to waste, that the Irish were pagans – assembled themselves into an inexorable conclusion: Queen Elizabeth's second kingdom would have to be resettled. Thanks to the dearth and disease which stalked the war in Munster, it wasn't difficult for prospective planters to convince themselves that the land was empty for the taking.[17]

Plantation was not a new solution to the problem of governing Ireland. Leix and Offaly had been renamed Queen's and King's Counties in 1557 as part of a planned extension of English influence to the west of the Pale, with English soldiers settling alongside loyal Irish septs. But farms proved difficult to defend against the O'Mores and O'Connors whose territory this traditionally had been. In 1579 Walsingham had to instruct the viceroy to spend more time in the forts of Maryborough and Philipstown to 'keep these Irish in awe and subjection', and encourage English settlers 'to inhabit and manure' the estates which they had been assigned.

The situation in Ulster was even more challenging. Sir Thomas Smith intended to take a hard line in the Ards peninsula in the early 1570s, expelling the 'wild Irish' and converting the more compliant into an underclass of agricultural labourers, forbidden to own land or wear English dress. Smith confidently placed his son in charge of the colony. But he reaped what he sowed when the younger Thomas was murdered by his Irish servants, his body boiled and fed to the dogs. The first Earl of Essex made matters worse by massacring the entire population of Rathlin Island, provoking violent reprisals against English soldiers and settlers.[18]

Elizabethan efforts to colonise Ulster were a kind of private enterprise, funded in Essex's case by mortgaging his estates to the queen and in Smith's by a joint-stock company. Learning a hard lesson from such high-profile failures, the crown took control of the Munster plantation from the outset. Walsingham set out the privy council's thinking in a letter to Wallop in January 1585. The way to draw men into Munster was for the queen to redistribute confiscated rebel lands, encouraging 'men of ability to go over from hence to inhabit there, who may be able to sustain the charges of the first planting, and tarry for their gain till after some years'. English settlers would have to ride out the early years when yields from farming and industry were low, and hold fast until their investment started to pay dividends. Recruit the wrong sort of person, warned Walsingham, and they would lease out their estates to the native Irish, 'who will not manure them but in such idle manner as hath been used before'.[19]

Before Munster could be repopulated, it would have to be mapped and measured. A small team of English commissioners meandered from Tipperary to Limerick, Kerry to Cork and Waterford, calculating what could be gleaned from the land. Stocks of corn and cattle, timber and minerals, and Church property were all recorded in a latter-day equivalent of England's Domesday survey. Arthur Robyns claimed personally to have assessed a hundred thousand acres 'both by line and instrument'.

If true, then this amounted to about one-third of the acreage granted to the settlers once the confiscations had been ratified by Parliament. Viewed from England, where land and the social capital which it bought were in increasingly short supply, the bounty on offer in Ireland seemed to be a gift from God. Thirty-five gentleman planters or 'undertakers' had been selected by 1587 out of the larger group who applied, and the process of settlement could begin.[20]

The plantation of Munster represented a personal triumph for the principal secretary. Walsingham had been promoting plats 'for the reformation of Ireland' since the landing of fitz Maurice and the revolt of the Earl of Desmond. His client Sir Edward Waterhouse had been the first to flag the opportunity to achieve 'a thorough reformation . . . if English be planted' in Munster. Waterhouse's preference was for a colony 'totally inhabited by natural English men', augmented if necessary by Old English brought in from the Pale; the 'natural inhabitants' of the province came a poor third. Edward Fenton described the region to Walsingham in terms which anticipated Richard Hakluyt's evocation of the new world: 'a fruitful and pleasant country such as the sun cannot shine on better', which if properly governed 'would maintain thousands of loyal and dutiful subjects' and add handsomely to the queen's coffers.

Fenton wrote before the worst of the famine, but the belief remained widespread that Ireland offered a ladder to those with some capital and a willingness to settle. Walsingham imagined a society strictly ranked, with the gentry at its summit and three classes of farmers ('chief', 'good' and 'other') as the middling sort, descending to copyholders and humble cottagers at its foot. A feudal hierarchy long since eroded at home could be reinvented in Ireland, complete with courts leet and courts baron, a demesne farm for the lord, and tenants who had to ride to war when summoned. The land was divided up into 'seignories' rather than parishes in another medieval throwback. The army officers who followed in the second wave of plantation found additional inspiration in the empire of Rome, whose soldiers had settled to farming and fashioned themselves as gentlemen. For a man like John Cooper of Somerset, one of the queen's ceremonial guards who acquired estates in Cork, the plantation in Munster was a chance to join the colonial aristocracy. A propaganda pamphlet claimed that a landowner could do better on £50 a year in Ireland than he could for £200 in England.[21]

One of the first English settlers to receive his seignory in Munster was Edward Denny, who became lord of six thousand acres at Tralee in County Kerry. In a public demonstration of his support for the plantations, Walsingham joined his cousin as an undertaker. His decision to invest may have been influenced by a report filed by Wallop describing a lucrative alum mine nearby. Walsingham had a number of mining interests in England, and had already used his agents to locate copper and silver mines near Youghal. He was also behind a scheme to grow woad and madder to supply dye to the infant Irish textile industry. Walsingham's experiment as an Irish planter didn't last for long, probably because of the debts he inherited following the death of Sir Philip Sidney. But it implies he was still close to his mother's family, thirty years since he had mentored the young Denny brothers during their exile in Basel.[22]

The resettlement of Munster was well under way by the time that Walsingham followed Sidney to the grave. Justices of the peace were proclaiming the good news up and down the English counties, encouraging skilled workers and their families to join the migration. Carpenters and thatchers, butchers and wheelwrights, all were needed for peopling of the Irish Utopia. The men travelled to Ireland first, sending for their wives and children once rudimentary houses had been put up to accommodate them. Reports filed by the undertakers in 1589 estimated the

English population in Munster as approaching three thousand. Convoys of ships left Southampton ferrying timber and harness to manufacture English ploughs, furnaces and ore to smelt iron. Preserved food sustained the colony until it could become self-sufficient.

The logistics of moving a grand household over to Ireland can be traced in the accounts of Sir William Herbert, beneficiary of more than thirteen thousand acres in Kerry. Herbert administered his seignory from the Earl of Desmond's former house at Castleisland, which was lavishly converted into an image of Elizabethan England. The interior was furnished with tapestries and linen and silver plate. A mill and a brewhouse were built, an orchard and hopyard planted and formal gardens laid out. New stables housed the horses which their master brought over from Wales. Only the well-stocked armoury, with its handguns and pikes and pair of cannon, warned that Herbert's Irish estates were a long way from the settled shires of home.[23]

After generations of conflict, it seemed that English roots were finally becoming planted in Irish earth. Walsingham's client Richard Bingham was not alone in writing of his concern for the ordinary folk of Ireland, condemned to live in poverty by their greedy Gaelic lords. Upending the existing social order could be justified on grounds of bringing justice and prosperity within the reach of the common people. All too often, however, such expressions of sympathy were nothing but empty rhetoric. Soldiers like Sir Nicholas Malby made no pretence of fellow feeling with the Irish poor. A scorched-earth policy was an effective means to bring rebels back into obedience; ethics didn't come into it. A regime of deliberate cruelty, 'to consume them with fire and sword, not sparing neither old nor young', made sound military sense.

Violence was inevitably met by violence, an ideology of

conquest by an ideology of resistance. James fitz Maurice Fitzgerald had introduced a note of patriotism into his appeals to the Old English community to defend 'this noble Ireland', 'our dear country' against the heresy of Elizabeth. This language of Irishness was picked up by Hugh O'Neill, leader of the rebellion in Ulster and an aspiring king of all Ireland, who linked faith and fatherland ever more explicitly in an attempt to maximise his appeal. Quite how deeply the English were rooted was revealed in 1598, when it took O'Neill's allies just two weeks to destroy the Munster colony. Both sides agreed that the uprising was fuelled by hatred between the local and the settler population. Far from solving the problem of ruling Elizabeth's second kingdom, the plantations championed by Walsingham and Burghley were sowing the seeds of a new Irish nationhood.[24]

The month of June 1586 found Walsingham's stepson Christopher Carleill as captain of the *Tiger*, a royal ship of 160 tons, bound for Roanoke Island on the Outer Banks of modern-day North Carolina. Martin Frobisher sailed nearby on the *Primrose*, while the fleet was commanded from the *Elizabeth Bonaventure* by Sir Francis Drake. Carleill had served a stint in Ireland as garrison commander at Coleraine, and would shortly return to Ulster to govern the massive Norman fortress at Carrickfergus. For the present, his orders were to offer passage home to the first tentative English settlers in America. The evacuees from Roanoke included the artist John White, whose drawings of Algonquian Indians at work and play remain a priceless record of their culture, and the scientist Thomas Harriot, who had taught himself some of the local language and went on to publish a best-selling *Report of the New Found Land of Virginia*.

Carleill was a trader as well as a naval commander and adventurer. His family's strong associations with the Muscovy Company made Christopher the ideal choice to escort a convoy of merchantmen sailing to Russia in 1582. But the war between Tsar Ivan the Terrible and Frederick II of Denmark meant that the Muscovy trade was losing money, hence his interest in pursuing other options. In 1583 Carleill published a *Discourse upon the Hethermoste Partes of America*, contrasting the hazards and expense of trading into Russia, Turkey and Italy with the relative ease of crossing the Atlantic. A trading colony situated about the 40° line of latitude (running between the modern cities of Philadelphia and New York) would benefit from the best of all worlds. The region to the north was rich in salmon and cod and whales, lush hides and thick furs, pitch and ships' masts. The west and south would supply the olives and wine currently imported into England from southern Europe; wild grapes could already be found in plenty, or so Carleill claimed. Wax and honey could be traded for 'trifles' with the local population, who might become a market for English cloth as their society improved.

There was another inducement for Carleill to prefer the new world over the old: the freedom to practise religion in the plain form intended by Christ. The *Discourse* promised that godly traders, their families and employees would have no 'confessions of idolatrous religion enforced upon them, but contrarily shall be at their free liberty of conscience'. Carleill's main concerns were the supply of commodities and the potential to make a profit; this was not quite yet the Puritan dream of a city on a hill. Nonetheless, the association between America and the freedom to worship plainly, at such an early date, is very striking. Carleill's stepfather would surely have approved.[25]

Manuscript copies of Carleill's proposals survive among the state papers, suggesting that he played the petitioning game as well as going into print. Another aspiring planter to benefit from Walsingham's position at court was Sir Humphrey Gilbert, who became the paper proprietor of vast estates in North America. Gilbert had been under something of a cloud since his adventure to the Netherlands in 1572, but Walsingham stood by him. Writing from his native Devon in 1578 before his first attempt to reach America, Gilbert reflected on the depth of his debt:

> Sir, knowing you to be my principal patron as well in furthering and procuring me her majesty's favour and licence for performance of this my sea voyage . . . as occasion shall serve, make me partaker of your good speeches to her majesty for the better supportation of my poor credit with her highness.

Gilbert fell out with a fellow commander before the expedition had even begun, prompting an angry vindication of his own good conduct; Elizabeth observed archly that he was not a man of 'good happ by sea'. The fact that he was allowed to sail again in 1583 owed everything to Walsingham, who subscribed £50 to his scheme to establish an English colony in America.[26]

Whether to accept the imperial destiny being presented to her by ambitious courtiers and explorers was a surprisingly tough calculation for Queen Elizabeth. The kingdom which she ruled was a comparatively weak power, lacking the resources to fund the military on the scale of France or Spain, and mired in a costly campaign in Ireland. If Philip II mobilised to defend his mastery of the new world, the consequences for England could be catastrophic. Then again, the imagery of empire offered Elizabeth new ways to assert her sovereignty at a time when domestic political tensions were running high. The extension of her dominions overseas might enable her to live up to the model of monarchy established by Henry VIII, whose memory Elizabeth selectively revered.

There was also the chance it might make her some money.

The news from America, whether eyewitness reports or speculation and hearsay, always returned to the same theme: the unexploited richness of the land. Elizabeth loved to gamble at cards, which gives some context to her decision to invest £1,000 in Martin Frobisher's 1577 return voyage to dig for gold on Countess of Warwick's Island (now known as Kodlunarn), where the trenches left by English miners can still be seen. Walsingham advanced £200 of his own money once Frobisher's sample of ore had been broken up and tested for its precious metal content. Even if the search for gold proved to be a fool's errand, the crown would still benefit from the import duties on any goods shipped from America. So too would Walsingham, who was granted the customs revenues from the western and northern English ports in 1585 in return for a fixed annual payment to the crown. Any increase in the value of the trade would go to him.[27]

Another consideration pressed on the queen's conscience. Licensing her subjects to occupy America in her name could prove to be strategically useful; it might even be profitable. But was it legal? For an answer based on something more than patriotic enthusiasm, she turned to John Dee. Elizabeth had faith in Dee, who had studied the heavens to cast the best day for her coronation and kept her up to date with developments in natural philosophy. An eclectic education and a magpie mind had given Dee some understanding of Roman law, codified by the emperor Justinian during the sixth century and theoretically still regulating international relations in sixteenth-century Europe. If English settlement in America were to go ahead, it was vital that foreign powers – most obviously, Philip of Spain – couldn't use it as a pretext for war.

Dee's solution, set out in a series of treatises and explained in personal audiences with Elizabeth, Burghley and Walsingham, was a palimpsest of Roman law and Arthurian myth which only he could have come up with. When Francis Drake returned from his circumnavigation laden with treasure looted from South America, sparking a stern protest from the Spanish ambassador, Dee had his answer already prepared. As the descendant of King Arthur, Elizabeth had a prior claim to North America (Dee called it Atlantis) which pre-dated Columbus's discoveries by a thousand years. Perhaps aware that not everyone would share his belief in Arthur's exploits (and Lord Burghley was certainly sceptical), Dee buttressed his case by appealing to ancient legal precedent. Spain may have asserted her sovereignty over the northern parts of America, but she had done nothing to occupy the land; and physical occupation, under Roman law, was an essential part of establishing legal title.[28]

The library which Dee had assembled in his house at Mortlake was one of the most extensive in England, far larger and more eclectic than the university or college libraries in Oxford and Cambridge; three thousand books and a thousand manuscripts, according to Dee's own calculation. It was also a storehouse for all sorts of equipment relating to exploration and discovery. Sea compasses and a lodestone, a quadrant, and two Mercator globes covered with Dee's own annotations were all on public display. An inner chamber was reserved for more arcane objects, such as the mirror of Aztec obsidian with which Dee could talk to angels. One chest was full of documents relating to 'divers Irelandish territories, provinces, and lands', while another contained Dee's collection of maps. Sooner or later, anyone who was serious about sailing to the new world had to beat a path to Dee's door. Martin Frobisher, who knew how to be a privateer but had no experience of sailing the north Atlantic, spent the six weeks prior to his first voyage of discovery being tutored by Dee in the theory of navigation. In November 1577 it was Gilbert's turn to visit the library. Three years later the queen herself came to Mortlake, returning the rolls of evidence with which Dee had sought to convince her of her right to occupy Atlantis.

Dee was in the habit of writing in the books which he owned, building up over the years to a kind of diary by marginalia. Public and personal events mingled with his observations of the tides, the stars and the weather. The first recorded meeting between Dee and Walsingham took place in November 1577, no doubt connected with the north-west passage and the publication of the *General and Rare Memorials*. Dee was also called on to explain the appearance of a comet shaped like a Turkish sword, and the macabre discovery of a doll of Queen Elizabeth in Lincoln's Inn fields with a pin driven through its breast. A year later he was briefed by Leicester and Walsingham before a trip to Germany on some sort of government service. In September 1579 Dee noted that he had had a dream about Walsingham. No details are recorded, although he had another dream the same night in which he saw himself naked with his skin patterned like velvet. In 1582 both men were involved in preparing a report for Burghley on the desirability of converting to the Gregorian calendar by jumping ten days, which would have put England in sync with papal Europe. Dee suspected that the Catholics had got their maths wrong and put forward an amended plan of his own, but the Archbishop of Canterbury rejected the whole notion unless a consensus could be reached among the Protestant churches. (The decision was postponed in Britain until 1752, by which time eleven extra days would be necessary.)

The web of connections between principal secretary and propagandist of empire continued to grow. On 23 January 1583 Walsingham paid a visit to Mortlake, an easy journey from Barn Elms or the court at Richmond, where he found Sir Humphrey's brother Adrian Gilbert, 'and so talk was begun of North-West Straights discovery'. The following day Dee and Gilbert met

Walsingham in secret at Robert Beale's house in Barnes, where 'we made Mr Secretary privy of the N. W. passage, and all charts and rutters were agreed upon in general', a rutter being a mariner's guide to sea routes and tides. In February it was Lady Walsingham who 'came suddenly into my house very freely', followed by her husband and the poet Edward Dyer, who shared Dee's enthusiasm both for westward expansion and for alchemy. In March 1590, only weeks before the death of her husband, Ursula Walsingham would stand as godmother to Dee's daughter Madinia.[29]

The fourth man around Beale's table on 24 January 1583 was John Davis, who had travelled up from Devon to seek official backing for his own attempt to find a way through the Arctic ice to China. Davis and his friend Adrian Gilbert had been involved in a dispute with Dee some years earlier, but were now sufficiently reconciled to make a joint appeal for funding from the merchant communities in London and Exeter. Dee then set off for Poland, at which point his house and library were ransacked, possibly by protesters against his magical practices, although associates and ex-pupils were certainly involved. Davis was among those helping themselves to books and instruments.

Walsingham took the lead in Dee's absence, drafting proposals for a north-west passage company with staple towns at London, Dartmouth and Plymouth. Gilbert entrusted the ensuing expeditions of 1585–7 to John Davis, and so it was that the Davis Strait between Baffin Island and Greenland acquired its European name. The discovery of a great cod bank in the strait created the opportunity to draw Lord Burghley into the enterprise. Burghley was less closely aligned with new world projects than Walsingham, consistent with his altogether more conciliatory foreign policy. But he was an avid collector of maps, including the 1570 world atlas by Abraham Ortelius, which he annotated with details of Martin Frobisher's voyage of 1576.

He was also keen to see a strong English fishing fleet, on grounds that subjects who were well fed were less likely to rob and to riot. When Davis returned to England with a sample of Canadian cod preserved in a barrel, Walsingham advised him to show a chunk of it to Burghley. He may have allowed himself a private smile at the thought of the lord treasurer being ceremonially presented with a slab of salted fish. But the tactic worked: Burghley became a sponsor of English expeditions to the St Lawrence to fish for cod and whale, and kill walrus for their ivory and oil – an alternative to Spanish olive oil for the soap-makers of Bristol.

On his third and final attempt, John Davis was able to sail into Baffin Bay and as far as the pack ice at 73° latitude before his dangerously depleted supplies forced him back to Devon. To get so far and find his way safely home again was an astonishing feat of navigation and daring, the equivalent in modern times to making it back from the Moon. The Spanish Armada and Walsingham's death put an end to Davis's search for a western route to the Indies, although he remained convinced that one existed. His main bequest to future explorers was the 'Davis backstaff', a new kind of quadrant which enabled the elevation of the sun to be measured more precisely. He remembered his patron by naming Cape Walsingham at 66° 1′ 60 N; other than an anonymous Victorian office on the site of Seething Lane, the only place where he is still commemorated.[30]

The prize which lured John Davis through Atlantic storms and ice, the sudden fogs and the constant fear of sailing uncharted waters in boats of less than sixty tons, was an exclusive English trade route to the wealth of the east. For others, the new world itself was the intended destination. One visitor to Mortlake who stood out from the rest was Sir George Peckham, a squire from an inland county with his own particular take on the opportunities to be grasped in the Americas. Peckham was a recusant Catholic, trusted to serve as Sheriff of Buckinghamshire but then imprisoned in 1580 for sheltering missionary priests. Unwilling to renounce either his allegiance or his faith, he resolved to establish a loyal Catholic colony in America. In company with Sir Thomas Gerard, a Lancashire Catholic who had subscribed to Frobisher's mining expedition of 1577, Peckham cast around for a potential commander. They found their answer in Sir Humphrey Gilbert: a ruthless enemy of Catholic rebels in Ireland but also a proven man of action, commissioned by the queen to search out and settle any 'remote, heathen and barbarous lands not actually possessed of any Christian prince or people'. Walsingham was all in favour of the plan, which gave Catholic loyalists an alternative to the conspiracy centres in Paris and Rome: emigration without political exile.

Thomas Gerard's sights had originally been set on Ulster rather than America. His offer to transport his tenants to be a buffer between the O'Neills and the clan MacDonald had been taken seriously by Lord Deputy Sidney, but Elizabeth was unwilling to fund him. A new-world colony, which ought to be able to pay for itself if half the tales were true, was a far more attractive proposition for the queen. In June 1582 Peckham became the lord of two million acres in what would one day become Rhode Island, pinpointed by Dee as the most auspicious place to settle. Gerard, who was granted one and a half million acres, and the other major proprietors (not all of them Catholic, since Philip Sidney was among them) made up a ruling council under Gilbert as governor. Just as in Ireland, a feudal hierarchy of settlers would stretch out below them, ranked according to the scale of their investment.

Gilbert and Peckham imagined their American colony in intricate detail. Every farmer of sixty acres should have a long-bow, arrows and a target, while two thousand acres demanded the provision of a warhorse – 'after such time as God shall send sufficient horses in these parts', as Gilbert added with a rare dash of realism. Country parishes would be no more than three miles square, with a resident minister and three hundred acres of glebeland. Bishops and archbishops would be provided with vast seignories of their own. A central treasure-house would be established to fund schools and offer loans, while lands were reserved for soldiers maimed in the wars; a recognition that the English occupation would not go unopposed. Ordinary settlers were to be supplied with a hatchet, saw and spade, and enough grain and beans to get them started on the land. Almost as an afterthought, special privileges would be offered 'to encourage women to go on the voyage', though what these could have been is not recorded.

While Gilbert set out to find a suitable site for the colony, Peckham turned to print to advertise the venture. His *True Reporte of the Late Discoveries and Possession of the New-Found Landes* was dedicated to Walsingham in 1583. Peckham added his own gloss to the alleged abundance of the new world: the stocks of fresh- and salt-water fish, the grapes as big as a man's thumb, potato roots and the 'grain called maize'. Gold, silver and precious stones could be cheaply bartered with the savages, who would benefit from the Christian gospel (no distinction being made between Catholic and reformed) and an education in 'mechanical occupations, arts, and liberal sciences'. What cause for complaint, asked Peckham with apparent sincerity, could they possibly have? Much was also made of the Welsh-sounding names to be found in the Americas, proving that Elizabeth's ancestor Prince Madog had settled in Florida in the twelfth century.

Sir William Pelham was one of several prominent figures to offer verses endorsing the *True Reporte*. To valiant minds, every land was a native soil. Other European powers had already woken up to the fact:

Our foreign neighbours bordering hard at hand,
Have found it true, to many a thousand's gain;
And are enriched by this abounding land,
While pent at home, like sluggards we remain.
But though they have, to satisfy their will:
Enough is left, our coffers yet to fill.

The English cause was wholly virtuous, and would receive the blessing of God:

Then *England* thrust among them for a share,
Since title just, and right is wholly thine.

Richard Bingham addressed his own exhortation to young patriots in search of adventure:

Then launch ye noble youths into the main,
No lurking perils lie amid the way:
Your travail shall return you treble gain,
And make your names renowned another day.
For valiant minds, through twenty seas will roam:
And fish for luck, while sluggards lie at home.[31]

Like Christopher Carleill, Peckham was at pains to emphasise 'the easiness and shortness of the voyage' to and from America. The truth was much harsher, and he knew it. By the time the *True Reporte* went into its second edition, Gilbert had already succumbed to the storms of the North Atlantic. Edward Hayes, the only captain to make it safely back to port, was able to tell Peckham what had happened. Gilbert's fleet of four ships had made initially for Newfoundland, where he landed at St John's harbour to read out the queen's commission and dig a piece of turf, duly witnessed by a cluster of European sailors. By symbolically cultivating the land Gilbert had possessed it for Elizabeth, like a medieval noble entering on his estates. The royal arms were erected 'engraven in lead, and inscribed upon a pillar of wood' as permanent markers of English sovereignty. His next destination was Sable Island off Nova Scotia, en route towards the projected colony in Rhode Island, but the sinking of one ship and near mutiny of a second compelled the rest to turn for home. Gilbert lost his life in a storm off the Azores, brazening the weather with a book in his hand. Hayes caught his last words on the wind, 'We are as near to heaven by sea as by land', before he and his crew were overwhelmed. The *Squirrel*, which Gilbert had insisted on taking as his flagship, was just eight tons.[32]

Peckham hoped to persuade Gilbert's executors to carry on his legacy, or failing that to recruit another backer. But Adrian Gilbert and Walter Raleigh had enterprises of their own, and Philip Sidney's dream had burst when the queen had forbidden him to sail. The scheme for loyal Catholic emigration swiftly foundered, taking its deviser with it. Within a year Peckham was in prison again, guilty of favouring the mass over holy communion. Far from becoming the proprietor of endless acres in America, he was forced to part with his family lands to pay his crushing recusancy fines. It was an obscure ending for a man who might have taken the heat out of the English Catholic question, to the acceptance of all sides. The best that can be said is that his celebration of the new world was widely circulated in Richard Hakluyt's *Principal Navigations of the English Nation*, and so helped to shape England's future relationship with North America and the sea.

If John Dee was the principal publicist of a British empire in the 1570s, then the same could be said for Hakluyt during the decade that followed. A Church of England clergyman, Richard Hakluyt (called 'the younger' to distinguish him from his cousin, a lawyer who advised the crown on its claim to America) used the stability of an Oxford college fellowship, a prebend in Bristol Cathedral and a Suffolk country parish to write books about exploration which would be read for generations. Hakluyt was more editor than writer, freely making use of the work of others. The 1589 first edition of *Principal Navigations* was dedicated to Walsingham with a warmth which was more than formulaic:

> whereas I have always noted your wisdom to have had a special care of the honour of her majesty, the good reputation of our country, and the advancing of navigation, the very walls of this our Island, as the oracle is reported to have spoken of the sea forces of Athens: and whereas I acknowledge in all dutiful sort how honourably both by your letter and speech I have been animated in this and other my travels, I see my self bound to make presentment of this work to your self, as the fruits of your own encouragements, and the manifestation both of my unfeigned service to my prince and country, and of my particular duty to your honour.[33]

An island with walls. Hakluyt's memorable image resurfaces a year or so later in Shakespeare's *Richard II* during John of Gaunt's 'sceptred isle' speech, perhaps indebted to *Principal Navigations*: 'this precious stone set in a silver sea, which serves it in the office of a wall, or as a moat defensive to a house' (II, I, 46–8). Hakluyt may also have been thinking about the very real sea-walls which Walsingham had ordered to fortify the harbour at Dover.

The phenomenal success of *Principal Navigations* is recalled in the many first editions which survive to this day – at Middle Temple and Cashel Cathedral, Harvard University and New York Public Library, three copies each in the Folger and the Huntington, ten distributed between the colleges of Oxford and Cambridge, and more besides. The preface tells the story of what amounted to Hakluyt's second conversion, to the cause of overseas discovery. Visiting his cousin at his legal chambers in London, the younger Hakluyt was shown the 'division of the earth' according to ancient knowledge and the findings of modern explorers. Transfixed by the map in front of him, his thoughts turned to the 107th Psalm: 'they which go down to the sea in ships, and occupy by the great waters, they see the works of the Lord, and His wonders in the deep'. A new sense of vocation quickened within Hakluyt, reflecting both his passionate Christian faith and his desire to see the English break out of their 'sluggish security'. To remain inert while England's enemies spread their net across the world was to expose crown and nation to danger. As if to alert his readers to all that might be lost, Hakluyt completed *Principal Navigations* on 17 November: Queen Elizabeth's accession day.

The dedication to Walsingham reflected a relationship which dated back to Hakluyt's days as a don at Christ Church. His earliest known work, a pamphlet recommending the seizure of the Strait of Magellan, was either commissioned by Walsingham or written to gain his attention. From 1580 onwards Hakluyt was collecting material and interviewing mariners in preparation for the plantation of North America. *Divers Voyages touching the Discoverie of America* appeared in 1582, fuelling the atmosphere of excitement in which Peckham and Humphrey Gilbert were able to stake their claims in New England. Walsingham praised Hakluyt for his efforts to publicise 'the discovery of the Western parts yet unknown', and encouraged him to continue both for his own private good – a hint of the preferment to come – as well as the 'public benefit of this realm'. In spring 1583 he was in Bristol, attempting to sell Christopher Carleill's projected voyage to the mayor and aldermen. The following September Walsingham sent him to France, the only foreign country which Hakluyt would see with his own eyes, as chaplain to the English ambassador Sir Edward Stafford. There was little love lost between Walsingham and Stafford, which makes it all the more interesting that Hakluyt was soon acting as the principal secretary's eyes and ears within the Paris embassy.

Using his chaplaincy as cover, Hakluyt was able to gather a

mass of information on French and Spanish interests in North America. A letter of January 1584 reveals the range of his activities in Paris. He promised Walsingham reports from Dieppe and St Malo. He visited a warehouse of Canadian pelts purchased by the royal furrier, and reported on gossip that the French were planning to send a mission of 'many friars and other religious persons' to the new world, although Hakluyt suspected that this might be misinformation: 'I think they not be in haste to do it'. He met the pretender to the Portuguese throne, Don Antonio, 'and five or six of his best captains and pilots', and had hopes of meeting a man from Savoy who had travelled to Japan. He rode to Rouen to investigate French plans to build a trading post in Maine or Nova Scotia, and he made contact with Walsingham's agents in the Basque country close to the Spanish border. Somehow Hakluyt got access to the royal library in the Abbey of St Martin, where he made notes on the voyages of Jacques Cartier to the Gulf of St Lawrence in 1534–6. He also monitored the activities of the English exile community in Paris, briefing the government on the Catholic response to Lord Burghley's propaganda tract *The Execution of Justice*. Given Stafford's double dealing, it is quite possible that Hakluyt kept a watch on him too. When Walsingham was sick, he dealt with Carleill instead. All told, he was a valuable asset.

The agents in Walsingham's service generally worked for money, laced with Protestantism to a greater or lesser degree. Hakluyt's motivation was subtly different. He welcomed the benefits which his patron could put his way, but he placed an even higher value on the chance to promote 'our western planting and discovery'. Sending news that he had approached the Genoese banker Horatio Palavicini 'to become an adventurer in those western voyages', Hakluyt appealed for lectures in mathematics and navigation in Oxford and London; if Walsingham agreed to fund them, it would be 'the best hundred pounds that was bestowed this five hundred years'. There was even the chance that Hakluyt would be released from his chaplaincy to sail westwards in person. Judging by the tone of his letters, this is what he truly yearned to do. He told Walsingham that he was ready to 'go myself into the action', 'in the service of God and my country to employ all my simple observations, readings and conference'. But as an Oxford academic with no experience of the sea, Hakluyt was more useful in Paris. By the time he was finally free to leave in 1588, it was too late: the Elizabethan experiment in empire was effectively over.[34]

Hakluyt's influence needs to be measured in words more than deeds. A busy editor and translator, he also made his own unique contribution to the cause of English overseas expansion. Hakluyt spent the summer of 1584 in London putting together his *Discourse of Western Planting*, twenty-one chapters which were part sermon and part practical guide to the settlement of America. The manuscript original which Hakluyt presented to the queen on 5 October is lost, but a contemporary copy survives in New York Public Library; this may be the one which Hakluyt paid a scrivener to prepare for Walsingham to keep. Hakluyt probably worked on the *Discourse* at Walsingham's house in Seething Lane, making use of the books and maps in his study. The title-page states that it was written at the 'request and direction' of Walter Raleigh, who had recently despatched two ships to assert the rights in America which he had been granted following the death of Humphrey Gilbert. Walsingham would come to resent Raleigh's easy manner with the queen, a tense situation made worse when Elizabeth granted her favourite the lands once belonging to Anthony Babington, but for the present the two worked together to get Hakluyt a hearing at court.

The *Discourse of Western Planting* is easily overlooked, its outline obscured by the far more famous *Principal Navigations*. The text wasn't printed until 1877, although the assumption that an idea is more important simply because it is published would have seemed strange to the Elizabethan mind. John Dee was highly selective about what he allowed to go into print; manuscript was the proper forum for advice and debate. By presenting his argument as the work of his own hand, Hakluyt played to the sensitivities of a queen who loathed the public discussion of state secrets. Long sections of the *Discourse* are quoted from Sir George Peckham, and the *Destruycion de las Indias* by Bartholomé de las Casas, and John Ribault's *Whole and True Discovery of Terra Florida*. Again, the modern equation between originality and impact can be misleading. Hakluyt skilfully selected his evidence, researching his subject and presenting his conclusion with all the care of an Oxford disputation. The ample examples, the repetition and the scrupulous citing of authorities were familiar techniques of academic rhetoric.

When Hakluyt does elect to speak in person, his voice comes through with conviction and a powerful sense of urgency. Explorers from many nations had found America to be 'a place wonderful fertile and of strong situation', its people naturally gentle and the climate so benevolent that two harvests could be gathered in a single year. The commodities on offer in this aromatic Eden run on for page after page, a shopping list for the senses: oranges and almonds, cloves and pepper, huge woods and mighty fish, silkworms and sassafras. The wealth of South America had elevated the monarchies of Spain and Portugal, rulers over parched and unyielding landscapes at home, to a scale of power and grandeur which they could scarcely have imagined. But there was ample space to settle north of Florida, 'if by our slackness we suffer not the French or others to prevent us'. The best part of America was still there for the taking, more suited to the industrious and godly nature of the English people than the torrid southern territories which had been conquered by Spain. Aware of the importance of dynastic continuity to the queen, Hakluyt threw in a prayer encouraging her to finish the work of her forebears:

God which doth all things in his due time, and hath in his hand the hearts of all princes, stir up the mind of her majesty at length to assist her most willing and forward subjects to the performance of this most godly and profitable action which was begun at the charges of King Henry the 7th her grandfather, followed by King Henry the eighth her father, and left as it seemeth to be accomplished by her.

Not for nothing did he sign himself to Walsingham as 'Richard Hakluyt, Preacher'.[35]

The key to all this wealth was what Hakluyt called 'traffic', the lawful exchange in the rich resources of the earth which was pleasing in the sight of God. Western planting would supply raw materials and skilled employment for a kingdom in which both were growing scarce. Hakluyt was happy to speak of colonies, but wanted it understood that the English would be far superior to the Spanish. His account of the violations inflicted on the subjects of New Spain brims over with anger and disgust. More than 'fifteen millions of souls', he calculated, had perished under Spanish tyranny. His choice of word for them, 'souls', is revealing. The native population was childlike rather than brutish in Hakluyt's estimation, willing to obey and eager to learn. The Catholic powers talked of converting them, but had brought only slavery and death. That was why the people of America 'cry out unto us their next neighbours to come and help them, and bring unto them the glad tidings of the gospel'. A reader familiar with the works of Thomas More would have been reminded of the citizens of *Utopia*, keen to soak up the Christian message.

Hakluyt edged further, treading carefully for fear of offending the queen. If England armed the natives of Florida 'as the Spaniards arm our Irish rebels', she would gain a powerful ally against a regime which aspired to dominate the globe. Combine this with a fortified plantation in Cape Breton, and the whole proud edifice of the Spanish empire might topple. Like the crow in Aesop's fable, his gorgeous feathers taken by the peacock and the magpie and the jay, Philip II would become 'a laughing stock for all the world'.[36]

Walsingham's timing in bringing Hakluyt back from Paris was impeccable. He arrived in England in late July 1584, just days after the assassination of William of Orange had thrown Protestant Europe into an uproar. Raleigh's two barques returned from their exploration of the Outer Banks in September, full of the welcome they had received at Roanoke and bringing two Indians who had decided to see the court of Elizabeth for themselves. A fortnight after Hakluyt's audience with the queen, Walsingham and Burghley led the privy council in signing the bond of association. In November Parliament was summoned, endorsing the bond and demanding harsher measures against Catholic priests and Jesuits. Walsingham, Drake and Sir Philip Sidney were all named to the Commons committee which met to confirm Raleigh's entitlements in the new world, a rare example of Walsingham taking an active interest in parliamentary procedure. Hakluyt's *Discourse* addressed any lingering concerns about the legality of colonisation, rebutting the pope's jurisdiction in America with a mixture of theology and legal reasoning laced with lively anti-Catholicism.

The queen yielded, wooed by Raleigh's poetry on the one side and Hakluyt's promises on the other. Raleigh was knighted on Twelfth Night 1585 and empowered to requisition 2,400 lb of gunpowder from the magazine in the Tower of London. His personal seal now styled him as 'Lord and Governor of Virginia', but Elizabeth could not bear to part with his company. So it was his Cornish cousin Sir Richard Grenville who led Raleigh's five ships out of Plymouth Sound in April, bound for 'her majesty's new kingdom of Virginia'. Two members of Walsingham's household, Master Atkinson and Master Russell, sailed with them to report on the establishment of the colony. Grenville later wrote to Walsingham regarding his share of the spoils from a Spanish cargo of sugar and ginger which the admiral seized after depositing the colonists, confirming that he had a personal stake in the first English colony in America. Walsingham also arranged for a Danish subject named Martin Laurentson to join the expedition to learn 'the art of naval warfare', acting on a personal request to Queen Elizabeth from her Protestant ally and former suitor Frederick II.[37]

Virginia had a more forgiving climate than either Nova Scotia or Newfoundland, but Roanoke Island was far from ideal as a place to settle. The Outer Banks form a crescent around the coast of modern North Carolina, two hundred miles from Cape Lookout in the south to Cape Henry and the entrance to the Chesapeake Bay. Roanoke lies four miles offshore, sheltered by the barrier islands from the worst of the Atlantic but windswept and unstable. The island has changed shape since the sixteenth century, losing the northern edge where an Indian village and an English-built jetty once stood. Much of the south and east is marshy. The forests of red and white cedar, pines and sweet gum which so impressed the first settlers have largely disappeared today. Gone too are the Secotan, the Indian nation who welcomed the newcomers with feasts of corn and smoked fish, traded their maize for knives and glass beads and baby dolls, and allowed John White to draw them. The Roanoke region, it turned out, was thickly inhabited; welcome news for those who believed that the colony's future lay in trade, but an unavoidable source of conflict if the English settled down to farming, logging and mining.[38]

That Roanoke was chosen as the first English foothold in America owed a good deal to Simão (or Simon) Fernandes, an

Azorean pilot who had seen the North American coastline for himself while learning his trade in the service of Spain. Fernandes was based in England by the early 1570s, plundering shiploads of sugar and exotic woods returning from the Indies. When the seizure of a Portuguese caravel landed him in jail amidst a storm of diplomatic protest, Walsingham secured his release on condition that he came to work for him. Fernandes was little better than a pirate, but his knowledge of Spanish overseas territories and naval strength made him a prize asset. He was also a Protestant convert; another cause of his searing hatred of Philip of Spain, who had absorbed Portugal into his empire following the death of Cardinal King Henry in 1580.

Fernandes guided Raleigh's two barques to Cape Hatteras in 1584, and it was he who piloted the colonists through an inlet, named Port Ferdinando in his honour, to Roanoke Island the following year. His determination to profit at Spanish expense helps to explain why the English ended up among the reefs and shoals of the Outer Banks, a good place to watch for the bullion ships making their way home from South America. For Raleigh too, laying permanent foundations for an English America was a secondary consideration; the glory, and the real money, lay with Philip II's treasure fleet. Walsingham's own hopes for Roanoke combined a tactical with a longer-term strategic approach. In the spring of 1585 he persuaded Elizabeth to authorise his 'Plot for the annoying of the King of Spain'. Drake, Carleill and Frobisher were unleashed to wreak havoc in Galicia and the West Indies, while Sir Walter Raleigh's brother Carew captured Spanish ships fishing off Newfoundland. Roanoke was one theatre within this undeclared naval war. And yet Walsingham's support for English plantation in Ireland suggests that it was simultaneously part of another story, the creation of an English Protestant sphere of influence beyond the traditional geographical boundaries of the crown. His patronage of Hakluyt and friendship with Dee pinpoint Walsingham as a believer in colonisation for its own sake, a generation before such ideas became conventional in English government.[39]

Whether as a naval base or a place to settle, Raleigh's colonists soon found that Roanoke had a major drawback. Sand-bars ran across both inlets to the island, impassable at high tide for any vessel of more than seventy tons. The hazards of taking a ship in too close were graphically illustrated when the *Tiger* ran aground at Wococon and nearly broke her back, an accident which the author of a shipboard journal blamed on the poor seamanship of pilot Fernandes. She was run onto the shore and saved, but only at the cost of 'great spoil of our provisions', sodden bags of wheat and rice which the colonists could ill afford to lose. Another casualty was their store of salt, essential for preserving meat over the winter months.

The *Tiger* was on loan from Queen Elizabeth, as was the first governor of Roanoke. Ralph Lane was a veteran of the war in Ireland, an experience which he shared with a number of the colonists under his command. Of the 109 men overwintering on Roanoke in 1585–6, more than half were soldiers in Raleigh's pay. Gentlemen adventurers formed another component, roundly condemned by Harriot for their 'nice bringing up' and their unwillingness to submit to military discipline, the balance being made up by craftsmen, a baker, a brewer and a cook. Joachim Ganz was a Jewish metallurgist from Prague, employed to test Indian copper (surveys of the site have turned up melted copper and a fragment of a crucible, implying that a furnace was built at Roanoke) and to assess the likelihood of more precious metal being found. Thomas Luddington may have been a fellow of Lincoln College, Oxford, in which case the colony had a chaplain to celebrate communion and baptise any Indian converts; the post which Hakluyt had probably hoped to secure for himself. The glaring omission is anyone skilled in farming. Soldiers could shoot game but would have been unwilling to till the land, even assuming that the rhythms of English agriculture could have adapted to suit different soil and seasons. Viable sugar cane and plantain had been transported from Hispaniola, but had suffered badly from the salt spray on deck.[40]

When Ralph Lane's men dug the ground, they did so in the cause of defence. Within a month of their arrival Lane was writing a letter to Walsingham 'from the new fort in Virginia', revealed by modern archaeology to be an angular structure with bastions and ramparts protecting the little settlement of two-storey cottages by its side. That the fort was built so swiftly suggests that Raleigh may have taken Hakluyt's advice to ship prefabricated gunnery platforms out to Virginia. Fort Raleigh, as its modern reconstruction is known, had symbolic as well as military significance. The English were announcing their lawful occupation of the land by constructing the means to defend it. Spanish raiders up from Florida would have been at the forefront of Lane's mind, but his guns and palisades were all too soon offering protection from a hostile local population. A silver cup went missing during a reconnaissance expedition to the mainland, perhaps a communion chalice which the English were showing to the Secotan in hope of explaining the Christian faith. Its alleged theft sparked harsh reprisals against the Indian village of Aquascogoc: 'we burnt, and spoiled their corn, and town, all the people being fled'. The phrase, all too sickeningly familiar, could have been taken from a report on the reduction of Ireland. John White, the next governor of Roanoke colony, was one of the company. If he spoke out against the destruction then his protests went unheard. The hasty actions of a handful of soldiers would have bitter consequences for the future of English settlement at Roanoke.[41]

Lane's letters to Walsingham, Philip Sidney and Richard

Hakluyt the elder, sent before the colony entered its winter isolation, show him clinging stubbornly to his preconceptions about the new world in defiance of the reality surrounding him. Virginia had 'the goodliest soil under the cope of heaven', supplying every commodity from flax to frankincense, maize which yielded both corn and sugar and sufficient drugs to satisfy any apothecary. Once horses and cattle had been sourced and the land inhabited by the English, 'no realm in Christendom were comparable to it'. Lane was paid to be upbeat and was true to his commission, despite a catastrophic falling-out with Grenville. But the cheery assurances that he was happier with 'fish for my daily food, and water for my daily drink' than all the luxury which the court could provide, are a more accurate reflection of life on Roanoke Island. Happy in the knowledge that he was adding a kingdom to the queen's dominions, Lane found further sustenance in his Protestant belief. He and his men were 'in a vast country yet unmanured', but the Lord would command the ravens to feed them. Faith in Christ would save them from the tyranny of Spain, 'being the sword of the Antichrist of Rome and his sect'. Every day that dawned revealed another province waiting to be 'civilly and Christianly inhabited'.[42]

Ralph Lane would willingly have remained in America. The account which he later gave to Raleigh describes the exploration of Virginia proper, skirmishes with the Algonquian and Iroquois of the Chesapeake Bay and the hunt for a gold or copper mine further up the Roanoke River. 'The discovery of a good mine,' as Lane was now prepared to admit, 'by the goodness of God, or a passage to the Southsea, and nothing else can bring this country in request to be inhabited by our nation'. What persuaded him to leave with Drake was the deteriorating relationship with the local Indians, on whom the English were heavily dependent for their food. The supply ship expected in

April 1586 had not arrived, and the colonists knew that they faced a thinner winter if they stayed. Angered by their repeated demands for corn and grief-stricken at the devastation which European disease had brought to his people, the ruler of the Secotan turned against the English and was killed during a parley. The appointed signal for Lane's men to open fire was 'Christ our victory'. The slaughter took place on 1 June, a week before Drake's fleet appeared on the horizon. Drake was willing to offer the colonists a boat and provisions for four months, but a massive storm forced her to cut her cables and put to sea. Lane read the sequence of events as a sign: 'the very hand of God as it seemed, stretched out to take us from thence'. Most of their books and papers were thrown overboard by the sailors rowing them through the reef. Grenville's relief party arrived two weeks later to find the settlement abandoned.[43]

We will never know what was lost in the hasty retreat from Roanoke: maps of the Chowan and Roanoke Rivers, Ganz's experiments in metallurgy, Harriot's handwritten dictionaries of the local languages were all likely casualties. Fortunately there were also some extraordinary survivals. Through the turbulent seas and hailstones the size of hens' eggs, John White clung onto his drawings of American flora and fauna and an Indian culture which could be civilised by the English. According to Theodor de Bry's edition of Harriot's *Report of the New Found Land of Virginia*, this was the reason that the queen had sent White to America: 'only to draw the description of the place, lively to describe the shapes of the inhabitants their apparel, manners of living, and fashions'. In the absence of any more tangible evidence, White's drawings made a compelling case for a return voyage to Virginia. He exploited their potential to the full, distributing copies to Hakluyt as well as Raleigh and Walsingham. The entomologist Thomas Penny received studies of a swallow-tail butterfly and a cicada, and John Gerard incorporated

White's Indian milkweed in his much-reprinted *Herball.* White also sold a set to de Bry, whose engravings opened them up to readers of German, French and Latin as well as English. The two men had been introduced by Hakluyt.[44]

White's experience and commitment made him the clear choice to govern Raleigh's second colony. In January 1587 the royal herald Garter King of Arms announced that he and twelve assistants had been incorporated to plant 'the City of Ralegh in Virginia'. White's Cornish gentry origins were sufficiently obscure to warrant a grant of arms in his own right. Among the others receiving arms were Ananias Dare, a tiler and bricklayer from London who had married White's daughter Eleanor, and Simon Fernandes, enjoying the final stage in his transformation from Portuguese pirate to English gentleman. Given the allegations of incompetence levelled against Fernandes in 1585, the fact that he took such a prominent role in the expedition which departed Plymouth in May 1587 may indicate that he was still under Walsingham's protection. As John White's narrative makes clear, it wasn't long before Fernandes returned to his old ways. One of the planters' boats was left behind in the night under a master who hadn't previously sailed to Virginia; a deliberate attempt to scupper the colony, or so White alleged. Valuable time was wasted in the West Indies while Fernandes waited for a Spanish prize.

Worse was to come when the little fleet reached the Outer Banks on 22 July. White had planned to lead the 116 men, women and children to the shores of the Chesapeake Bay, where (quoting Harriot's survey of 1585–6) 'we found the soil to be fatter, the trees greater and to grow thinner, the ground more firm and deeper mould, more and larger champions, finer grass and as good as any we saw ever in England'. But when they landed on Roanoke Island to search for survivors of Grenville's holding party of 1586, Fernandes ordered his men not to let the colonists back on board. His reason was 'that the summer was far spent' – in other words, he would soon miss his chance to intercept the Spanish treasure fleet. White had little option but to clear the cottages of the vines and pumpkins which had grown up since his departure the previous year, and to set to work repairing Ralph Lane's fort.[45]

Fernandes's maverick behaviour is difficult to explain. Having refused to land the settlers on the mainland, he then spent a leisurely four weeks scouring the bilges of his ships and felling timber to sell in England before setting sail. The second Roanoke colony was less fully provisioned than Governor White had intended, thanks again to the actions of Fernandes on the outward journey. White had wanted to put in at Puerto Rico at a place where oranges and plantains could be grubbed up for replanting in Virginia, 'but our Simon denied it, saying that he would come to an anchor at Hispaniola'. When Hispaniola was sighted the pilot sailed straight on, depriving the colonists of the cattle which they had hoped to take on board. As White presents it, Fernandes was effectively guilty of sabotage.

The link between Fernandes and Walsingham has allowed a conspiracy story to be constructed, with Walsingham marooning the colonists of 1587 to take revenge against Raleigh for snatching the spoils of the Babington plot. There is no denying that Fernandes was out for his own gain. But in his defence, he did take the time to unload the colonists' equipment and provisions, and he did leave them with a pinnace capable of sailing back to England. Roanoke could be fortified more quickly than a newly built town on the Chesapeake. Ralph Lane, who was a capable military commander, had nothing but praise for Fernandes in 1585. Ultimately the problem is one of evidence. As the only known survivor of the second Roanoke colony, John White was keen to preserve his reputation from slanderers and sceptics when he got back to London. Other than the report which he passed on to Hakluyt, historians have little to go on; no equivalent, for instance, of Lane's letters to Walsingham in 1585. Granted, Walsingham was not a friend of Raleigh. But his many positive connections with the sponsors of English expansion – Hakluyt and Dee, Peckham and the Gilberts, Davis and Carleill – make it difficult to believe that he would willingly have sent three boatloads of English Protestant families into the void, simply to settle a private grievance. In the long-anticipated war with Spain, it would be better to have Raleigh as an ally than an enemy.[46]

White's vision as governor had been to create a civil society rather than a military encampment, a deep-rooted colony which was capable of sustaining and reproducing itself. But this could not be achieved at Roanoke. Tragedy struck in their first week when George Howe, one of the nine assistants who had sailed with White, was felled by Indian arrows and beaten to death while catching crabs. A reprisal raid went disastrously wrong when the English attacked a friendly group from Croatoan Island to the south, including women and children who were gleaning in the fields. The settlers had been expecting to farm a rich soil, but found that it was already too late in the year to plant. Someone would have to sail back with Fernandes to requisition more supplies, and the word of the governor would carry most weight. According to White's account, the 'whole company' of assistants and planters petitioned him to go in person. White was reluctant, for oddly ignoble reasons: he feared his 'great discredit' in London, and he was worried that his possessions might be 'spoiled and pilfered' during the planned trek to a better site on the mainland. In the end he was persuaded, though only once the colonists had given him a sealed affidavit that they had full confidence in his leadership. Addressed to 'you, her majesty's subjects of England' from 'your friends and countrymen, the planters in Virginia', this document offers a fascinating glimpse into the self-perception of the very first English colonists: an identity which was linked and yet distinct, as if being in America had already changed them. White sailed for England on 27 August 1587, three days after the baptism of his granddaughter Virginia Dare, the first English child to be born in America. It was less than five weeks since he had led the first colonists ashore at Roanoke. No European would see any of them again.[47]

In the preface to the 1589 edition of his *Principal Navigations*, Richard Hakluyt triumphantly placed before Walsingham everything that had been achieved since he had been forced to listen to the sneers of the French while serving as a Protestant chaplain in Paris. English consuls and traders could now be found in Constantinople and Tripoli, in Persia and in Goa. English ships had braved the Strait of Magellan and the Cape of Good Hope, trafficked with the Moluccas and Java and returned home 'most richly laden with the commodities of China'. Commerce with the Philippines and Japan would one day bring their people 'the incomparable treasure of the truth of Christianity'. If Henry VIII had been King David, laying the foundations of the temple of God, then Elizabeth had proved herself another Solomon by constructing it. No one could deny the ambition and the courage of the English:

> they have been men full of activity, stirrers abroad, and searchers of the remote parts of the world; so in this most famous and peerless government of her excellent majesty, her subjects through the special assistance and blessing of God, in searching the most opposite corners and quarters of the world, and to speak plainly, in compassing the vast globe of the earth more than once, have excelled all the nations and people of the earth.[48]

Hakluyt's sermon was a shrewd piece of propaganda, defending England from the baseless taunts of foreigners while exhorting its people to aspire to greatness. The same combination of patriotism and godliness can be caught in the writings of Christopher Carleill and the letters of Ralph Lane. Like his client Hakluyt, Francis Walsingham could find comfort in the fact that the English crown and nation had woken up at last to the dangers of their 'sluggish security'. But there was a nagging absence from Hakluyt's litany of successes by sea. Where were the settlers who had sailed to Roanoke with John White and Simon Fernandes? By the time that *Principal Navigations* was published, nothing had been heard from them for more than two years. The supplies which they had entreated their governor to bring them had never reached the colony, despite White's frantic efforts to find a way around the general prohibition on English ships putting to sea which the privy council had imposed in October 1587 to preserve the nation's defences against an armada from Spain.

It was March 1590 by the time that White was able to negotiate a place on a privateer crossing the Atlantic, and another five months before he stepped ashore on Roanoke Island. The search party found a fire burning and fresh footprints left by the Indians, but there was no reply to their shouts or the English tunes played by their bugler. Scrambling up the sand dunes, they made a discovery which set their hearts racing and has been a source of mystery ever since. Carved on a tree were the letters 'CRO' in Roman script, though without the accompanying Maltese cross which White had agreed would be the colonists' signal that they were in imminent danger. Its meaning became clear when they reached the English village, recently refortified but emptied of everything that could be carried. A post at the entrance had been stripped of its bark, 'and 5 foot from the ground in fair capital letters was graven

CROATOAN without any cross or sign of distress'. Croatoan Island was the home of Manteo, one of the two Indians who had sailed to England, who had been baptised at Roanoke a few days before Virginia Dare. A shout from the sailors directed White to where his sea-chests had been buried in a trench before the planters had left. The contents had been dug out and scattered, 'my books torn from the covers, the frames of some of my pictures and maps rotten and spoiled with rain, and my armour almost eaten through with rust'. Four artillery pieces and some shot were found 'thrown here and there, almost overgrown with weeds', evidently too heavy to transport to wherever the colonists had gone.[49]

The marker trees were clear enough, though their message was very strange. Croatoan, or Hatteras Island as it is now known, was less suitable even than Roanoke if the English wanted to settle to farming. The planters had agreed with White that they would move the colony to a better site fifty miles inland while their governor brought help from England, leaving him a 'secret token' carved into a tree or a door-jamb to let him know where to seek them. Croatoan made no sense unless they had divided into two groups, the main party heading towards the Chesapeake while a smaller group waited for White at Roanoke and then left with Manteo in 1588 or 1589 when the relief ships did not come. 'Greatly joyed' at this proof that the settlers were at least alive, White persuaded his captain to set course for Croatoan only for a storm to snap their anchor cable and sweep them out to sea. Contrary winds meant that the plan to winter in Trinidad before trying again had to be abandoned, and the ships were forced to head for home. It was White's last chance to rejoin his family and the colonists in his care.

Wherever the lost colonists lived out the rest of their lives, it was not on Roanoke Island. Perhaps their boat was wrecked on the way towards their new Eden, pitching them into the water.

If they did manage to found their 'City of Ralegh' on the mainland, they could easily have been wiped out by Indians resentful of their need for food and their competition for land. But there is another possibility, pure speculation unless archaeology turns up some trace of an Elizabethan English village, but still regarded as the most likely scenario by David Beers Quinn, who did more than anyone to ensure that their story is told from the evidence. He imagines the settlers finding a new home somewhere in Norfolk County in Virginia, clinging onto their language and religion while learning a new kind of agriculture from the Indians, marrying within the colony when they could but looking to the local population to find wives for their many young men. Years later, when the colony at Jamestown was well established, the Indian leader Powhatan confessed to Captain John Smith that he had had the English settlers killed after they had intermingled with his people for twenty years, producing a brass gun and a musket-barrel as evidence. Intriguingly, later generations of Croatoans believed that they had white ancestors. Writing his last letter to Hakluyt from Raleigh's plantation in County Cork in 1593, John White could only commit 'my discomfortable company the planters in Virginia' to the merciful help of the Almighty, 'whom I most humbly beseech to help and comfort them, according to his most holy will and their good desire'.[50]

8 Eleventh Hour

The panel portrait of Francis Walsingham which hangs in London's National Portrait Gallery captures his features with unflinching precision. The face is long and rather narrow, coming to a point in a closely trimmed beard. Frown lines have etched themselves into his forehead. Walsingham was in his early fifties when he sat for the painting, and no effort has been made to conceal the encroaching signs of age. The eye sockets are sunken, the dark hair receding under his scholar's cap. A few streaks of silver fleck through his moustache. The fur trim on his black gown hints at a man who had begun to feel the cold. The obligatory starched ruff and fancy cuffs seem oddly out of place on a man like Walsingham; a photographer's gimmick, grudgingly put on and quickly discarded. The only other adornment is a cameo of Queen Elizabeth, a symbol of his power but also a reminder of its ultimate source. The globes and guns and coats of arms crammed into more conventional portraits of Elizabethan courtiers have been deliberately left out of the frame. Instead the viewer's attention is drawn inexorably to Walsingham's eyes, watchful and piercingly blue.

Although the panel isn't signed, we can be pretty confident about the identity of the artist. John de Critz was first-generation English, the son of a Dutch Protestant family living in London since the reign of Edward VI. His parents had assimilated within the Church of England by the time that they arranged for John to be apprenticed to another Dutch exile, the painter Lucas de Heere in 1571. De Heere had carried out commissions for both Philip II and Catherine de' Medici before the revolt in the

Netherlands forced him to take shelter in England in the 1560s. Young John must have watched him working on the group portrait of the Tudor royal family which the queen gave to Walsingham in celebration of the treaty of Blois. Maybe he took a hand in filling in some of the background detail, a common task for an artist's apprentice.

It was probably through this connection that John de Critz came to Walsingham's notice. An aspiring artist naturally wanted to see the court culture of Renaissance Europe for himself, and the principal secretary had the means to grant a passport under the privy seal. By April 1582 he was in Paris, 'resting dutifully at your honour's discretion in anything that I shall undertake'. His letters home refer to him buying art on Walsingham's behalf: a study of St John, and a painting of the sea-god Neptune ravishing Cœnis and transforming her into a man. A sexually charged story taken from Ovid's *Metamorphoses* seems a risky choice for de Critz to send to Walsingham; more suited to the Holy Roman Emperor's 'chamber of wonders' at Prague, where visitors could see a similar work by the Flemish Mannerist Bartholomeus Spranger, than to the walls of Barn Elms. The likely solution seems even stranger, albeit more in keeping with what we know about Walsingham's interests and friendships. Ovid's entwined and androgynous couples were read by contemporaries in terms of alchemical philosophy: the union of the fixed male, represented by mercury, and the more volatile female, or sulphur. John Dee would certainly have picked up the reference when he came visiting from Mortlake. De Critz may also have been a source of the artefacts or 'curiosities' which Walsingham was known to collect, complementing the books in his library and the exotic flora in his garden.

Perhaps this is all that John de Critz was doing in France, touring 'fair houses here about the country' to marvel at their workmanship and gather works of art for his patron. But the fact that his correspondence was filed in the state papers rather than in Walsingham's lost personal archive implies that something else may have been going on. His occupation as a painter gave de Critz an unusual degree of freedom to travel between courts without arousing suspicion. His chosen destination of Paris was the focal point for the English Catholic community in exile. Its streets were awash with conspiracy stories which could be bought for money or the promise of a royal pardon. De Critz's offer to send 'some rare piece of work' from the palace at Fontainebleau may have held some deeper meaning, confided to his courier to explain to Walsingham in person. A letter of October 1582 talks of moving on to Italy, but fees paid out by the treasury reveal that de Critz was in Paris on several further occasions between 1583 and 1588 on some sort of official business. Did he make contact with Richard Hakluyt, another English shadow at the French royal court? De Critz was certainly a political survivor, outlasting the Tudor dynasty to work on Queen Elizabeth's tomb at Westminster and ending up as serjeant-painter to the Stuart kings.[1]

Walsingham probably commissioned his own portrait; Elizabeth preferred her courtiers to foot the bill for the cult of devotion surrounding her. The occasion may have been the signing of the 1585 treaty of Nonsuch committing England to the defence of the Protestant cause in the Netherlands. It had been a long and wearying road to reach this point. Walsingham had been pressing for intervention in the Dutch revolt ever since he had joined the government in 1573. Taking the fight to the Habsburgs was not only the queen's clear duty to God; it was the best guarantee of her own safety. The assassination of William of Orange in July 1584 had prompted Walsingham to draw up a list of leading questions to be debated by the privy council:

> Whether Holland and Zealand, the Prince of Orange being now taken away, can with any possibility hold out unless they be protected by some potent prince.
>
> Whether it be likely that the King of Spain, being possessed of these countries, will attempt somewhat against her majesty . . .
>
> What way there may be devised to annoy the King of Spain.

By the time that Burghley tabled a similar set of proposals in October, Walsingham had acquired proof positive that Philip II intended to strike against Elizabeth. Papers found on the Scottish Jesuit William Crichton revealed that the invasion plans touted by Francis Throckmorton hadn't died with him. They had merely been postponed pending a time when the Spanish king 'shall be rid of his Low Countries troubles'. Crichton had previously been maddeningly out of reach, shuttling between Rome and Paris in an attempt to draw the pope, the Duke of Guise and Philip II behind a plan to invade England and free the Queen of Scots. A tip-off that he was sailing for Scotland had given Walsingham his chance, and his boat was intercepted by a Dutch naval patrol. Crichton tore up his plans and tried to throw them overboard, but enough fragments were blown back on deck to enable an outline of his story to be pieced together. He was taken for interrogation at Seething Lane, where Walsingham was able to fill in the rest.

Two further revelations reached the court within days of each other in the spring of 1585, both of them a consequence of the wars of religion in France. On 6 March the council learned that Henry III had rejected the sovereignty which the States-General had offered him in the wake of Orange's death. The fate of the Protestant Netherlanders now lay in Elizabeth's hands. Still more alarming was the news which Walsingham confided in a letter to the English ambassador in Paris, Sir Edward Stafford, on 22 March. A secret agreement had been reached at Joinville between the pope and the King of Spain, 'whereof they have chosen the Duke of Guise to be the executioner'. The treaty promised Spanish money and soldiers for the Catholic League, in return for military assistance in the Netherlands and the eradication of Protestant heresy in France. Although nothing specific had been said about England, the threat of invasion had suddenly come a lot closer.

This reading of events seemed to be confirmed when Philip II placed an embargo on foreign shipping in May, impounding the ninety-one English ships in harbour. London learned about the outrage from the 150-ton *Primrose*, which fought her way out with four Spanish officials still on board. According to a pamphlet published by Humphrey Mote, her crew were resolved 'to die and be buried in the midst of the sea rather than suffer themselves to come into the tormentor's hands'. The same mood of patriotic defiance is captured in a letter which Walsingham received in June from Sir George Carey, governor of the royal garrison in the Isle of Wight. Carey had heard about the aggressive stance of the Spanish king, and he wanted Walsingham's opinion on what the queen meant to do about it. If open war was coming, then he was ideally placed to intercept the Spanish freighters which he suspected of carrying money to the army in Flanders concealed in boxes of oranges. If her majesty preferred her subjects to recover their own losses, then Carey asked for leave to join the band of adventurers 'as either will lose part of what they have, or gain more from the King of Spain'. Philip II had thrown down a challenge to English honour, and that demanded 'amends and satisfaction' – whether by public war or private revenge.[2]

The treaty of Nonsuch committed Elizabeth to supply five thousand foot-soldiers and a thousand cavalry to the Dutch revolt, in return for naval support from the States if an enemy fleet got as far as the Narrow Seas. The 'cautionary towns' of Brill and Flushing would be taken as collateral until the campaign was won and her loans repaid. Elizabeth wasn't interested in becoming queen of the Netherlands and Walsingham seems to have agreed with her, feeding a list of 'reasons why her majesty should rather accept the title of protector than of a sovereign' into the treaty negotiations. Elizabeth's reluctance might appear odd in light of her obsession with recovering Calais, but in fact her decision was consistent with her broader understanding of monarchy. Calais was part of the hereditary estate of the English crown, while Burgundy was an ancient territory in its own right. To absorb the Low Countries into her dominions, even at the express request of the States-General, was dangerously similar to what the tyrannical Habsburgs were attempting to do. As Walsingham put it, the queen's conscience had previously been 'free from all note of ambition and avarice'. Besides, the drain on the treasury could be open-ended. Taking on the rule of the Netherlands would prompt a 'perpetual quarrel' between the crowns of England and Spain 'which may be the root of long bloody wars'. A decisive campaign to shore up Protestantism and pre-empt a Spanish attack was one thing; a permanent war of religion quite another. Walsingham knew that in the long term, England's resources couldn't hope to match those of the most powerful monarchy in the known world.[3]

For once, the queen and her principal secretary were in agreement on an issue of foreign policy. The problem was her commander on the ground, who took a very different line on the sovereignty question. If Elizabeth had dealt him a different hand, the Earl of Leicester might have been a king of England; now the position of governor-general of the Low Countries proved just too tempting to resist. When she heard that Leicester had accepted the offer from the States, Elizabeth was incandescent that she hadn't been consulted. Worse, he had made a mockery of her claim to stand for the ancient liberties of the Netherlanders rather than her own best interests. Walsingham had a hard fight to save Leicester from being forced to renounce his new title, weakening his own credit with the queen in the process. Elizabeth relented in the end, but the episode left her even less willing to authorise the payments to the army for which Leicester was appealing with increasing desperation. Relations with Walsingham reached a new low when the queen threw a slipper in his face, furious that she hadn't been told about a hostile navy allegedly assembling at Lisbon. Smarting from the humiliation, Walsingham recalled happier times spent in the Protestant city of Basel: 'The opinion of my partiality continueth, nourished by faction, which maketh me weary of the place I serve in and to wish myself amongst the true-hearted Swiss'. By the time that Leicester was recalled in November 1586, £115,000 had been spent in trying to stall the advance of the Duke of Parma – getting on for half the ordinary annual revenue of the crown. The battle of Zutphen had claimed the life of Sir Philip Sidney, leaving Walsingham's daughter Frances a widow at nineteen.[4]

The only good news came courtesy of Francis Drake, and even this would turn out to be a mixed blessing. The queen's decision to unleash her sea-dogs against the Spanish Empire fell short of an outright declaration of war, but it undoubtedly strengthened the case being put by Philip II's advisers for the invasion of England. The fleet which Drake led out of Plymouth in September 1585 made initially for the Spanish port of Vigo, where a number of the English merchantmen had been impounded. Christopher Carleill, captain of the *Tiger* and overall military commander of the expedition, forwarded Walsingham an account of the raiding party sent upriver by Drake. A coffer was discovered containing the vestments and treasures from the cathedral, 'whereof one cross was as much as a man might carry, being very fine silver of excellent workmanship'. Carleill's men skirmished with a company of

Spanish harquebusiers, and a captured English looter was beheaded. The Governor of Bayona offered a truce, at which point Drake allowed some local gentlemen 'to view and see our ships' as a pledge of good faith. But it had been an ugly incident, with blood spilled on both sides and the ritual plunder of church property.

Drake clearly relished the symbolism of having landed on Spanish soil, although he later discovered that the delay might have cost him the treasure fleet from Panama. Subsequent attacks on the Leeward Islands, Hispaniola and Cartagena in Colombia offered scant compensation for the casualties sustained. The queen and other investors in the 1585–6 voyage got back only fifteen shillings in the pound, contrasting with the spectacular returns on Drake's navigation of the globe. Honour had been served and the colonists on Roanoke Island saved from an uncertain fate, but the escapade had done nothing to fill the coffers of the crown. Nor had it improved the lot of English cloth-workers suffering the collapse of their foreign markets. By the time that Drake returned to Plymouth in July 1586, food riots were breaking out across the west of England. The beacon fires standing ready to warn of an invasion had come worryingly close to signalling a popular uprising against the gentry.[5]

In January 1586 Philip II instructed his captain-general of the ocean seas to draw up a plan for the invasion of Britain. It was the moment which the Marquis of Santa Cruz had been waiting for. A vast armada must be made ready, with 150 warships and the auxiliaries to supply them, plus enough transports to carry artillery, cavalry horses and an astonishing fifty-five thousand infantry: a fleet of 510 ships in all. He calculated that the cost would approach four million ducats or about £1,000,000 sterling, equivalent to three years' income for the English crown. Philip welcomed the idea, but paled at the expense. An alternative was put forward by his nephew the Duke of Parma, simpler and cheaper while being every bit as daring: thirty thousand troops floated over to England in flat-bottomed Flanders barges, a blitzkrieg across the Channel in just one night. As Spain's most capable general, Parma was content to keep the navy in a supporting role. He was also critical of Santa Cruz's strategy of targeting the first wave of landings against English power in Ireland. Philip himself was drawn one way and the other, with the result that the Armada which finally sailed in 1588 was a composite of both proposals: a smaller naval force than Santa Cruz had hoped and lacking the surprise element which Parma regarded as essential, but still posing a mortal threat to the Elizabethan regime.

Francis Walsingham had a copy of Santa Cruz's report in his hands by April 1586, only days after Philip himself had seen it. This extraordinary intelligence coup was achieved by Antony Standen, an English Catholic émigré who had come to rest in Florence and assumed a new identity as Pompeo Pellegrini. Walsingham was sometimes prepared to overlook the activities of his agents' families when the quality of information was high, which may explain why Standen agreed to work for him. Or perhaps it came down to patriotism, an unwillingness to see England overrun by Spain in the name of religion. Whatever his motivations, he was a first-class spy with unrivalled access to the enemy camp. As a friend of the Tuscan ambassador to the Spanish court, Standen was able to take soundings of current opinion on the English question. He also recruited an agent of his own, the brother of a trusted servant of the Marquis of Santa Cruz, who sent letters to Standen from Lisbon by way of the diplomatic bag at Madrid. Standen travelled to Spain in person in the spring of 1588, from where he was able to report to Walsingham directly. His reward would be 'reintegration to her highness's favour' and a pension of £100 – the same sum that Gilbert Gifford received for unearthing the Babington plot.[6]

Thirty years before, Philip of Spain had helped his wife Mary Tudor to shepherd the English people back into the fold of the true faith. Now the chance to resume the re-Catholicisation of England stirred him to the core. And yet some doubts remained: the military wisdom of opening up another front before the Netherlands was finally reduced to order, and the sharply political problem of what to do with Elizabeth once her kingdom had been conquered. She was, after all, his sister-in-law and a former candidate for his hand in marriage. Officially Philip and Parma continued to talk the language of peace until the last possible moment, though Walsingham dismissed this as a feint to split the States from their English allies and buy time to assemble an armada. Lord Howard of Effingham, admiral of the fleet, shared his sense of scepticism: 'Sir, there was never, since England was England, such a stratagem and mask made to deceive England withal as is this treaty of peace'. Whatever his previous reservations, the martyrdom of Mary Stuart in February 1587 convinced Philip that God would absolve him of striking against an anointed monarch. Having shed tears over Mary and ordered a requiem mass, he gave the word to assemble the fleet at Lisbon. In the words of Walsingham's counterpart at the Spanish court, it was time to put England 'to the torch'.[7]

Faced with a decision which might provoke a war, Elizabeth's instinct was usually to back away. But for a few critical weeks in the spring of 1587, the balance of power at court was turned upside down. Enraged and shaken that Mary had been executed without her express command, Elizabeth did as she had never done before and banished Burghley from her presence. Suddenly Walsingham and Leicester had the opportunity to present their case for war without interference from the lord treasurer. Intelligence gathered in Portugal and Spain had the desired effect on the queen, and she duly authorised Drake 'to impeach the joining together of the King of Spain's fleet'. Drake was exultant. He set out from Plymouth on 2 April 1587 with a farewell salute to Walsingham. It is a biographer's dream of a letter:

> I thank God I find no man but as all members of one body to stand for our gracious queen and country against Antichrist and his members . . . The wind commands me away. Our ship is under sail. God grant we may so live in His fear as the enemy may have cause to say that God doth fight for her majesty as well abroad as at home, and give her long and happy life, and ever victory against God's enemies and her majesty's.

In his haste to engage the enemy, Drake succeeded in outrunning the letter countermanding his orders which he correctly anticipated would soon be chasing him. Ignoring the fortified harbour at Lisbon, he sailed onward south and east to the port of Cadiz. For its sheer daring as well as its role in disrupting preparations for the Spanish Armada, the raid on Cadiz has never been forgotten. Walsingham's heart must have surged when he read Drake's description of the scene: five merchantmen and one of Santa Cruz's own galleons looted and sunk, four cargo ships taken and a further two dozen stripped and burned at anchor, and a squadron of Philip's galleys repulsed and humiliated, all under a hail of artillery fire from the shore. The English fleet then sailed to Sagres on the Algarve, where the castle was bombarded into surrender and a monastery was ransacked and set on fire. Drake told the tale in the language of the Old Testament, casting the Catholic Spanish as 'upholders of Baal or Dagon's Image, which hath already fallen before the ark of our God with his hands and arms and head stricken off'.

But there was also hard detail in his reports to Walsingham, wooden casks to the weight of 1,600 tons 'consumed into smoke and ashes' along with the nets on which the Spanish navy depended for its supply of salted fish. Drake's ships and soldiers were not in Sagres for long, but they succeeded in deterring Philip's Mediterranean fleet from joining the force assembling at Lisbon. If Elizabeth's countermand had reached him in time, the Spanish Armada might well have launched a year earlier than it did.[8]

The delay proved a godsend to those charged with readying England's defences. The threat of a French invasion back in the 1530s had been met by a chain of coastal forts and gun batteries to the latest designs, paid for with the proceeds of the dissolution of the monasteries. But once Henry VIII's Reformation windfall had been spent, the full burden of maintaining fortress England had fallen on the ordinary revenues of the crown. The consequences were all too predictable. The Elizabethan military engineers tasked with preparing to repel a Spanish attack discovered that once-proud castles had been weakened and left obsolete by two generations of neglect. A survey of artillery forts in Dorset in the early 1580s found their wooden platforms rotten and their guns dismantled. Walls were in danger of sliding into the sea. Spanish forces landing in Cornwall or Devon would have encountered defences which had hardly altered since the days of Henry VIII. There had long been talk of a new fort on Plymouth Hoe, but nothing was achieved until several years after the Armada had come and gone. The massive bulwarks at Pendennis Castle above Falmouth harbour and Star Castle in the Isles of Scilly both date from the 1590s rather than any earlier.

The royal docks at Portsmouth fared rather better. In February 1584 Walsingham had authorised the hiring of several hundred pioneers to repair and extend the fortifications around the town.

But the earthworks were far from complete by the time the Armada sailed, partly because the labour force had been reduced to just a hundred on the orders of the queen. On the opposite side of the Solent, the lion's share of the money spent on Carisbrooke Castle had gone on a superior new dwelling for Sir George Carey. Upnor was a rare example of a new-build Elizabethan castle, offering some protection to the Medway and the important anchorage at Chatham, yet incapable of defending itself from an attack on the landward side; a fault which it shared with many Tudor fortifications. The Essex port of Harwich was allocated £1,000 for defences only in 1588, while Ipswich had to fend for itself by employing Walsingham's surveyor and counterfeiter Arthur Gregorye to build it a gun platform.[9]

In the words of the privy council to the citizens of Hastings, 'the strength of her majesty's navy is their surest defence, and of the whole realm'. Given the chronic degree of overstretch in the royal finances, the strategic decision to concentrate on warships rather than shore defences made good sense. A campaign of construction and purchase since the early 1570s had furnished Elizabeth with a fleet of thirty-four ships by 1587, although a dozen were of less than 250 tons' burden and only ten had been designed with gunnery rather than close-quarter grappling in mind. Supplemented by vessels taken up from trade or supplied by the London livery companies, the entire English fleet numbered fewer than sixty ships. With a fair wind and a blessing from God, they could hope to deflect and defeat an invasion armada if not to destroy it outright. But even the newest race-built ships needed harbours where they could shelter and replenish, and here the geography of the coastline east of Portsmouth presented the government with a major headache. The ancient ports of Winchelsea, Rye and Sandwich had all silted up by the later sixteenth century, making them useless to the great galleons of the royal navy. That left only Dover at the narrowest point of the Channel, a scrape between two cliffs offering limited protection from the fierce tides and prevailing winds. Until, that is, Francis Walsingham initiated one of the most impressive civil engineering projects undertaken by the Elizabethan state.

Walsingham had become aware of Dover's potential in 1576, when he appointed the navigator William Borough to report on the possibility of building a better haven for the navy. A plan was hatched to take advantage of a great bank of shingle which had drifted down from the remnants of earlier Tudor experiments to create a harbour. After several false starts, Walsingham found the right overseer in the mathematician and MP Thomas Digges. A pupil of John Dee and his acknowledged 'mathematical heir', Digges had already proved his worth by surveying the strength of Dutch fortifications during Walsingham's and Cobham's embassy in 1578. He was also a committed Protestant, a prime mover of the 1584 bond of association to legislate for a provisional government in the event of Elizabeth's assassination and a keen supporter of intervention in the Netherlands. Digges's theoretical understanding of the formidable challenges at Dover was complemented by the practical experience of Paul Ive, a military engineer who had also seen service in the Low Countries. Ive would dedicate his treatise *The Practise of Fortification* jointly to Walsingham and Cobham in 1589.

Walsingham handled virtually all the paperwork generated by the works at Dover. Reginald Scot's history of the project praised him as 'the man without whom nothing was done, directing the course, and always looking into the state thereof'. Walsingham's manuscript journal of 1583–4 gives us a glimpse of him running the operation from Seething Lane, despatching orders and authorising payments for men and materials. Hydraulic experts were brought over from Flanders to refine the sophisticated system of groynes and sluices devised by Digges and Ive. But it was local know-how from Romney Marsh which underpinned the strength of Dover harbour. The key to success turned out to be the mixture of chalk and 'ooze', or mud, used in constructing the walls. Digges recognised that Romney men were 'the only and fittest workmen' for the task, so long as they were properly supervised. Throughout the summer of 1583, hundreds of Kentish carts transported building materials down to Dover. The chronicler Raphael Holinshed recorded the songs and laughter of the drivers as they tipped their loads into the water. As the local gentleman Sir Thomas Scott triumphantly reported to Walsingham, two months of effort achieved what had been expected to take two years, and at a fraction of the cost of using timber and stone. For the first time, the English navy had a usable harbour on the Channel coast closest to the continent.[10]

The tremor radiating out from Francis Drake's 1587 assault on Cadiz was felt by Walsingham's sources across Europe. Watching the Spanish reaction from his viewpoint in Florence, Antony Standen described how the Devon pirate (who had his own symbol, 22, in Standen's cipher alphabet) 'hath put a great terror among that people'. According to Edward Stafford, the pope was now sneering that the King of Spain was 'a coward that suffered his nose to be held in the Low Countries by a woman'. Philip had been humiliated in his own realm by a mere mariner. Captain Thomas Fenner, who took part in the raid, judged it a miracle 'that so great an exploit should be performed with so small loss'. Drake basked in the adulation, but was under no illusions about Spain's ability to recover. His despatches to Walsingham and Leicester contained the same urgent warning: 'the like preparation was never heard of nor known, as the King of Spain hath and daily maketh to invade England'. Philip had powerful allies, and his store of provisions was sufficient to keep an army of forty thousand in the field for a whole year. Singeing his beard at Cadiz had only delayed the inevitable. Drake's appeal to Walsingham sounded an alarum as clearly as in any Shakespeare play: 'Prepare in England strongly, and most by sea. Stop him now, and stop him ever. Look well to the coast of Sussex . . . It is the Lord that giveth victory.'[11]

The challenge facing Walsingham and the council lay less in establishing the existence of the Armada, which was obvious, than in working out what Philip II intended to do with it. Reports were frequently contradictory, not least because Spanish plans were themselves so fluid. When the fleet still wasn't ready by the winter of 1587, Philip amazed the Duke of Parma by urging him to launch an assault across the Channel without it. Further confusion was caused by a turnover in the Spanish high command. Santa Cruz's death in February 1588 meant that the helm passed to the Duke of Medina Sidonia, an amiable grandee who by his own admission 'had no experience either of the sea or of war' and was a martyr to sea-sickness. Santa Cruz's battle plans and files were jealously guarded by his secretary, and his successor had to make an impassioned appeal to the king to be allowed to see them. Medina Sidonia did his best to make sense of the chaos at Lisbon harbour, but his natural deference to his sovereign was a poor substitute for the robust decision-making of Santa Cruz.

Drake suspected that the Armada might drop anchor off the Sussex coast, where the Throckmorton plotters had hoped to welcome a Spanish landing back in 1583, but in truth the intended landing-zone kept on shifting. Ireland remained a plausible target until late in the day, where Catholic insurgents might be expected to do Philip's work for him. The Isle of Wight was also considered as a bridgehead, a plan which would very quickly have exposed Sir George Carey's folly in building a fine house before reinforcing the defences at Carisbrooke. Meanwhile every month that the Armada didn't sail cost the Spanish crown another seven hundred thousand ducats, testing the discipline and sapping the morale of soldiers and sailors confined to port. Finally the Isle of Thanet was decided upon, an unfortified spur of land on the eastern tip of Kent. Parma's seventeen-thousand-strong Flanders army would be joined by a similar number who had sailed from Spain, while the faster ships of the Armada patrolled the approaches to the Medway and the Thames. Thanet was also symbolically important, the place where St Augustine of Canterbury had begun his mission to convert the Anglo-Saxons to Catholic Christianity. By choosing to land here, Philip II could portray his invasion as the second liberation of the English people from pagan heresy, nearly a thousand years since the first.

Comparatively little thought seems to have gone into the shape of the post-invasion regime in England. It was deeply unlikely that Philip would want to rule in person, while the execution of the Queen of Scots had put paid to ideas of a puppet government under Mary and the Duke of Parma. The sealed orders which Medina Sidonia intended to hand to Parma plotted more than one possible outcome. The Armada was to avoid battle unless forced into it, focusing on preserving its artillery pieces and marines and making its rendezvous at Gravelines. Once the troop transports had been escorted across the Channel, everything would depend on the scale of English resistance. If the landing became bogged down or failed, Parma was authorised to negotiate with Queen Elizabeth. Spanish terms would be, firstly, the free exercise of the Catholic faith in England, and a passport for religious exiles to return home; secondly the surrender of the cautionary towns to King Philip, together with any other parts of the Netherlands in English hands; and finally the payment of damages for acts of piracy against Spanish interests. As for the queen's ministers, Lord Burghley might just have survived – he had, after all, made his peace with the Spanish once before – but Walsingham's execution would have been non-negotiable.[12]

To see the Spanish Armada as a kind of gunboat diplomacy, an attempt to enforce Catholic toleration rather than to annihilate English liberty and religion, goes against more than four centuries of national myth-making. To be fair, Parma's sealed orders would only come into play if the land campaign began to falter; conquest was the prime objective, at least in the eyes of the commander in the field. But a parallel strategy of negotiating from a position of military strength makes some sense of Philip II's protracted peace talks, dismissed as a ruse by Walsingham. It would also be consistent with the attitude of a man who, even though he had once been King of England, displayed little interest in ruling it again.

Following Drake's capture of the *Nuestra Señora del Rosario* on the first day of the battle, the English had the chance to question her officers and crew about the intentions of the Armada. The aristocrat Don Pedro de Valdés was haughty and obstructive, maintaining that it wasn't the place of a subject 'to judge the actions of his prince', but other prisoners of war in London's Bridewell were quicker to talk. Their replies suggest that, as in many large armies, speculation was rife among the soldiers and mariners who made up the Armada. The master of the *Rosario* claimed not to know where the army would have disembarked, though he was clearer about its purpose – 'to conquer the land and to set up the mass' rather than to subjugate the English people, many of whom were expected to rise up in support of their liberators. The ship's doctor wondered if Philip's nephew the Viceroy of Portugal might have been installed as Governor of England, whereas the captain of the *Rosario* reckoned that Parma was the likelier candidate. 'It was a question among them,' as he told his interrogators, 'if the Duke of Parma should conquer this land, who should then enjoy it, either the king or the duke; and it was suspected that it would breed a new war between them'. Regarding tactics, however, all were agreed: captains and ordinary soldiers had determined 'to put all to the sword that should resist them'.[13]

At the eleventh hour, Walsingham received a report which alleged that the Armada would not be sailing at all. Sir Edward Stafford had informed his brother-in-law Howard of Effingham that Spanish forces earmarked for the enterprise of England had been stood down. Howard was unsure what to make of it. 'If it be true,' he wrote to Walsingham, 'I would not wish the queen's majesty to be at this charges that she is at; but if it be but a device, knowing that a little thing makes us too careless, then I know not what may come of it'. Historians are now certain of what Walsingham merely suspected, that Stafford had been in the pay of Philip II since 1587. The opening gambit had come from Stafford himself, who told his Spanish handlers that he wanted to be revenged on Walsingham and Leicester for their hostility towards him. He also claimed, rather less plausibly, that no English warship could be made seaworthy without his first passing on a warning to the Spanish. Mendoza and Philip were both hooked, and so Stafford became the asset known variously as 'Julio' and the 'new correspondent' in return for substantial cash payments.

Agent Julio was as good as his word. Mendoza got the lists and statistics of Queen Elizabeth's fleet which he had been promised, although it should also be said that they exaggerated English firepower by a substantial degree. Either Stafford was acting as a loyal servant of the crown, deliberately making out Elizabeth's navy to be far stronger than it was, or he had been discovered by Walsingham and was being fed false information to pass on to his paymasters. The loss of the ambassador's papers makes it difficult to be sure which of these two paths he had chosen. As for his mysterious letter to Howard of Effingham, in 1583 Stafford had forewarned the queen that his cables might contain passages specifically intended to deceive anyone intercepting his correspondence, indicated by a mark known only to writer and recipient. Since the original letter to Howard no longer exists, we cannot be sure whether it was intended to be read as fact or fiction. Maybe Stafford was engaged in an elaborate double bluff, earning his keep from Mendoza by encouraging Elizabeth to let down her guard while silently tipping off the privy council. As with Walsingham and the Italian banker Roberto di Ridolfi, it is difficult to tell who was ultimately fooling whom. But any argument in favour of Stafford's sincerity has to account for some uncomfortable aspects of his career, not least the stream of misinformation which he continued to send Walsingham after the Armada had set sail: that plague had sent it scurrying back to Spain, that odds of six to one against Spanish ships reaching the Channel were being offered in Paris, and – most amazingly of all – that a fleet of 160 Turkish galleys was even now beating its way towards Spanish Italy.[14]

Stafford's report that Philip had given up on his Armada was contradicted by Howard's own sources. In February 1588 he forwarded 'news fresh of the wonderful preparations in Spain', and wanted to know if Walsingham could confirm the story: 'this is the year that makes or mars, and it were a great deal better that some did weep than all England should cry'. John Hawkins, treasurer of the navy and commander of the *Victory*, added his own voice to the chorus assembling around Walsingham and the queen. England was faced with the starkest choice imaginable: between a peace that was dishonourable and uncertain, and a determined and resolute war. 'If we stand at this point in a mammering and at a stay,' declared Hawkins with a passion, 'our commonwealth doth utterly decay'. Further delay could only benefit the enemy, allowing Philip to prepare at leisure while eating up the limited resources of the crown. Open war would give every subject who loved God and the queen the chance to 'do somewhat for the liberty and freedom of this country', at the same time as forcing Jesuits to declare themselves. Inaction could only lead to 'servitude, poverty and slavery'. As a trader in human cargo between Sierra Leone and Spanish America, whose coat of arms depicted a Moor bound about the neck with a cord, John Hawkins knew what it meant to be a slave.

Hawkins was preaching to the converted. Walsingham shared his conviction that popery and tyranny were two sides of the same coin. But he was also full of foreboding, his sense of depression deepened by his collapsing state of health. A seizure brought on by a severe urinary complaint in summer 1587 left him dangerously ill for several months. In January 1588 he was bedridden once again, tormented by a discharge of fluid from one of his eyes. His mood was worsened by the peace negotiations in which the queen still placed an unwarranted degree of faith, what Walsingham called 'our cold and careless proceeding' at a time of imminent danger. His thoughts turned to divine providence as they so often had before, though without the optimism of Drake and Hawkins that the English nation would prove itself worthy. 'Unless it shall please God in mercy and miraculously to preserve us,' he lamented to the Earl of Leicester, 'we cannot long stand'.[15]

At least the queen had come to recognise that good intelligence was worth the investment. A docket in the state papers counter-signed by the signet clerk Thomas Lake notes the funds released to Walsingham in the later 1580s 'to be paid over to such persons as her majesty hath appointed him' – to agents and informers, in other words. The royal signet was less open to audit than the lumbering procedures of the Tudor exchequer, hence a useful means of authorising cash payments without too many questions being asked. The £500 made out to Walsingham in 1585 leapt to £2,100 the following year, a response to the Babington plot and the growing threat from Spain. A further £2,800 was paid out before the Armada set sail, placing substantial powers of patronage in the principal secretary's hands. According to William Camden, Walsingham topped up these official resources with subventions from his own private income, paid out of the profits from his farm of the customs and various offices including the chancellorship of the duchy of Lancaster. Added to the debt which he had inherited from Philip Sidney, this would help to explain the financial difficulties which weighed Walsingham down during the final years of his life. The contrast with Lord Burghley, who profited handsomely from Tudor service and founded a political dynasty on the back of it, could hardly be more poignant.[16]

Walsingham received his first realistic report of the Armada as late as April 1588, only two months before it moved out of Lisbon harbour to brave the unseasonable storms lashing the coast. Previous estimates of Spanish strength had varied wildly. Thomas Fenner picked up a nightmarish rumour in March of a fleet of four hundred sail and fifty galleys, provisioned with vast quantities of bacon and fish, rice and cheeses. A more accurate assessment came courtesy of Nicholas Oseley, an English merchant who had stayed on in Spain in order to spy for the privy council. His story is fleshed out in a letter addressed to Walsingham in July 1588 from her majesty's ship *Revenge*, where he had been allowed to join Drake as a reward for his loyal service. Oseley described the three months he had spent riding from port to Spanish port, gathering news to send to Walsingham. He also reminded his patron of 'the long time I was prisoner for a spy', and the bribes he had been forced to pay to be released.

Mendoza had known about his activities as early as July 1587, reporting to Philip II that Walsingham judged Oseley to be one of the cleverest men he knew. Given this fact, it seems strange that he was allowed to buy his way out of prison. One possibility is that the Spanish chose to leave agents such as Standen and Oseley untouched, on the assumption that their despatches could only increase the sense of fear among the English. Since the existence of the Armada could hardly be concealed, it could be turned into a form of propaganda. Speculation was ended in May 1588 when Medina Sidonia's report on his 130 ships was printed in Lisbon and Madrid in all its detail, from its sixteen thousand pikes and ten thousand corselets of armour to the mules which would pull its artillery pieces and the friars who would pray for its success. The agent who copied out the book for Walsingham noted that 'in this fleet there goeth many English, some voluntaries and some for pay'. Three English pilots sailed on Medina Sidonia's ship alone.[17]

Beyond a certain point, the size of the Armada was academic: no additional English ships and mariners could be conjured up to oppose it. A more pressing question was where it intended to make landfall, and who might be there to greet it. Exasperated at the queen's orders to 'ply up and down' every possible invasion route against both England and Ireland, a strategy which he described as a 'thing unpossible', Howard of Effingham vented his anger to Walsingham: 'I would to God her majesty had thought well for it that she had understood their plot, which would have been done easily for money'. An official memorandum set out the reasons why the Spaniards might choose to land in the Isle of Wight, easily overrun and an ideal base to launch raids against the mainland. The Lord Lieutenant of Hampshire was fearful that his county was about to become the front line of the invasion. But Walsingham's reply was adamant: 'their whole plot and design is against the City of London, and they will bend their whole forces that way'. This was fact rather than opinion, 'very certainly discovered', though Walsingham did not explain how. The privy council sent a similar letter to the Lord Lieutenant of Sussex, explaining that 'they do not think that the Spanish navy will or dare attempt to land on that coast'. Walsingham's source was sufficiently trustworthy to justify the concentration of Elizabeth's army at Stratford and Tilbury on the flat north bank of the Thames, which the Spanish would prefer (or so Elizabeth's council of war predicted) over fighting their way through Kent.[18]

As for Parma's welcoming parties of English Catholics, they entirely failed to materialise. Recusants were made to give up their weapons and a number of gentlemen were confined to quarters or imprisoned, but otherwise Catholics were treated with restraint and even a degree of dignity under Walsingham's direction. The mayor and corporation of Reading were thanked for discovering a cache of 'popish books', which were ordered to be burnt, and some priest's vestments which were defaced before being handed out to the poor of the parish. But the privy council also received numerous declarations of loyalty from among the Catholic gentry. Some sank their differences with the Church of England, attending 'divine prayers and sermons' for the duration of the crisis, while others offered to enlist as common soldiers in order to prove their devotion to queen and country.[19]

From the moment that the beacon fires warned of the Armada's sighting off the Lizard on 19 July, the privy council sat in session at Richmond and St James's. Walsingham was present at every meeting, sweating over the deployment of troops and weapons and communicating with the lords lieutenant in the counties. Keeping the navy supplied with gunpowder and ammunition soon became a major problem. 'For the love of God and our country', pleaded Howard in his letter of 21 July informing Walsingham of his first engagement with the enemy, 'let us have with some speed some great shot sent us, and some powder with it'. The city of London was searched for any private stores of gunpowder, while the Governor of Upnor Castle was ordered to send his powder and gunners to the Earl of Leicester's army in Essex. Decisions made by the council were passed down the military chain of command. Lieutenant of the Ordnance Sir Robert Constable was urged to send as many wheelbarrows as he could find, or else 'twenty dozen of baskets or more', to assist in strengthening the blockhouse which Henry VIII had built at Gravesend. Brewers in Dover and the Cinque Ports were set to work 'with all expedition' to provide beer for the navy. The master smith of the royal ordnance in Ireland was authorised to manufacture pikes and muskets, so long as 'the Irishry might not be permitted to buy the same to arm themselves'.

More intimidating even than the scale of the Armada was the discipline with which it held together. At first contact with the enemy, the English had watched in awe as the Spanish reorganised themselves into a defensive crescent, a complex manoeuvre perfected against Turkish forces in the Mediterranean and in convoy duties in the Atlantic. The formation proved difficult to break. English gunners maintained an impressive rate of fire without making a decisive impact on ships or mariners. The *San Lorenzo*, an oar-and-sail galleass which subsequently ran aground at Calais, was found to be intact in its hull despite a bruising encounter with Martin Frobisher off Portland Bill. The stalemate was only ended by a freshening wind from the south-west on 25 July, pushing the Armada onward towards its intended rendezvous with the Duke of Parma. Walsingham responded rapidly, redeploying the English squadron in the Narrow Seas to patrol the waters off Dunkirk. Anchoring off Calais on 27 July, Medina Sidonia was horrified to find the Flanders army still six days away from embarkation. Now dangerously short of ammunition and powder, Howard was persuaded to use 'hell-burners' against the Spaniards. On the night of 28–29 July, eight English fireships were packed with pitch and set adrift among the Armada. Ordnance was charged with shot and primed to explode. Many vessels scattered in the ensuing panic, leaving them vulnerable to the predations of Drake and Frobisher. For a time it looked as if the entire Spanish fleet might be wrecked in the shallows off Zealand, but at the last moment a change in the wind allowed it to beat into the North Sea. On 2 August, contact with the Armada was lost.[20]

Remarkably, the peacetime business of the privy council managed to carry on amidst the mêlée. An investigation was launched into a house burglary in Worcestershire, and a fraud case pursued through the ecclesiastical Court of Arches. A dispute over lands in Cork and Limerick was dealt with at the same meeting which discussed the best strategy for defending the Thames. The council also found time to monitor the spiritual welfare of the nation. The Archbishop of Canterbury was requested to lead his bishops and clergy 'in public prayers to Almighty God, the giver of victories, to assist us against the malice of our enemies'. A book of Armada prayers was hastily printed for use in parish churches, recalling God's past mercies in 'preserving our most gracious queen, thine handmaid, so miraculously from so many conspiracies, perils and dangers'. Elizabeth was compared to King David, the slayer of Goliath. A broadside prayer for the armed forces called on God to 'strengthen them with courage and manliness, that they may suppress the slights of Antichrist'.[21]

The surge of patriotism and propaganda reached its high-water mark in Queen Elizabeth's visit to Tilbury on 8 and 9 August. The decision to concentrate royal forces in Essex had come late in the day, a response to the latest intelligence that the Armada was aiming for London. A letter from Burghley to Walsingham dated 19 July refers to five thousand foot-soldiers and a thousand horsemen 'for defence of the enemy landing in

Essex', and Leicester was confirmed as captain-general four days later. Reinforced with troops from the coastal counties which the Armada had already passed by, the army that welcomed Elizabeth to the 'camp royal' at Tilbury had swollen to 16,500: equivalent in size to the one which had sailed from Spain. A boom of ships' cables and anchored lighters was thrown across the Thames. Leicester described his soldiers to Walsingham as 'forward men, and all willing to meet with the enemy, as ever I saw', though how they would have coped in combat against experienced Spanish *tercios* and mercenaries is an unanswerable question.[22]

As the organiser of many of Elizabeth's progresses around her kingdom, Leicester had seen for himself the invigorating effect which the queen could have on her subjects. 'I trust you will be pleased with your poor lieutenant's cabin', he wrote in his letter inviting Elizabeth to review the troops at Tilbury. Her decision to accept his offer was braver than it may seem. The crowds of Londoners cheering the royal row-barges setting off from the privy stairs at Whitehall cannot have known which side was faring better in the atrocious weather now sweeping the North Sea. The Duke of Parma also remained an unknown quantity. The queen was having dinner in Leicester's tent when a report arrived that Parma had set sail and 'would be here with as much speed as he possibly could'. Walsingham picked up the same rumour a few days later, though was able to discount it on Drake's advice that the neap tides would now prevent any troopships from being able to leave Dunkirk.

Walsingham was far from happy about the queen leaving London. Nevertheless, as he explained to Leicester, he decided 'to steal to the camp when her majesty shall be there' to see the assembled army for himself. Recording Elizabeth's visit to Tilbury was a young poet named James Aske, who rushed to register a pamphlet turning its pageantry into verse. *Elizabetha*

Triumphans depicted the Spanish Armada as the latest in a long line of 'damned practices that the devilish popes of Rome have used ever since her highness's first coming to the crown'. The rebellious northern earls and the Desmonds in Ireland, Francis Throckmorton and 'proud Babington with all his wretched crew', had all been destroyed like moths in a flame; yet the pope still plotted to destroy Christ's flock. Now he had met his match in Elizabeth, cast variously as the Virgin Queen and a nursemaid suckling the English nation. Aske described the 'sacred goddess of this royal soil' arriving at Tilbury blockhouse to a salute of guns, the army falling to its knees and dipping its ensigns as her jewelled coach passed by. Elizabeth spent her second day riding around the camp on horseback, reviewing the troops with a marshal's baton in her hand,

In nought unlike the Amazonian Queen,
Who beating down amain the bloody Greeks,
Thereby to grapple with Achilles stout,
Even at the time when Troy was sore besieg'd.

According to Aske, it was as she was heading back to her barge that the queen stopped to offer a parting message to her troops, delivered from her coach to Sergeant-Major Nicholas Dawtry. If she did claim to have the 'heart and stomach of a king' as later generations believed, then Aske made no mention of it. What he did describe was still a rousing piece of oratory: an offer to lead her troops into battle in person, marching 'in the midst and very heart of them' rather than cowering behind castles or palaces of stone. Nor is there any reason to doubt what she said. More than thirty years before, her sister Mary had donned armour to rally her forces against Wyatt's rebellion; now Elizabeth could prove her leadership in a just and holy war. As Walsingham reported ruefully to Burghley, 'your lordship seeth that this place breedeth courage'.[23]

Even as the queen delivered her speech, the crisis of the Armada was passing. The Spanish fleet began its desperate journey home around the coasts of Scotland and Ireland, while the English levies were released to the urgent task of gathering in the harvest. Prayers for deliverance were replaced by services of thanksgiving. Captured Spanish flags were displayed in St Paul's and on London Bridge. The queen's accession day in November was chosen to mark a double celebration, of victory over her enemies and thirty years of unbroken rule. It should have been a time of personal triumph for Walsingham, whose agents had supplied crucial intelligence about the scale and the strategy of the Armada. As the squadron commander Lord Henry Seymour put it in a letter of 18 August, 'I will not flatter you, but you have fought more with your pen than many have in our English navy'.

And yet Walsingham could take little joy in the apotheosis of Elizabeth. Writing to Burghley during the queen's progress to Tilbury, he had aired his sense of shame that 'our half doings breed dishonour, and leave the disease uncured'. The Armada had been dispersed but not defeated, and that by the weather as much as the English navy. Like the East Anglian Puritan Oliver Pigge, Walsingham feared that the hatred of the Spaniards 'is not yet quenched, but rather we may be assured, much more increased, so as they will but wait opportunity to set upon us again'. The Lord must have had some purpose in allowing the Armada to sail, yet there was little sign of the national repentance which it should have summoned into being. The privy council and shire lieutenants had risen effectively to the challenge of the invasion. But worrying cracks had also appeared in the structure of the English state, its ability to sustain a defensive campaign for any length of time and the unwillingness of some commanders to co-operate across county boundaries. Troubled by these unsolvable problems and exhausted by the strain of constant service, Walsingham succumbed to his old illness. He would never be fully well again.[24]

Stoked up by the victory over Spain and the papacy, the cult of Elizabeth reached an unprecedented intensity of praise and devotion. George Gower's Armada portraits depicted the queen with a globe and an empress's crown, her serenity contrasting with the chaos being inflicted on the Spanish fleet behind her. Walsingham's gifts to Elizabeth to mark the new year of 1589 included a velvet cloak lined with cloth of silver, and a white satin doublet embellished with Venice gold. Dame Ursula gave presents too, a pair of perfumed gloves laced with symbolic pearls of chastity, and a 'skimskin' embroidered with golden birds, beasts and trees. Walsingham's relationship with his royal mistress had warmed a little since the crisis of Mary Stuart's execution. The queen asked after his health in the wake of the Armada, though her 'many gracious and comfortable words' had to be coaxed out of her by Clerk of the Signet Sir Thomas Windebank. But Barn Elms was honoured with a two-day royal visit in May 1589, while Windebank was allowed to share some of the burden of attending on Elizabeth.[25]

Although Walsingham often wished himself free from the shackles of royal service, the idea of actually retiring seems never to have occurred to him. The situation at court was in a state of flux. The death of Philip Sidney in 1586 had dealt a heavy blow to those who believed that England had an international Protestant mission to fulfil. Now Leicester had followed his nephew to the grave, carried off by a malarial infection less than a month after he had hosted the queen at Tilbury. Mortality probably held few terrors for Francis Walsingham. Calvinists usually included themselves among the elect, while the torment of purgatory was just so much monks' cant. But Leicester's passing deprived him of a powerful ally as well as a friend. It was also a sharp reminder that the queen, who was Leicester's exact contemporary, would not be around for ever. Age would inevitably accomplish what foreign invasion and an assassin's bullet had so far failed to achieve, yet the royal succession remained unresolved. A war by proxy in the Netherlands had escalated into a full-scale conflict with Spain, compounding the tension in court politics. One observer commented that he had never seen 'such emulation, such envy, such back-biting as is now at this time'.

The impending extinction of the Tudor line left several possible contenders for the English throne. As the son of Catherine Grey and the Earl of Hertford, Lord Beauchamp enjoyed the strongest claim according to the provisions of Henry VIII's will, but his parents' secret marriage had been declared invalid by the queen, and Beauchamp never seriously entered the running. James VI of Scots was descended on both his father's and his mother's side from King Henry VII, whose daughter Margaret had married into the house of Stuart. James's cousin Arabella Stuart had the same pedigree with the added advantage of being English by birth, but the support she received from Catholic circles effectively ruled her out (after decades of female rule, her gender may have been another factor). The King of Scots was a committed Calvinist, though this had not prevented him from engaging in brinkmanship with the English at the time of the Armada. Catholicism remained a real presence among the Scottish nobility, and James was able to play on English fears of a war on two fronts to extract a promised pension from Elizabeth. It was a game of high stakes, as Walsingham observed to Sir Robert Sidney. 'If he should lose the possibility that he pretendeth to have to this crown after her majesty's decease by growing to a pike with us', then neither Spain nor France would be quick to help him regain it.

Judging James to have been 'ill counselled', Walsingham offered him some advice of his own. A letter of December 1588 praised the good intentions of the young monarch while warning of the perils when 'every great personage in that realm pretendeth to be a king'. What was necessary for sound government, along with an impartial council of advisers, was a parliament and Star Chamber to check the nobility and enforce the rule of law. Offering English solutions to Scottish problems was Walsingham's way of bringing the two nations closer together, smoothing the path towards an increasingly inexorable union. To achieve anything more would have required a clear statement about the succession from the queen, and for that she kept her councillors guessing until the hour of her death.[26]

Regarding the hostilities with Spain, Elizabeth took a much clearer line. A reprisal raid must be launched to 'distress the ships of war' which had limped back to take refuge in the ports of Santander and San Sebastián. Walsingham was all in favour of a counter-attack against Philip II, questioning Howard as early as August 1588 about the feasibility of harrying the Azores and capturing the treasure fleet, but the navy was in urgent need of being careened and re-rigged. When the expedition finally departed in April 1589, its commanders had a markedly different set of priorities from the queen's. Drake was at the helm once more, leading a huge counter-armada of seven royal vessels and seventy merchantmen plus a further sixty Dutch troop transports. Elizabeth forbade her favourite the Earl of Essex to join Drake at Plymouth, but he ignored her and boarded the *Swiftsure* further down the coast at Falmouth. When she demanded that the captain be arrested and Essex returned to court, Walsingham saw to it that the order wasn't sent.

Events proceeded in the same vein. Drake led a wholly

ineffective assault on Corunna before landing his forces on the Portuguese coast in a bizarre attempt to restore the pretender Don Antonio as king. A forty-five-mile march ended in an unsustainable siege of Lisbon and personal frustration for Essex, who drove his lance into the city gates in disgust that no one would accept his challenge to a duel. Ralph Lane, the former governor of Roanoke who served as muster-master of the army, wrote a report for Walsingham commending Essex's bravery but criticising the behaviour of Drake and Sir John Norris. They were characterised as 'two overweening spirits, contemning to be advised and disdaining to ask advice'. Spanish galleys succeeded in capturing several English ships and would have taken more, claimed Lane, had it not been for the intervention of God. Elizabeth was incensed at the loss of men and materiel, and with good cause. Her temper was hardly improved when the privy council decreed that eighty ships belonging to German merchants, taken by Drake as prizes on the pretext that they were trading in contraband, should be restored to their rightful owners. Walsingham urged the queen to listen to her councillors debating the issue, but nothing he could say would persuade her to attend.[27]

Walsingham had only recently returned to the council table, having suffered repeated bouts of illness between February and June 1589. In August he was bedridden but still working, instructing his secretaries to read Burghley's letters out loud and dictating his replies. On 12 December he signed his will, with Robert Beale standing as one of the witnesses. Sensing that the end must be approaching, Walsingham's thoughts turned at last to his family. There was no son to inherit his influence at court; any lasting political legacy would depend on his brother-in-law Beale. But he and Ursula did have their daughter Frances, 'wonderfully overthrown' by the death of Philip Sidney and their stillborn child, and still only nineteen years old. Sidney and

Essex had forged a powerful bond during the campaign in the Netherlands, where the young earl served as colonel-general of cavalry. The dying Sidney had bequeathed Essex his sword, symbolically conferring on him the role of a Protestant knight which Sidney had crafted for himself. Given this close connection, it is not so surprising that Essex should choose to marry Sidney's widow. And Frances could not have hoped for a higher-ranking husband: master of the horse and a knight of the Garter, an intimate favourite of the queen and also arrestingly handsome, if Nicholas Hilliard's miniature 'Young Man among Roses' is indeed the Earl of Essex.

The date of Frances's marriage to Essex has never been known for sure, but it must have taken place after December 1589, when Walsingham's will referred to his daughter by her widow's title of Lady Frances Sidney. Their first child was born in January 1591: a boy, named Robert after his father, and destined to command the parliamentary army against King Charles I during the civil war. The timing implies that Frances and Essex were married shortly before Walsingham's death in March 1590; perhaps at his request, although it may also have been for love. The couple went on to have five further children, and Essex also assumed responsibility for his stepdaughter Elizabeth Sidney. Another boy and two girls would result from Frances's third marriage, to the Irish peer the Earl of Clanricarde, following Essex's execution for treason in 1601. Clanricarde drew on his Galway estates to build a fine house for Frances in Kent.[28]

Walsingham continued to attend meetings of the privy council until late March 1590. On the night of 1 April he suffered a fit, at which point Thomas Windebank stepped in to petition the queen 'for speedy easing of your honour'. Elizabeth's response was typically lofty. She would shortly 'call another to the place', but until then Walsingham should be reminded to make 'speedy despatch' of Irish business. The letter informing him of the queen's decision was probably the last that he read. On 3 April he sold some land to a consortium including his secretary Francis Mylles, perhaps to reward him for his role in rounding up the Babington plotters. Three days later, Walsingham's lifelong struggle against illness was over. Lurid stories were soon trading hands in Catholic circles – that 'his urine came forth at his mouth and nose with so odious a stench that none could come near him', or that his body had become so corrupted that he poisoned one of the pall-bearers at his funeral. John Dee's diary for 6 April 1590 states simply that 'good Sir Francis Walsingham died at night *hora undecim*', at the eleventh hour. Updates from Richard Bingham detailing the seizure of Irish cattle and corn reached Seething Lane too late for Walsingham to read them. The problem of Ireland was still there, just as it had been when he first joined the privy council.[29]

Walsingham's will was found 'in a secret cabinet' the day after his death. As was conventional, his first bequest was his own soul: 'to God the father my creator, to God the son my only redeemer, and God the holy ghost the true comforter', affirming him to be an orthodox believer in the Trinity. Less formulaic was the section which followed it,

> assuring myself that Jesus Christ my true and only Saviour of his great and infinite mercy and goodness will vouchsafe not only to protect and defend me during the time of my abode here in this transitory earth with his most merciful protection (especially in this time wherein sin and iniquity doth so much abound), but also in mercy to grant unto me, by increase of faith, strength and power to make a good and Christian end.

All the elements of a godly Protestant belief were there: the sufficiency of Christ for salvation, with no mention of the Virgin Mary or the saints; the impermanence and corruption of the world; a yearning for the gift of faith, and for the stoical death which would be proof of election. There was even a nagging thorn of doubt, 'assuring myself' managing to convey both the certainty and the fear of being uncertain which coexisted in the Protestant mind. In his will, we finally have the chance to hear Walsingham in prayer.

Having committed his soul to the keeping of his redeemer, Walsingham had little time for his body. He asked to be buried 'without any such extraordinary ceremonies as usually appertain to a man serving in my place', citing the greatness of his debts. Walsingham was troubled about the 'mean state' in which he would be leaving Dame Ursula. A later inquest into his estates listed the manor of Bradford in Wiltshire as well as farms and orchards in Barnes, including twelve acres of arable which by then had passed to Robert Beale. Even with Barn Elms and the lands which he had sold before his death, this wasn't much to show for twenty years as an ambassador, principal secretary and the queen's chief of security.

In keeping with his wishes, Walsingham was buried quietly on the evening of 7 April in the north aisle of old St Paul's, within sound of the preachers and booksellers who clustered around Paul's Walk. Ursula and Frances chose to place him in the same grave as Philip Sidney. There was no effigy, nor even a tomb: merely a wooden tablet with an inscription in two languages. A summary of his career in Latin praised Walsingham's role in making peace, serving the state and protecting his country from danger, while an English epitaph reflected more specifically on his work as a spymaster:

In foreign countries their intents he knew,
Such was his zeal to do his country good,
When dangers would by enemies ensue,
As well as they themselves he understood.

The initial letters of each line spelled out 'Sir Francis Walsingham' as an acrostic. The memorial was recorded in the early seventeenth century but destroyed in the Great Fire of 1666. Sidney's modern admirers have erected a slate plaque to his memory in the crypt of St Paul's Cathedral, but of Walsingham there is no mention.

In the absence of a state funeral, it was left to the poet Thomas Watson to reflect on Walsingham's passing. Watson had probably worked for the crown as an intelligencer before settling down to a literary career. He had also recently served a term in Newgate prison for manslaughter, the price of intervening in a brawl to save the life of Christopher Marlowe. Watson's verses to mark Walsingham's death were crammed with classical allusions. England became Arcadia, while courtiers and statesmen were recast as characters from Virgil's *Eclogues*. Queen Elizabeth appeared as Diana, the 'glory of her sex and kind'. Watson recalled Walsingham as 'a sound pillar of our common wealth'. His death had deprived Diana of the protection which she had enjoyed for so long:

> Now in the fields each corn hang down his head,
> Since he is gone, that weeded all our corn:
> And sprouting vines wither till you be dead,
> Since he is dead, that shielded you from storm.

Rooting out the weeds from the commonwealth, and shielding his queen from harm: a tribute that would have satisfied even Walsingham.[30]

Acknowledgements

Neil Belton at Faber and Faber has been a heroically patient editor, incisive and gracious in his comments. This was his idea for a book; I hope it has been worth the wait. Kate Murray-Browne helped to make it a better-written story than it would otherwise have been. Numerous colleagues, friends and family have assisted along the way. Robert Armstrong, Jason Eldred, Jonathan Fagence and Matthew Grimley kindly commented on drafts. Simon Ditchfield translated Tomasso Sassetti's Italian account of Francis Walsingham and the Sieur de Briquemault, and Stuart Carroll helped me understand the geography of sixteenth-century Paris. Advice and encouragement was offered by Kenneth Bartlett, Claire Booth, John Bossy, Jonathan Blunden, Jon Crawford, Thomas Healy, Jan James, Harry Kelsey, Peter Mancall, Bill Sherman, Penry Williams and Jonathan Woolfson. Blair Worden lent me his copy of Conyers Read's three-volume biography of Walsingham, and Stephen Alford arranged for me to see the portrait in King's College, Cambridge. Aspects of the argument were tested out in seminars at the Universities of Cambridge, London, Liverpool and York. A Francis Bacon Fellowship at the Huntington Library gave me time to read about western planting; Juan Gomez and the staff of the Ahmanson Reading Room were hospitable beyond the call of duty. My deepest debt of gratitude is to Suzanne Fagence Cooper, who read the entire book in draft and coaxed me to complete it.

Notes

†

ABBREVIATIONS

BL	British Library
NPG	National Portrait Gallery, London
TNA	The National Archives, Kew
APC	*Acts of the Privy Council of England*, ed. J. R. Dasent et al. (London, 1890–1964)
CSP Dom.	*Calendar of State Papers, Domestic Series, of the Reigns of Edward VI, Mary, Elizabeth*, ed. R. Lemon et al. (London, 1856–71)
CSP For.	*Calendar of State Papers, Foreign Series, of the Reign of Elizabeth*, ed. J. Stevenson et al. (London, 1863–1950)
CSP Scot.	*Calendar of State Papers relating to Scotland, and Mary, Queen of Scots*, ed. J. Bain et al. (Edinburgh, 1898–1969)
CSP Ven.	*Calendar of State Papers and Manuscripts, relating to English Affairs, existing in the Archives and Collections of Venice*, ed. Rawdon Brown et al. (London, 1864–1947)
HMC	Historical Manuscripts Commission
STC	*A Short-Title Catalogue of Books . . . 1475–1640*, ed. W. A. Jackson, F. S. Ferguson and Katharine F. Pantzer (London, 1986–91)
VCH	Victoria County History of England
EHR	*English Historical Review*
ELH	*English Literary History*
HJ	*Historical Journal*
HLQ	*Huntington Library Quarterly*
JEH	*Journal of Ecclesiastical History*
PP	*Past and Present*
SCJ	*Sixteenth Century Journal*
TRHS	*Transactions of the Royal Historical Society*
WMQ	*William and Mary Quarterly*

PROLOGUE

1 Briquemault and Sassetti: John Tedeschi, 'Tomasso Sassetti's Account of the St Bartholomew's Day Massacre', in A. Soman (ed.), *The Massacre of St Bartholomew: Reappraisals and Documents* (The Hague, 1974), 143, where Briquemault is called Bricamore; 'Journal of Sir Francis Walsingham from Dec. 1570 to April 1583', ed. C. T. Martin, *Camden Miscellany* 6 (London, 1870–1), 4–5, 10, 13; Dudley Digges, *The Compleat Ambassador, or, Two Treaties of the Intended Marriage of Qu. Elizabeth* (London, 1655), 270–1, 345. The Briquemault incident is not mentioned in Conyers Read's account of St Bartholomew: *Mr Secretary Walsingham and the Policy of Queen Elizabeth* (Oxford, 1925), I, 219–22.

1: EXODUS

1 Walsingham family, London and Kent: E. A. Webb, G. W. Miller and J. Beckwith, *The History of Chislehurst: Its Church, Manors, and Parish* (London, 1899), 30–6, 111–32; Karl Stählin, *Die Walsinghams bis zur Mitte des 16 Jahrhunderts* (Heidelberg, 1905); William B. Robison, 'Sir Edmund Walsingham' and Reavley Gair, 'Sir Thomas Walsingham' in *Oxford DNB*; Conyers Read, *Mr Secretary Walsingham and the Policy of Queen Elizabeth* (Oxford, 1925), I, 1–13; Joseph Foster, *Register of Admissions to Gray's Inn* (London, 1889), 2. Baptismal rite: Eamon Duffy, *The Stripping of the Altars: Traditional Religion in England c. 1400–c. 1580* (New Haven and London, 1992), 280–1. Henry VIII jewel: PRO, PROB 11/42B, fol. 137v. Aldermanbury: PRO, PROB 11/25, fol. 70v; John Stow, *A Survey of London*, ed. C. L. Kingsford (Oxford, 1908), under 'Cripplegate warde'.

2 Key of all England: John Chandler, *John Leland's Itinerary* (Stroud, 1993), 245. Society and church in Kent: Peter Clark, *English Provincial Society from the Reformation to the Revolution* (Hassocks, 1977), 3–23; Michael Zell, 'The Coming of Religious Reform', in Michael Zell (ed.), *Early Modern Kent 1540–1640* (Woodbridge, 2000), 177–206; Diane Watt, 'Elizabeth Barton' in *Oxford DNB*.

3 Act of Appeals: *Statutes of the Realm* (London, 1810–28), III, 427. Rebellion of youth: Susan Brigden, 'Youth and the English Reformation', *PP* 95 (1982), 37–67. Rood of Boxley: Zell, 'Religious Reform', 199.

4 William Walsingham's will: PRO, PROB 11/25, fol. 70v. Sir John Carey: Read, *Walsingham*, I, 13–14. Hunsdon: Simon Thurley, *The Royal Palaces of Tudor England* (New Haven and London, 1993), 49, 80–1.

5 Cambridge and King's: King's College, Cambridge Archive Centre, KCAR 4/1/6 commons book 1549–50, KCAR 4/1/1 mundum book 1547–53; Read, *Walsingham*, I, 14–16; D. R. Leader, *A History of the*

University of Cambridge, volume I: to 1546 (Cambridge, 1988), 69–71, 228 and chapter 13; Victor Morgan, *A History of the University of Cambridge*, volume II: 1546–1750 (Cambridge, 2004), 16–17, 119–21.

6 Chapel glass: H. G. Wayment, *The Windows of King's College Chapel Cambridge* (London, 1972), 1–6, 55–6.

7 Provosts of King's: Malcolm Kitch, 'George Day' and Alan Bryson, 'Sir John Cheke' in *Oxford DNB*. Bucer: Winthrop S. Hudson, *The Cambridge Connection and the Elizabethan Settlement of 1559* (Durham, North Carolina, 1980), 58–60. Gardiner: C. H. Cooper and T. Cooper, *Athenae Cantabrigienses* (Cambridge, 1858), I, 515. Cheke and Cecil: Stephen Alford, *Burghley: William Cecil at the Court of Elizabeth I* (New Haven and London, 2008), 17–21.

8 King Edward and the Reformation: Diarmaid MacCulloch, *Tudor Church Militant: Edward VI and the Protestant Reformation* (London, 1999), 14–41, 102; Peter Marshall, *Reformation England 1480–1642* (London, 2003), 58–85.

9 Portraits: R. Ormond and M. Rogers (eds), *Dictionary of British Portraiture* (London, 1979), I, 146; NPG 1704, 1807. St Paul's epitaph: Henry Holland, *Monumenta Sepulchraria Sancti Pauli* (1614), STC 13583.5 [17–19]; Cooper, *Athenae Cantabrigienses*, II, 89–90. Gray's Inn: Foster, *Gray's Inn*, 22; Stow, *Survey of London*, under 'The suburbes without the walles'; Greg Walker, *Plays of Persuasion: Drama and Politics at the Court of Henry VIII* (Cambridge, 1991), 33–5. Religion in London: Susan Brigden, *London and the Reformation* (Oxford, 1989), chapters 10–12; Andrew Pettegree, *Foreign Protestant Communities in Sixteenth-Century London* (Oxford, 1986), 272.

10 Edward's illness: W. K. Jordan (ed.), *The Chronicle and Political Papers of King Edward VI* (Ithaca, 1966), 117. Mary's accession and Wyatt's rebellion: D. M. Loades, *Two Tudor Conspiracies* (Cambridge, 1965), map; Anna Whitelock and Diarmaid MacCulloch, 'Princess Mary's Household and the Succession Crisis, July 1553', *HJ* 50 (2007), 265–87; Brigden, *London and the Reformation*, chapter 13; J. P. D. Cooper, *Propaganda and the Tudor State: Political Culture in the Westcountry* (Oxford, 2003), 163–70. Walsingham relatives: Read, *Walsingham*, I, 22.

11 Nicodemism and conventicles: Brigden, *London and the Reformation*, 559–60, 600–4. Cecil and the mass: Alford, *Burghley*, 74.

12 Basel: C. H. Garrett, *The Marian Exiles: A Study in the Origins of Elizabethan Puritanism* (Cambridge, 1938), 55–7, 143–4, 319–20, 357–8; H. G. Wackernagel (ed.), *Die Matrikel der Universität Basel* (Basel, 1951), II, 91; Read, *Walsingham*, I, 25; Diarmaid MacCulloch, *Reformation: Europe's House Divided* (London, 2003), 194, 261. Padua: Jonathan Woolfson,

Padua and the Tudors: English Students in Italy, 1485–1603 (Toronto, 1998), 221–2, 231, 280–1.

13 Walsingham to his nephew: printed in Read, *Walsingham*, I, 18–20. Sidney to Denny: printed in James M. Osborn, *Young Philip Sidney 1572–1577* (New Haven and London, 1972), 537–40.

14 Activism in the Veneto: Kenneth R. Bartlett, 'The English Exile Community in Italy and the Political Opposition to Queen Mary I', *Albion* 13 (1981), 223–41; 'The Misfortune that is Wished for Him: The Exile and Death of Edward Courtenay, Earl of Devon', *Canadian Journal of History* 14 (1979), 1–28.

15 Cecil in Mary's reign: Alford, *Burghley*, 65–82. Thomas Walsingham and Pole: *APC* V (1554–6), 83.

16 Restoration and persecution: Eamon Duffy, *Fires of Faith: Catholic England under Mary Tudor* (New Haven and London, 2009), reference to 'microscopic' scrutiny at 131; Eamon Duffy and David Loades (ed.), *The Church of Mary Tudor* (Aldershot, 2006); Judith M. Richards, *Mary Tudor* (London, 2008), chapter 10; Gina Alexander, 'Bonner and the Marian Persecutions', *History* 60 (1975), 374–91. Stratford-le-Bow: John Foxe, *Actes and Monuments* (London, 1570), 2,097.

17 Radical political thought: Robert M. Kingdon, 'Calvinism and Resistance Theory, 1550–1580', in J. H. Burns (ed.), *The Cambridge History of Political Thought 1450–1700* (Cambridge, 1991), 193–218.

2: MASSACRE AT PARIS

1 Elizabeth's conformity during Mary's reign: David Starkey, *Elizabeth: Apprenticeship* (London, 2000), 122–4, 164–5. Bishops: Penry Williams, *The Later Tudors* (Oxford, 1998), 237.

2 Bossiney: History of Parliament, *The House of Commons 1558–1603*, ed. P. W. Hasler (London, 1981), III, 571–2; J. P. D. Cooper, *Propaganda and the Tudor State: Political Culture in the Westcountry* (Oxford, 2003), 182–4. Elizabethan religious settlement: Jennifer Loach, *Parliament under the Tudors* (Oxford, 1991), chapter 6; Winthrop S. Hudson, *The Cambridge Connection and the Elizabethan Settlement of 1559* (Durham, North Carolina, 1980); Williams, *Later Tudors*, 233–7, 456–7.

3 Freedom of speech: T. E. Hartley (ed.), *Proceedings in the Parliaments of Elizabeth I* (Leicester, 1981), I, 426. Reformations by public authority: Conyers Read, *Mr Secretary Walsingham and the Policy of Queen Elizabeth* (Oxford, 1925), II, 264–5.

4 Lyme Regis and Surrey: Hasler, *Commons 1558–1603*, III, 571. My brother Beale: BL Harley 6035, fol. 47v, 57r.

5 Archives: Robert Beale, 'A Treatise of the Office of a Councillor and

Principal Secretary', BL Additional 48161, reproduced in Read, *Walsingham*, I, 431; Stephen Alford, 'State Papers of Edward VI, Mary I and Elizabeth I: the Archives and the Documents', *State Papers Online, 1509–1714* (Cengage Learning, Reading, 2007). Gyrfalcon: TNA SP 59/24/445. Trees and gardens: BL Harley 6035, fol. 73, 96; 'Journal of Sir Francis Walsingham' from Dec. 1570 to April 1583', ed. C. T. Martin, *Camden Miscellany* 6 (London, 1870–1), 9; Read, *Walsingham*, III, 432.

6 Sarsenet was a soft silk fabric, 'Saracen' in origin. Anne Carleill and Parkbury: PRO, PROB 11/47, fol. 241v. Muscovy Company: Read, *Walsingham*, III, 370–1. Appointment as JP: Hasler, *Commons 1558–1603*, III, 571.

7 Ursula: PRO, PROB 11/100, fol. 92r–v; PRO, PROB 11/75, fol. 262v; 'Journal of Sir Francis Walsingham', 7; C. H. and T. Cooper, *Athenae Cantabrigienses* (Cambridge, 1858), II, 87; NPG 1705. Don Antonio's diamond: Read, *Walsingham*, II, 56–7, 81–2.

8 Barn Elms: 'Journal of Sir Francis Walsingham', 38–40, 48; John Nichols, *The Progresses and Public Processions of Queen Elizabeth* (New York, 1973), II, 440 and III, 27–8. Horses: TNA SP 12/224, fol. 160–3. Odiham: TNA SP 12/109, fol. 11r; Simon Adams, Alan Bryson and Mitchell Leimon, 'Sir Francis Walsingham' in *Oxford DNB*. Portrait, house and garden: Roy Strong, *The Artist and the Garden* (New Haven and London, 2000), 47 and plates 49, 50. Dutch gables and banqueting houses: Mark Girouard, *Elizabethan Architecture* (New Haven and London, 2009), 96, 104–6, 171, 274. Cosyn and Bacheler: S. Sadie (ed.), *The New Grove Dictionary of Music and Musicians* (London, 1980), I, 880–1 and IV, 827.

9 English royal arms: John Guy, *My Heart is My Own: The Life of Mary Queen of Scots* (London, 2004), 95–6, 105.

10 Cecil and the 'casket letters': ibid., chapters 25–6; Stephen Alford, *Burghley: William Cecil at the Court of Elizabeth I* (New Haven and London, 2008), 151–3.

11 Franchiotto: TNA, SP 12/47, fol. 84; TNA SP 70/101, fol. 4; TNA SP 12/48, fol. 50; TNA SP 70/122, fol. 167; *HMC Salisbury* (London, 1883–1976), I, 361. Security: Walsingham to Cecil 20 Dec. 1568, TNA SP 12/48/61, fol. 165r.

12 The earls' proclamation: BL Harley 6990, fol. 90. Northumberland's confession: TNA SP 15/21, fol. 108–15. Other details from K. J. Kesselring, *The Northern Rebellion of 1569* (Basingstoke and New York, 2007); Mervyn James, 'The Concept of Honour and the Northern Rising, 1569', *PP* 60 (1973), 49–83; Julian Lock, 'Thomas Percy, seventh Earl of Northumberland' in *Oxford DNB*.

13 Ridolfi and his plot: TNA SP 12/59, fol. 11–13, 81–2, 84–5, 86, 102; TNA SP 12/74, fol. 43–5; Alford, *Burghley*, chapter 12; Robyn Adams, 'The Service I am Here For: William Herle in the Marshalsea Prison, 1571', *HLQ* 72 (2009), 217–38. The Papey: John Stow, *A Survey of London*, ed. C. L. Kingsford (Oxford, 1908), under 'Aldgate warde'.

14 Atrocity stories: Natalie Zemon Davis, 'The Rites of Violence: Religious Riot in Sixteenth-Century France', *PP* 59 (1973), 51–91; Mack P. Holt, *The French Wars of Religion* (Cambridge, 2005), 62–3.

15 Saint Marceau: John Tedeschi, 'Tomasso Sassetti's Account of the St Bartholomew's Day Massacre', in A. Soman (ed.), *The Massacre of St Bartholomew: Reappraisals and Documents* (The Hague, 1974), 143, 'si salvò nel borgo di San Marceo in casa del medesimo ambasciatore'. Read followed Karl Stählin in placing Walsingham's house in the Faubourg Saint Germain, and every other account has followed Read. Visitors to the embassy: 'Journal of Sir Francis Walsingham', 3, 8, 10 (Languet), 12 (Franchiotto), 13 (Sassetti and Ramus).

16 Walsingham's dinner: Dudley Digges, *The Compleat Ambassador, or, Two Treaties of the Intended Marriage of Qu. Elizabeth* (London, 1655), 28. Cooks in my kitchen: TNA, SP 70/146, fol. 29. Man in black: Read, *Walsingham*, I, 93.

17 Continual increase of charges: TNA, SP 70/120, fol. 59r. Advancement of the gospel: Digges, *Compleat Ambassador*, 121. God's glory and the queen's safety: TNA, SP 70/117, fol. 179v.

18 Coligny: Digges, *Compleat Ambassador*, 135; Susan Doran, *Monarchy and Matrimony: The Courtships of Elizabeth I* (London and New York, 1996), 99–101, 120. Massacre at Wassy: Stuart Carroll, *Martyrs and Murderers: The Guise Family and the Making of Europe* (Oxford, 2009), 12–19. Cardinal of Lorraine: N. M. Sutherland, *The Massacre of St Bartholomew and the European Conflict 1559–1572* (London, 1973), 66–74.

19 Walsingham's instructions: Digges, *Compleat Ambassador*, 18–20. Mary's possible release: Alford, *Burghley*, 161–3.

20 Anjou's appearance: Digges, *Compleat Ambassador*, 29. His sexuality: Katherine B. Crawford, 'Love, Sodomy, and Scandal: Controlling the Sexual Reputation of Henry III', *Journal of the History of Sexuality* 12 (2003), 513–42. Elizabeth's first speech to Parliament: Leah S. Marcus, Janel Mueller and Mary Beth Rose (eds), *Elizabeth I: Collected Works* (Chicago and London, 2000), 56–8 (the Lansdowne version).

21 Ursula Walsingham as Leicester's cousin: Digges, *Compleat Ambassador*, 96. Not for lack of goodwill: ibid., 90.

22 Elizabeth's conditions: ibid., 62–6.

23 Walsingham, Burghley, and Anjou's religion: ibid., 67–70, 89–92; Doran, *Monarchy and Matrimony*, 107–10.

24 Anjou's demands: Digges, *Compleat Ambassador*, 83–6. Book of Common Prayer: ibid., 98–9.

25 Rarest creature: Digges, *Compleat Ambassador*, 101. De Foix's prediction: TNA, SP 70/11, fol. 141v. Her majesty's state: Digges, *Compleat Ambassador*, 97. De l'Archant: Doran, *Monarchy and Matrimony*, 114–15. Plain dealing: Digges, *Compleat Ambassador*, 112. Straiter alliance and confederacy: ibid., 134.

26 My disease: TNA, SP 70/120, fol. 59r; 'Journal of Sir Francis Walsingham', 12, 'I began my diet'. Pheasants and peacocks: TNA, SP 70/146, fol. 29.

27 Devilish Italian practice: TNA, SP 70/122, fol. 153r. Assassination plot, Norfolk and the Queen of Scots: Alford, *Burghley*, 184–95.

28 Smith's embassy: Mary Dewar, *Sir Thomas Smith: A Tudor Intellectual in Office* (London, 1964), chapter 12. Four orders of friars: TNA, SP 70/122, fol. 29v. Fire and water: Digges, *Compleat Ambassador*, 170.

29 Treaty of Blois: ibid., 199; Read, *Walsingham*, I, 189–97; James M. Osborn, *Young Philip Sidney 1572–1577* (New Haven and London, 1972), 39–43.

30 The enterprise of Burgundy: BL Harley 168, fol. 54r–57v. Conyers Read apparently missed this important treatise. Its attribution to Walsingham rather than Burghley is discussed in *Oxford DNB*. God and the Prince of Orange: Digges, *Compleat Ambassador*, 226.

31 Rascal multitude: François Hotman, *A True and Plaine Report of the Furious Outrages of Fraunce* (1573), STC 13847, 59. Massacre: Carroll, *Martyrs and Murderers*, 20. On St Bartholomew see Holt, *French Wars of Religion*, chapter 3; Davis, 'Rites of Violence'; Barbara B. Diefendorf, *Beneath the Cross: Catholics and Huguenots in Sixteenth Century Paris* (New York and Oxford, 1991), especially 102–3; Philip Benedict, 'The Saint Bartholomew's Massacres in the Provinces', *HJ* 21 (1978), 205–25.

32 On Marlowe and Walsingham see below, chapter 5. *De Furoribus Gallicis*: Robert M. Kingdon, *Myths about the St Bartholomew's Day Massacres 1572–1576* (Cambridge, Mass. and London, 1988), 118–19, 129; Sutherland, *Massacre of St Bartholomew*, 317–18.

33 Ursula: 'Journal of Sir Francis Walsingham', 6; Read, *Walsingham*, I, 261 and III, 425 n. 3. Sidney: Osborn, *Young Philip Sidney*, 67–70. A very sanctuary: Timothy Bright, *An Abridgement of the Booke of Acts and Monumentes of the Church* (1589), STC 11129, and see also below, chapter 6. Spanish ambassador: Read, *Walsingham*, I, 222 n. 3.

34 Absence of eyewitness accounts: Carroll, *Martyrs and Murderers*, 193. Discourse after the murder in Paris: BL Cotton Titus, F. III, fol. 302r–308v.

35 Ursula's attempted escape: Arlette Jouanna, *La Saint-Barthélemy: Les Mystères d'un Crime d'État* (Paris, 2007), 188.

36 Spiritual comfort: Digges, *Compleat Ambassador*, 250–1. Disquietness of this state: ibid., 253–8.

3: ARMED WITH INNOCENCE

1 St Bartholomew's service: *A Fourme of Common Prayer Necessarie for the Present Tyme and State* (1572), STC 16511. Public fasts: Alexandra Walsham, *Providence in Early Modern England* (Oxford, 1999), 146.

2 Allegory of the Tudor Succession: Karen Hearn (ed.), *Dynasties: Painting in Tudor and Jacobean England 1530–1630* (London, 1995), 81–2; Roy Strong, *Gloriana: The Portraits of Queen Elizabeth I* (London, 1987), 71–7. John N. King in *Tudor Royal Iconography* (Princeton, 1989), 223–4 argues for a date of *c.*1570 for this painting, interpreting it as an admonition to Walsingham to adopt the queen's own cautious Protestantism instead of a more active foreign policy. This seems too early: Walsingham did not formally take up the post of resident English ambassador until 1571, and did not join the council until 1573.

3 Appointment as principal secretary: TNA PC 2/10, 178; 'Journal of Sir Francis Walsingham from Dec. 1570 to April 1583', ed. C. T. Martin, *Camden Miscellany* 6 (London, 1870–1), 13. Daily attending: Smith to Burghley, 6 Mar. 1575, BL Harley 6991/61. Smith as secretary: Mary Dewar, *Sir Thomas Smith: A Tudor Intellectual in Office* (London, 1964), chapter 15. Ulster: Christopher Maginn, 'Thomas Smith (1547–73)' in *Oxford DNB*.

4 Signet and seals: Penry Williams, *The Tudor Regime* (Oxford, 1979), 39–45; G. R. Elton, *The Tudor Constitution* (Cambridge, 1960), 116–17.

5 Progresses: 'Journal of Sir Francis Walsingham', 19–22; John Nichols, *The Progresses and Public Processions of Queen Elizabeth* (New York, 1973), I, 396; Dewar, *Sir Thomas Smith*, 176; Mark Girouard, *Elizabethan Architecture* (New Haven and London, 2009), 149–50, 181–4; Mary Hill Cole, *The Portable Queen: Elizabeth I and the Politics of Ceremony* (Amherst, Mass., 1999), 37.

6 Privy council: Conyers Read, *Mr Secretary Walsingham and the Policy of Queen Elizabeth* (Oxford, 1925), I, 424; Williams, *Tudor Regime*, 27–33; Elton, *Tudor Constitution*, 101–4; Christopher Haigh, *Elizabeth I* (Harlow, 1988), chapter 4. Star Chamber: John Guy, *The Court of Star Chamber and its Records to the Reign of Elizabeth I* (London, 1985), 1; 'Journal of Sir Francis Walsingham', 17 (5 Feb. 1574), 'I sat in the Star Chamber'.

7 State of the whole realm: TNA PC 2/10, 232–4; Read, *Walsingham*, I, 428.

8 Advice manuals: Robert Beale, 'A Treatise of the Office of a Councillor and Principal Secretary', BL Additional 48161, reproduced in Read, *Walsingham*, I, 423–43; Charles Hughes, 'Nicholas Faunt's Discourse touching the Office of Principal Secretary of Estate, 1592', *EHR* 20 (1905), 499–508.

9 Managing the queen: Read, *Walsingham*, I, 437–8; Pam Wright, 'A Change in Direction: The Ramifications of a Female Household, 1558–1603', in David Starkey (ed.), *The English Court* (Harlow, 1987), 147–72. Walsingham and Huntingdon: Huntington Library Hastings correspondence, box 2, HA 5356, 13064, 13065, 13067; Claire Cross, 'Katherine Hastings, Countess of Huntingdon' in *Oxford DNB*.

10 Cumber and variableness: Hughes, 'Nicholas Faunt's Discourse', 499–500, 503. Falling sick: 'Journal of Sir Francis Walsingham', 17–18. Thwarts and hard speeches: TNA SP 12/109, fol. 11r. A Christian man: Huntington Library Hastings correspondence, box 2, HA 13053.

11 Protestantism in the Netherlands: Geoffrey Parker, *The Dutch Revolt* (London, 1985), 36–7, 57–63, 75–80. Turning-point: ibid., 84.

12 Exiles and Sea Beggars: ibid., 109–10, 118–21; Penry Williams, *The Later Tudors* (Oxford, 1998), 264.

13 Pope's champion: Dudley Digges, *The Compleat Ambassador, or, Two Treaties of the Intended Marriage of Qu. Elizabeth* (London, 1655), 120–1. War: ibid., 127–8; BL Harley 168, fol. 54r–57v.

14 Meanest sums of money: Digges, *Compleat Ambassador*, 57. Opportunity of revenge: Read, *Walsingham*, I, 150.

15 Without licence or knowledge: *CSP For.* 1583, addenda, 496–8. For Gilbert see also below, chapter 7.

16 Christ and Belial: Baron Kervyn de Lettenhove, *Relations politiques des Pays-Bas et de l'Angleterre sous le reigne de Philippe II* (Brussels, 1882–1900), VII, 402; Geneva Bible, II Corinthians 6:14–15. To lull us asleep: Read, *Walsingham*, I, 310. Slumber as she doth: BL Harley 6991, fol. 110.

17 Not for sovereignty but for safety: TNA SP 70/136, fol. 214–15. The case for Walsingham as author of this unsigned paper is made by Read, *Walsingham*, I, 317. The argument and language are both similar to BL Harley 168, fol. 54–7.

18 Champagney: Read, *Walsingham*, I, 319–21. Slipper in the face: Haigh, *Elizabeth I*, 72.

19 Marvellously exasperate her majesty: BL Egerton 1694, fol. 12. Walsingham's advice to Orange: TNA SP 70/140, fol. 154–5.

20 Don John and Peruvian treasure: Parker, *Dutch Revolt*, 180–3, 188–9.

21 John Casimir of the Palatinate: ibid., 192–3. 1578 embassy: Lettenhove, *Pays-Bas*, X, 536, 549–54, 567, 591, 594, 596–7,

613–15, 814–15; TNA SP 83/8/27; Read, *Walsingham*, I, chapter 7; Julian Lock, 'William Brooke, tenth Baron Cobham' in *Oxford DNB*.

22 Doubly inscrutable: Digges, *Compleat Ambassador*, 'To the reader'. One way or the other: ibid., 408. Dudley Digges, who was Leicester's godson, had a diplomatic career in Russia and the United Provinces under James I. *The Compleat Ambassador* was published from his copies of the original manuscripts sixteen years after his death. Horrible spectacle: BL Harley 1582, fol. 49.

23 Advantages of the Alençon match: Smith to Burghley 10 Jan. 1572, TNA SP 70/122, fol. 50r; Dewar, *Sir Thomas Smith*, 134; Susan Doran, *Monarchy and Matrimony: The Courtships of Elizabeth I* (London and New York, 1996), 133–4. Although Francis succeeded as Duke of Anjou in 1576, I will continue to refer to him as Alençon (as English observers often did) to distinguish him from his older brother.

24 Frogs: David Bindman, 'How the French Became Frogs: English Caricature and a National Stereotype', *Apollo* August 2003. Corrupt courtiers: Digges, *Compleat Ambassador*, 343; Read, *Walsingham*, I, 207. Refuge and succour: Doran, *Monarchy and Matrimony*, 131. Clear their bodies: ibid., 197.

25 Elizabeth to Walsingham 23 and 27 July 1572: Digges, *Compleat Ambassador*, 226–30. Perplexity: Doran, *Monarchy and Matrimony*, 136.

26 Such further matter: Digges, *Compleat Ambassador*, 228.

27 Alençon's appeal: Leighton to Walsingham 22 May 1574, TNA SP 70/131, fol. 51. Montgommery: TNA SP 70/130, fol. 136; Stuart Carroll, *Martyrs and Murderers: The Guise Family and the Making of Europe* (Oxford, 2009), 207. Dwarfs: Read, *Walsingham*, I, 288.

28 For the love of God: TNA SP 52/26, fol. 153–4. Casimir's army: Read, *Walsingham*, I, 289–90.

29 The case will be hard: TNA SP 83/8/13.

30 Mildmay, Burghley and Sussex: Mitchell Leimon, 'Sir Francis Walsingham and the Anjou Marriage Plan, 1574–1581' (PhD thesis, University of Cambridge, 1989), chapter 6; Natalie Mears, 'Counsel, Public Debate, and Queenship: John Stubbs's *The Discoverie of a Gaping Gulf*, 1579', *HJ* 44 (2001), 635–7; Doran, *Monarchy and Matrimony*, 159–60.

31 Diseased state of the realm: BL Harley 1582, fol. 46–52; Leimon, 'Walsingham and the Anjou Marriage Plan', 120–2. Some broil in England: TNA SP 12/133/23, fol. 50v.

32 Sermons and pamphlets: Doran, *Monarchy and Matrimony*, 160–4. A frog he would a-wooing go: an earlier frog ballad was published in Scotland in 1548, of which this English version could be a variant. *OED* has 'roly-poly' as a synonym for rascal in the early seventeenth century. *The*

Moste Strange Wedding of the Frog and the Mouse was licensed by the Stationers' Company in 1580.

33 To seduce our Eve: John Stubbs, *The Discoverie of a Gaping Gulf whereinto England is Like to be Swallowed by Another French Marriage* (1579), STC 23400, sig. A2r, A3v, F3r–4v. Scaffold speech: Mears, 'Counsel, Public Debate, and Queenship', 629–30.

34 Walsingham and Stubbs: *CSP Ven.* 1558–80, 621; Mears, 'Counsel, Public Debate, and Queenship', 631–4, 638; Leimon, 'Walsingham and the Anjou Marriage Plan', 123– 5.

35 Walsingham and Sidney: Blair Worden, *The Sound of Virtue: Philip Sidney's* Arcadia *and Elizabethan Politics* (New Haven and London, 1996), 48–55, 112–13. Letter to Queen Elizabeth: Katherine Duncan-Jones and Jan van Dorsten (eds), *Miscellaneous Prose of Sir Philip Sidney* (Oxford, 1973), 46–57.

36 Councillors as sieves: Read, *Walsingham*, II, 22. Sieve portraits and their patrons: Strong, *Gloriana*, 94–107; Susan Doran (ed.), *Elizabeth: The Exhibition at the National Maritime Museum* (London, 2003), 80, 82–3; Hearn, *Dynasties*, 85–6; N. G. Jones, 'Sir Christopher Wray' in *Oxford DNB*. Strong notes that George Gower's 1579 sieve portrait of Elizabeth was painted from a template rather than a sitting with the queen.

37 French delegation of 1581: 'Journal of Sir Francis Walsingham', 41–2; Nichols, *Progresses and Public Processions*, II, 312–29; Doran, *Monarchy and Matrimony*, 180–3. Walsingham the Moor: *HMC Salisbury* (London, 1883–1976), II, 40.

4: THE ENGLISH MISSION

1 Tregian: A. L. Rowse, *Tudor Cornwall* (London, 1941), 346–54; R. F. Trudgian, *Francis Tregian 1548–1608* (Brighton, 1998). Mayne's interrogation: TNA SP 12/118, fol. 105; *APC* IX (1575–7), 375, 390. Agnus Dei: statute 13 Eliz. I, c. 2, *Statutes of the Realm* (London, 1810–28), IV, 529–30; Keith Thomas, *Religion and the Decline of Magic* (London, 1971), 33, 60.

2 Council of Trent: Christopher Haigh, 'The Continuity of Catholicism in the English Reformation', *PP* 93 (1981), 46. Rebellion in Edward VI's reign: J. P. D. Cooper, *Propaganda and the Tudor State: Political Culture in the Westcountry* (Oxford, 2003), 62.

3 Martyred clergy: *Oxford Dictionary of the Christian Church* (London, 1974), under 'Forty Martyrs of England and Wales'.

4 Walsingham's admirers: for example Conyers Read, *Mr Secretary Walsingham and the Policy of Queen Elizabeth* (Oxford, 1925), II, 266–70, 338–9. Mission untainted by politics: Patrick McGrath, *Papists and*

Puritans under Elizabeth I (London, 1967), 122 – the Catholic revival resulted from 'the efforts of men who were not concerned with politics and who strove to bring their countrymen back to the Roman Church by spiritual means'. Fabrication of the Babington plot: Francis Edwards, *Plots and Plotters in the Reign of Elizabeth I* (Dublin, 2002), 125 – 'no historian of any colour could deny that the principal contriver was Francis Walsingham'.

5 Engine of the state: Robert Naunton, *Fragmenta Regalia*, ed. John S. Cerovski (Washington, 1985), 59.

6 Hunting: 'Journal of Sir Francis Walsingham from Dec. 1570 to April 1583', ed. C. T. Martin, *Camden Miscellany* 6 (London, 1870–1), 32. Knighthood and Garter: History of Parliament, *The House of Commons 1558–1603*, ed. P. W. Hasler (London, 1981), III, 571. Garter ceremonial: Diarmaid MacCulloch, *Tudor Church Militant: Edward VI and the Protestant Reformation* (London, 1999), 30–6.

7 Secretary: John Bossy, *Under the Molehill: An Elizabethan Spy Story* (New Haven and London, 2001), 29. Papists marvellously increase: Bishop of London to Walsingham 21 June 1577, in Read, *Walsingham*, II, 280. Recusancy: Peter Holmes, *Resistance and Compromise: The Political Thought of the Elizabethan Catholics* (Cambridge, 1982), 83–9.

8 Bonfires: Christopher Haigh, *English Reformations* (Oxford, 1993), 242–3. Predestination: the seventeenth of the thirty-nine articles of religion (1571). St Piran: *Nicholas Roscarrock's Lives of the Saints: Devon and Cornwall*, ed. Nicholas Orme (Exeter, 1992), 106, 166.

9 Church fabric: Eamon Duffy, *The Stripping of the Altars: Traditional Religion in England c. 1400–c. 1580* (New Haven and London, 1992), 570–7. Clergy: Haigh, 'Continuity of Catholicism', 40; Eamon Duffy, *The Voices of Morebath* (New Haven and London, 2001), 176, 186–7.

10 Lumbye's burial: John Bossy, *The English Catholic Community 1570–1850* (London, 1975), 140.

11 Elizabeth's faith: Richard Rex, *Elizabeth I: Fortune's Bastard* (Stroud, 2003), 54–60. Latin prayerbook, observed by the visiting Duke of Stettin-Pomerania: Leanda de Lisle, *After Elizabeth* (London, 2005), 9. Pius IV: Alexandra Walsham, *Church Papists* (Woodbridge, 1993), 17. Louvainist loyalty: Holmes, *Resistance and Compromise*, 13–17.

12 Church papists: Walsham, *Church Papists*, 9; Bossy, *Catholic Community*, 110–12, 121–4; McGrath, *Papists and Puritans*, 27–31.

13 Tunicle: Duffy, *Morebath*, 178.

14 Prayerbook and accession day: David Cressy, *Bonfires and Bells* (London, 1989); Cooper, *Propaganda*, 233. Catholic prisoners: *APC* VIII (1571–5), 264, 269. Bishop Horne: McGrath, *Papists and Puritans*, 109.

15 Allen and missionary priests: Bossy, *Catholic Community*, 12–19; Haigh, *English Reformations*, 5–6, 254, 261–2; Patrick McGrath, 'Elizabethan Catholicism: A Reconsideration', *JEH* 35 (1984), 424 n. 57; Peter Lake and Michael Questier, 'Prisons, Priests and People in Post-Reformation England', in Nicholas Tyacke (ed.), *England's Long Reformation 1500–1800* (London, 1998), 202.

16 Colleges founded: Penry Williams, *The Later Tudors* (Oxford, 1998), 117. Oxford University and seminary priests: James McConica (ed.), *The Collegiate University* (Oxford, 1986), 378–86, 407–8.

17 July conference: Read, *Walsingham*, II, 280–2. Feckenham re-arrested: *APC* X (1577–8), 4, 13. Garlick: Haigh, 'Continuity of Catholicism', 54.

18 Census of recusants: *CSP Dom.* 1547–80, 558; McGrath, *Papists and Puritans*, 117 n. 3. Population: D. M. Palliser, *The Age of Elizabeth* (London, 1983), 34.

19 Country-house Catholicism: Bossy, 'The Character of Elizabethan Catholicism', *PP* 21 (1962), 39–43, 48; Christopher Haigh, 'From Monopoly to Minority: Catholicism in Early Modern England', *TRHS* 5th series, 31 (1981). Newcastle: TNA SP 12/178, fol. 36–7.

20 Aysgarth: Duffy, *Stripping of the Altars*, 570.

21 Chapels: Bossy, *English Catholic Community*, 125–8. Music: Craig Monson, 'William Byrd' in *Oxford DNB*.

22 Priest-hunters: *John Gerard: The Autobiography of an Elizabethan*, ed. Philip Caraman (London, 1951), 41–2. Priest-holes: Michael Hodgetts, *Secret Hiding-Places* (Dublin, 1989) and 'Nicholas Owen' in *Oxford DNB*; *John Gerard*, ed. Caraman, 201.

23 Candlemas: Ronald Hutton, 'The English Reformation and the Evidence of Folklore', *PP* 148 (1995), 96–8.

24 Prisons: TNA SP 12/165/5, fol. 23r and BL Harley 286, fol. 97 (Newgate), TNA SP 12/194/32, fol. 55r (Dorchester); *John Gerard*, ed. Caraman, 5, 78 (the Marshalsea and the Clink); Lake and Questier, 'Prisons, Priests and People'; Alexandra Walsham, 'Thomas Bell [alias Burton]' in *Oxford DNB*.

25 Theatre of the gallows: Peter Lake and Michael Questier, 'Agency, Appropriation and Rhetoric under the Gallows', *PP* 153 (1996); Michael E. Williams, 'Ralph Sherwin' in *Oxford DNB*. Walsingham on martyrs: Read, *Walsingham*, II, 312–13.

26 Burghley: Robert M. Kingdon (ed.), *The Execution of Justice in England by William Cecil, and A True Sincere and Modest Defense of English Catholics by William Allen* (Ithaca, 1965), 9–10, 29, 39. Espials: scouts, spies.

27 Allen: Kingdon (ed.), *Execution of Justice*, 60–1; Eamon Duffy, 'William

Allen' in *Oxford DNB*, where he describes Allen's postbag as 'stuffed with the explosive matter of high espionage'.

28 *Regnans*: Geoffrey Elton, *The Tudor Constitution* (Cambridge, 1960), 416–18; McGrath, *Papists and Puritans*, 69–72; Julian Lock, 'John Felton' in *Oxford DNB*. Treason: statutes 13 Eliz. I, c. 1 and 2, *Statutes of the Realm*, IV, 526–31.

29 Arundell: *CSP Dom.* 1547–80, 353, 369; Pamela Stanton, 'Arundell family 1435–1590' and Thomas M. McCoog, 'John Cornelius' in *Oxford DNB*; Rowse, *Tudor Cornwall*, 332–3. Fines: McGrath, *Papists and Puritans*, 54, 176.

30 Burghley's fears: Kingdon (ed.), *Execution of Justice*, 6–7.

31 Paris and exiles: Catherine Gibbons, 'The Experience of Exile and English Catholics: Paris in the 1580s' (PhD thesis, University of York, 2006), 169–92.

32 Apartheid: 2 Corinthians vi, 14–15; Walsham, *Church Papists*, 34–5. Sander: Holmes, *Resistance and Compromise*, 26–30; T. F. Mayer, 'Nicholas Sander' in *Oxford DNB*; Kingdon (ed.), *Execution of Justice*, 13.

33 Ideological turning-point: Holmes, *Resistance and Compromise*, 129–35. Mayne and Bell: TNA SP 12/118/46, fol. 105; Peter Holmes, 'James Bell' in *Oxford DNB*.

34 Roscarrock: *CSP Dom.* 1547–80, 649; *APC* XII (1580–1), 264–5; Orme (ed.), *Lives of the Saints*, 1–14.

5: SECURITY SERVICES

1 Throckmorton and his plot: *A Discoverie of the Treasons Practised and Attempted against the Queene's Majestie and the Realme by Francis Throckmorton*, reprinted in *The Harleian Miscellany* (London, 1808–13), III, 190–200; John Bossy, *Under the Molehill: An Elizabethan Spy Story* (New Haven and London, 2001), 31–3, 84–6, 120 n. 40; Stuart Carroll, *Martyrs and Murderers: The Guise Family and the Making of Europe* (Oxford, 2009), chapter 10. Salisbury Court: John Bossy, *Giordano Bruno and the Embassy Affair* (New Haven and London, 1991), 203.

2 Englefield: *Discoverie of Treasons*, 191 bis. Pretention, intention and torture: ibid., 191–2 bis, 200. The dearest thing to me: ibid., 195. Ballad: Alexandra Walsham, 'A Very Deborah? The Myth of Elizabeth I as a Providential Monarch', in Susan Doran and Thomas S. Freeman (eds), *The Myth of Elizabeth* (Basingstoke, 2003), 152.

3 Feron: Bossy, *Under the Molehill*, 46–61, 105–6. Fagot: ibid., 35–6; Bossy, *Giordano Bruno*, 15, 18–21.

4 Camden: William Camden, *Annals, or the Historie of the Most Renowned and Victorious Princesse Elizabeth*, trans. Robert Norton (London, 1635),

394; Hugh Trevor-Roper, 'Queen Elizabeth's first historian: William Camden', in his *Renaissance Essays* (London, 1986), 133. Naunton: Robert Naunton, *Fragmenta Regalia*, ed. John S. Cerovski (Washington, 1985), 59.

5 Secret service: Sidney Lee, 'Sir Francis Walsingham' in *Oxford DNB*. Office of Strategic Services: Benjamin R. Foster, 'Conyers Read' in *American National Biography*.

6 Walsingham's web: Conyers Read, *Mr Secretary Walsingham and the Policy of Queen Elizabeth* (Oxford, 1925), II, 335–6; Bossy, *Under the Molehill*, 144; Alison Plowden, *The Elizabethan Secret Service* (Hemel Hempstead, 1991), 52–5. Subtiltie: Geneva Bible, Genesis 3:1: 'Now the serpent was more subtil than any beast of the field which the Lord God had made'.

7 Local society: Keith Wrightson, 'The Politics of the Parish in Early Modern England', in Paul Griffiths, Adam Fox and Steve Hindle (eds), *The Experience of Authority in Early Modern England* (Basingstoke, 1996). Cucking-stools: David Underdown, 'The Taming of the Scold', in Anthony Fletcher and John Stevenson (eds), *Order and Disorder in Early Modern England* (Cambridge, 1985), 123–5. Treason: J. P. D. Cooper, *Propaganda and the Tudor State: Political Culture in the Westcountry* (Oxford, 2003), 87–93. Oaths: S. J. Gunn, *Early Tudor Government 1485–1558* (Basingstoke, 1995), 181; C. S. L. Davies, 'The Cromwellian Decade: Authority and Consent', *TRHS* 6th series, 7 (1997), 185. Cromwell: R. B. Merriman, *Life and Letters of Thomas Cromwell* (Oxford, 1902), I, 99; Geoffrey Elton, *Policy and Police* (Cambridge, 1972), 327–33.

8 1571 legislation: statutes 13 Eliz. I, c. 1 and 2, *Statutes of the Realm* (London, 1810–28), IV, 526–31. Mildmay: Patrick McGrath, *Papists and Puritans under Elizabeth I* (London, 1967), 174–5.

9 1581 legislation: statute 23 Eliz. I, c. 1, *Statutes of the Realm*, IV, 657–8. The mark, an obsolete monetary unit, was worth two-thirds of a pound sterling.

10 Jesuits in disguise: *John Gerard: The Autobiography of an Elizabethan*, ed. Philip Caraman (London, 1951), 15–18.

11 Persons: John Bossy, 'The Heart of Robert Persons', in Thomas M. McCoog (ed.), *The Reckoned Expense: Edmund Campion and the Early English Jesuits* (Woodbridge, 1996), 141–56. Greenstreet House Press: McGrath, *Papists and Puritans*, 169–71. 1585 legislation: statute 27 Eliz. I, c. 2, *Statutes of the Realm*, IV, 706–8.

12 Seething Lane: John Stow, *A Survey of London*, ed. C. L. Kingsford (Oxford, 1908), under 'Sydon lane' or 'Sything lane'. Walsingham's table book: BL Stowe 162. Secret cabinet: PRO, PROB 11/75, fol. 262v. Maps: BL Harley 6035, fol. 35v; BL Harley 286, fol. 78r.

13 Puritan household: Read, *Walsingham*, II, 261. Herle: Robyn Adams,

'The Service I am Here For: William Herle in the Marshalsea Prison, 1571', *HLQ* 72 (2009), 217–38; 'The Letters of William Herle', ed. Robyn Adams, (Centre for Editing Lives and Letters, 2006, http://www.livesandletters.ac.uk/herle/index.html). Williams: BL Harley 6035, fol. 33v; 'Journal of Sir Francis Walsingham from Dec. 1570 to April 1583', ed. C. T. Martin, *Camden Miscellany* 6 (London, 1870–1), 13, 41; TNA SP 12/155, fol. 56–7, 58–9, 71, 112; TNA SP 12/156, fol. 35–6; Bossy, *Under the Molehill*, 44–6, 48, 55–6, which improves on Read, *Walsingham*, II, 325–7.

14 Sores of this diseased state: *CSP Scot.* V (1574–81), 99; Read, *Walsingham*, II, 345–54. Poison of this estate: transcribed in ibid., II, 305–8.

15 Gentlemen exiles: estimated at four hundred by Catherine Gibbons, 'The Experience of Exile and English Catholics: Paris in the 1580s' (PhD thesis, University of York, 2006), 148–9; Cobham to Walsingham 3 Mar. 1582, *CSP For.* 1581–2, 511; Stafford to Walsingham 27 Dec. 1583, *CSP For.* 1583–4, 281–2.

16 News from Rouen: Becknor to Walsingham 31 Aug./10 Sep. 1584, *CSP For.* 1584–5, 39. Banking: Stafford to Walsingham 15 Dec. 1583, *CSP For.* 1583–4, 269; Gibbons, 'Experience of Exile', 95 n. 28. By statute 13 Eliz. I, c. 3, 'against fugitives over the sea', profits from the lands of unlicensed exiles were forfeit to the crown, although there is some doubt whether the law was strictly applied; see *Statutes of the Realm*, IV, 531–2.

17 Progresses: Mary Hill Cole, *The Portable Queen: Elizabeth I and the Politics of Ceremony* (Amherst, Mass., 1999), 38–9.

18 Stafford: *CSP For.* 1583–4, 435, 457; *CSP For.* 1586–8, 34–5; Mitchell Leimon and Geoffrey Parker, 'Treason and Plot in Elizabethan Diplomacy: The Fame of Sir Edward Stafford Reconsidered', *EHR* 111 (1996); James McDermott, 'Sir Edward Stafford' in *Oxford DNB*.

19 Needham: Read, *Walsingham*, III, 246–7.

20 Foreign espials: Robert Beale, 'A Treatise of the Office of a Councillor and Principal Secretary', BL Additional 48161, reproduced in Read, *Walsingham*, I, 435–6. Sundry foreign places: TNA SP 12/232, fol. 25.

21 Hoddesdon: *CSP For.* 1577–8, supplementary letters 4, 15, 18; 'Journal of Sir Francis Walsingham', 28; Read, *Walsingham*, II, 360–1; James Hodson, 'Sir Christopher Hoddesdon' in *Oxford DNB*.

22 Harborne's carpet: *CSP For.* 1583–4, 329. Elizabeth's orator: Christine Woodhead, 'William Harborne' in *Oxford DNB*. Turkish alliance: Walsingham to Harborne 8 Oct. 1585, deciphered and reproduced in Read, *Walsingham*, III, 226–8.

23 Corpus buttery books: Park Honan, *Christopher Marlowe: Poet and Spy* (Oxford, 2005), 84–8. Privy council meeting: *APC* XV (1587–8), 141. Marlowe and Burghley: David Riggs, *The World of Christopher Marlowe* (London, 2004), 181. Marlowe and Thomas Walsingham: Honan, *Marlowe*, 128–32, 324; Reavley Gair, 'Sir Thomas Walsingham' in *Oxford DNB*, which mistakenly refers to Sir Francis Walsingham as Thomas's uncle.

24 Baines: Charles Nicholl, *The Reckoning: The Murder of Christopher Marlowe* (London, 1993), 122–32; Roy Kendall, 'Richard Baines and Christopher Marlowe's Milieu', *ELH* 24 (1994).

25 Catlyn: BL Harley 286, fol. 102, 266–7; *CSP Dom.* addenda 1580–1625, 172–4; *CSP Dom.* 1581–90, 35, 336–7; Read, *Walsingham*, II, 327–30 and III, 181. The Latin tag *hic et ubique*, which is also used by Shakespeare's Hamlet, was Catlyn's attempt to flourish a little learning.

26 Privy seal payments: *CSP Dom.* 1581–90, 636; Read, *Walsingham*, II, 370–1 and III, 418 n. 2. Crown income: Penry Williams, *The Tudor Regime* (Oxford, 1979), 71.

27 Bewray: to reveal or betray. Beale's advice: Read, *Walsingham*, I, 436. Entrapment: Camden, *Annals*, 394.

28 Rogers alias Berden: TNA SP 12/167, fol. 5; TNA SP 12/176, fol. 117–18, 119–20; TNA SP 12/178, fol. 36–7, 83–4, 163; TNA SP 12/187, fol. 181–2; TNA SP 12/189, fol. 56–8; TNA SP 12/209, fol. 36, 215; Read, *Walsingham*, II, 316–17, 330–5, 415–19.

29 Gifford: Francis Edwards, *Plots and Plotters in the Reign of Elizabeth I* (Dublin, 2002), 137; Peter Holmes, 'Gilbert Gifford' in *Oxford DNB*; Read, *Walsingham*, II, 337. Stafford: J. H. Pollen, *Mary Queen of Scots and the Babington Plot* (Edinburgh, 1922), 126.

30 Tyrell: TNA SP 53/19, fol. 69; Michael Questier, *Conversion, Politics and Religion in England, 1580–1625* (Cambridge, 1996), 44–5, 160–1, 175–6; Peter Holmes, 'Anthony Tyrell' in *Oxford DNB*.

31 Machiavellian precision: Sidney Lee, 'Francis Walsingham' in *Oxford DNB*. Militants and pacifists: Edwards, *Plots and Plotters*, 87.

6: BONDS AND CIPHERS

1 Somerville and his plot: TNA SP 12/163, fol. 17, 54, 56–7; *CSP Dom.* 1581–90, 128–30, 182; BL Harley 6035, fol. 32–5; *VCH Warwickshire* 4 (London, 1947), 45, 62; William Wizeman, 'John Somerville' and 'Edward Arden' in *Oxford DNB.* Torture: Robert Hutchinson, *Elizabeth's Spy Master: Francis Walsingham and the Secret War*

that Saved England (London, 2006), 72–8; Conyers Read, *Mr Secretary Walsingham and the Policy of Queen Elizabeth* (Oxford, 1925), II, 378–9.

2 To avoid a greater evil: *CSP Dom.* 1581–90, 161. Breathing nothing but blood: William Camden, *Annals, or the Historie of the Most Renowned and Victorious Princesse Elizabeth*, trans. Robert Norton (London, 1635), 257.

3 Cult of Elizabeth: J. P. D. Cooper, 'O Lorde Save the Kyng: Tudor Royal Propaganda and the Power of Prayer', in G. Bernard and S. J. Gunn (eds), *Authority and Consent in Tudor England* (Aldershot, 2002), 190–3; Henry Foulis, *The History of Romish Treasons and Usurpations* (London, 1681).

4 Bond of association: examples include TNA SP 12/174/1, BL Additional 48027, fol. 248, and BL Cotton Caligula C. IX art. 41, fol. 122, the latter reproduced in Leah S. Marcus, Janel Mueller and Mary Beth Rose (eds), *Elizabeth I: Collected Works* (Chicago and London, 2000), 183–5; David Cressy, 'Binding the Nation: the Bonds of Association, 1584 and 1696', in D. J. Guth and J. W. McKenna (eds), *Tudor Rule and Revolution* (Cambridge, 1982). Spontaneity: Patrick Collinson, 'The Monarchical Republic of Elizabeth I', in John Guy (ed.), *The Tudor Monarchy* (London, 1997), 124; Stephen Alford, *Burghley: William Cecil at the Court of Elizabeth I* (New Haven and London, 2008), 256–7.

5 Surety of the queen's person: statute 27 Eliz. I, c. 1, *Statutes of the Realm*, IV, 704–5. Links of your goodwills: Marcus et al. (eds), *Elizabeth I: Collected Works*, speech 16, March 1585, 181–2. Plowden and the king's two bodies: E. H. Kantorowicz, *The King's Two Bodies: A Study in Medieval Political Theology* (Princeton, 1957), 7.

6 Parry: BL Additional 48027, fol. 244–5; John Bossy, *Under the Molehill: An Elizabethan Spy Story* (New Haven and London, 2001), 96–9; Julian Lock, 'William Parry' in *Oxford DNB*; Penry Williams, *The Later Tudors* (Oxford, 1998), 303.

7 Throckmorton's cipher: *A Discoverie of the Treasons Practised and Attempted against the Queene's Majestie and the Realme by Francis Throckmorton*, reprinted in *The Harleian Miscellany* (London, 1808–13), III, 197. Morgan: Leo Hicks, *An Elizabethan Problem: Some Aspects of the Careers of Two Exile-Adventurers* (London, 1964); John Bossy, *Giordano Bruno and the Embassy Affair* (New Haven and London, 1991), 66–8; Alison Plowden, *The Elizabethan Secret Service* (Hemel Hempstead, 1991), 56–7.

8 Alum is aluminium sulphate. Mary's recipe for secret ink: John Guy, *My Heart is My Own: The Life of Mary Queen of Scots* (London, 2004), 474. Gregorye: BL Harley 286, fol. 78–9; Camden, *Annals*, 305. Gregorye served Burghley's son Robert Cecil after Walsingham's

death, and petitioned James I for a grant of confiscated Catholic land 'for recompense for my services': Hutchinson, *Elizabeth's Spy Master*, 98–9.

9 Orange juice: TNA SP 12/156, fol. 35–6. Lopez and Walsingham: Dominic Green, *The Double Life of Doctor Lopez* (London, 2003), 39–44, 51–6.

10 Codes and ciphers: David Kahn, *The Codebreakers: The Story of Secret Writing* (New York, 1996); Simon Singh, *The Code Book: The Secret History of Codes and Code-Breaking* (London, 1999), chapter 1. Strictly speaking codes involve the replacement of words or whole phrases, while ciphers substitute letters of the alphabet with an encrypted equivalent.

11 St Aldegonde and Don John's plans: Baron Kervyn de Lettenhove, *Relations Politiques des Pays-Bas et de L'Angleterre sous le Reigne de Philippe II* (Brussels, 1882–1900), IX, 405–14; Read, *Walsingham*, I, 315, 323–4 and II, 355–8; Kahn, *Codebreakers*, 119–21.

12 Phelippes: *CSP For. 1578–9*, 37; *CSP Dom.* addenda 1580–1625, 68–9, 86; History of Parliament, *The House of Commons 1558–1603*, ed. P. W. Hasler (London, 1981), III, 219–20; William Richardson, 'Thomas Phelippes' in *Oxford DNB*; Edward Fenton (ed.), *The Diaries of John Dee* (Charlbury, 1998), 46.

13 Frequency analysis: Singh, *Code Book*, 17–29. Walsingham ordering new and old ciphers: BL Harley 6035, fol. 7r, 45v.

14 Shorthand and cryptography: Page Life, 'Timothy Bright' in *Oxford DNB*.

15 Trithemius and Dee: Benjamin Woolley, *The Queen's Conjuror: The Science and Magic of Dr Dee* (London, 2001), 72–81; Kahn, *Codebreakers*, 130–6.

16 Mary's cipher: J. H. Pollen, *Mary Queen of Scots and the Babington Plot* (Edinburgh, 1922), lv; Guy, *My Heart is My Own*, 480; Singh, *Code Book*, 37–8.

17 Move to Chartley: Pollen, *Babington Plot*, lii.

18 Mary at Buxton: Guy, *My Heart is My Own*, 447–8.

19 Gifford's appearance: Pollen, *Babington Plot*, liii, quoting a memoir by Châteauneuf. William Gifford and Walsingham: Read, *Walsingham*, II, 428–33.

20 Mary's shoes: Guy, *My Heart is My Own*, 480. Phelippes at Chartley: Read, *Walsingham*, III, 10.

21 Rich, pleasant witted, and learned: Camden, *Annals*, 302. Babington's first confession: Pollen, *Babington Plot*, 49–66, transcribing BL Additional 48027, fol. 296–301.

22 Ballard and Babington: Pollen, *Babington Plot*, 53.

23 Savage's oath: William Cobbett, *Cobbett's Complete Collection of State Trials* (London, 1809–23), I, 1,129–31.

24 Babington's dilemma: Pollen, *Babington Plot*, 54. Friends and conspirators: Penry Williams, 'Anthony Babington' and Enid Roberts, 'Thomas Salisbury [Salesbury]' in *Oxford DNB*. Tilney's conversion: Cobbett, *State Trials*, I, 1,149. Portraits: Camden, *Annals*, 304; Cobbett, *State Trials*, I, 1,138.

25 Abington's kidnap plan: Pollen, *Babington Plot*, 57. Sabotage and assassination: ibid., 60. Poley: Read, *Walsingham*, III, 8, 21–2, 25–6. Babington's offer of service to Walsingham: Pollen, *Babington Plot*, 56.

26 Mary's delayed letter: ibid., 15–16; Read, *Walsingham*, III, 31. Betwixt two states: Pollen, *Babington Plot*, 58.

27 Babington to Mary ?6 July 1586: ibid., 18–22.

28 Mary to Babington 17 July 1586: ibid., 26–46.

29 Killing Elizabeth: ibid., 66, 74, 80; Cobbett, *State Trials*, I, 1,131. Babington on the run: Camden, *Annals*, 306.

30 Trials, 13–15 Sep. 1586: Cobbett, *State Trials*, I, 1,127–40.

31 Executions: BL Additional 48027, fol. 263–71; Camden, *Annals*, 308. Tichborne, ciphers and Star Chamber: Pollen, *Babington Plot*, 75, 94–5. *Parce mihi domine*: Job 7:16. Pamphlet: William Kemp[e], *A Dutiful Invective Against the Moste Haynous Treasons of Ballard and Babington* (1586–7), STC 14925; see also George Carleton, *A Thankfull Remembrance of Gods Mercie* (fourth edition, 1630), STC 4643, chapter 9.

32 Gifford's flight: Read, *Walsingham*, III, 45. Nau: ibid., III, 37; Alford, *Burghley*, 267.

33 Morgan's loyalty: William Murdin, *A Collection of State Papers left by William Cecill Lord Burghley* (London, 1759), 513–14; Bossy, *Giordano Bruno*, 246; Pollen, *Babington Plot*, xxxiii–xxxv; Hicks, *An Elizabethan Problem*, 113–15.

34 Animate, comfort and provoke: Cobbett, *State Trials*, I, 1,134. Mary as an absolute prince: Alford, *Burghley*, 272, quoting BL Harley 290, fol. 191r; Cobbett, *State Trials*, I, 1,169.

35 Mary's trial: BL Additional 48027, fol. 569*r; Cobbett, *State Trials*, I, 1,169. Phelippes's facsimile: Guy, *My Heart is My Own*, 491.

36 Walsingham's creed: Cobbett, *State Trials*, I, 1,182; Alford, *Burghley*, 275; Guy, *My Heart is My Own*, 491–2. Walsingham to Leicester 15 Oct. 1586: Read, *Walsingham*, III, 54, quoting BL Cotton Caligula C. IX, fol. 502.

37 Walsingham to Burghley 6 Oct. 1586: TNA SP 12/194, fol. 34r. Speedy execution: Cobbett, *State Trials*, I, 1,189–95. London proclamation: BL Additional 48027, fol. 569*v.

38 Grief of my mind: TNA SP 12/197, fol. 6v. Rather lookers-on: TNA SP 12/195, fol. 111r. Dangerous alteration: printed in full in Read, *Walsingham*, III, 58–9.
39 A cordial for Walsingham: Alford, *Burghley*, 287.
40 Mary's execution: BL Additional 48027, fol. 650*; Cobbett, *State Trials*, I, 1,207–12.
41 Hatton's speech: ibid., I, 1,138, 1,140. Captain Fortescue: ibid., I, 1,150.
42 Tichborne's speech: ibid., I, 1,157–8.
43 Extremities of the kingdom: Pollen, *Babington Plot*, 81. Drawn by the heels: Cobbett, *State Trials*, I, 1,147. Huntingdon to Walsingham 16 Mar. 1581: Huntington Library Hastings correspondence, box 2, HA 5356. Babington's predictions: Pollen, *Babington Plot*, 82, 86–7.

7: WESTERN PLANTING

1 Dee and empire: John Dee, *General and Rare Memorials pertayning to the Perfect Arte of Navigation* (1577), STC 6459, 'An advertisement to the reader'; William H. Sherman, *John Dee: The Politics of Reading and Writing in the English Renaissance* (Amherst, 1995), 148–70; Margery Corbett and Ronald Lightbown, *The Comely Frontispiece: The Emblematic Title-Page in England, 1550–1660* (London, 1979), 49–56. Philosopher's stone: Glyn Parry, 'John Dee and the Elizabethan British Empire in its European Context', *HJ* 49 (2006), 663. Inuit man: James McDermott, *Martin Frobisher: Elizabethan Privateer* (New Haven and London, 2001), 149.
2 Globes: Roy Strong, *Gloriana: The Portraits of Queen Elizabeth I* (London, 1987), 90–107.
3 Muscovy Company and licences to export: Conyers Read, *Mr Secretary Walsingham and the Policy of Queen Elizabeth* (Oxford, 1925), III, 371–2, 380–2.
4 Hakluyt on Ireland: 'Discourse of Western Planting, 1584', in E. G. R. Taylor (ed.), *The Original Writings and Correspondence of the Two Richard Hakluyts* (London, 1935), II, 212. Carleill: Rachel Lloyd, *Elizabethan Adventurer: A Life of Captain Christopher Carleill* (London, 1974), 95–6, 121–5, 136–7. Reduce: Huntington Library Bridgewater and Ellesmere, EL 1701, fol. 2r; David Harris Sacks, 'Discourses of Western Planting: Richard Hakluyt and the Making of the Atlantic World', in Peter Mancall (ed.), *The Atlantic World and Virginia, 1550–1624* (Chapel Hill, 2007), 436–7, 444–6.
5 Walsingham's Irish archive: BL Stowe 162, fol. 2–3, 46–65. King James in the State Paper Office: TNA SP 14/107, fol. 24.

6 Edmund Tremayne and his discourse: Huntington Library Bridgewater and Ellesmere, EL 1701; 'Journal of Sir Francis Walsingham from Dec. 1570 to April 1583', ed. C. T. Martin, *Camden Miscellany* 6 (London, 1870–1), 15–16; History of Parliament, *The House of Commons 1558–1603*, ed. P. W. Hasler (London, 1981), III, 526; Jon G. Crawford, *Anglicizing the Government of Ireland: The Irish Privy Council and the Expansion of Tudor Rule, 1556–1578* (Dublin, 1993), 10–11, 389–93; S. J. Connolly, *Contested Island: Ireland 1460–1630* (Oxford, 2007), 165.

7 Sovereignty: Huntington Library Bridgewater and Ellesmere, EL 1701, fol. 3r; *The Walsingham Letter-Book or Register of Ireland May 1578 to December 1579*, ed. James Hogan and N. McNeill O'Farrell (Dublin, 1959), 89–90. Surrender and re-grant: Connolly, *Contested Island*, 105–10.

8 Agarde: TNA SP 63/55/169; Crawford, *Anglicizing the Government of Ireland*, 163–9. Gerard: TNA SP 63/56/108; TNA SP 63/57/62–3, 66–8; Penry Williams, 'Sir William Gerard' in *Oxford DNB*.

9 Agriculture and diet: David Beers Quinn, *The Elizabethans and the Irish* (Ithaca, NY, 1966), 14–15, 63–6. Royal soil: John Derricke, *The Image of Irelande with a Discoverie of Woodkarne* (1581), STC 6734, sig. E3r. Bryskett: TNA SP 63/81/12; Nicholas Canny, *Making Ireland British, 1580–1650* (Oxford, 2001), 1–10, 36.

10 Walsingham's affinity in Ireland: Rory Rapple, *Martial Power and Elizabethan Political Culture: Military Men in England and Ireland, 1558–1594* (Cambridge, 2009), 150–1, 157–61, 253. Ireland and Calais: ibid., 208. Her majesty had a country: Pelham to Walsingham 6 Sep. 1579, TNA SP 63/69, fol. 18. Elizabeth's instructions to Essex: Nicholas Canny, 'The Ideology of Colonization: From Ireland to America', *WMQ* 3rd series 30 (1973), 580.

11 Irish language as contaminant: Patricia Palmer, *Language and Conquest in Early Modern Ireland* (Cambridge, 2001), 76–80. Old English priests: Steven Ellis, *Tudor Ireland: Crown, Community and the Conflict of Cultures, 1470–1603* (London, 1985), 221–2.

12 Stucley, Fitzgerald and the Desmond rebellion: *APC* X (1577–8), 236, 245, 257–8; Rapple, *Martial Power*, 75, 113–18; Peter Holmes, 'Thomas Stucley' in *Oxford DNB*.

13 Enniscorthy: *Calendar of the Carew Manuscripts* II (1575–88), 343; David Edwards, 'The Escalation of Violence in Sixteenth-Century Ireland', in David Edwards, Pádraig Lenihan and Clodagh Tait (eds), *Age of Atrocity: Violence and Political Conflict in Early Modern Ireland* (Dublin, 2007), 71–2. Youghal: TNA SP 63/70, fol. 47v; *Walsingham Letter Book*, 257.

14 Smerwick: TNA SP 63/78, fol. 72–3; Vincent P. Carey, 'Atrocity and History: Grey, Spenser and the Slaughter at Smerwick', in Edwards, *Age of Atrocity*, 79–94. Edward Denny: TNA SP 63/78, fol. 62v. Bingham's Irish career and relationship with Walsingham are examined in Rapple, *Martial Power*, chapter 7.

15 Sidney's defence: Ciarán Brady (ed.), *A Viceroy's Vindication? Sir Henry Sidney's Memoir of Service in Ireland 1556–1578* (Cork, 2002), 13–16; *Calendar of the Carew Manuscripts* II (1575–88), 334–60. The right Antichrist: TNA SP 63/78, fol. 62–5; Carey, 'Atrocity and History', 90–3.

16 Death in Munster: Malby to Walsingham 12 Oct. 1579, TNA SP 63/69, fol. 108v; Bingham to Walsingham 20 Sep. 1580, TNA SP 63/76, fol. 103r; Meade to Walsingham 8 Feb. 1582, TNA 63/89, fol. 52r; figures and analysis indebted to Anthony M. McCormack, 'The Social and Economic Consequences of the Desmond Rebellion of 1579–83', *Irish Historical Studies* 34 (2004), 1–15.

17 Irish as pagans: Huntington Library Bridgewater and Ellesmere, EL 1701, fol. 2v; Canny, 'Ideology of Colonization', 583–6.

18 Queen's and King's Counties: *Walsingham Letter Book*, 42; Connolly, *Contested Island*, 116–18, 148–50. Smith and Essex in Ulster: Ellis, *Tudor Ireland*, 266–8.

19 Crown control: Michael MacCarthy-Morrogh, *The Munster Plantation: English Migration to Southern Ireland 1583–1641* (Oxford, 1986), 46. To go over from hence: TNA SP 63/114, fol. 124v–125r.

20 Surveying the land: MacCarthy-Morrogh, *Munster Plantation*, 4–16.

21 Thorough reformation: Waterhouse to Walsingham 4 Nov. 1579, TNA SP 63/70, fol. 7v; Waterhouse to Walsingham 20 April 1580, TNA SP 63/72, fol. 147r; Fenton to Walsingham 11 July 1580, TNA SP 63/74, fol. 41r; 'A plot touching the peopling of Munster', TNA SP 63/121, fol. 193; Canny, *Making Ireland British*, 121–34. John Cooper (no relation): MacCarthy-Morrogh, *Munster Plantation*, 74–5.

22 Walsingham as undertaker: *Calendar of the Carew Manuscripts* II (1575–88), 450–1; MacCarthy-Morrogh, *Munster Plantation*, 23, 40.

23 Herbert at Castleisland: ibid., 124–7.

24 Bingham: Rapple, *Martial Power*, 259. Fire and sword: Malby to Walsingham 17 Mar. 1577, TNA SP 63/57/40. Faith and fatherland: Mícheál Mac Craith, 'The Gaelic Reaction to the Reformation', in Steven G. Ellis and Sarah Barber (eds), *Conquest and Union: Fashioning a British State, 1485–1725* (London, 1995), 144–6.

25 Carleill and the *Tiger*: Lloyd, *Elizabethan Adventurer*, 111, 133–4. Salmon, cod and the godly: TNA SP 12/155, fol. 201–10;

Christopher Carleill, *A Breef and Sommarie Discourse upon the entended Voyage to the Hethermoste Partes of America* (1583), STC 4626.5, sig. A3r.

26 My principal patron: Gilbert to Walsingham 23 Sep. 1578, in D. B. Quinn (ed.), *The Voyages and Colonising Enterprises of Sir Humphrey Gilbert* (London, 1940), I, 199–200. Of not good happ by sea: Gilbert to Walsingham 7 Feb. 1583, ibid., II, 339–41. Walsingham's £50 subscription: Read, *Walsingham*, III, 403.

27 Gold mining: McDermott, *Frobisher*, 154–9, 186. Walsingham's farm of the customs: Read, *Walsingham*, III, 383–91, where his profits on the lease are averaged out at over 58 per cent.

28 Questions of sovereignty: Ken MacMillan, *Sovereignty and Possession in the English New World* (Cambridge, 2006), chapter 2; Sherman, *Dee*, 182–9; David Armitage, 'The Elizabethan Idea of Empire', *TRHS* 6th series, 14 (2004), 269–77; *The Private Diary of Dr John Dee*, ed. J. O. Halliwell (London, 1842), 4–9.

29 Dee's library and its visitors: Sherman, *Dee*, 30–8; R. Julian Roberts, 'John Dee' in *Oxford DNB*; *Private Diary of Dr John Dee*, 3, 9, 18–19; McDermott, *Frobisher*, 132. Walsingham, Dee and the Gregorian calendar: Benjamin Woolley, *The Queen's Conjuror: The Science and Magic of Dr Dee* (London, 2001), 193–4. Adrian Gilbert: Raleigh Trevelyan, *Sir Walter Raleigh* (London, 2002), 4, 66–8. Ursula as godmother: *Private Diary of Dr John Dee*, 33.

30 Gilbert, Davis and the north-west passage company: Read, *Walsingham*, III, 404–5; Michael Hicks, 'John Davis' in *Oxford DNB*. Raid on Mortlake: Woolley, *Queen's Conjuror*, 306–8. Cod for Lord Burghley: David Beers Quinn, *England and the Discovery of America, 1481–1620* (London, 1974), 316. Burghley's Ortelius: Stephen Alford, *Burghley: William Cecil at the Court of Elizabeth I* (New Haven and London, 2008), 236.

31 Catholics in America: George Peckham, *A True Reporte of the Late Discoveries and Possession of the New-Found Landes* (1583), STC 19523; Quinn, *Enterprises of Sir Humphrey Gilbert*, II, 245–78; Quinn, *England and the Discovery of America*, 371–81; James McDermott, 'Sir George Peckham' in *Oxford DNB*.

32 Claiming Newfoundland: Peckham, *True Reporte*; MacMillan, *Sovereignty and Possession*, 111–13.

33 The very walls of this our Island: Richard Hakluyt, *The Principall Navigations, Voyages and Discoveries of the English Nation* (1589), STC 12625, sig. *3r. Hakluyt the elder: Taylor, *Original Writings*, I, 116; MacMillan, *Sovereignty and Possession*, 76–7, 124–5.

34 Hakluyt and Walsingham: Taylor, *Original Writings*, I, 196–7, 205–7; Richard Hakluyt, *A Particuler Discourse concerninge the Greate Necessitie and*

Manifolde Commodyties that are Like to Growe to this Realme of Englande by the Westerne Discoveries Lately Attempted, ed. D. B. and A. Quinn (London, 1993), xv–xxxi; Peter C. Mancall, *Hakluyt's Promise: An Elizabethan's Obsession for an English America* (New Haven and London, 2007), 102–3, 115–21, 128–35. Palavicini: Hakluyt, *Particuler Discourse*, 199.

35 *Discourse of Western Planting*: Taylor, *Original Writings*, II, 211–326; Sacks, 'Discourses of Western Planting'; MacMillan, *Sovereignty and Possession*, 50, 67–8, 80. Richard Hakluyt, Preacher: Taylor, *Original Writings*, I, 207.

36 Traffic: ibid., II, 274. Fifteen million souls: ibid., II, 259. Glad tidings of the gospel: ibid., II, 216. Aesop's crow: ibid., II, 249.

37 Commons committee: D. B. Quinn (ed.), *The Roanoke Voyages 1584–1590* (London, 1955), I, 122–6. Raleigh's seal and the kingdom of Virginia: ibid., I, 147, 199. Atkinson and Russell: ibid., I, 197–8. Walsingham as adventurer: Grenville to Walsingham 29 Oct. 1585, in ibid., I, 218–21. Martin Laurentson: ibid., I, 226–8.

38 Secotan nation: Lee Miller, *Roanoke: Solving the Mystery of England's Lost Colony* (London, 2000), 263–7. Considering English sources alongside Algonquian linguistic and ethnological evidence, Miller finds no evidence for Quinn's separate Roanoke tribe; the Secotan country extended to the island as well as the mainland.

39 Fernandes and Walsingham: Quinn, *England and the Discovery of America*, chapter 9. To annoy the King of Spain: Read, *Walsingham*, III, 102–3.

40 The *Tiger* aground: Lane to Walsingham 12 Aug. 1585, in Quinn, *Roanoke Voyages*, I, 201–2; the *Tiger* journal in ibid., I, 189. Composition of the 1585 colony: D. B. Quinn, *Set Fair for Roanoke: Voyages and Colonies, 1584–1606* (Chapel Hill and London, 1984), 88–96. Nice bringing up: Quinn, *Roanoke Voyages*, I, 323.

41 Archaeology of Roanoke: Quinn, *Set Fair for Roanoke*, chapter 20. Roanoke fort: Taylor, *Original Writings*, II, 322; MacMillan, *Sovereignty and Possession*, 125–7, 163–5. Burning of Aquascogoc: the *Tiger* journal in Quinn, *Roanoke Voyages*, I, 191.

42 Goodliest soil: Lane to Hakluyt 3 Sep. 1585, in ibid., I, 207–10. A vast country: Lane to Walsingham 12 Aug. 1585, in ibid., I, 203. Christianly inhabited: Lane to Walsingham 8 Sep. 1585, in ibid., I, 213.

43 Lane's report to Raleigh: ibid., I, 255–94, as printed by Hakluyt.

44 The description of the place: ibid., I, 400.

45 Grants of arms: ibid., II, 506–12, 571. Fatter soil: ibid., I, 382. Grenville and Fernandes: Quinn, *England and the Discovery of America*, 258–9. White's report: Quinn, *Roanoke Voyages*, II, 515–38.

46 Oranges and plantains: ibid., II, 520–2. The case for Walsingham's complicity in sabotage is made by Miller, *Lost Colony*, especially 166–71, 178–82, 187–9.

47 George Howe's murder: Quinn, *Roanoke Voyages*, II, 530–1. White's return: ibid., II, 532–5.

48 Stirrers abroad: Hakluyt, *Principall Navigations*, sig. *2v–*3r.

49 Ships prohibited from sailing: *APC* XV (1587–8), 254. White's return to Roanoke: Quinn, *Roanoke Voyages*, II, 610–18. Manteo's baptism: ibid., II, 531.

50 Lost colonists: Quinn, *Set Fair for Roanoke*, chapter 19. White to Hakluyt 4 Feb. 1593: Quinn, *Roanoke Voyages*, II, 716.

8: ELEVENTH HOUR

1 Walsingham's portrait: NPG 1807. De Critz: TNA SP 15/27, fol. 132, 187, 246; Mary Edmond, 'John de Critz' in *Oxford DNB*. Curiosities: Richard L. Williams, 'The Visual Arts', in Susan Doran and Norman Jones (eds), *The Elizabethan World* (Abingdon, 2010), 583–4.

2 Walsingham's privy council memorandum: transcribed in Conyers Read, *Mr Secretary Walsingham and the Policy of Queen Elizabeth* (Oxford, 1925), III, 73–5. Treaty of Joinville: TNA SP 78/13, fol. 163v. Crichton: TNA SP 12/173, fol. 4–12; Read, *Walsingham*, II, 177, 373–8, 386, 398–9. Spanish embargo: Humphrey Mote, *The Primrose of London with her Valiant Adventure on the Spanish Coast* (1585), STC 18211, sig. A3r; James McDermott, *England and the Spanish Armada: The Necessary Quarrel* (New Haven and London, 2005), 152–3. Amends and satisfaction: Carey to Walsingham 25 June 1585, in Julian S. Corbett (ed.), *Papers relating to the Navy during the Spanish War 1585–1587* (London, 1898), 33–6.

3 Treaty of Nonsuch: R. B. Wernham, *Before the Armada: The Growth of English Foreign Policy 1485–1588* (London, 1966), 371. Protector rather than sovereign: TNA SP 84/2, fol. 95r; Read, *Walsingham*, III, 106 n. 2.

4 Leicester as governor-general: Wernham, *Before the Armada*, 376–9. True-hearted Swiss: Walsingham to Leicester 28 Mar. 1586, quoted in Read, *Walsingham*, III, 143.

5 Drake's expedition 1585–6: Carleill to Walsingham 4–11 Oct. 1585, in Corbett, *Spanish War*, 39–49; Edward Wynter to Walsingham 24 Oct. 1585, in ibid., 49–51; 'Statement of the Queen's account', in ibid., 94–5; Harry Kelsey, *Sir Francis Drake: The Queen's Pirate* (New Haven and London, 1998), chapter 9. Beacon fires: Buchanan Sharp,

In Contempt of All Authority: Rural Artisans and Riot in the West of England, 1586–1660 (Berkeley, 1980), 16.

6 Santa Cruz and Parma: De Lamar Jensen, 'The Spanish Armada: The Worst-Kept Secret in Europe', *SCJ* 19 (1988), 621–41; McDermott, *Necessary Quarrel*, 162–3. Standen: Read, *Walsingham*, III, 288–92, where a detailed case is made for the identification of Pompeo Pellegrini with Antony Standen.

7 Philip's sense of mission: Geoffrey Parker, 'The Place of Tudor England in the Messianic Vision of Philip II of Spain', *TRHS* 6th series, 12 (2002), 167–221. Peace negotiations: Read, *Walsingham*, III, 260–79. Since England was England: Howard to Walsingham 27 Jan. 1588, in John Knox Laughton (ed.), *State Papers relating to the Defeat of the Spanish Armada* (London, 1894–5), I, 48–50.

8 Burghley's disgrace: Stephen Alford, *Burghley: William Cecil at the Court of Elizabeth I* (New Haven and London, 2008), 291–5. For queen and country: Drake to Walsingham 2 Apr. 1587, in Corbett, *Spanish War*, 102–4. Cadiz and Sagres: Drake to Walsingham 27 Apr. 1587, in ibid., 107–9; Drake to Leicester 27 Apr. 1587, in Simon Adams (ed.), 'The Armada Correspondence in Cotton MSS Otho E VII and E IX', in Michael Duffy (ed.), *The Naval Miscellany VI* (Aldershot, 2003), 52–3; Drake to Walsingham 17 May 1587, in Corbett, *Spanish War*, 131–4; Kelsey, *Queen's Pirate*, chapter 10.

9 Defences: John Summerson, 'The Defence of the Realm under Elizabeth I', in H. M. Colvin (ed.), *The History of the King's Works* (London, 1982), IV, part II, 402–14; Martin Biddle, H. M. Colvin and John Summerson, 'The Defences in Detail', in Colvin, *King's Works*, 468–70 (Dorset coast), 471 (Harwich and Ipswich), 480–1 (Upnor), 518–27 (Portsmouth; see also TNA SP 12/168, fol. 20–1), 531–2 (Carisbrooke), 590–3 (Scilly) and 598–601 (Falmouth).

10 Their surest defence: *APC* XVI (1588), 203; McDermott, *Necessary Quarrel*, 176–81. Dover harbour: BL Harley 6035, fol. 3r–v, 7r, 27v; Martin Biddle and John Summerson, 'Dover Harbour', in Colvin, *King's Works*, 755–64; Eric H. Ash, *Power, Knowledge and Expertise in Elizabethan England* (Baltimore and London, 2004), chapter 2, 'Expert Mediation and the Rebuilding of Dover Harbor'; Paul Ive, *The Practise of Fortification* (1589), STC 1708.5; Stephen Johnston, 'Thomas Digges' in *Oxford DNB*.

11 Reaction to Cadiz: Pellegrini/Standen to Walsingham 16 July 1587, TNA SP 98/1, fol. 20–1; Stafford to Walsingham, TNA SP 78/17, fol. 249r. So great an exploit: Adams, 'Armada Correspondence', 55–8. Prepare in England: Drake to Walsingham 27 Apr. 1587, in Corbett, *Spanish War*, 107–9.

12 Medina Sidonia: Garrett Mattingly, *The Defeat of the Spanish Armada* (London, 1959), 182–4. Parma's orders: Jensen, 'Worst-Kept Secret', 639–40; Geoffrey Parker, 'If the Armada had Landed', *History* 61 (1976), 358.

13 Prisoners in Bridewell: TNA SP 12/214, fol. 53, 55–65; *APC* XVI (1588), 200, 210–11. Valdés: Laughton, *Spanish Armada*, II, 27–9.

14 But a device: Howard to Walsingham 24 Jan. 1588, in Laughton, *Spanish Armada*, I, 46–8; Adams, 'Armada Correspondence', 45–7; Mitchell Leimon and Geoffrey Parker, 'Treason and Plot in Elizabethan Diplomacy: The Fame of Sir Edward Stafford Reconsidered', *EHR* 111 (1996). Turkish fleet: TNA SP 78/18, fol. 243r.

15 This is the year: Howard to Burghley and Walsingham 23 Feb. 1588, in Adams, 'Armada Correspondence', 68–70. Liberty and freedom: Hawkins to Walsingham 1 Feb. 1588, in Laughton, *Spanish Armada*, I, 58–62. Mammering: wavering or hesitating. We cannot long stand: BL Cotton Galba D. ii, fol. 192v.

16 Signet payments: TNA SP 12/229, fol. 115.

17 Bacon and fish: Fenner to Walsingham 3 Mar. 1588, in Laughton, *Spanish Armada*, I, 90–3. Oseley: Oseley to Walsingham 23 July 1588, in ibid., I, 301–2; Read, *Walsingham*, III, 292–3; McDermott, *Necessary Quarrel*, 364 n. 11. There goeth many English: BL Harley 168, fol. 160–1; Jason E. Eldred, 'Imperial Spain in the English Imagination, 1563–1662' (PhD thesis, University of Virginia, 2010), 167; Bertrand T. Whitehead, *Brags and Boasts: Propaganda in the Year of the Armada* (Stroud, 1994), 65–7.

18 Ply up and down: Walsingham to Howard 9 June 1588, in Laughton, *Spanish Armada*, I, 192–3. Had understood their plot: Howard to Walsingham 13 June 1588, in ibid., I, 195–9. Isle of Wight: ibid., I, 190–2. Whole plot and design: Walsingham to Sussex 24 July 1588, in Adams, 'Armada Correspondence', 80–2; *APC* XVI (1588), 168, 176.

19 Catholics and the Armada: *APC* XVI (1588), 167–8, 214, 218–19; McDermott, *Necessary Quarrel*, 244–7.

20 Some great shot: Howard to Walsingham 21 July 1588, in Laughton, *Spanish Armada*, I, 288–9. Privy council orders: *APC* XVI (1588), 166–7, 174, 176, 183, 186–7, 191. Crescent formation: Mattingly, *Defeat of the Spanish Armada*, 236–7. Fireships: McDermott, *Necessary Quarrel*, 266–8.

21 Public prayers: *APC* XVI (1588), 172; Whitehead, *Brags and Boasts*, 82–4, 94–5; David Cressy, 'The Spanish Armada: Celebration, Myth

and Memory', in Jeff Doyle and Bruce Moore (eds), *England and the Spanish Armada* (Canberra, 1990), 157–9.

22 Army in Essex: Burghley to Walsingham 19 July 1588, in Laughton, *Spanish Armada*, I, 284–5; *APC* XVI (1588), 198, 208–9; Neil Younger, 'If the Armada had Landed: A Reappraisal of England's Defences in 1588', *History* 93 (2008), 328–54; Adams, 'Armada Correspondence', 80 n. 1.

23 Camp at Tilbury: TNA SP 12/213, fol. 90r, 113–14; James Aske, *Elizabetha Triumphans* (1588), STC 847 (amain, with full force or speed); Leah S. Marcus, Janel Mueller and Mary Beth Rose (eds), *Elizabeth I: Collected Works* (Chicago and London, 2000), 325–6; Miller Christy, 'Queen Elizabeth's Visit to Tilbury in 1588', *EHR* 34 (1919), 43–61. McDermott, *Necessary Quarrel*, 279–81 dates the visit as 7–8 August, but Walsingham wrote to Burghley describing events 'at the court, in the camp' on 9 August. Rumours of Parma's departure: Adams, 'Armada Correspondence', 87–8. This place breedeth courage: Walsingham to Burghley 9 Aug. 1588, in Laughton, *Spanish Armada*, II, 82–3.

24 Harvest: *APC* XVI (1588), 221–2. Fought more with your pen: Seymour to Walsingham 18 Aug. 1588, in Laughton, *Spanish Armada*, II, 126–7. Half doings: Walsingham to Burghley 8 Aug. 1588, BL Harley 6994, fol. 138. Oliver Pigge: Cressy, 'Celebration, Myth and Memory', 158, 160.

25 Armada portraits: Roy Strong, *Gloriana: The Portraits of Queen Elizabeth I* (London, 1987), 132–3; Kevin Sharpe, *Selling the Tudor Monarchy* (New Haven and London, 2009), 381–2. Gift exchange and Barn Elms: John Nichols, *The Progresses and Public Processions of Queen Elizabeth* (New York, 1973), III, 8–9, 27–8; Lisa M. Klein, 'Your Humble Handmaid: Elizabethan Gifts of Needlework', *Renaissance Quarterly* 50 (1997), 459–93. Windebank: Read, *Walsingham*, III, 326, 349, 447–8.

26 Such emulation: Penry Williams, *The Later Tudors: England 1547–1603* (Oxford, 1998), 341. After her majesty's decease: Walsingham to Sidney 7 Sep. 1588, in Read, *Walsingham*, III, 338–9. Pretendeth to be a king: ibid., 343–4.

27 Azores: Howard to Walsingham 27 Aug. 1588, TNA SP 12/215, fol. 104. Lisbon expedition and Essex: Walsingham to Windebank 2 May 1589, TNA 12/224, fol. 12; Lane to Walsingham 27 July 1589, TNA SP 12/225, fol. 77–8; Kelsey, *Queen's Pirate*, chapter 12. Contraband: Read, *Walsingham*, III, 350–2.

28 Working in bed: BL Harley 6994, fol. 189r. Wonderfully overthrown: Read, *Walsingham*, III, 424. Essex as Sidney's heir: Paul E. J. Hammer, 'Robert Devereux, second Earl of Essex' in *Oxford DNB*.

29 Speedy easing: TNA SP 12/231, fol. 116. Selling land: inquisition post mortem, 27 Sep. 1592, printed in E. A. Webb, G. W. Miller and J. Beckwith, *The History of Chislehurst: Its Church, Manors, and Parish* (London, 1899), 361–2; for Mylles see also Read, *Walsingham*, II, 319–20, 336 and III, 45. Walsingham's death: *The Private Diary of Dr John Dee*, ed. J. O. Halliwell (London, 1842), 33 (16 April according to Dee's own version of new-style dating); Alexandra Walsham, *Providence in Early Modern England* (Oxford, 1999), 240. Bingham's letter: Rory Rapple, *Martial Power and Elizabethan Political Culture: Military Men in England and Ireland, 1558–1594* (Cambridge, 2009), 285.

30 Walsingham's will: PRO, PROB 11/75, fol. 262v–263r. Bradford and Barnes: Webb, *History of Chislehurst*, 361–2. Burial inscription: Henry Holland, *Monumenta Sepulchraria Sancti Pauli* (1614), STC 13583.5, 17–19, 'ut a multis periculis patriam liberavit, servarit Rem-publicam, conformarit pacem'. Pillar of our common wealth: Thomas Watson, *An Eglogue upon the Death of the Right Honorable Sir Francis Walsingham* (1590), STC 25121; Albert Chatterley, 'Thomas Watson' in *Oxford DNB*.

Index